Summer Cottages
in the
White Mountains

Summer Cottages in the White Mountains

THE ARCHITECTURE OF
LEISURE AND RECREATION

1870 to 1930

≈

Bryant F. Tolles, Jr.

University Press of New England ≈ HANOVER AND LONDON

University Press of New England, Hanover, NH 03755
© 2000 by Bryant F. Tolles, Jr.
All rights reserved
Printed in Singapore
5   4   3   2   1
CIP data appear at the end of the book

Grateful acknowledgment for financial assistance in the publication of this book is made to Furthermore, the publication program of The J. M. Kaplan Fund.

Frontispiece: "The Castle" (1891–92), Jackson, N.H. Photograph by the author.

Contents

Illustrations

4. RANDOLPH/JEFFERSON

5. BETHLEHEM/LITTLETON

6. FRANCONIA/SUGAR HILL

7. CAMPTON/WATERVILLE

8. HOLDERNESS/SANDWICH/MOULTONBOROUGH

10. OUTLYING LOCATIONS

Preface

My interest in and enthusiasm for researching and writing this book originated largely with two previous publications. During the mid-1970s, when I was working on *New Hampshire Architecture: An Illustrated Guide* (University Press of New England for the New Hampshire Historical Society, 1979), I first became acquainted with the more visible and interesting of the White Mountain summer cottages. It was not until nearly twenty years later, however, after I had expanded my knowledge of this unusual and intriguing facet of residential architecture, that I fully recognized the potential for an illustrated volume on this subject. This occurred when I was compiling my 1998 book, *The Grand Resort Hotels of The White Mountains: A Vanishing Architectural Legacy*, published by the David R. Godine company of Boston. As I examined hotel architecture in the region and its related history, I focused closely on summer resort communities, and the integral relationship between their hotels and the summer houses built in proximity to them. In doing so I realized the importance of these single-season residences to the architectural, social, cultural, and economic history of the mountains. They are as essential to the story of summer life there as the hotels, and, as this book will demonstrate, emanated directly from them.

Perhaps the most compelling reason for pursuing the topic is the near total lack of general knowledge about the summer cottage phenomenon in the White Mountain area. To date, with the exception of brief specialized studies, or references in local histories or articles, virtually nothing has been published on these buildings and the life surrounding them. Furthermore, a substantial number of the cottages have long gone unrecognized by local residents and the general public, in part because of the remote locations of many of them. Others have been lost to fire, or have been demolished due to structural deficiencies or burdensome property taxes. Given the lack of readily available published materials, the principal sources of information on these cottages include local and tourist newspapers, county deed and probate records, photographs, maps, architectural drawings, family correspondence, and oral history interviews with house owners and local residents. The best and most reliable documentation, however, are the cottages themselves—fortunately, of the approximately one hundred under study here, over 65 percent of them are still standing, most in a reasonably good state of preservation. Due to the generous hospitality of house owners, I was able to visit the interiors of most of these, and recapture the essence and nature of the summer life-style they formerly accommodated and sustained.

With any successful architectural and historical study of this kind, it is necessary and desirable to establish logical subject parameters. Chronologically, the book commences with the earliest hotel-built and privately constructed cottages in the 1870s, and extends to 1930, after which the Great Depression and World War II had an understandably dampening effect on the summer cottage movement, and dramatically altered the American vacation ritual. The geographical scope of the region treated is defined as the area, extending south to north, from Plymouth and the northern edge of the Lakes Region to upper Coos County; and, east to west, from the Maine state boundary to a line running from Plymouth up the Baker River Valley north to Warren, then to Littleton and up the northern Connecticut River Valley to Colebrook. All houses discussed in the book were designed and erected primarily or exclusively for summer use—farmhouses or other buildings adopted for summer vacation purposes are not included unless they were subjected to major, transforming renovations and/or were incorporated into residential facilities largely the product of new construction. Significant outbuildings or other dependent structures are considered within the proper purview of this work providing that they served functions relating to summertime leisure and recreation. As defined in the introduction to this book, the summer cottage is intended to encompass buildings, from the modest to the extravagant, located in towns, villages, and more rural or even isolated settings, either functionally independent, or at the core of working agricultural complexes or estates.

The book commences with an introductory essay that treats the origins and development of the summer cottage and cottage communities (or colonies). The defining characteristics of the distinctive cottage building type and its stylistic expressions are examined in the context of American historical patterns and themes, with attention to influential regional as well as national factors and trends. The introduction also treats the first cottage owners, and their architects and builders, for the most part, not mentioning subsequent owners unless they were responsible for major renovations or additions. The area constituting the White Mountains is presented and interpreted as a highly important sample study region that tells us much about what art historian Vincent J. Scully, Jr., has termed "the architecture of the American summer" (*The Architecture of the American Summer* [New York: Rizzoli, 1989]). Following the introduction are nine separate sections grouping the houses geographically according to the summer communities in which they are or were located. Under each section heading individual essays describe the houses, arranged chronologically, after a brief general essay outlining the history and characteristics of each community. A tenth and final section incorporates those few examples that were physically isolated, and not part of a defined social unit. The architecture, origins, and early history of each house are critically reviewed, with additional commentary about initial owners/financiers, and, where known, architects and builders. The volume concludes with an epilogue commenting on the changing concept of the summer cottage and its architectural and historical legacy, an appendix listing identified architects and their commissions, and an exhaustive bibliography. Accompanying and essential to an understanding and appreciation of the text are a collection of color, and black and white photographs, the majority of which I shot while conducting field surveys throughout the mountains.

The summer cottage phenomenon in the White Mountains—and its physical legacy, the buildings themselves—has long rested in obscurity, with only the barest of recognition by scholars, more popular writers, and the public. It is my hope and intent that this book will shed new light on a subject, though previously overlooked, that tells us a great deal about how earlier generations of Americans built for and enjoyed their summer vacation experiences in one of the oldest, largest, and most popular resort regions in the United States.

Center Sandwich, New Hampshire   B.F.T., Jr.
January 1999

Acknowledgments

There are numerous institutions and organizations, their staffs, as well as individuals, to whom I wish to express my deep appreciation for their assistance in the researching of this book. While my own personal White Mountain collection provided the basis for preliminary investigation of the subject, the bulk of my research was undertaken at the following libraries or archival repositories: the New Hampshire Historical Society, Concord (William N. Copely, librarian; Cathy Zusy, curator; and Donna-Belle Garvin, registrar); the White Mountain Collection, Dartmouth College Library, Hanover, N.H. (Stanley W. Brown, curator of rare books); the Mount Washington Observatory Resource Center, North Conway, N.H. (Guy Gosselin, executive director); the Appalachian Mountain Club, Boston (Jessica Gill, librarian); the New England Historical Genealogical Society, Boston; the Hugh M. Morris Library, University of Delaware, Newark; the Loeb Library, Graduate School of Design, Harvard University, Cambridge, Mass.; the Avery Architectural and Fine Arts Library, Columbia University, New York City (Janet Parks, curator, and Don Kany, assistant, Architectural Drawings and Archives); the New Hampshire State Library, Concord; The Athenaeum of Philadelphia (Bruce Laverty, curator of architecture); the Boston Architectural Center (Susan Lewis); the Boston Athenaeum (Rodney Armstrong, librarian); the American Antiquarian Society, Worcester, Mass.; the Fine Arts Department, Boston Public Library (Janice H. Chadbourne, curator of fine arts, and Kim Tenney, fine arts librarian); the Society for the Preservation of New England Antiquities, Boston (Laura Congdon, archivist); the Winterthur Museum Library, Winterthur, Del.; the Fine Arts Library, University of Pennsylvania, Philadelphia; the Historical Society of Pennsylvania, Philadelphia; the New York Genealogical Society, New York City; the Maine Historical Society, Portland (Nicholas Noyes, librarian); the New Jersey Historical Society, Newark (Elsa Meyers, librarian); the Massachusetts Historical Society, Boston; the Wilmington Free Library, Del.; the Essex Institute Library, Salem, Mass. (Mary Fabiszewski); the Harvard University Archives, Cambridge, Mass. (Patrice Donoghue, assistant curator, and Danielle Green, curatorial assistant); the Museum of American Textile History, North Andover, Mass. (Claire Sheriden); The Art Institute of Chicago (Leischon A. Potuznik, coordinator of photographic rights); the Lamson Library, Plymouth State College, N.H.; the Brooklyn (N.Y.) Historical Society; the Worcester

(Mass.) Historical Museum (William Wallace, director); the Connecticut Historical Society, Hartford; the Smith College Archives, Northampton, Mass. (Marjorie Sly and Margaret Jessup); the Forbes Library, Northampton; the University of Massachusetts-Amherst Library; the Robert Frost Library, Amherst College, Amherst, Mass.; the Carroll County Registry of Deeds, Ossipee, N.H.; the Grafton County Registry of Deeds, Woodsville, N.H.; and the Coos County Registry of Deeds, Lancaster, N.H. Of those individuals who were particularly helpful to me, I wish to offer my sincere thanks to Douglas A. Philbrook, Gorham, N.H.; Earle W. Shettleworth, Jr., director, Maine Historic Preservation Commission, Augusta; Roger G. Reed, Brookline Historical Commission, Brookline, Mass.; James L. Garvin, New Hampshire Division of Historical Resources, Concord; Charles O. Vogel, West Townsend, Mass.; Steven Jerome, Brookline, Mass.; Richard Guy Wilson, University of Virginia; and Phyllis Kihn and Karl P. Stofko, East Haddam, Conn. For financial support essential to fulfillment of the project goals, I would like to credit the College of Arts and Science, University of Delaware, for two one-year Supplemental Funds Grants and one Project Development Award. I also owe a great debt of gratitude to the university for a half-year sabbatical in 1993–94, which enabled me to compile much of the text of this volume within a concentrated time frame.

To establish a solid research foundation for the book, I devoted over two years to the search for appropriate source materials as well as to field survey and photography throughout the entire White Mountain region. Many people kindly invited me to visit their homes. For the summer cottages of North Conway and Lower Bartlett (incorporating Intervale), I received invaluable aid from the Archives and Records Center, University of Pennsylvania, Philadelphia; Richard Balboni, Quincy, Mass.; Ann Cullinan, Henney Historical Room, Conway Public Library; Eileen Davis, Wildflowers Guest House; David Emerson and Ann Levesque, Conway Historical Society; Mrs. Charles P. (Mary N. H.) Dethier, Blue Hill, Maine; Robert Duncan; Carrie Gleason, librarian, North Conway Public Library; Chalmers Hardenbergh, Yarmouth, Maine; Mr. and Mrs. Charles E. Houghton, Jr.; Carl E. Lindblade, Red Jacket Mountain View Motor Inn; Dr. Thomas J. McDonough; Peter Rattay, Stonehurst Manor; Rev. F. Lee Richards, historiographer, Episcopal Diocese of Pennsylvania, Philadelphia; Mr. and Mrs. Arlond C. Shea; Aaron B. Webber, student archivist, Olin and Chambers Libraries, Kenyon College, Gambier, Ohio; and Mrs. Robert G. (Helen) von Bernuth. In studying the houses of Jackson, I was offered help by numerous individuals, including George Beal, South Newbury, N.H.; Mr. and Mrs. Bradford L. Boynton; Mr. and Mrs. Roland E. Christie, Jr.; Mr. and Mrs. James Cooper, the Inn at Thorn Hill; Mrs. J. Arthur (Rachel) Doucette; Dr. Ashton Emerson; Mrs. Rodney (Alta M.) Gale, Eagle Rock, Calif.; Mrs. Buhrman B. (Margaret) Garland; J. Ritchie, Frederick, Arnold and Nancy Garrison; Robert T. Halloran; Mrs. Delmar F. (Charlotte) Haskell, Donald A. Jackson; Helen M. Kerr, Lexington, Mass.; Paul Lodi; Mr. and Mrs. Cronan Minton; Mrs. John B. (Alice) Pepper, Jackson Historical Society; Dr. William D. Sohair; Mrs. John J. (Joanne) Sutton; and Laurie Tradewell, the Inn at Jackson. My task of researching the single-season residential architecture of Randolph and Jefferson was immeasurably facilitated by Malcolm G. Call; Mr. and Mrs. H. Adams Carter; Mr. and Mrs. Charles G. Chlanda; Rupert E. Corrigan; Evelyn Foss, Lancaster, N.H.; Ruth Harris, Whitefield Historical Society; Mrs. Stephen (Deborah) Ives, New Boston, N.H.; Helen Merrill, Jefferson Historical Society; and Benjamin R. Sears, Bedford, Mass. In Gorham and Shelburne, I was assisted by Mrs. Howard Gorham; Connie and Anne Leger, Philbrook Farm Inn; Francis Peabody, Gorham Historical Society; Mr. and Mrs. Douglas A. Philbrook; and Scott Wilfong.

Given the high number of summer dwellings constructed there, the town of Bethlehem required the most research inquiries of all the vacation resort communities in the mountains. I am extremely grateful to Hardy Banfield, "Adair"; the late Martha L. Batchelder, Milton, Mass.; Mr. and Mrs. Charles F. Batchelder III, Rome, N.Y.; Neil Brody; Mrs. Floyd S. (Murial) Brown, librarian, Bethlehem Public Library; Harold Brown; Mrs. Robert E. (Cheryl) Burns; Leslie Dreier; Mr. and Mrs. George Epstein; Barbara Ferringo; Abe M. Goldstone; Curt Gowdy, Boston; Richard Hamilton; Rodney Haywood; Frances Heald and Arthur F. March, Jr., Littleton Area Historical Society; Mr. and Mrs. Kenneth King, Dover, Mass.; Nigel Manley, director, The Rocks Estate, Society for the Protection of New Hampshire Forests; Mrs. Steven (Frances) Marszalkowski; Michael McHose; Tim McKeever, Lisbon, N.H.; Robert MacLean; Leonard Reed; Richard Reinhold; Mrs. Mark Salton, Hartsdale, N.Y.; Mr. and Mrs. Gus C. Sanborn; Mr. and Mrs. Howard Sanborn; Roland Shick; Louise Sims; Doris Stevenson; Nancy Stevenson; Kathryn Taylor, librarian, Littleton Public Library; Mickey Whitcomb; Mrs. Victor R. (Ruth) Whitcomb; and Mr. and Mrs. Neil Winton.

Of the remaining towns with concentrations of summer houses, Franconia and Sugar Hill offered unusually rich research possibilities, and I am indebted to several individuals in each town. My thanks are due to Mrs. Roger H. (Nancy) Aldrich; Richard Burwell; Peter de Vries, Knoxville, Tenn.; Mrs. Albert E. Dower, Fort Meyers, Fla.; Joseph Fobes, Manchester, N.H.; George E. Foss; Paul W. Foss; Rosemary Mallery Gregg; Gordon E. Hyam, The Inn at Forest Hills; David Mallery, Philadelphia, Pa.; Susan Packard; Barbara Serafini; Virginia Sohn, Beverly Farms, Mass.; John D. Starr, Littleton; Donald G. Straw; Mr. and Mrs. Steven K. Trooboff; Mrs. Mitchell C. (Jane L.) Vincent, curator, Sugar Hill Historical Museum; and Robert Whitney. For the Mathews houses in West Campton, I was assisted by Margaret K. Campbell; Rev. Bayard Hancock; and Carol H. Newcomb. For information on properties in the area comprising Holderness, Sandwich, and Moultonborough, I am grateful to the late Julia Coolidge; Howard Corsack; Dennis Cushing, Bald Peak Colony Club; Robin Dustin, director, Sandwich Historical Society; James Gray, Purity Springs Company; Mr. and Mrs. Peter Kampf, Piedmont, Calif.; Barry H. Rodrique, Quebec

City, Quebec, Canada; J. Paul Sticht, Purity Springs Company; Mrs. John (Kip) Scott; Mr. and Mrs. John H. Valentine, Jr., Carlisle, Mass.; Wayne Wakefield, Bald Peak Colony Club; and Mr. and Mrs. Laurence J. Webster III. In Tamworth, particularly the Chocorua, Wonalancet, and Great Hill sections, I most appreciate the assistance of Mr. and Mrs. Samuel I. Bowditch, New London, N.H.; Judy Rubel Bradford; David Brown; Bernice M. Burke; Mrs. Peter A. (Joan A.) Casarotto; Mrs. Richard T. Gill, Fort Lauderdale, Fla.; Virginia B. Harlan; Mrs. John B. (Mabel) Hidden; Kay M. Hubbell, Conway, N.H.; Margaret Johnson; William H. Kiser, Atlanta, Ga.; John F. Lewis, Malvern, Pa.; David Loring; Mr. and Mrs. Wayne Mock; Scott Paul; Mrs. Peter (Marty Bemis) Perry, Concord, Mass.; Mr. and Mrs. John Peter; Mrs. Thomas (Donna T.) Rourke, Venice, Fla.; Alan A. Smith, Concord, Mass.; Mr. and Mrs. Peter M. Snyder, Cambridge, Mass.; Rev. William H. Thompson; Mr. and Mrs. Stephen M. Weld, Boston; Mrs. Leonard (Cornelia B.) Wheeler, Cambridge, Mass.; Mr. and Mrs. John F. Woodhouse, Houston, Tex.; Major and Mrs. Jack M. Wellinghurst; and George Zink. For cottages in outlying locations, I wish to thank Stephen A. Barba, president, The Balsams Grand Resort Hotel, Dixville Notch; Joel and Cathy Bedor, and Charles Ricardi, Mount Washington Hotel and Resort, Bretton Woods; Ed Butler, The Notchland Inn, Harts Location; and Faith Kent, curator, Lancaster Historical Society.

Last, I want to express my gratitude to my wife, Carolyn, and my daughter, Thayer, for their valuable critical comments about the manuscript, Alex Zafiroglu and Becky McAndrews of my office staff for their diligent devotion to the task of word processing, and Linda Magner and Thom Thompson for their superb photo laboratory work which produced most of the illustrations included in this book. To individuals whom I have had inadvertently overlooked, I also extend my considerable thanks.

B.F.T., Jr.

Summer Cottages
in the
White Mountains

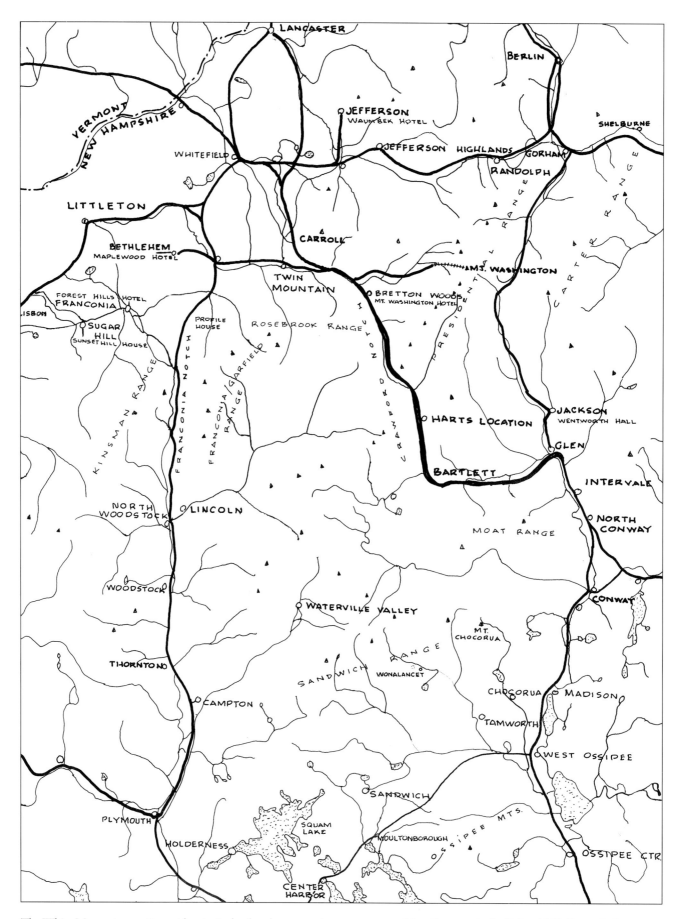

The White Mountains, c. 1893, with principal railroad routes and cottage communities. Cartography by Robert T. Holloran, Jackson, N.H.

Introduction

The Historical and Architectural Background

The summer cottage, the supreme architectural expression of family leisure and recreation, had its American origins in the mid-nineteenth century, achieving full-blown maturity by World War I. The phenomenon of the cottage, and the life-style associated with it, has persisted in a variety of forms, and is still strikingly evident in our contemporary culture. In the architectural lexicon, there is near unanimity as to the meaning of the term, "summer cottage." *Webster's New Twentieth Century Dictionary of the English Language* (1980), like most dictionaries, defines it as "a house at a resort or in the country, used for vacations or as a summer home." For many people the summer cottage is the ultimate symbol of professional, social, and financial success, and the epitome of what they perceive is virtuous and exemplary in our national society. As such, this distinctive residential structure is a fascinating and enlightening reflection of American social, cultural, and economic history, meriting our close scrutiny. In New Hampshire's White Mountains, the summer cottage and the resort hotel have long existed as complementary building types, providing valuable physical documentation of single-season vacation life over nearly a century and a half.

During the four decades before the Civil War, the United States underwent rapid and dramatic economic and social change, producing conditions that fostered tourism and made possible the origins and development of resort communities in the Northeast and elsewhere. From the 1820s to the 1850s, the American economy became more diversified, with traditional agrarian, maritime, and artisan activities supplemented, and ultimately eclipsed by industrialism and big business. As a consequence, the national economy greatly expanded, particularly in the years immediately following the Civil War, and per capita income rose, especially in the growing middle class. Hence, in this pre–income tax era, people possessed more disposable income as well as time to devote to leisure and material pursuits, including enjoyment of the resort experience. Simultaneously, technological advances, which launched the American Industrial Revolution, resulted in improved means of transportation: road systems were expanded; the steamship was invented, and steamship routes established; and, most important, the steam railroad engine was conceived, and railroad lines opened, reaching desirable rural locations from the 1840s to the 1880s. Actual as well as potential resort areas, therefore, became more accessible

"Maplewood Cottages on the Avenue" (Bethlehem Street), Maplewood Hotel and Cottages, Bethlehem, N.H., from booklet *Maplewood Hotel, Bethlehem, N.H.* (c. 1895). Author's collection.

and attractive, as travel time was significantly reduced and travel conditions more tolerable.

Other national factors, less quantifiable but equally important, encouraged tourism and fueled enthusiasm for resort communities and their distinctive hotel and cottage architecture. Urbanization in the mid- and late nineteenth century, with its many negative features, encouraged people to escape from the cities to the American countryside, seacoast, and wilderness areas to avoid summer heat, disease, congested and noisy living and working conditions, and the often intense competition of their professional careers and private social lives. In an effort to cope with these mounting pressures, many people, seeking nostalgia and historicity, gravitated to the seemingly simple, unsophisticated, morally upright, and older seacoast and inland towns and villages of New England (many of which became resort communities) and their romanticized Colonial pasts. Not to be discounted as a valid factor is the almost obsessive American interest in the novel, the unusual, and the fashionable, which resort life, with its separateness, exclusiveness, and glamour, often exemplified. Also lending impetus to the summer resort movement was the growing romanticization of the outdoor landscape and its spiritual, aesthetic, health, and recreational benefits. Nineteenth-century American literary giants such as Thoreau, Longfellow, Emerson, Whittier, and Bryant, and accomplished artists led by Cole, Kensett, Bierstadt, Inness, Durand, Doughty, and Thomas Hill helped to publicize and popularize the natural landscape, and draw people to the new and burgeoning resorts from the cities and the suburbs. Ironically, many summer "rusticators," as they were sometimes called, found the vacation resort the perfect stage set in which to engage in the kind of material and social competition that most people sought to minimize in their everyday lives at home.

Beginning in the 1820s and 1830s, the White Mountain district began to ascend to prominence as a summer resort area. By the end of the nineteenth century, it was one of the most publicly visible, heavily marketed, and frequently visited centers of summer tourism in North America. Just what regional (as opposed to national) factors allowed it to achieve such exalted status? First and foremost were the rare beauty and the compelling historic associations of the district, and the specific natural attractions popularized by the writings of early explorers and adventurers, scientists, and American as well as European travelers. Once discovered, the White Mountains—with their lofty, sometimes exposed and rocky summits (Mount Washington, Mount Chocorua, Mount Mousilauke, Mount Lafayette, and so on), distinctive geological curiosities (The Profile, The Flume, Indian Head, The Basin, Elephant's Head), virgin forests, lakes (Echo, Profile, Saco, Chocorua), rivers and streams, many with lovely cascades (Glen Ellis Falls, Crystal Cascade, Flume Cascade, Georgiana Falls, Ripley Falls) —became sources of inspiration to numerous poets, novelists, and nonfiction writers, whose works brought the region further to the attention of the American public. This highly influential group included Bryant, Whittier,

Lucy Larcom, Edna Dean Proctor, James Fields, George Waldo Browne, John H. Spaulding, Benjamin G. Willey, Samuel Adams Drake, and Rev. Thomas Starr King, whose 1860 book *The White Hills* perhaps did more than any other nineteenth-century literary work to lure people to the White Mountains. Starting in the 1850s with their first publication, illustrated guidebooks (such as Tripp's, Appleton's, Eastman's, Chisholm's, and Osgood's/Sweetser's) educated the public about the area and its assets. Artists, commencing with the leading lights of the pre–Civil War Hudson River School, had a similar impact, most notably through printed reproductions of their sketches and paintings contained in serial and book publications, or issued independently. They were followed in the latter part of the century by an indigenous group of painters—led by Benjamin Champney, Frank H. Shapleigh, and Edward Hill, the brother of Thomas—whose luminous landscapes illustrated the virtues of summer life in and near the mountains, and the inherent value of close contact with nature.

The White Mountains achieved recognition as the ideal vacation solution for several other, equally significant reasons. The region benefited tremendously from its geographic proximity to the major population centers of the Northeast (Boston, New York, Philadelphia, Baltimore, Washington) as well as to the British Isles and Europe, from which it drew a surprising number of visitors each year. The mountains thereby enjoyed a marketing advantage over parts of North America that were farther removed from the East Coast and Europe and where the population was less concentrated. Competition from the western United States and Canada was minimal until after 1900, largely due to the lack of adequate transportation links and traveler's amenities. Starting in the 1850s, early railroad companies such as the Atlantic and St. Lawrence, the Northern, the Eastern, the Portland and Ogdensburg, and the Boston, Concord, and Montreal, supplemented or altogether replaced the stage routes, opening up the entire district from the east, south, and west. Once they became well established after the Civil War, the railroads and the hotels symbiotically joined in a common economic enterprise, aggressively promoting the assets of the mountain region and attracting hordes of tourists. Once there, substantial numbers of them became converted to the possibilities and advantages of the resort experience, and its varied social, recreational, and cultural offerings. Between 1890 and 1915, the state of New Hampshire published a series of promotional booklets (with titles like *New Hampshire Farms for Summer Homes*), which further convinced people of the merits of summer residency in the North Country.

The cottage phenomenon in the White Mountains was the direct outgrowth of the hotel development there. Many of the region's earliest cottage owners were former hotel guests, who stayed in cottages either owned and operated by the hotels, or financed with private money and built on hotel grounds. Among the larger hotels most active in providing the cottage option were the Profile House at Franconia Notch, Wentworth Hall at Jackson, the Waumbek at Jefferson, the Waterville Inn at Waterville Val-

The Hayes/Fernald cottage (c. 1889), Jackson, N.H. Photograph by the author.

"Profile House and Cottages," Franconia Notch, N.H., from booklet *Franconia Notch, White Mountains, N.H.* (c. 1910). Author's collection.

"Conni Sauti" (1892–93), Chocorua, Tamworth, N.H. Photograph by the author.

ley, the Maplewood at Bethlehem, and the Sunset Hill House at Sugar Hill. Cottage dwellers at the hotels developed residency habits and patterns which were consistent with a separate living environment, and reflected an independent life-style. In the associated cottages many sought privacy, solitude, and flexibility not possible in the often regimented, artificial, "sociological fishbowl" existence of the hotels. Yet, almost without exception, the private family cottage communities grew up in proximity to the hotels that spawned them.

Whether or not they were introduced to the cottage concept through the hotels, people were frequently motivated to create their own vacation residences because of the appeal and prestige derived from property ownership, as well as the wish for a real estate investment and a financial "stake" in a North Country community. Once there, many cottage owners established a strong presence in their communities, in some cases exercising philanthropy, and contributing their money as well as time to worthy causes, good works, and local church groups and organizations. Separate living conditions also provided cottagers the opportunity to bring together family groups in private, personalized settings, and to accommodate and entertain guests according to their own standards. Through cottage ownership, many summer vacationers satisfied a desire to create special, individualized living environments as expressed in architecture, interior furnishings and decor, site layout, landscaping, and carefully contrived mountain and valley vistas. Examples of such devotion to planning may still be observed in each of the prominent White Mountain cottage colonies.

"Toad Hall" (Krantz family, c. 1910 and after), Franconia, N.H. Photograph by the author.

"Highland Croft" (1909–10), Littleton, N.H., photograph from *New Hampshire Farms for Summer Homes* (10th ed., 1912), p. 12. Author's collection.

Another attraction of cottage life was the opportunity it offered people to pursue individual interests. Many saw the summer residence in the mountains as the perfect rural retreat at which to carry on professional activities or hobbies such as music, writing, art, horticulture, and natural history. Others, such as the Glessners in Bethlehem, the Astons in Shelburne, or the Websters in Holderness, used their extensive properties to practice forms of agriculture, including crops production, fruit culture, and animal husbandry. These large landholders, and the great majority of their summer neighbors, had a fervent interest in preserving natural resources, and made every effort to follow up-to-date forestry methods. Substantial numbers of people found the summer cottage the ideal staging base for the pursuit of outdoor recreational or athletic activities such as trail hiking, fishing, bowling, croquet, boating, hunting, swimming, horseback riding, badminton, tennis, and golf. As a consequence, property owners often constructed their own tennis and badminton courts, boathouses, pitch and putt courses, indoor bowling alleys, game rooms, and riding and hiking trails as adjuncts to their cottages and outbuildings.

The arrival of the automobile to the White Mountains around the turn of the century provided further impetus to the cottage movement over the subsequent three decades. Offering increased freedom, flexibility, and mobility, this remarkable new invention gradually supplanted the railroads as the primary form of transportation to, from, and within the region. While railroad access was restricted to specific points of embarkation and disembarkation, the automobile could go anywhere there were passable roads. The new transportation technology permitted cottage owners to travel literally door to door, from their winter residences to their summer retreats. Furthermore, the automobile allowed families to build cottages virtually anywhere they could acquire land, which gave them access to the most advantageous sites with the best aesthetic as well as practical features.

The Fitz cottage (c. 1888), Jackson, N.H. Photograph by the author.

"Kilmarnock" (1906), Cleveland Hill, Tamworth, N.H., photograph from *New Hampshire Farms for Summer Homes* (4th ed., 1906), p. 12. Author's collection.

Who then were the people who were drawn to the White Mountains, and who financed and built privately owned, single-family summer houses there? Most members of this group were accomplished in their respective fields, with high public profiles. A few were wealthy, and nearly all were of comfortable financial means, and able to commit the time required to enjoy fully the summer vacation experience. The vast majority represented the upper socioeconomic echelons of their communities, for the most part the larger cities and suburbs of the Northeast. Not surprisingly, people from Boston and other New England urban centers tended to populate the resorts of the Eastern Slope Region of the White Mountains, while those from Connecticut southward based themselves more often in the readily accessible west side district; Chocorua and Jackson were distinctly Bostonian, for example, while Bethlehem and Sugar Hill drew from the Mid-Atlantic states. Fully thirty-seven of nearly one hundred vacation house owners mentioned in this book were the subjects of profiles in major biographical reference works (*Dictionary of American Biography*, *The National Cyclopaedia of American Biography*), or were listed in *Who Was Who in America*, *Who's Who in America*, or similar volumes. Constituting the group were businessmen, lawyers, physicians, ministers, educators, government officials, writers, artists, and some people of leisure, living off their financial resources. While many of the summer cottage dwellers were married couples with families, in several instances, single women or men acquired property, and built and occupied houses to their liking. Nearly all were committed to Protestant denominations. A significant percentage were college educated (there was a large contingent of Harvard alumni), and a number, particularly the academics and theologians, possessed advanced degrees. The majority were highly cultured, well-read individuals, with

"El Fureidis" (first, c. 1883–84), Blair's Colony, West Campton, N.H. Photograph courtesy of Carol Newcomb, West Campton, N.H.

"Arden Cottage" (1881), Wentworth Hall and Cottages, Jackson, N.H. Photograph by the author.

travel experience and exposure to sophisticated social life in both urban and rural settings.

It has been exciting and rewarding to research the identity of the individuals who designed and built the summer cottages and related outbuildings in the White Mountain region. Available sources disclose that the great majority of these structures were planned by professional architects and architectural firms, in most instances with offices in the cities where their clients maintained year-round residences. Only a small number of buildings were designed by New Hampshire architects. Some were the creation of people untrained in architecture, but skilled in related fields such as structural engineering or the visual arts. Still others were conceived by a small group of highly talented North Country contractors, carpenters, or builders, who occasionally performed the dual role of architect and builder, frequently relying on published design sources to influence and guide them in their work. The major names in the region were Sylvanus D. Morgan of Lisbon, Eugene C. Gale of Jefferson, Waldo C. Whitcomb of Bethlehem, Andrew C. Harriman of Jackson, and Larkin D. Weed of Sandwich. These men were remarkably flexible and enterprising in their contracting management and work patterns, capable of functioning independently or in tandem with big-name architects or firms far removed from northern New Hampshire. Upon occasion, cottage owners themselves played a highly

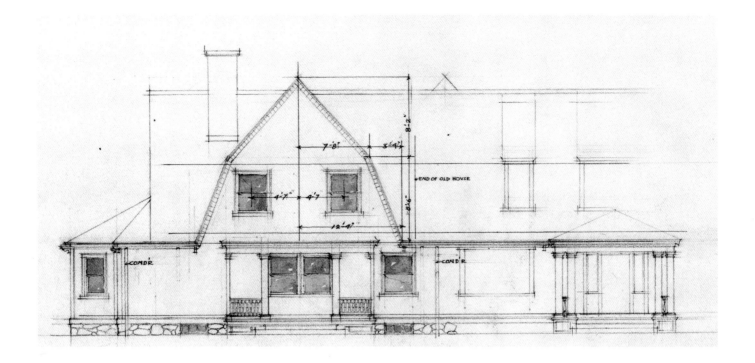

"Addition to House for E. C. Clarke Esq., Tam-
worth, N.H., Peabody & Stearns, Architects."
Drawing, c. 1897. Peabody and Stearns Collection,
Boston Public Library. Reproduced courtesy of the
Trustees of the Boston Public Library.

active role in the design and construction processes, expressing and implementing their own ideas about the form they wished their houses and other
buildings to assume. The appendix lists approximately forty architects and
firms, along with the names, locations, and dates of their commissions, and
the names of their clients. Their names range from some of the most highly
respected and recognized professionals in the United States—Stanford
White, Charles Follen McKim, William R. Emerson, Charles A. Platt,
John Calvin Stevens, C. Howard Walker, and Robert S. Peabody and John
G. Stearns—to lesser-known figures in the field whose careers are barely
mentioned, if at all, in architectural serials, reference volumes, or other historical works.

Between 1860 and 1930, these architects and builders produced a collection of summer cottages in the White Mountains that represented an evolution of national architectural styles, with regional variations. With some
notable exceptions, these buildings possessed the common qualities of simplicity, rusticity, moderate size, and practicality. In most cases the houses of
the mountain region were the antithesis of the great vacation "cottages" of
other major resort areas in the Northeast—eastern Long Island, Newport,
Manchester-by-the-Sea, the Berkshires of western Massachusetts, and Bar
Harbor. Far less monumental and extravagant, they were generally smaller,
were built almost exclusively of native materials, and were linked aesthetically and functionally to the natural environment of the mountains.
Furthermore, they accommodated a much less sophisticated, and more
informal, relaxed, and flexible life-style than their English and European-
inspired counterparts at these other resorts. The great majority were constructed on two stories, the second floor accommodating living quarters,

and the first a large, multipurpose common room or parlor, supplemented by dining, kitchen, hallway, porch, and other spaces. Almost by definition, the White Mountain cottages were indigenous to the land—they were built to coexist rather than conflict with nature, to be compatible instead of to stand out conspicuously as did so many of the mansions at the other fashionable summer communities.

The White Mountain district is a fascinating and informative case study region for investigating the architectural styles of the American summer cottage during this period. Fundamentally inspired by the Gothic Revival, the first, relatively small cottages of the area were unostentatious expressions of the Stick and Swiss chalet vernaculars—excellent examples were "Buckeye Cottage" (1873) and the Maplewood Hotel cottages (c. 1875 and after) at Bethlehem; the first "Stonehurst" (1871–72; 1875–77), "Kilbarchan" (1879), and "Bergenheim" (c. 1880) at the Intervale colony, North Conway; the Waterville Inn cottages (c. 1870) at Waterville Valley; the Profile House cottages (1868 and after) in Franconia Notch; "Ossipee Mountain Park" (c. 1880–81) at Moultonborough; and the Bemis cottage (1856–68) at Hart's Location. The American country version of the Queen Anne style was present in the marvelous cottages of Wentworth Hall hotel (1881 and after) and the Wigglesworth house (c. 1888) in Jackson; "The Stone House" (1884–85) in Shelburne; and the "Big House" (1883) at "The Rocks" estate and "The Gables" (1893–94) at Bethlehem. Most of these buildings may still be seen today.

The summer cottage phenomenon in the White Mountains achieved its most pronounced expression in three styles extremely popular in this coun-

East elevation, "Burleigh Brae" (1910–11), Holderness, N.H. Photograph by the author.

try from around 1880 into this century—the Shingle, the Colonial Revival, and the Craftsman. Of these three, the Shingle and the Craftsman—both highly versatile, imaginative, and concerned with the interplay of materials and nature—were most appropriate for the region, while the Colonial Revival—restrictive, formalistic, and academic—in many respects seemed out of place. Several outstanding examples of the Shingle style were constructed at White Mountain summer communities, and nearly all survive. Foremost of this group were "Wyndham Villa" (1884–85) in Shelburne; the McCabe cottage (1892–93) in Jefferson Highlands; "The Outlook" (1890–91) and "The Glamis" (1904–5) in Bethlehem; the second "Stonehurst" (1895), "The Knoll" (1885–86), "Nirvana" (c. 1885–86), and "Concordia Hut" (1888–89) in Intervale; the Fitz cottage (c. 1888), "The Satyr" (1892), and "Maple Knoll" (1896–97) in Jackson; "The Homestead" (1896) in Holderness; and "Conni Sauti" (1892–93), "Willowgate" (1899–1900), and "Avoca" (c. 1905–6) in the Chocorua section of Tamworth. Despite its seeming incompatibility with its surroundings, the Colonial Revival made its mark in "The Boulders" (1895) in Jackson; "The Hummocks" (1897–98) in Jefferson Highlands; "Edgemont" (c. 1903), the Frank house (1923–24) and "Adair" (1927–28) in Bethlehem; and "Heavenly Hill" (1898–99) and "Birch Knoll" (1913) in Chocorua. The Craftsman style, inspired primarily by the work of the California firm Greene and Greene, left its mark in the White Mountains in such houses as "Lone Larch" (1917) and "Upland Cottage" (1918) in Bethlehem; "Mount Prospect Lodge" (1912–13) in Lancaster; "Kilmarnock" (1906) in Tamworth; "Juniper Lodge" (1910–11) in Chocorua; "Burleigh Brae" (1910–11) in Holderness; and "Highland Croft" (1909–10) in Littleton. Other architecturally notable houses drew from these and other style vocabularies, some European and Asian in derivation—unusually outstanding, highly eclectic examples were "The Lodge" (1892) and "The Bells" (1892) in Bethlehem; the Waumbek Hotel cottages (c. 1890–c. 1900) in Jefferson; "Lucknow" (1911–14) in Moultonborough; and "Funfield" (1916) in Sugar Hill.

The summer cottage movement in the White Mountains originated and flourished there for very compelling reasons. The original financiers/owners, as well as their architects and builders, were almost without exception talented and visionary people with a genuine affection for and an innate sense of the region. The illustrated essays contained in this book illuminate in some detail their architectural legacy to New Hampshire, New England, and the nation. Unlike the White Mountain hotels, which, with a few notable exceptions, have passed to history, the cottages have largely survived as physical documents of a once active, multifaceted, and yet tempered summer life-style.

Summer Cottages and Cottage Communities in the White Mountains

Cottage life among tourists to the White Mountains is rapidly growing in popularity. . . . This new phase of summer life possesses many attractions. While on the one hand cottagers can live in a quiet and semi-exclusive manner, on the other they can at pleasure share in the excitement and festivities of the . . . hotels. Cottage life is the connecting link between the charm of repose and the sweetness of activity, and possesses the attractions of both.

Among the Clouds *11, no. 7
(18 July 1887), p. 4*

1 ≈

North Conway/ Intervale

Comprising the northwest portion of Conway township, the village of North Conway saw in the 1820s its economic base begin to shift from agriculture, commerce, and artisanry to tourism. This occurred as word of the natural attractions of the Saco Valley and the surrounding mountains reached the population centers of the Northeast, and better road transportation made the area more accessible from Boston, Portland (Maine), and other cities. The oldest of the White Mountains' summer tourist centers, North Conway saw its earliest hostelries, the McMillan, Moat Mountain, and Washington houses, before 1820, followed by the famous Kearsarge Tavern, established by Samuel W. Thompson in about 1825. Through Thompson's enterprising efforts, the village was widely promoted as a summer resort, and the first members of what would eventually become the noted White Mountain School of painters visited the valley. During the 1850s, the landscape scenes of John F. Kensett, Benjamin Champney, and other artists, coupled with the work of printmakers and photographers, further directed attention to North Conway's many assets. Among the first bona fide hotels constructed were the North Conway House (1858), the Kearsarge House (1861 and after), Randall House (1864), the Sunset Pavilion (1867), and Mason's Hotel (1871). The arrival of the railroads—the Portland and Ogdensburg (later the Maine Central) and the Great Falls and Conway (subsequently the Boston and Maine)—in 1872 and 1873 provided even greater impetus to the tourist industry, resulting in further hotel expansion. Eastman House was put up around 1872, and in Kearsarge Village, on the east side of North Conway, Russell Cottages was opened around 1863, and The Ridge in 1885.

A direct outgrowth of local hotel development were summer residences, virtually all of which were located at Kearsarge Village, and at Intervale on the north end of the village and in the southeastern section (Lower Bartlett) of the adjacent town of Bartlett. One of the pioneers of the hotel trade, W. H. H. Trickey, anticipated the coming of tourism to Intervale when he erected the Intervale House, later to assume grand resort hotel status, in 1868. The new railroad routes (which converged at Intervale) further spurred hotel development, resulting in the establishment of Pendexter Mansion (c. 1874), East Branch House (before 1874), Langdon House (1884), Pitman Hall (1888–89), Maple Villa (1895), and The Fairview (1896) in Bartlett, and the Idlewild (1870s), Bellevue House (1871–72), and Clarendon House (1890–91) south of the town line in North Conway.

A number of visitors to the area, some former patrons of these facilities, chose to erect single-season cottages in the North Conway district of Intervale, thereby creating a summer colony closely associated with hotel life. Originating from Boston, New Haven, New York, and Philadelphia, many of these people were connected to Harvard University and were linked also by common social, intellectual, and religious lifestyles. Setting the precedent for the larger summer houses was Erastus B. Bigelow, the carpet manufacturing magnate from Massachusetts, who built the first Bigelow/Merriman family dwelling, "Stonehurst," in 1871–72. The products of Boston-area architects, other cottages soon appeared in a variety of late Victorian architectural styles for the Schoulers (1879), the Fettes (c. 1880), the Curries (c. 1885–86), the Hurds (1885–86), and the Nichols (1888–89).

North of the town line in Lower Bartlett, other much more modest summer residences (such as "Sylva-of-the-Pines," c. 1902) were built along the main road, now Route 16A, and two religious communities were established: the Intervale Park Colony, by Rev. Dr. Charles Cullis of Boston in the 1880s on a foothill of Bartlett Mountain; and the New Church Divine group, initiated by Swedenborgian Dr. John Worcester from Massachusetts, based at "Worcester Cottage" on Worcester Hill Road. Among the houses at Kearsarge Village, those raised for the Pratt family (1894) and Miss Carruth (c. 1911) are most significant architecturally. "Birchmont" (1890–93), the Tucker estate south of North Conway village on Sunset Hill, was isolated from the Intervale and Kearsarge communities, but was an important and integral part of the history of the North Conway/Intervale summer cottage movement.

"Stonehurst"

1871–72; 1875–77; 1895

(Mr. and Mrs. Erastus B. Bigelow)

(Rev. and Mrs. Daniel S. Merriman)

North Conway (Intervale)

"Stonehurst" (first, 1871–72), Intervale, North Conway, N.H., photograph from glassplate negative. Courtesy of the Conway (N.H.) Historical Society.

CONCEIVED AND DEVELOPED over the course of a quarter of a century by the Bigelows of Massachusetts, "Stonehurst" is the epitome of the English country estate in New Hampshire's White Mountains. In this region it was the supreme statement of rural elegance, rivaled only by "The Rocks" in Bethlehem and "Wyndham Villa" in Shelburne. In contrast to these other working farm complexes, however, "Stonehurst" has retained all of its original major buildings. Despite physical alterations and changes in ownership and function over the years, the site conveys much the same impression as it did a century ago, and provides important physical evidence of upper-class summer architecture and life in late-Victorian America.

The man behind the creation of "Stonehurst" and Intervale's first summer resident was Erastus B. Bigelow (1814–79), the wealthy and well-known carpet manufacturer from Clinton, Massachusetts. Born in nearby West Boylston, he attended the district school and held various jobs during his teenage years. As a boy he pursued several intellectual and artistic activities, including arithmetic and music, his favorite pastime. By 1830, he had saved enough money to enter Leicester Academy, and he had visions of attending Harvard and studying medicine. Lacking his father's backing and having exhausted his financial resources, he instead entered the dry goods business of S. F. Morse & Company in Boston, mastered stenography, and published a small work on the subject, which did not sell well. He was destined, however, to become an inventor and economist. His first major invention, in 1837, was a power loom for the production of coach lace, which established the technological basis for the many other power looms that would follow. In Leicester in 1838, he, his brother Horatio N., and two other men, formed a new manufacturing enterprise, The Clinton Company, to build and operate the new looms. Over the next twenty years, Bigelow's mechanical discoveries multiplied, and included power looms for the fabrication of Brussels, Wilton, tapestry and velvet carpetings, as well as counterpanes, silk brocatel, ginghams, pile fabrics, and wire cloth. The town of Clinton, the center of the Bigelow manufacturing empire, grew up around the first mill, with additional factories at Lowell, Massachusetts, and Derby, Connecticut. Over his career, he constantly improved and refined methods of carpet production, and his contributions to the industry were widely recognized, in both the United States and Europe.

While Erastus Bigelow is most often associated with his many important mechanical inventions, he also established a reputation as an economist. He wrote about the tariff issue, and expressed his advocacy of import duties in several articles and two books—*The Tariff Question Considered in Regard to the Policy of England and the Interests of the United States* (1862) and *The Tariff Policy of England and the United States Contrasted* (1877). He served as the first president of the National Association of Wool Manufacturers. In addition, he ran for United States Congress in 1860, but was defeated. He followed closely the field of scientific education, serving in 1861 as a member of the founding committee for the Massachusetts Institute of Technology. Yale, Harvard, Williams, Dartmouth, and Amherst marked his many achievements with honorary degrees. In "Stonehurst," Bigelow found a place for relaxation, repose, and social entertaining, but also delighted in applying his penchant for invention in farming and irrigation.[1]

Erastus Bigelow made his initial land purchase in Intervale in 1870, acquiring the former Willey farm from Stephen Mudgett of Conway. He and his wife had some knowledge of the area from staying at Eastman's boarding house in 1865. Between 1870 and 1872, he added several adjacent tracts, until he had amassed a substantial estate comprising several hundred acres.[2] For the location of the family house, he and his wife, Eliza, chose a lovely site on the crest of a slight ridge, looking out over the Saco River Intervale toward Cathedral and White Horse Ledges, the Moat Mountain Range, and the Presidential peaks in the distance. According to a marvelously rich family diary, "Annals of Stonehurst," in the manuscript archives of the Massachusetts Historical Society, construction on the house

"Stonehurst" (third, 1895), Intervale, North Conway, N.H., photograph from *New Hampshire Farms for Summer Homes* (6th ed., 1908), frontispiece. Author's collection.

"Stonehurst" (third, 1895), Intervale, North Conway, N.H. Photograph by the author.

began in 1871 and was completed by May 1872, when the Bigelows took up occupancy. Materials for the building project were shipped by wagon from Conway Center and Fryeburg, Maine.

Commissioned as architects was the Boston firm of Snell and Gregson. The senior and best known of the partners, George Snell (1820–93), came to the United States from England in 1850, and established a broad reputation as the designer of private homes, public buildings, and warehouses in Boston. Somewhat of a departure from Snell's Massachusetts work, the Bigelow cottage was a large Stick-style structure with such common features as steep-pitched truncated (jerkinhead) main and dormer roofs; scalloped eaves verge boards; thin, fragile-looking eaves and porch trusses; and variegated wall siding with clapboards, flat boards, and half-timbering. The plan was asymmetrical, with an attached veranda, porte cochere, and rear ice house topped by a pyramidal roof with cupola/ventilator. Unfortunately, this provocative building was totally leveled by fire on 12 February 1875, but the Bigelows promptly rebuilt. Over the next two years, using the original Snell and Gregson plans, they recreated the destroyed cottage, so that it was an almost exact duplicate. They moved into the new house in September 1877.[3]

Sadly, Erastus Bigelow was able to enjoy "Stonehurst" for only a brief few years before his death. The entire property was inherited by his only child, Helen Bigelow Merriman, who in 1874 had married the Reverend Daniel S. Merriman. Educated at Williams College and Andover Theological Seminary, Merriman (1838–1912) served for twenty-three years as pastor of the Central Church in Worcester, Massachusetts. During his tenure there he was a trustee of several educational institutions including Williams, Atlanta University, Worcester Polytechnic Institute, and Abbot Academy, also in Massachusetts. In addition, Merriman was the first president of the Worcester Art Museum from 1896 until his death. He received honorary degrees from both Williams and Yale, and was known to be an eloquent, learned, and vigorous speaker.[4] He and his wife took a great interest in the North Conway community, particularly the local Congregational church; and it was they who brought the Worcester architect Stephen C. Earle (1839–1913) to the village to design the new North Conway Congregational Church in 1884 (see "Kilbarchan" and "Bergenheim," both North Conway). They also influenced friends to buy land and construct summer residences in Intervale, and served as the focal point for much of the social, intellectual, and cultural life of the small colony. Helen Merriman, an artist, writer, and philanthropist, served as president of the North Conway Public Library, founded the Memorial Hospital in memory of her parents, held annual fundraisers, and was active in local land and forest preservation.[5] Although they were primarily summer residents, the Merrimans probably had a greater impact on their community than any other vacation cottage owners of their era in the mountains.

In 1895, desiring a larger, more lavish, and more fashionable summer residence, Helen Merriman orchestrated a complete refurbishing and enlargement of the main house at "Stonehurst." The project took ten months to complete. The result, in what she called the English Manor Style, was an imposing Shingle-style building in which the shape of the 1875–77 cottage is barely visible. Irregular in the configuration of its elevations and floor plan, the new Merriman house was sheathed with dark-stained shingles, with which the mortared fieldstone foundations and porte-cochere support posts very effectively contrast. The fenestration is irregular (the original shutters have been removed), with double sashes containing small panes. The second story projects slightly over the first, with the shingles flared above the demarcation line. Topping the house and providing an ample attic story are a series of intersecting gable roofs, clipped at their ends and penetrated by dormers similarly treated. The eaves overhangs are pronounced, with rafter heads exposed. On the front (west) facade, two second-story sleeping porches and a large first-story veranda offer superb valley and mountain vistas. Although the original furnishings are gone, today the twenty-three-room interior is replete with magnificent English oak woodwork, including fireplace, doorway and window surrounds, doors, beamed ceilings, built-in bookcases, textured wall panels, and decorative carvings. The "Annals of Stonehurst" indicate that family friend Stephen Earle visited the estate during the construction period (he was present in October when the furniture was moved in), suggesting that he was indeed the architect. Another Worcesterite, C. O. Wheeler, served as supervising contractor, directing the efforts of a crew of stonemasons and carpenters.[6]

The Bigelow and Merriman residences stood at the center of a model working farm and cottage colony, the buildings of which are nearly all intact today. Almost as soon as he had acquired the Mudgett property, Erastus Bigelow and his family took up summer residency in the farmhouse, altering it to meet their needs. Immense barns, a carriage house/stable, and other outbuildings, supposedly planned by Bigelow himself, joined the complex in 1871–72, on the west side of the Conway-Jackson road. These structures all reflect the form of the first main house, with clipped gable (jerkinhead) roofs, board and batten siding, and cupola/ventilators. North of the main house, acquired as guest overflow facilities by the family, are the "Red Cottage" (on the main road), originally built by William C. Seavey in about 1865, and the "Brown Cottage" (Neighbors Row), erected in about 1895. The latter building is a fine, representative example of the transition in summer cottage architecture from the Queen Anne to the Shingle style.[7]

In the summer of 1907, while the Merrimans were traveling in England, the "Stonehurst" estate achieved notice as the temporary "British Embassy" for Viscount James Bryce (1838–1922), the British ambassador to the United States. Bryce, his wife, and his entourage occupied the main house, the two adjacent cottages, as well as space at the nearby Bellevue House hotel. A previous visitor to the White Mountains in 1870 (a visit he recorded in his travel journal), Bryce was a noted politician, diplomat, conservationist, historian, and legal scholar, and in 1888 published *The American Commonwealth*, which had great influence on the attitudes of his countrymen toward the United States. During that memorable, halcyon summer, "Stonehurst" was at the center of international diplomatic exchange, the Bryces' active and glamorous social life, and the ambassador's many hiking expeditions throughout the mountains. His favorite hiking companion was Rev. Harry P. Nichols (see "Concordia Hut," North Conway), with whom he cut Bryce's Path to Cathedral Ledge during his stay in North Conway.[8]

After Helen Merriman's death, the main house stood vacant for eleven years, and then was sold out of the family. Since 1946, it has served as an attractive, upscale country inn, which now includes the original house, a connected motel, condominiums, and recreational facilities.[9] Although the grounds of the estate have lost some integrity, the grand "Stonehurst" mansion has retained its historic character and passed to the current generation largely intact, recalling the time when it was the locus of the invigorating, carefree late-Victorian summer life of the Intervale colony.

≈

"Kilbarchan"

1879

(Mr. and Mrs. James Schouler)

North Conway (Intervale)

~ "KILBARCHAN," THE SCHOULER cottage at Intervale, North Conway, is one of only a few houses in the White Mountain region to receive national exposure in an architectural periodical at the time of its construction. The 8 March 1879 issue of *The American Architect and Building News* featured a full-page plate (see illustration) containing a perspective view, floor plans, and an interior detail. Accompanying this plate is the following brief paragraph:

> This cottage, built during the past season, is situated near the Intervale House [a neighboring grand resort hotel] and commands a charming prospect of the Saco [River], the meadows, and the mountains. It is designed as a quiet summer residence, and has been treated very simply, inside as well as outside. The finish being of white pine without paint and the floors plain hard pine. A. Thurber, of North Conway, was the contractor. The cost was $5,000.[10]

Erected on land acquired from Mary D. Pendexter, a local boarding house proprietor, in 1877, this distinctive, rustic, yet quite sophisticated twelve-room Stick-style building bears many characteristics of a nineteenth-century Swiss Alpine chalet.[11] Among its most prominent original features were steep-pitched sweeping roof planes, eaves truss brackets, unfinished tree-trunk porch columns, and an east-side, second-story balcony (removed some years ago) with turned balusters and contoured support brackets. Only slightly modified over the years, the Schouler cottage is historically significant as one of the earliest single-season dwellings built in the White Mountains region.

The designer of "Kilbarchan" (the name derives from the Schouler ancestral home in Scotland) was Stephen C. Earle (1839–1913), a somewhat obscure, nonetheless impressively productive Massachusetts architect. Ed-

"Cottage Built in North Conway for James Schouler, Esq. of Boston," plate from *American Architect and Building News* 5 (8 March 1879), no. 167. Courtesy of the University of Delaware Library, Newark, Delaware.

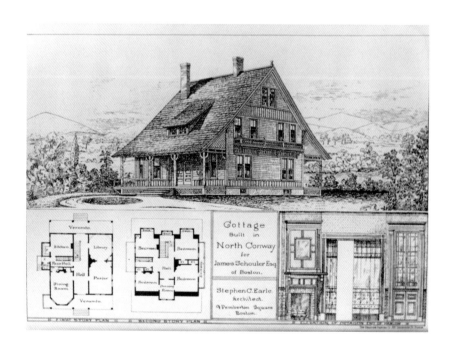

"Kilbarchan" (1879), Intervale, North Conway, N.H. Photograph by the author.

ucated at MIT, Earle established an office in Worcester in 1866, forming a partnership with James E. Fuller and preparing plans for a number of buildings in the city over the next six years. After this partnership was dissolved, Earle maintained an independent practice in Boston, but returned to Worcester in 1891 to establish another partnership with Clellan W. Fisher. Under the firm name Earle & Fisher, the two men were active for twenty years, planning churches and educational and public buildings in the Worcester area and elsewhere in New England. Among their most noteworthy commissions in Worcester were the Art Museum, the Free Public Library, St. Matthews Episcopal and Central Congregational churches, and structures at Clark University and Worcester Polytechnic Institute. Earle is known to have done very little residential work, and how he came to design the Schouler cottage remains a mystery.[12] He may have met the Schoulers through their Intervale neighbors, the Merrimans (see "Stonehurst," North Conway), however, as Merriman was the minister at Central Congregational Church in Worcester.

The conceiver and first owner of "Kilbarchan," James Schouler, belongs to a small honored group of White Mountain summer cottagers for whom biographical sketches are included in the *Dictionary of American Biography* (1935). Born in West Cambridge (Arlington), Massachusetts, in 1839, he graduated from Harvard in 1859, studied law, and was admitted to the Massachusetts bar in 1862. Hampered by deafness incurred while serving in the Union army during the Civil War, he entered the legal profession in Boston in 1863. Here he developed a lucrative practice based on war claims cases, and opened a branch office in Washington in 1869. Because of his disability, he committed himself to legal writing, establishing a broad reputation for his expertise, and earning substantial royalties. From the 1880s until 1908, he gave courses of lectures at the law schools of Boston University and the National University in Washington, and at Johns Hopkins University to American history graduate students. Schouler is perhaps most noted for his seven-volume *History of the United States of America under the Constitution* (written between 1880 and 1913), the first lengthy scholarly work to treat the period from the Revolution to Reconstruction (1783–1877). While his reputation as a political and constitutional historian rests largely with this work, he also wrote biographies of Alexander Hamilton and Thomas Jefferson, and books on state and federal constitutional studies, ideals of the American republic, and Americans at the time of independence.[13] During their many summers at Intervale, Schouler and his wife, Emily, were extremely active socially, and made notable cultural and civic contributions to the North Conway community, with particular interest in the public library. Schouler Park in the center of town is named after them. After his wife's death in 1904, Schouler lived year-round at his Intervale cottage, until he died in 1920, and the house then passed out of the family to other owners.[14]

⁓

"Bergenheim"

c. 1880

(Mr. and Mrs. William Eliot Fette)

North Conway (Intervale)

"Bergenheim" (c. 1880), Intervale, North Conway, N.H. Photograph by the author.

～ DURING THE LATE 1870s, Bostonians William Eliot Fette and his wife, Eliza H., were likely introduced to the White Mountains and the Intervale summer colony by Helen Bigelow Merriman, a first cousin of William Fette. In fact, it is quite conceivable that the Fettes' interest in the area, and the prospect of owning a summer cottage there, may well have kindled as a result of visits to "Stonehurst," the Bigelow/Merriman estate in Intervale. In 1879, they made a long-term real estate commitment by the purchase of a house lot, a few hundred yards north of "Stonehurst," on the opposite (west) side of the North Conway–Bartlett main road. It was on this spot around 1880 that the Fettes erected their charming and provocative cottage, "Bergenheim," the name inspired by family connections with central Europe. Like the nearby Schouler cottage, "Kilbarchan," the Fette house commands a marvelous westward view across the Saco River intervale to the Moat Range, and to the Presidential peaks, dominated by Mount Washington.[15]

An outstanding example of a Stick-style chalet, "Bergenheim" is unquestionably one of the White Mountain's most significant summer residences. Unlike most of its counterparts, it is virtually unaltered since the time of its construction and is in an excellent state of preservation. While the form of the building is a conventional rectangular box, the ornamentation is inordinately rich and varied. In typical Stick fashion, the walls are sheathed with yellow-painted board and batten siding, and are divided into sections by green vertical corner and horizontal sill and first-story-level flat boarding. The projecting eaves of the low-pitched roof are supported by large scroll brackets. Two substantial square brick chimneys with elaborate corbeled patterns rise above the main roof at the ridgepole. The windows are arranged in pairs, with two-over-two double sash under multiple square-paned transom lights. In the center of the south long wall, servicing the principal entrance, is a highly articulated pitched-roof porch, supported by turned posts and embellished with a saw-cut balustrade and entablature. On the front (east) gable end, at the second-floor level, is a picturesque bracket-supported balcony screening two sets of paired windows. The presumed date marker, "A.D. 1880," may be seen above these windows. The entire house rests securely on a mortared granite foundation. Slightly southwest of the house is a small one and a half story carriage barn, displaying compatible detailing.[16]

The architect of "Bergenheim" has yet to be identified, but there is ample room for speculation. Based on his Intervale connections, as well as stylistic similarities to his other works in North Conway, there is strong reason to believe that this individual may have been Stephen C. Earle (1839–1913) of Worcester, Massachusetts. Earle had close ties with the Merrimans, owners of "Stonehurst," in Worcester where Rev. Merriman was the pastor of Central Congregational Church (see "Kilbarchan," North Conway). It is believed that the Merrimans probably recommended Earle to their friends the Schoulers as architect for their quite similar Stick-style cottage. Erected in 1879, a year before "Bergenheim," "Kilbarchan" is a documented Earle commission. Furthermore, Earle was commissioned by the Merrimans in 1884 to design the North Conway Congregational Church, an outstanding amalgam of the Queen Anne and Shingle styles. Although it postdates the Fette cottage, this neighboring edifice is proof of Earle's continuing relationship with the Merrimans and the local community.[17]

William Eliot Fette (1839–99) was another of several Harvard-associated members of the Intervale summer society. Born in St. Louis, Missouri, he received his bachelor's degree from Harvard in 1858, returning to his alma mater in 1867–68 for a master's degree. After completing his bachelor's he opened a fashionable private school for boys in Boston, gradually transforming it from an intermediate to a classical preparatory institution. The West End Latin School, as it was known after 1867, graduated many distinguished Bostonians, several of whom went on to Harvard. In 1875, Fette left his school, and traveled in Europe for the next two years with his wife. Returning to Boston, he entered business, and for many years served as the president of the Danvers and Marblehead Gas Works. Always public-spirited, he was deeply involved in efforts to preserve the front of the Massachusetts State House, designed by Charles Bulfinch, and the Boston Common at the time it was threatened by subway development. Fette was also an occasional writer, publishing two series of *Dialogues of Dickens* in 1871 and 1872. The Fettes traveled to Europe again in 1885, and to the American West and South in 1897, during which time they rented their Intervale cottage. The house is still owned and inhabited by their descendants.[18]

~

"The Knoll"

1885–86

(Mr. and Mrs. Melancthon M. Hurd)

North Conway (Intervale)

"A Mountain Cottage at Intervale, N.H.—C. Howard Walker, Architect, Boston," plate from *The Sanitary Engineer and Construction Record*, 11 February 1886, p. 248. Peabody and Stearns Collection, Boston Public Library. Reproduced Courtesy of the Trustees of the Boston Public Library.

"The Knoll" (1885–86), Intervale, North Conway, N.H. Photograph by the author.

～ "THE KNOLL" AT INTERVALE was erected for Mr. and Mrs. Melancthon Hurd of New Haven, Connecticut, and New York City on a small tract of land acquired from Mary D. Pendexter, of the local hotel family, in September 1885.[19] Construction commenced soon thereafter, and extended into the spring of 1886. During the building period, an obscure periodical, *The Sanitary Engineer and Construction Record*, published a fine perspective view and description of this "moderate-cost," rambling, Shingle-style residence:

> This house . . . is intended as a summer cottage, with broad piazzas and many doors and windows. It is [set] upon cedar posts, and is finished with stained shingles and broad sidings upon piazzas. The interior has ash finish in [the] principal rooms, and marble mantels with brick facings and hearths. The windows have mill sashes.[20]

The same source identifies the architect as C. Howard Walker (1857–1936) of Boston, the designer of several vacation cottages in Chocorua, about twenty miles to the southeast (see "Pine Cone," Chocorua).[21] In contrast with Walker's Chocorua commissions, however, "The Knoll" possesses nearly symmetrical principal (west-facing) and side elevations; square, wood, knee-brace veranda columns instead of fieldstone; square, wood veranda balustrades, also in place of fieldstone; brick as opposed to stone chimneys; and other very pronounced features associated with its style (second-story flared shingle overhangs, curved gable-end attic ventilator hoods, geometric wall panels, and so on). With its long, low lines and balanced proportions, the Hurd house easily qualifies as one of the most outstanding Shingle-style dwellings in the White Mountain region.[22]

Drawn to Intervale because of his friendship with the Merrimans, Melancthon Montgomery Hurd (1828–1913) was born in Bridgeport, Connecticut, and took his education at local schools. In 1851 he married a home-town girl, Clara Hatch, and they had seven children, five of whom survived to adulthood. He joined with H. O. Houghton in 1864 to found the highly prominent publishing firm of Hurd and Houghton, which merged with James R. Osgood & Company in 1878 to become Houghton, Osgood and Company (taking the name of Houghton Mifflin Company in 1908). According to family sources, Hurd achieved business success early in his career, and decided to retire in 1871 when he was only in his forties.[23] In pursuit of leisure, pleasure, and intellectual stimulation, the Hurds took numerous trips to Europe, a practice they continued long after their Intervale cottage was built. Local newspapers reported several summer seasons when the Hurds rented "The Knoll" to other families from the Northeast or Midwest. When they were at Intervale, however, the Hurds were active participants in the life of their immediate neighborhood and the town of North Conway.[24]

"Nirvana"

c. 1885–86

(Rev. Dr. and Mrs. C. George Currie)

North Conway (Intervale)

"Nirvana" (c. 1885–86), Intervale, North Conway, N.H. Photograph by the author.

ON THE NORTH SIDE of Neighbors Row, on a rise overlooking Intervale village and the site of the Intervale House, is "Nirvana," the large Shingle-style summer cottage first owned by the Reverend Dr. and Mrs. C. George Currie of Philadelphia. It was erected in about 1885–86 on a small tract of land the Curries purchased from the local Dinsmore family in 1885.[25] Most impressive about the house is its irregular massing, consisting of substantial wings, porches, bay windows, and dormers with steep-pitch gable and hipped roofs. The pronounced pyramidal form of the main hipped roof echoes the silhouetted shapes of nearby Mount Kearsarge, as well as the adjacent hills. The overhanging, closed gables of the wings display half-timbering of the kind normally associated with English Tudor eclectic architecture. This is unusual in Shingle-style buildings. Balancing the strong horizontal lines of the house are vertical accents provided by the tall, white, brick chimneys, white-painted corner molding boards, and thin, bracketed porch columns.[26]

The design of "Nirvana," with its systematically articulated components and their refined embellishment, bespeaks the hand of a professional architect. Thus far, however, no evidence has surfaced to substantiate who this individual might be. Current Intervale residents have conjectured that Boston architect C. Howard Walker (1857–1936), who, around the same time, planned "The Knoll" next door for the Hurds, might also have been commissioned by the Curries to do their house. Furthermore, Walker's own cottage, "Pine Cone," which he designed and built at the Chocorua colony in about 1891–92, bears a close resemblance to "Nirvana." Another possibility, though less likely, is the well-known Philadelphia architect and art historian Mantle Fielding (1865–1941), who is known to have designed a year-round dwelling for Currie and his second wife in the Germantown section of Philadelphia in 1899. Widely recognized for his residential designs, Fielding would only have been twenty years old at the time, though he was listed in Philadelphia directories as an architect as early as 1886, after one year of study at MIT, which was then located in Boston.[27] Perhaps the most promising prospect is the Worcester and Boston architect Stephen C. Earle (1839–1913), friend of the Daniel Merrimans, the owners of the nearby estate "Stonehurst," after 1879. As a result of the Merriman contract, Earle is know to have drafted plans for the Schouler cottage ("Kilbarchan") in Intervale in 1879, and may also have designed the Fette cottage ("Bergenheim") just to the north of it the following year. It is not inconceivable, therefore, that the Merrimans or their Intervale neighbors recommended Earle to the Curries when they were seeking the services of an architect.

The Reverend Charles George Currie (1837–1918) was an accomplished theologian, a world traveler, and a man of means. Born in Edinburgh, Scotland, he was educated at Trinity College in Glen Almand. Upon graduation he married Margaret Aiken of Glasgow, and they immediately sailed for the United States. Settling in Gambier, Ohio, the home of Kenyon College, the young Currie completed his theological studies at Bexley Seminary, an independent Episcopal divinity school founded along with Kenyon by Bishop Philander Chase. While finishing his studies, he taught Greek, Latin, and Hebrew at Kenyon. Upon graduating from Bexley in 1857, Currie launched his career preaching in Louisiana, followed by a brief pastorate in Cincinnati, and eight years (1860–68) as rector of Trinity Parish, Covington, Kentucky. He followed this experience with a ten-month stay at St. Matthew's Church, Wheeling, West Virginia, after which he was called to Grace Church, Providence, Rhode Island, until 1873. His next assignment was at St. Luke's (later the Church of St. Luke and the Epiphany) in Philadelphia, where he remained until 1888 when he resigned due to poor health. While at St. Luke's, in 1877, he was granted a doctorate of divinity from the University of Pennsylvania.

His first wife died in 1881, and after a few years he married Sarah C. Zantzinger, a widowed member of his congregation. It was with his second wife that he purchased the Intervale property and built "Nirvana." The Curries and their children then went to Germany for a few years, returning to the United States in 1890 when Currie became rector of Christ Church, Baltimore. After six years there another illness forced him to resign, and he and his family went to France about 1896 where he studied, wrote, and preached, taking trips to the United States during the summers. The Curries stayed in Paris eight years until Sarah Currie's son, Philip Zantzinger (later to be a well-known Philadelphia architect) finished his training. For the next six years the Curries resided in London, returning to Chestnut Hill near Philadelphia about 1910 where Rev. Currie eventually passed away. Despite frequent relocation and long periods abroad, the Curries managed to travel regularly to the White Mountains, and were integral members of the Intervale summer colony.[28]

"Concordia Hut"

1888–89

(Rev. and Mrs. Harry P. Nichols)

North Conway (Intervale)

"Concordia Hut" (1888–89), Intervale, North Conway, N.H. Photograph by the author

↝ THIS DIGNIFIED, RUSTIC Shingle-style cottage was erected for Rev. and Mrs. Harry Peirce Nichols in 1888–89 on two acres of land acquired from Mary D. Pendexter of the Intervale inn-keeping family. While living in New Haven, Connecticut, during the 1880s, Harry Nichols first visited Intervale as a guest of the publisher Melancthon M. Hurd at his house, "The Knoll." A lifelong hiking enthusiast, from his youth Nichols had been infatuated by the White Mountains, but ideally wished for a house site in Randolph, closer to the highest peaks of the Presidential Range. His wife, Alice Shepley Nichols, preferred a more populated and

Sketch of end view, cottage for Rev. H. P. Nichols, Intervale, North Conway, N.H., by Rotch & Tilden, Architects, Boston, c. 1888. Courtesy of Mary H. Dethier, Blue Hill, Maine.

active setting, however, so the couple opted for Intervale, with its many hotels, summer cottages, artists, and easy railroad access to Boston and New York. For the name of their new house, the Nichols chose "Concordia Hutte" (later anglicized to "Hut"), named after a climber's shelter in which Rev. Nichols stayed while hiking the Jungfrau in Austria. The cottage is one of only a few in the White Mountains that is still owned and used by the descendants of the builders and first owners.[29]

Harry Peirce Nichols (1850–1940) was a remarkably versatile, energetic and accomplished man, with a broad range of interests. Born in Salem, Massachusetts, he received his bachelor of arts from Harvard in 1871, his bachelor of divinity from Andover (Massachusets) Theological Seminary in 1875, a diploma from the Philadelphia Divinity School in 1876, and his doctorate in divinity from New York University in 1904. During his long and distinguished career of service to the Episcopal Church, he was rector at St. Paul's, Brunswick, Maine, 1877–83; assistant rector, Trinity, New Haven, Connecticut, 1883–92; rector, St. Mark's, Minneapolis, Minnesota, 1892–99; and rector, Holy Trinity, New York City, 1899–1922. He was a member of the Appalachian Mountain Club from 1881 until his death, and in 1902 was one of the founders of the American Alpine Club, serving as its president and for many years as a member of its council. After 1889 he spent most of his summer vacations in Intervale, hiking throughout the White Mountains whenever time permitted. The tourist newspaper *Among the Clouds* contains numerous notices of family hiking trips launched from "Concordia Hut," including Nichols' annual tramps the length of the Presidential Range. He was known as a superb storyteller, conversationalist, cardplayer, and devotee of nature. During the summers he presided at church services at various communities in the mountains, and in August 1915, delivered the historical address at the dedication of the new Mount

Sketch of first floor plan, cottage for Rev. H. P. Nichols, Intervale, North Conway, N.H., by Rotch & Tilden, Architects, Boston, c. 1888. Courtesy of Mary H. Dethier, Blue Hill, Maine.

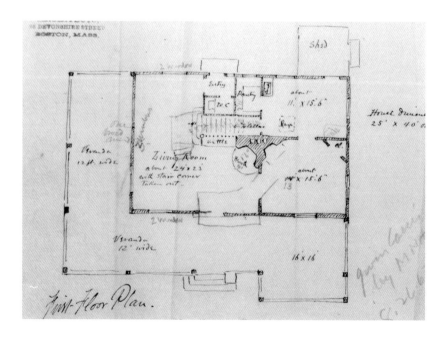

Washington Summit House. He and his wife were much involved in the cultural, religious, intellectual, and social life of Intervale and their home was a focal point for occasional social gatherings.[30]

In terms of scale, massing, and detail, "Concordia Hut" is a simple but meritorious example of the Shingle style. Exhibiting forceful horizontal lines, the house is protected by several intersecting hipped roofs, all with sharply overhanging eaves. The roof surfaces are punctuated by center brick and end fieldstone chimneys, and three-sided dormers. A long L-shaped veranda is present on the front (north) and west sides, its square support posts sheathed with the same natural shingles that cover the wall surfaces. Portions of the veranda and second-story bays have been screened for use as sitting or sleeping porches in warm weather. Typical of its style, the building is asymmetrical in plan, with no two elevations alike. Additions and alterations made in 1897, 1898, and in this century, have augmented interior space, but have not compromised the basic architectural character of the cottage. It seems well suited to its rural environment and to the role it has been called upon to play for over a century.[31]

Sketch plans, formal designs, and manuscript correspondence and records in possession of Nichols descendants reveal that "Concordia Hut" was designed by the well-known Boston architectural firm of (Arthur) Rotch (1850–1894) and (George Thomas) Tilden (1845–1919). Working with the designers as superintending contractor was John L. Nute of North Conway. Rotch and Tilden were associated in partnership from 1880 to 1895. During this period they maintained one of the most active offices in New England, designing many buildings there as well as in New York City, Washington, D.C., and Charleston, South Carolina. In Massachusetts, the firm's most important projects included the Art Museum at Wellesley College, Plymouth High School, Jesup Hall at Williams College, the Town Hall in Milton, the Sargent Normal School and Gymnasium in Cambridge, the Blue Hill Observatory in Milton (with which the Mount Washington Observatory has had a long relationship), and the American Legion Building, Church of the Ascension, and Church of the Messiah, all in Boston. Rotch and Tilden also designed many suburban and country homes, including estates in Lenox, a socially upscale summer community in the Massachusetts Berkshires. Rotch was perhaps best known for founding the Rotch Traveling Scholarship Fund, under the aegis of the American Institute of Architects, to provide training in Europe for American architecture students. Upon Rotch's death, Tilden was appointed trustee of the fund.[32] How the partners made contact with the Nicholses is not absolutely certain, but it is believed that it occurred through mutual friends or associates in Boston. Nichols and Rotch were Harvard classmates, and it is possible that this connection encouraged the establishment of a business relationship.[33]

"Birchmont"

1890–93

(Mr. and Mrs. Payson Tucker)

North Conway

"Birchmont" (1890–93), North Conway, N.H., winter photograph, 1951. Courtesy of Bob Duncan, North Conway.

⌐ ERECTED IN 1890–93, "Birchmont" (originally "Birchmonte") was the "elegant mansion" of Mr. and Mrs. Payson Tucker of Portland, Maine.[34] Until the destruction of the main house by fire in 1970, this magnificent estate was regarded as the residential showplace of North Conway. It derived its name from its proximity to several large white birch trees on Sunset Hill, a prominent ridge commanding excellent views to the west and northwest of the Saco River Valley, Mount Chocorua, the Moat Range, and Mount Washington and the other Presidential peaks. The house site is said to be the spot where in 1851 the artist John F. Kensett painted the well-known picture, "Mount Washington from the Valley of Conway," reproduced as an engraving by the American Art Union the same year. This superlative location and others along the ridge have remained popular with White Mountain artists to this day.[35]

The Tuckers were attracted to the Eastern Slope Region as a consequence of Mr. Tucker's executive career with the Maine Central Railroad, which acquired the major route from Portland to North Conway and through the mountains in 1888. Late in the following year, Tucker purchased the land upon which "Birchmont" would be built from Elizabeth J. Plummer of Conway.[36] The major portion of the house, the adjacent stable (extant), and other outbuildings were completed the spring and summer of 1890. The Tuckers christened their stately new summer home in September with an opening party for their Portland friends and associates. Local residents were immediately impressed by the "picturesque" and "lovely" house, one commenting, "by night, when the many windows twinkle with lights, it looks down on us like some storied castle in the Rhineland."[37] The grounds (which ultimately reached fifty acres) were beautifully landscaped, with expansive lawns, carefully selected shade trees and shrubs, and a curving drive, accessed through a large iron gateway, with stone towers on either side.[38]

In 1893, the Tuckers added a southern wing to "Birchmont," containing a music hall on the first floor, with bedrooms on the second.[39] This created a balanced composition as viewed on the front (west) elevation—nearly identical two-and-one-half-story cubical masses with steep-hipped roofs were linked by an unobtrusive one-story connecter. A long veranda or piazza extended across the entire front facade and bent around each end corner. A large ell, part of the 1890 portion, extended to the rear of the north block. The roof surfaces were broken by several shed-roof dormers containing either two or three double-sash windows in each. A disjointed collection of shapes and forms, lacking distinctive decoration, the whole, elongated, L-shaped building mass was virtually impossible to fit into any late-Victorian architectural vocabulary of style.

The designer of "Birchmont" is unknown, but it is reasonably safe to assume that he was from Maine, possibly Portland. Prior to 1905, two of Maine's most distinguished nineteenth-century architects, Francis H. Fassett (1823–1908) and John Calvin Stevens (1855–1940) (see "Wilson Cottage," Jackson, and "Peabody Cottage," Gorham), secured commissions in the White Mountains, either for hotels, hotel additions, or residences. In fact, around 1889, Stevens prepared an elevation rendering of an "Observatory at North Conway for Mr. Payson Tucker," which today may be seen in the Stevens Collection at the Avery Library, Columbia University. To date, however, no evidence has been discovered associating Fassett, Stevens, or any other professional architect with "Birchmont" or other buildings in the complex.[40]

While the exterior of the Tucker house may not merit high praise for its aesthetic qualities, the interior was imaginatively laid out and adorned. An unusually thorough description from *Among the Clouds* highlights the best features of the first-floor main rooms:

> On entering, one passes from the hallway directly into the library, a charming little room, the walls of which are decorated with quiet green and light brown palms on a background of grayish red. It is lower paneled with oak, and at either end is a knowledge panel, worked into a soft tone. At the entrance to the library from the passageway is a beautiful arch of grill work done in oak. The floor is of hardwood, and the ceiling clouded with delicate blue tints. The music room surpasses any other in elegance. The hardwood floor is incased with an inlaid border, and a large chimney of terra cotta brick with an open fire-place is opposite the entrance. The walls are hung with Empire brocade, and lower paneled like the library. A narrow moulding of carved oak and torch relief frieze makes an effective finish at the top. The ceiling is clouded with delicate blue and pink tints, outside of which is run around a bead and torch relief moulding. In each of the four corners are emblems of musical instruments artistically painted by hand. An oaken staircase leads from the music room to the great chambers above.[41]

Such lavish interior decor was not characteristic of the more rustic, basic White Mountain summer cottages, but seemed well suited to "Birchmont" and the transplanted, sophisticated urban life-style that the Tuckers clearly enjoyed there.

"Country Seat of Payson Tucker, Sunset Hill, North Conway, N.H.," lithograph from *Town and City Atlas of the State of New Hampshire* (Boston: D. H. Hurd & Co., 1892). Author's collection.

Parlor, "Birchmont" (1890–93), North Conway, N.H., photograph from the *White Mountain Echo* 32, no. 11 (18 September 1909): 2. Courtesy of the Appalachian Mountain Club Library, Boston.

Stable (left) and ice house (right), "Birchmont" (1890–93), North Conway, N.H. Photograph by the author.

Soon after the sudden death of Payson Tucker in 1900, the entire estate was put up for sale by his executors, passing to James L. Gibson in 1901, and then to G. C. Tyler of Boston in 1904. The Tylers altered the use of the complex, operating it as an inn, yet retaining much of its original appearance. About 1910, Mrs. M. T. (Louisa) Jones of Houston, Texas, purchased the property, converting it back to a private residence, and resurrecting aspects of the Tucker era ambience. Then in 1935, the estate took on a new life when the Manufacturers Trust Company (Harvey Dow Gibson of North Conway was president) acquired "Birchmont" and for the next twenty years ran it as a year-round private vacation retreat for its employees. From 1955 to 1957, it was owned and again operated as a public inn by the former caretaker, a man with the most appropriate name of Joseph Birch. Mr. and Mrs. Robert Knapp, proprietors of the nearby Cranmore Inn, were the last owners.[42]

Payson Tucker, the planner and financier of "Birchmont," was born in 1840 in Lowell, Massachusetts, and attended public schools in Portland and the New Hampshire Conference Seminary in Tilton, New Hampshire. He began his railroad career in 1853 at the Portland office of the Portland, Saco & Portsmouth Railroad, remaining with this company in various capacities until 1872. For the next three years he was the general agent for the Boston and Maine Railroad at Portland. In 1875 he joined the Maine Central Railroad, serving as superintendent to 1880, general superintendent from 1880 to 1882, and vice president and general manager from 1882 until 1896, when he was replaced as a result of a management reorganization. After leaving the Maine Central, Tucker devoted his business interests to running the Maine and New Hampshire Granite Company, of which he was the treasurer. A promoter at heart, he was a member of the group that built the famed Union Station in Portland, and the consortium that erected the Cantilever Bridge in St. John, New Brunswick, connecting the railroad systems of the United States and the Canadian Maritime Provinces. Tucker was a director of the Casco National Bank of Portland and other Maine banks, a director of the Maine Mutual Benefit Association, and president of the Maine Eye and Ear Infirmary. Afflicted with alcoholism for many years, he established a Keeley Institute treatment center for alcoholics at the former Artist's Falls House, part of his "Birchmont" estate holdings in North Conway. A major figure in the development of rail systems and tourism in northern New England, he apparently found his estate in the White Mountains the perfect place to witness their impact, and yet escape from their sometimes questionable consequences.[43]

⌇

The Pratt Cottage

1894

(Mr. Fred I. Pratt)

North Conway (Kearsarge)

The Pratt cottage (1894), Kearsarge, North Conway, N.H. Photograph by the author.

⌁ FRED I. PRATT and his family were members of the Kearsarge summer colony for well over a decade, from around 1893 when Pratt acquired forty acres of land from Albert Barnes, to some time around 1908 when this property was sold.[44] Situated between two hotels, the Ridge and the Orient House, on Kearsarge Ridge, the site that Pratt selected for his house was magnificent, looking westward over the Cathedral Woods and the Saco River intervale to the mountains, from the Sandwich Range to the south to the Presidential Range to the north. The new cottage, which remained unnamed during the Pratt ownership, was completed in time for the 1894 summer season. Local residents regarded it as "a handsome addition to the private summer homes of Kearsarge."[45]

Little is known about Fred Pratt, other than the fact that he worked in the hotel business in New York, and considered the city to be his principal place of residence. From the mid-1890s to at least 1905, he also was owner of the Langham Hotel in Boston, and often used it as his business address.[46] It is here that he likely met architect Frederick Pope (1838–c. 1915), a bachelor, who for many years maintained an apartment at the hotel. With offices in downtown Boston, Pope carried on an architectural practice for over forty years, planning and superintending the construction of many Boston buildings. These included several large wholesale department stores, blocks of offices, and Back Bay residences.[47] Apparently, Pope did little or no work in New Hampshire during his career, but he did consent to design the Pratt family house there. The tourist newspaper *Among the Clouds* specifically attributed the design to Pope in its 30 August 1894 edition.[48]

The Pratt cottage is a rather plain, late-Shingle-style building, with characteristic sweeping main and dormer roof lines, shingle wall siding, and extensive front and side porches. A slight suggestion of the more recent Colonial Revival mode is evident in the round and tapered Doric porch columns, and the semicircular window in the front dormer gable. When the house was first placed on the market in 1904–5, *Among the Clouds* advertised that it possessed "all the modern conveniences, purest of mountain spring water, bathroom, electric lights, cemented cellar, large Smith & Anthony furnace, . . . eleven rooms, including seven large chambers, . . . [a] large store attic, . . . [and] three open fireplaces."[49] The advertisement also referred to a separate but connected building put up in 1898[50] and containing "two regulation [bowling] alleys, [a] fine large casino [for music and billiards] covering 1200 feet, 14 feet stud, finished in hard wood, (sheathed and polished), with floor prepared for dancing, and a grand fireplace capable of accommodating a four foot log."[51] Despite the presence of area hotels, this unusual structure was said to have filled "a long felt gap at Kearsarge,"[52] making local "social life lively."[53] Evidently, Pratt's inclination to extend hospitality as a hotelman carried over into his private life. In fact, even while he was on vacation, he could not draw himself away from the trappings and amenities of his profession: next door at "The Ridge" hotel, Pratt had "a private dining room, granted by the proprietor for his exclusive uses if desired."[54]

❧

"The Manor House"

c. 1911

(Ellen Carruth)

North Conway (Kearsarge)

"The Manor House" (c. 1911), Kearsarge, North Conway, N.H. Photograph by the author.

❧ IN 1905, THE second hotel bearing the name "The Ridge and Cottages" burned on Kearsarge Ridge in North Conway, leaving a gaping hole just to the south of the Pratt cottage. For several years this highly desirable elevated site, with its superlative views of the Saco River intervale and mountains to the west, remained vacant. Finally, late in 1910, Ellen Carruth (1846–1923), a single woman from the Dorchester section of Boston, purchased the land from the Dow and Barnes families, previous owners of the hotel. Here, on the foundations of "The Ridge," she began the next year to build her new summer cottage, known today as "The Manor House."[55]

Ellen Carruth was apparently the beneficiary of inherited money, and did not herself pursue a professional career. Her father, Nathan (1808–81), a native of North Brookfield, Massachusetts, entered the drug business in Boston in the late 1820s, managing several enterprises under the family name until his death. He had also actively promoted the introduction of the railroads to Massachusetts, helped form the Old Colony Railroad, and became its first president and general manager, as well as the treasurer of the Northern Railroad of New Hampshire, which reached to North Conway—which may explain why his daughter Ellen ultimately decided to acquire property there. The Carruths became residents of Dorchester in 1847, when the family moved to a substantial estate in the Ashmont district.[56]

To design "The Manor House," Ellen Carruth selected Bradford Hamilton, a relatively obscure and modestly productive architect from Milton, Massachusetts, who from 1896 to 1918 maintained professional offices in Boston. This choice was neither accidental or surprising; building inspector reports for the city of Boston reveal that between 1889 and 1892, Hamilton had designed four one-family wooden dwellings (likely real estate speculation or rental properties) in Dorchester for Ellen Carruth's brother, Herbert Shaw Carruth, a Boston city official. During those years and later, Hamilton also planned houses for other clients in Dorchester. Whether by referral or direct association, when the time came for Carruth to decide on an architect for her Kearsarge house, she clearly knew about Hamilton's previous commissions. The original undated Hamilton floor plans (cellar, first floor, and second floor) have been restored and framed, and hang in the upstairs hallway of "The Manor House" today.[57]

This spacious, rambling residence defies easy stylistic classification; it probably exhibits more qualities of the late Shingle style than any other in vogue at the time. Protected by a main hipped roof with hipped secondary roofs, the building possesses asymmetrical elevations on all sides, with uneven fenestration. Cream-colored, painted cedar shingling covers the wall surfaces. To take advantage of the outstanding vistas, the west side of the house is fitted with six sets of large triple windows, three sets accommodated in projecting bays. At the southwest corner, where the principal mass of the house is joined with an angled south service wing, is the primary visual feature—a low, two-story tower capped by a concave pyramidal roof with finial. A hint of the neoclassical may be seen in the rounded Doric columns of the east sun porch (converted from a former porte-cochere), and end and west elevation porches. Before modern spatial rearrangements, the interior contained fourteen principal rooms: a large entrance hall, living room, dining room, sun porch, and kitchen on the first floor; and a stair hall, four bed chambers, two sleeping porches, and two maid's rooms on the second floor.[58] Inside and outside, "The Manor House" displays a unity and integrity that reflects well on its creators. It also expresses distinctly its function as a comfortable and serviceable single-season vacation abode, typifying upper-middle-class aspirations and cultural tastes during the years immediately preceding World War I.

~

"Sylva-of-the-Pines"

c. 1902

(Miss Marion Weston Cottle and

Miss Cedelia May Cox)

Bartlett (Intervale)

"Sylva-of-the-Pines" (c. 1902), Bartlett, N.H. Litho-graph from *New Hampshire Farms for Summer Homes* (2nd ed., 1904), p. 19. Author's collection.

∽ "SYLVA-OF-THE-PINES" was built around 1902 as a summer res-idence for Marion Weston Cottle of New York City and Cedelia May Cox of Boston, who became acquainted while students at Wellesley College. They were attracted to the mountains of New Hampshire due to their common affection for trail hiking and other outdoor activities, as well as their desire for a place of beauty, rest, and solitude. Their small rusticated cottage, situated on a bluff overlooking Intervale Village in lower Bartlett, provided the ideal environment for them to pursue their interests, and ben-efit from a rural retreat far removed from their active professional lives.

Cottle and Cox share the honor of being listed in the 1914 edition of *Women's Who's Who of America.*[59] A graduate of New York University Law School, Cottle commenced law practice in 1905; she was eventually admit-ted to the bars of New York, New Hampshire, and other states, and was granted the right to practice in the United States Supreme Court in 1911. A registered patent attorney, she specialized in surrogate's law and bank-ruptcy practice, as well as real estate law and the management of incompetents' estates. An outstanding courtroom lawyer, it was said that she rarely lost a case. She often lectured on women's suffrage and belonged to several organizations devoted to the suffrage cause. From 1909 to 1912 she served as president of the Woman Lawyers' Club of New York. She maintained offices in New York City and at Intervale, where she had a small stone law office building erected, still standing at the entrance of the road leading to the cottage (see illustration).[60]

A teacher of voice culture, Cox studied music in Germany and the United States before beginning her career in Boston in 1900. Like her cottage companion, she strongly favored women's suffrage, and also committed her time to suffrage organizations. The two women had a mutual interest in music, a further basis of their friendship.[61]

The 1904 edition of *New Hampshire Farms for Summer Homes* contains an excellent description of "Sylva-of-the-Pines":

> The site for their home decided, they [Cottle and Cox] busied themselves over plans, talked learnedly of 'specifications, foundation,' and became for the moment their own architects and contractors. Their plans made and the various cosey corners and fireplaces, book shelves, and other feminine touches planned, 'the carpenter did the rest,' and the result is a picturesque cabin in the heart of the woods. . . .
>
> They have scoured the country round in search of old-fashioned furniture and quaint relics of bygone days with which to furnish their home. The large open fireplace in the living room is built of pasture stone, and is crowned by a magnificent deer head. It is adorned with ancient irons and a huge kettle, over a century old. Quaint old chairs and tables, braided rugs, and rag carpets make the interior cosey, while the broad porch in which the hammocks are swung is shaded by the pines and cooled by balsam-laden zephyrs.
>
> Off the living room is a cosey little 'Japanese room,' in which souvenirs of the Orient are prominent; the music room is by no means least important in the make-up of the menage, as both Miss Cox and Miss Cottle are musicians of more than average ability. The dining-room, with its dainty glass and silver, plate racks, and chafing dishes, is the joy of all feminine beholders.[62]

This cheerful, well-appointed, but modest cottage was conceived in the tradition of the small dwellings erected by Rev. Dr. Charles Cullis and his followers for their neighboring Intervale Park religious community in the 1880s.[63] The architect was a personal friend, Anne Grant of New York City.[64] Several regular guests of the nearby Maple Villa hotel were so impressed by the appearance and ambience of the new cottage that in the summer of 1902 they purchased lots adjacent so that they could create similar summer homes. One of the new landholders was Cottle's father, Octavius O. Cottle from Buffalo, New York.[65]

2 ～

Jackson

The still serene, lovely river valley town of Jackson arrived as a significant summer resort later than North Conway, Intervale, or other White Mountain communities. By the end of the nineteenth century, however, it had become one of the region's most active and successful tourist centers. In 1858, the first major hotel, the Jackson Falls House, was opened, followed by the Thorn Mountain House (later Wentworth Hall and Cottages) in 1869, the Glen Ellis House in 1876, the first Eagle Mountain House in 1879, and the second Iron Mountain House and the first Gray's Inn in 1885. The presence at these hotels of guest cottages, some for group and others for single-family use, established precedent in the town for privately owned summer residences, ultimately of considerable size and sophistication. Commencing with the relatively modest cottages of Augustus F. Jenkins (1885), G. C. Hayes (c. 1889), and Charles W. Kellogg (1893), the summer colony blossomed with the construction of the larger and more ornate Strahan (c. 1887–88), Fitz (c. 1888), Wigglesworth (c. 1888), Wentworth (1891–92), Wormeley (1894–95), Ditson (1895), Goff (1896), Shapleigh (1896–97), Baldwin (1902–3) and Saunders (1904–6) houses. Smaller cottages and converted farmhouses augmented this core group, all situated on the surrounding hillsides within relatively easy walking distance of the village center. The complexion of the summer colony was decidedly Bostonian, though there were some members from New York and other eastern locales. The list of their architects, both documented and conjectured, is impressive, including such names as William A. Bates, Charles F. McKim, and Stanford White of New York, and William R. Emerson, John P. Putnam, Arthur G. Everett, and Samuel W. Mead of Boston. The legacy of these men is a superlative collection of domestic buildings representing the architectural styles fashionable in the White Mountains area between the Civil War and World War I.

Wentworth Hall
and Cottages

1881–c. 1930

Jackson

"Wentworth Hall and Cottages, Jackson, N.H.,"
lithograph from *Town and City Atlas of the State of
New Hampshire* (Boston: D. H. Hurd & Co., 1892).
Author's collection.

⁓ OF THE THIRTY grand resort hotels that were once present in the White Mountain region, Wentworth Hall and Cottages in Jackson village is highly unusual, if not unique. At its height, the complex boasted a diverse collection of almost forty principal, service, recreational, and residential units operated under the English-inspired "cottage system" of hotel operation. In contrast to the Profile House at Franconia Notch and the Waumbek at Jefferson, all Wentworth buildings were owned and maintained by the hotel corporation. Like these other hostelries, guests in adjacent cottages at the Wentworth centered their social, recreational, cultural, and dining pursuits on the main hotel facility. Those individuals desiring privacy, flexibility, and freedom in their housing arrangements found the cottages particularly suited to their vacation life-styles.[1]

Whereas most of its buildings were erected in the 1880s and after, Wentworth Hall and Cottages had much earlier origins. In 1868–69, Joshua Trickey of Jackson built a modest inn, Thorn Mountain House, for his daughter Georgia upon the occasion of her marriage to another local resident, General Marshall C. Wentworth (see "The Castle," Jackson). With this gift, General Wentworth commenced a lengthy and distinguished career in the hotel business. Around 1880, using Thorn Mountain House as the core, he began the daunting task of creating his ideal mountain resort colony. To guide him in this undertaking, he contracted New York City architect William A. Bates (1853–1922), widely respected for his residential, hotel, apartment, and country club commissions in or near the city. Particularly skilled in the execution of buildings in the then-popular English Queen Anne style, Bates was an ideal choice to implement Wentworth's vision. His ties with Wentworth and his subsequent visits to the new hotel

"Cottage for M. C. Wentworth, Esq., Thorn Mt. House, Jackson, N.H.," plate from *American Architect and Building News* 9 (1 January 1881), no. 262. Courtesy of the University of Delaware Library, Newark, Delaware.

would firmly connect Bates with Jackson, and would result in other work for him there (see "The Castle" and "The Boulders").[2]

In 1881, Bates launched General Wentworth's grand scheme, to be carried out exclusively in the Queen Anne vein. The initial building to be completed was "Arden Cottage," just behind and to the northeast of the Thorn Mountain House. Although it was a group as opposed to a single-family residence, it was "the first flower of the growing plant," setting a design precedent for the cottages that were to follow. A comparison of Bates' front elevation perspective (see illustration) from the *American Architect and Building News* with a recent photograph reveals similarities as well as differences. One can see today the general main facade configuration and Queen Anne embellishment of the original plan, "in the true old English style from the old-fashioned knocker on the 'Dutch door' to the very peak of its gable roof." Remarkably, fifteen rooms of various sizes, supplemented by first-floor general spaces, were contained in this highly stylized structure.[3]

After the opening of Arden Cottage and the completion of Wentworth Hall, the main hotel facility, in 1882–83, Wentworth waited two more years before continuing his ambitious undertaking. Again under Bates' direction, three more cottages—"Thornycroft," "Glenthorne," and "Elmwood" —were built to the west and north of the existing buildings, increasing the total guest capacity of the complex to 250. In 1889, "Wildwood Cottage"

"Arden Cottage" (1881), Wentworth Hall and Cottages, Jackson, N.H. Photograph by the author.

was raised slightly to the east on the edge of the Wildcat River (it was later moved to its current site when the road in front of Wentworth Hall, "Thornycroft" and "Arden" was relocated). Floor plans of these cottages signed by Bates, appearing in promotional booklets published by the hotel between 1885 and 1900, provide vital information about the functional layout of each. As a group the cottages built between 1881 and 1886 displayed distinctive Queen Anne traits: asymmetry in floor plans and wall elevations; variety in wall texture and color; fancy-cut and variously arranged shingles; elaborate chimneys; intersecting pitched roofs; polygonal corner towers; gable-roof dormers; bay windows; small-paned (diamond or square) glass fixed or moveable window sashes; ample verandas; and balconies. Joined by covered piazzas and open walkways, the buildings in the complex, while individual aesthetic statements, were bound in a unified whole.[4]

Wentworth Hall and Cottages continued its physical growth into the 1920s. A new casino and large stable, both designed by William Bates, joined the complex in 1886–87. "Sunnyside Cottage," was put up in 1915 slightly north of "Arden." Conceived to blend in with the older Queen Anne buildings, this seemingly anachronistic dwelling may also have been planned by Bates late in his career. "Fairlawn" and "Amster" cottages, both group annexes, were built during the 1920s on the south side of the main hotel, and essentially completed General Wentworth's "miniature cottage city." In 1982, several of the original hotel structures were declared obsolete

"Sunnyside Cottage" (left, c. 1885) and "Wildwood Cottage" (right, 1889), Wentworth Hall and Cottages, Jackson, N.H. Photograph by the author.

"Wentworth Hall and Cottages, Jackson, N.H.," floor plans for "Thornycroft," "Arden," and "Glenthorne" cottages, from *Wentworth Hall and Cottages* promotional booklet, c. 1900. Author's collection.

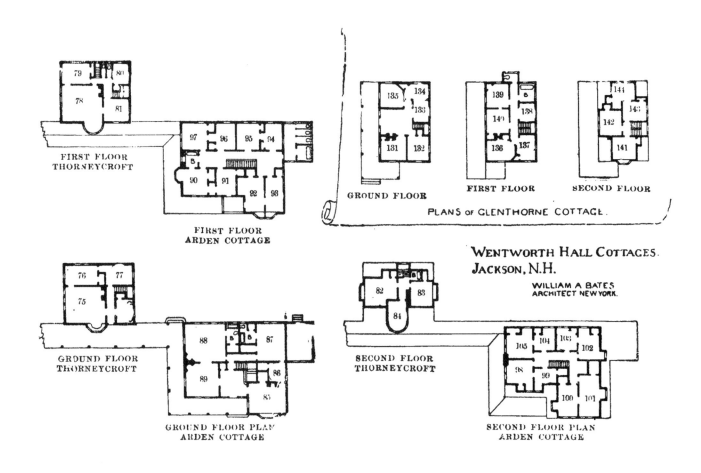

The Hurlin cottage (1896), Wentworth Hall and Cottages, Jackson, N.H. Photograph by the author.

or structurally unsound by new ownership, and were destroyed. Seven others survive today as centerpieces for the Wentworth Resort Hotel condominium community—Wentworth Hall, "Arden," "Thornycroft," "Wildwood," "Sunnyside," "Fairview," and "Amster." Fortunately, enough physical evidence remains on the site to provide the present generation with a quite vivid impression of White Mountain hotel and cottage life a century ago.[5]

Across the road east of the Wentworth Hall complex, and neatly aligned on the hillside along the Wildcat River, are three additional cottages historically associated with the resort. According to local oral sources, the lowermost and largest of these was erected for General Wentworth by the talented Jackson contractor Andrew C. Harriman (see "Thorn Lodge" and "Hilldrift") to serve as the residence of J. Brackett Hurlin, Wentworth's superintendent of buildings and grounds. Raised in 1896, this example of "the old colonial style" shares certain features with the hotel cottages, and may have been designed by their architect, William A. Bates. Just above the Hurlin house is "The Parsonage" (c. 1890), formerly used by the Freewill Baptist Church and Jackson Protestant Chapel Association for their ministers and their families. This compact, well-sited cottage exhibits such distinctly Colonial Revival features as a main gambrel roof with flared overhangs, octagonal bays, classical porch columns, and elliptical gable windows bounded by keystone-accented molding. Positioned at the top of the row is the third and smallest of the dwellings, built by Wentworth Hall around 1900 for James Pratt, the hotel chauffeur. As in certain of the Bates buildings below, the dominant form is the two-story octagonal corner tower with spire roof cap. Harriman may have also acted as head contractor for "The Parsonage" and the Pratt house, as well as other Wentworth Hall structures.[6]

≈

"The Parsonage" (c. 1890), Wentworth Hall and Cottages, Jackson, N.H. Photograph by the author.

"Thistleton"

c. 1887–88

(Mr. and Mrs. Thomas F. Strahan)

Jackson

◈ SITUATED UNDER Tin Mountain, on the Five-Mile Circuit Road north of Jackson Center, was a handsome, rambling, Shingle-style cottage, erected about 1887–88 for Mr. and Mrs. Thomas F. Strahan of Chelsea, Massachusetts. Set on an open knoll, surrounded by lawns and lovely, natural landscaping, "Thistleton," as the house was originally named, presented its main elevation to the north, toward Black Mountain, Carter Notch, and the Wildcat and Carter ranges. The still sparsely settled, largely forested mountain surroundings of the site recall the late 1800s when the Strahan's neighbor, Frank H. Shapleigh (see "Maple Knoll," Jackson), one of the giants of the post–Civil War White Mountain School of artists, sketched and painted farm and landscape scenes from hillside locations in the immediate area.

Like others who built summer cottages in Jackson, the Strahans probably became acquainted with the town through visits to local hotels, but this fact remains undocumented. In September 1887, in the name of Mrs. (Esther) Strahan, the couple purchased a one-hundred-acre tract from Oren W. and Hannah M. Hackett of Jackson, and, it is believed, financed and supervised construction there during the remainder of the fall and into the following year.[7] Plans for the house have yet to be discovered, but the last owners of the house conjectured that it may have been designed by a Providence, Rhode Island, architect. Containing over a dozen rooms, "Thistleton" comprised a principal rectangular block core, a south ell, and an east service wing, expanded from its original size by the insertion of an infill section, likely during Strahan ownership. Protected by a gambrel roof, the building exhibited two large double-window dormers and a long, closed veranda on its north side. On the west end were a first-story bay

"Thistleton" (c. 1887–88), Jackson, N.H. Photograph by the author.

Stable (left) and guest house/laundry (right), "Thistleton" (c. 1887–88), Jackson, N.H. Photograph by the author.

window, a bracketed and balustraded balcony above, and second-story single windows flanking a green-painted thistle motif, topped by a bracketed overhang. The most striking room in the interior was the large southwest parlor, featuring built-in cabinetry embellished with classical detail in wood and pressed pulpwood incrusta. To the east rear of the cottage site stand four outbuildings—a barn, carriage house, and ice house, all painted red and predating the Strahans' arrival—and, a small, rather fetching Colonial Revival cottage, put up by the Strahans to serve as a residence for their chauffeur (first story) and laundry (basement). The property possessed most of the requisite qualities of a turn-of-the-century, northern New England country estate, in its heyday affording a variety of opportunities for relaxation and recreational activity.[8]

Born in Scotland in 1847, Thomas Strahan emigrated to the United States at a young age, settling in Arlington, Massachusetts, where he attended the public schools and Cotting Academy. He proceeded to Phillips Exeter Academy, where he took a collegiate course as preparation for the ministry, but at age nineteen decided on a career in business. As a wallpaper dealer in Boston, he experienced quick success, and in 1867 he moved to Chelsea where he established his own small wallpaper manufacturing business. What eventually became the Thomas Strahan Company (1885), grew to be nationally prominent in its field and is still in business today (not surprisingly, "Thistleton" once displayed a variety of Strahan wallpapers in its public rooms, hallways, and bed chambers). In addition to fabricating and selling wallpaper products, Strahan was granted numerous patents, both in the United States and Great Britain, for blending colors, and for converting cotton and jute fabrics to appear like silk damask hangings. While carrying on a large and prosperous business, he still found time to engage in social and political affairs, serving as mayor of Chelsea in 1883–84, chairman of the school committee, a state representative, a member of the Masons and Odd Fellows, a trustee of the public library, and a trustee and president of the Chelsea Savings Bank. In Chelsea the Strahans led a comfortable, perhaps even sumptuous life at their brick and stone mansion atop Mount Bellingham, overlooking the city of Boston and the harbor. They frequently entertained guests there. This fascinating residence, its appearance preserved in old photographs, burned to the ground in the great Chelsea fire of April 1908, taking with it valuable works of art, which the Strahans had collected from around the world. Despite this great loss, they continued to enjoy their Jackson property.[9] Thomas Strahan once said, "It should be possible for everyone to live in a harvest of beauty and color"[10]— in his wallpapers he achieved this objective for his many customers, while for his family he realized his dream in the beauty and integrity of "Thistleton" and its environment.

≈

The Wigglesworth Cottage

c. 1888

(Dr. and Mrs. Edward Wigglesworth)

Jackson

"Cottage for Dr. Edw. Wigglesworth, Jackson, N.H.," plate from *American Architect and Building News* 24 (15 September 1888), no. 664. Courtesy of the University of Delaware Library, Newark, Delaware.

⌁ SITUATED PROMINENTLY ON a grassy knoll overlooking Jackson village, the Wigglesworth cottage features a truly spectacular setting, one of the finest possessed by any White Mountain summer residence built before 1930. From its north-facing piazzas, one may view a sweeping panorama highlighted by Mount Washington and the Presidential Range, and the foothills in the foreground. Like many other North Country cottages of its era, the house, in virtually every respect, is predicated on the advantages of its location. This is reflected in its siting, exterior form, and interior layout—the fertile product of successful collaboration between owner, architect, and contractor.

The man who initiated this building project, like several of his Jackson neighbors, enjoyed a national reputation in his professional field. Born in Boston of old Yankee stock in 1840, Dr. Edward Wigglesworth graduated from Harvard College in 1861, and from Harvard Medical School in 1865; he studied in Europe from 1865 to 1870. Returning to his native city, he quickly established himself as dermatologist, founding and maintaining the Boston Dispensary for Skin Diseases from 1872 to 1877. For many years he headed the Department of Diseases of the Skin at Boston City Hospital, while also teaching at Harvard Medical School.[11] For reasons unknown, he

The Wigglesworth cottage (c. 1888), Jackson, N.H. Photograph by the author.

was attracted to Jackson in the late 1880s, and, with his brother-in-law, Walter Scott Fitz (see the Fitz cottage, Jackson), acquired his first piece of land (about eighty acres) there in 1887 from Adeline Wentworth of the local family (see "The Castle," and Wentworth Hall and Cottages).[12] It was on this tract that the house was built. Over the subsequent six years, Wigglesworth extensively supplemented his real estate holdings with purchases (some with Fitz) from the Gray and Chesley families, and other Jackson landowners.[13] Upon his death in 1896, his wife, Sarah W. Wigglesworth fell heir to the house and much of the land, which she retained until after World War I.[14]

The architect of the Wigglesworth cottage, John Pickering Putnam of Boston (1847–1917), was known better for his inventions and publications relating to plumbing, heating, and sanitation, than he was for his architectural design work. Like his client, he was a graduate of Harvard (1868). He received his architectural training at the renowned Ecole des Beaux Arts, Paris (1869), and at the Royal Academy of Architecture, Berlin (1870–71). His many publications included *The Open Fire Place in All Ages* (1882), *The Principles of House Drainage* (1885), *Improved Plumbing Appliances* (1887), *The Outlook for the Artisan and His Art* (1892), and *Plumbing and Household Sanitation* (1911).[15] Little is known about his building commissions. His association with the Wigglesworth project, however, is solidly documented by a front elevation perspective sketch with first floor plan, published as a full-page plate in the 15 September 1888 issue of *The American Architect and Building News* (see illustration).[16] How he became connected with Edward Wigglesworth, one can only conjecture—they came from well-established Boston families with strong Harvard ties, and may well have known each other socially.

The Wigglesworth cottage has passed largely intact to the modern generation. On the exterior, only the shutters, a small open porch, and a portion of the front piazza are missing from the original Putnam plan. With powerful vertical accents and a tall hipped roof mimicking the form of the surrounding hills, the house incorporates many features of the Queen Anne style, then so popular in the United States. Among these are the asymmetrical elevations and floor plan, differing roof and window types, notably tall chimneys, an array of dormers piercing the roof planes, extensive verandas, cylindrical and semioctagonal projecting bays, and variegated wall shingle treatments.[17] A slight hint of the newer Shingle style may be seen in the shingled porch columns, and the flared gambrel roof on the west wing. Typical of the Queen Anne mode, the house features irregularity in plan and massing, variety of texture and shape, and general picturesqueness. An expression of Victorian whimsy and imagination, the house passes a true test of its dominant style—its principal north and south elevations are so strikingly dissimilar that they scarcely seem from the same building.

～

The Fitz Cottage

c. 1888

(Mr. and Mrs. Walter Scott Fitz)

Jackson

The Fitz cottage (c. 1888), Jackson, N.H., stereo view, privately commissioned, c. 1896. Author's collection.

～ POSITIONED SLIGHTLY to the east of the Wigglesworth cottage on the gradual slope of Thorn Hill, the Fitz cottage enjoys the same magnificent view of the distant high peaks of the White Mountains, the Wildcat and Glen Ellis river valleys below, and the adjacent hills. Surrounded in part by forest growth today, it once offered completely unobstructed vistas in all directions (see illustration). Early photographs of this imposing

The Fitz Cottage (c. 1888), Jackson, N.H. Photograph by the author.

Shingle-style house depict a building of outstanding architectural merit, thoughtfully conceived, meticulously assembled, and embellished with a fascinating profusion of period details. Fortunately, it has passed to the current era little altered, and in an excellent state of preservation, allowing us still to view one of the White Mountain region's most important examples of late Victorian domestic architecture.

The sophisticated and imaginative design of the Fitz cottage strongly suggests that it was planned by a major architect or architectural firm. But architectural drawings and related records, which could provide easy identification, apparently no longer survive.[18] A recent search of the Bethlehem tourist weekly, *White Mountain Echo*, though, revealed a citation attributing the design of the "handsome residence of Mr. W. S. Fitz" in Jackson to "Mr. W. R. Emerson, the Boston architect."[19] This exciting discovery adds another documented commission to the growing list of Emerson's work, which architectural historians have compiled in recent years.[20] In Jackson, the Fitz cottage joins the company of the Shapleigh house, "Maple Knoll" (1896–97), and the public library (1900–1901), both constructed from Emerson plans.

Until the late 1960s, William Ralph Emerson (1833–1917) was unrecognized as a significant contributor to the development of American residential architecture—despite the fact that his career was remarkably productive, spanning more than half a century, and including at least sixty known projects. One of his recent biographers considers him to be "one of the earliest and finest designers of Shingle style country and suburban houses" after the late 1870s—the Fitz cottage and "Maple Knoll" alone lend strong support to that claim. Born in Illinois, Emerson (a distant cousin of Ralph Waldo Emerson) spent his boyhood living in Kennebunk, Maine, and Boston, where he attended public schools. Here his formal education stopped, unlike increasing numbers of architects of his time, who went on to college and then received architectural training. Essentially self-taught in his trade, he initially worked with Jonathan Preston, a Boston architect-builder, beginning in 1854, and formed a partnership with him from 1857 to 1861. He then practiced alone in the early sixties, was associated with Carl Fehmer from 1864 to 1873, and was independent again from 1874 to 1909. He was a charter member of the Boston Society of Architects, and often lectured at meetings on the adaptability of American Colonial design elements for contemporary New England architecture. Like many architects focusing primarily on residential work, Emerson developed networks of clients, and concentrations of his houses, as well as other buildings, once existed in Milton, Massachusetts (the home of his second wife, Sylvia Watson), and the resort communities of the Massachusetts North Shore and Mount Desert Island, Maine. He was regarded by his professional colleagues as an extraordinarily gifted and creative free spirit, which is particularly reflected in his summer cottages.[21]

The connection between Emerson and his client Walter Scott Fitz (1838–1900) is unknown; perhaps their paths crossed in the Boston area, where both resided. Biographical data concerning Fitz is extremely sparse, and the details of his youth and education are a mystery. A family history, however, discloses that he prospered in the Boston-based China trade, and made donations of Chinese art to the Boston Museum of Fine Arts. In 1888 he married Henrietta Goddard (Wigglesworth) Holmes (it was her second marriage), the sister of Edward Wigglesworth of Boston.[22] Apparently, Fitz and Wigglesworth knew each other earlier, and, sharing a love for and commitment to the White Mountains, negotiated a joint land purchase in Jackson in 1887. The house was constructed on this land the following year. Fitz, usually in partnership with his brother-in-law Wigglesworth, continued to acquire tracts in Jackson until 1893. The properties on which the two houses and outbuildings are located have traditionally been known as the "Fitz-Wigglesworth estate," though they were sold by the original families long ago.[23]

With its longitudinal axis running east and west, the Fitz cottage, as is characteristic of the Shingle style, possesses totally contrasting asymmetrical principal elevations. Reached by a circular gravel drive enclosing a low hummock, the front main (south) facade is marked by an active combination of roof forms (main gambrel, closed gable pavilion, conical tower); a recessed front entrance porch behind a double arcade; a second-story four-sided angular window bay topped by a hipped-roof dormer; a two-story attached cylindrical tower; varied fenestration (multiple diamond-pane or square-pane upper over single-pane lower sash; multiple-square or diamond-pane fixed sash); and a tall, narrow stairway light with a paneled base and arched top displaying a molded archivolt and keystone. The rear (north) elevation is distinguished by projecting bays (three-sided), gabled dormer and pavilion roofs, tall brick chimneys piercing the main gable roof plane, and fenestration similar to that of the main facade, with the exception of the molded elliptical and arch-topped gable windows with keystones (these provide a hint of the Colonial Revival). Across the west end of the house, really a cross-gabled wing, there is a one-story, balustraded, square-columned veranda terminating in a semicircular projection, angled off the northwest corner. At the east end of the building is a two-story, gable-roof service wing. Less obvious but charming details of the cottage include patterned shingling (square butt, diamond, fish-scale, engrailed) on the wall surfaces, second-story cantilevered joists, corbeled with square ends, ogee crown molding in the gables, and matched and beaded veranda ceiling board. The Fitz residence blends Emerson's exemplary design with this symphony of integrated, beautifully crafted architectural elements.

≈

The Wormeley Cottages

1889–95

(Miss Katherine P. Wormeley)

Jackson

"The Satyr" (c. 1892), Jackson, N.H. Photograph by the author.

≈ DURING THE 1890s, Katherine ("Kate") Prescott Wormeley (1830–1908), the noted Newport, Rhode Island, author, translator, and philanthropist, became a significant presence in the Jackson summer community. Between 1891 and 1895, she renovated an old farmhouse and built two new houses on Thorn Hill Road, eventually assuming year-round residency. In the 1902 edition of the state publication *New Hampshire Farms for Summer Homes*, she expressed her motivation for coming to the area and acquiring property:

I located my summer home in Jackson because of the extreme beauty of the spot I chose and because I was tired of summer hotels. The land, bought in parcels at intervals of a year or two, cost rather more than $4,000. . . . Why do I like New Hampshire as a place of vacation residence? The climate suits me; the scene from my house and the varied drives about Jackson are unsurpassed; and I have friends who have summer residences around me for the same reasons.[24]

Such a statement encapsulated well the sentiments of many late-nineteenth-century summer cottage owners, not just in Jackson, but throughout the White Mountains.

Wormeley's first real estate in the town was acquired from Warren G. Gray and his wife, Abbie, in 1889. She supplemented this with additional contiguous purchases from the Grays in 1892 and 1893. Known historically as Gray's Farm, the property contained a substantial but quite conventional farmhouse, with connecting ell to a large barn, and small outbuildings. Over the next couple of years, Wormeley made interior alterations to the house, and also added a large front gable-roof dormer (with two sets of paired windows) and a veranda to take advantage of the spectacular views north toward the Presidential and Carter ranges. In addition, to ensure privacy, she had the road by the house relocated to the west to avoid the noise and disruption of sightseeing groups passing by in carriages. After she erected her other houses nearby, Wormeley often rented "The Poplars," her first Jackson residence, ultimately selling it to the Bradbury Bedells of Philadelphia in 1904.[25]

In 1892, Wormeley, wishing even greater privacy and a more advantageous location, decided to construct a cottage farther up the hillside, screened from the road by forest growth. To design her new single-season dwelling, displaying "the lady's taste," she enlisted the aid of architect Charles Follen McKim (1847–1909) of the internationally recognized New York City firm of McKim, Mead and White. She first met McKim in Newport, where the partnership had so many noteworthy commissions from the 1870s until after 1900. In fact, McKim had designed her winter residence (1876–77) there on Red Cross Avenue. It is possible also that McKim was responsible for the renovations to "The Poplars" and other adjacent structures, but available published evidence is inconclusive.[26]

Wormeley chose to call the new cottage "The Satyr," meaning "upland meadow" in Norwegian. With walls covered with natural cedar shingles (the roof surfaces were originally of similar materials), this plain wood-frame Shingle-style house is notable for its low gambrel roof with non-matching, hipped-roof dormers above an open veranda. Supporting the roof projection over the veranda are nicely scaled, rounded Doric columns. First- and second-story sketch floor plans, in possession of the current owning family, reveal that only the western half of the building was ever constructed, eliminating a proposed dining room, bedroom, and pantry on the first floor, and two bedrooms, a dressing room, and a bathroom on the second. As a result, a spacious parlor on the first floor has doubled for din-

"Brookmead" (1894–95), Jackson, N.H. Photograph by the author.

ing purposes, and there are just three modestly sized utilitarian bedrooms on the second floor, under the low-angled roof planes. A small one-story ell appended to the southeast corner makes up for some loss of space. The parlor is graced by an unusual paneled overmantle with flaming torches and a data marker, and a hearth with side panels of brass. The plans appear to have been drafted and inscribed by Wormeley herself, very likely under the direct guidance and supervision of McKim. To date, no formal drawings, specifications, or other records pertaining to "The Satyr" have turned up in McKim, Mead and White archival collections.[27]

Late in 1894, Wormeley decided to build a larger year-round residence in Jackson so that she could spend the winters there if she desired. For the site of the new cottage, she purchased approximately five acres of land from the Trickey family, down the hill and across the road from her other houses, with easy access to the center of the village. The house, "Brookmead," was completed by the following summer, under the direction of Orman S. Spring of Hiram, Maine, the chief contractor (see "The Boulders"). According to local tradition, Stanford White (1853–1906), the highly esteemed partner of Charles F. McKim in the firm of McKim, Mead and White, prepared the designs. No solid evidence has thus far appeared, however, to support such a claim, either in Jackson, in manuscript documents generated by the firm, or in published sources. Nor do floor plans appear to exist in Wormeley's hand, as they do for both "The Satyr" and the Baldwin cottage (see "Gray Manor"), the other building in Jackson attributed to White. On the other hand, Wormeley may well have known White in Newport, possibly through her friend McKim, and committed him to work for her.

Lending some additional credence to the White theory is the external appearance of "Brookmead." Like "Gray Manor," as well as McKim's "The Satyr," the building possesses a low sweeping main gambrel roof, bulky rectangular form, and generous verandas (today altered and partially enclosed). Similarly, it exhibits limited architectural detail. Nonetheless, one can still see the impact of the Shingle and Colonial Revival styles. Since Wormeley's death in 1908, the building has been used as a small inn under the ownership of Pitmans, the Moodys, and other families and individuals. During the 1950s a wing was added on the south side, and since then other modifications have been made. In recent years, the house has been known as "Thorn Hill Lodge" and "The Inn at Thorn Hill."[28]

What of Katherine Wormeley herself, the creator and financier of the three houses? Like several of her other summer neighbors in Jackson, she was of national stature in her field, and hence merited biographical sketches in a number of published reference works. Born in Ipswich, England, the daughter of a rear admiral in the Royal Navy, she emigrated with her family to the United States when she was eighteen. Before she left, however, she had extensive contact with English and French society and European literary figures. During the Civil War she was active in relief work for the Union army, and later served as superintendent of a hospital for convalescent soldiers in Portsmouth, Rhode Island, writing books about her experiences. Upon settling in Newport after the war, she participated in public affairs, most notably sanitation, charitable organizations, female domestic science, and the Girl's Industrial School of Newport, which she founded and funded. Among her best known translations, largely of French writers are: *The Works of Balzac* (1885–1896); Paul Bourget's *Pastels of Men* (1891–92); several works of Alexandre Dumas (1894–97); *The Works of Alphonse Daudet* (1898–1900); *Memoirs of the Duc de Saint-Simon* (1899); and Charles Augustin Sainte-Beuve's *Portraits of the Eighteenth Century* (1905). She had an unparalleled understanding and scholarly knowledge of French culture, and also wrote *A Memoir of Honore de Balzac* (1892). The last years of her life in Jackson provided a quiet and nurturing pastoral environment for exercise of her considerable literary talents.[29]

≈

"The Castle"

1891–92

(General and Mrs. Marshall C. Wentworth)

Jackson

WHILE DEVELOPING THEIR grand resort hotel, Wentworth Hall and Cottages in Jackson village, General Marshall C. Wentworth and his wife, Georgia T., shared a vision for their ideal summer residence. Both the general and his wife had grown to adulthood in an era when Alfred Lord Tennyson's *Idylls of the King* had filled its readers' minds with romantic images of "medieval knights, dangerous dragons, and mysterious castles." General Wentworth himself traced his family roots to English nobility, being a direct descendent of Sir Thomas Wentworth, the first Earl of Stafford and Prime Minister to King Charles I. Descendants of the first family member to emigrate to America, Elder William Wentworth of Exeter, New Hampshire, arrived in Jackson in 1816, establishing a farmstead on the road to Carter Notch, two miles north of the future site of the hotel. Steeped in this heritage, both English and American, the Wentworths set

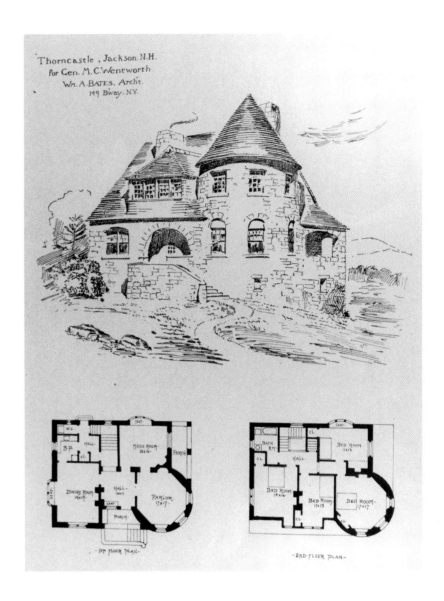

"Thorncastle, Jackson, N.H., for Gen. M. C. Wentworth," from *Building* 3, no. 15 (December 1885), Plate 242. Author's collection.

out to create a baronial mansion that would recall pleasant vestiges of the past, and at the same time incorporate the best qualities and amenities of late Victorian domestic life.[30]

Not surprisingly, the Wentworths turned to William A. Bates (1853–1922), the New York City architect of the Wentworth Hall buildings, to prepare the plans for their new summer abode. For the location of the house, they selected a near-perfect site about a thousand feet north of the hotel on a rocky prominence, commanding superb views of Jackson and the Wildcat and Glen Ellis river valleys below. Working closely with Bates from the mid-1880s, they initially conceived a relatively modest stone masonry cottage, combining on its exterior characteristics of the Romanesque Revival, the Queen Anne, and the Shingle styles. A design plate published in the December 1885 issue of the architectural serial *Building* presents an artistic front elevation perspective sketch, and first- and second-floor plans. Christened "Thorncastle," the house was to feature a cylindrical corner

"Residence of Gen. Marshall C. Wentworth, Jackson," photograph from James A. Wood, *New Hampshire Homes* (1895), vol. 1, p. 147. Courtesy of the New Hampshire Historical Society, Concord.

tower with a flared conical roof cap, a central hipped-roof dormer set on a steep-pitched tile roof, and round and segmental-arch door, window, and porch apertures. The first floor was intended to include an entrance hallway, music room, dining room, and circular (tower) parlor, while the second was to consist of a hall, bathroom, three rectangular bedrooms, and one circular (tower) bedroom. Construction based on this design was for some reason deferred and, ultimately, never was carried out.[31]

Six years later, in 1891, General Wentworth and his wife, again working with architect Bates, decided to proceed with the building of their cottage. On this occasion, though the original proposed site was unchanged, their financial resources, life-style aspirations and aesthetic tastes called for a much more ambitious and elegant residence. Borrowing from the 1885 plan, Bates conceptualized a thirteen-room house derived from the same eclectic stylistic idioms. In June 1891, the Wentworths and invited guests celebrated the laying of the corner stone at a special ceremony, during which "a glass vessel containing photos of the General's family, and a record of the building of the house, hermetically sealed, were placed under the stone, Mrs. Wentworth sprinkling water over it from the Helene Spring, newly discovered, which is to furnish the supply of pure drinking water."[32] The new cottage was first known as "Montecito," but within two years it was renamed "The Towers." In this century, its more popular appellation has been "The Castle."[33]

A comprehensive description of "The Castle," published during the 1891 construction phase, merits attention:

The house will be built entirely of [field] stone. . . . On the front will be two circular towers ending in conical [slate] roofs. . . . The house will have a solid [seven-foot-thick] foundation of stones in their natural state from the hills. The handsome first floor entrance will be through a [stone-arched] porch, and will have a library, parlor, dining-room, butlers' pantry, kitchen, and store room. On the second floor there will be three chambers with open fireplaces, a boudoir, two bath-rooms, and a sitting room and alcove with a tasty balcony front [protected by a lattice screen with a circular aperture]. The top floor [under steep-pitched slate roofs with dormers] will have three servants' rooms, two spare rooms, and a novelty of a room [in one of the towers] called 'Mystic Chamber,' decorated to represent the heavens and planets in position just as they were at the moment of the birth of General and Mrs. Wentworth, who are strong believers in astrology, and think the planets have a great deal to do with one's success in this life.[34]

The Wentworth's "astrological and spiritual temple," as they were prone to call their cottage, also contained a hand-painted tent ceiling in one of the octagonal tower bedrooms, a hand-painted first-floor entrance hall ceiling with the Wentworth coat of arms, eight fireplaces with carved wooden surrounds and overmantels, and oak and birch paneling, wainscoting, bookcases, cupboards, and door and window molding. Completed by 1893, virtually all of this highly articulated and lavish detail has survived intact.[35]

The exterior of "The Castle" conveys a powerful sense of permanence, stability, and solidity, much like the contemporaneous Romanesque-inspired buildings of the famous Boston architect Henry Hobson Richardson. Harmonizing with its natural surroundings, the house seems to grow out of the land, a perception enhanced by the forested hilltop site and the use of native wood and stone materials. Flanked by the identical round corner towers on the front facade, the main arched entranceway, as with certain Shingle-style dwellings of the era (Tuxedo Park, New York, for example), presents an inviting appearance, figuratively pulling the onlooker into the interior. The house has a princely, monumental quality, a successful reflection of the collaborative goals of the owners and the architect. Upon its completion, architect Bates undoubtedly received many commendations for the way in which "The Castle" combined historic architectural forms and elements with what were then modern building practices and technology.

The financier and coplanner of "The Castle," General Marshall C. Wentworth, was a local boy made good, much like Karl Abbott in Bethlehem (see "Upland Cottage") and John S. Runnells in Chocorua (see "Willowgate"). Born in 1844 in Jackson, the young Wentworth was raised on his father's farm, and attended the district school eight miles away. At sixteen years of age, during the Civil War, he enlisted in the Army of the Potomac, participating in some twenty-seven battles, and experiencing exciting military escapades and narrow escapes. He was twice wounded. After the war, he returned to Jackson, entering local hotel management at Thorn Mountain House, erected for his wife, Georgia, by her father Joshua Trickey, owner of the adjacent Jackson Falls House. The successor enterprise, Went-

West side elevation, "The Castle" (1891–92), Jackson, N.H. Photograph by the author.

worth Hall and Cottages, experienced great business success during the 1880s and 1890s, attracting many people of wealth and culture to enjoy its renowned casino, ballroom, recreational facilities, and social functions. Wentworth also managed hotels at some of the principal resorts of the country, including the Laurel House and the Lakewood at Lakewood, New Jersey; La Pintoresca and the Raymond at Pasadena, California; and the New Frontenac in the Thousand Islands of the St. Lawrence River. In addition, he built the Hotel Huntington in Pasadena. Also active in politics and civic affairs, in 1881–82 he was quartermaster general on the staff of New Hampshire Governor Charles H. Bell (from which he received the title of "General"); in 1884 was a member of the Republican electoral college; and for many years he served as chairman of the state forestry commission. A generous and engaging personality, he took a great interest in the welfare, growth, and future of Jackson, supporting many useful local causes and projects. After his death in 1915, his wife continued to live at "The Castle" year-round until she passed away in 1930. Considering their many contributions to Jackson and its hotel industry, it was fitting that for so many years, the Wentworth family occupied this magnificent residence overlooking the town center.[36]

∾

"Thorn Lodge"

c. 1891

(Mr. and Mrs. Isaac Y. Chubbuck)

"Hilldrift"

1904–1906

(Mr. and Mrs. George E. Saunders)

Jackson

"Thorn Lodge" (c. 1891), Jackson, N.H. Photograph by the author.

∾ SITUATED ON THE SIDE of Copps Hill overlooking Jackson village and the site of the Jackson Falls House hotel are two summer cottages of contrasting size and architectural character. They are linked historically, however, by their common association with the highly proficient local builder, Andrew C. Harriman. In about 1891, Harriman erected the older and smaller of these, "Thorn Lodge," for Isaac Y. Chubbuck, a business-

"Hilldrift" (1904–6), Jackson, N.H. Photograph by the author.

"West Elevation, House for Mr. George E. Saunders, Jackson, N.H.," Everett & Mead, Architects, Boston, c. 1904. Courtesy of Alta M. Gale, Los Angeles, Calif.

man engaged in book binding, from Roxbury, Massachusetts. Chubbuck had acquired the one-acre piece of land upon which the house stands from Nelson and Jennie Tricky, of the local hotel-owning family, in August 1890.[37] A charming, simple, symmetrical, one-and-one-half-story wooden structure, "Thorn Lodge" offers evidence of excellent workmanship, particularly the first-story wrap-around piazza with slender, turned support columns, and the attic-story double dormer recessed into an expansive front (west-facing) roof plane. A square, brick chimney, turned forty-five degrees so that one corner faces forward, rises above the roof at the exact midpoint of the ridgepole. Owned by descendants of the Chubbucks, the house has been only slightly altered over the years by enlargement of the east ell (a second story was added around 1900), and kitchen remodeling.[38] Still present is the ambience of informal, late Victorian, mountain region, summer vacation life.

In July 1901, George E. Saunders and his wife, Elizabeth H., of Cambridge, Massachusetts, purchased from members of the Trickey family a tract just under and directly abutting the Chubbuck property.[39] George Saunders (b. 1853 in Boston), who was admitted to Harvard in 1870, but never attended, was a successful banker, who served as president of the Harvard Trust Company in Cambridge. He was an avid hiker, which may partially explain his desiring real estate in Jackson. Obviously impressed by Harriman's work for the Chubbucks and other local clients, the Saunders contracted with him in 1904 to build a residence for them on their new

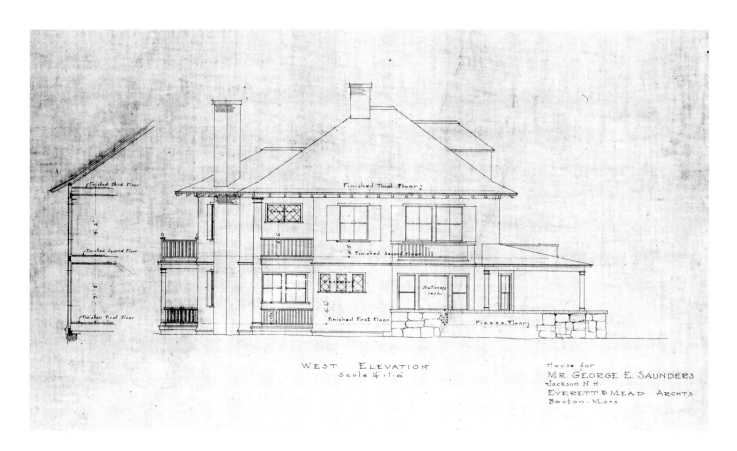

WEST ELEVATION
Scale ¼"·1'·0"

House for
MR. GEORGE E. SAUNDERS
Jackson N.H.
EVERETT & MEAD ARCHTS.
Boston Mass

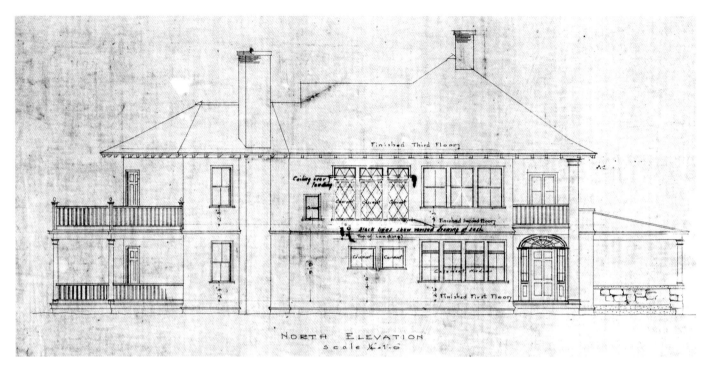

"North Elevation, House for Mr. George E. Saunders, Jackson, N.H.," Everett & Mead, Architects, Boston, c. 1904. Courtesy of Alta M. Gale, Los Angeles, Calif.

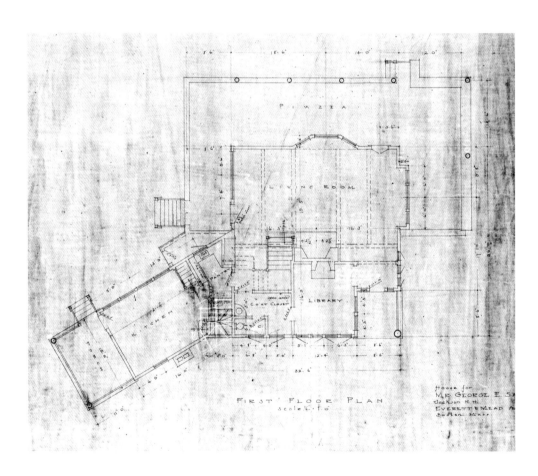

"First Floor Plan, House for Mr. George E. Saunders, Jackson, N.H.," Everett & Mead, Architects, Boston, c. 1904. Courtesy of Alta M. Gale, Los Angeles, Calif.

land. Completed in 1906, the house was named "Hilldrift," which apparently was derived from both geological terminology and Elizabeth Saunders' maiden name, Hildreth.[40] Harriman and his fellow builders were closely guided in their efforts by architectural plans prepared by the Boston architectural firm of (Arthur Greene) Everett (1855–1925) and (Samuel W.) Mead (18??–19??). Initially associated with Edward Clark Cabot (1818–1901), the designer of the Boston Athenaeum, the Boston Theatre, and other landmark buildings in the city, Everett and Mead remained in partnership for many years, planning libraries, college dormitories, other public buildings, and "numerous suburban homes in the New England area, typical examples of the [rambling and] picturesque rural style of the late nineteenth century."[41]

The Saunders' "Hilldrift" typifies the best of the firm's residential commissions. As it may be viewed today, the house, inside and out, is virtually unchanged from its pre–World War I appearance. Eminently practical, with a suggestion of Shingle-style elegance and inventiveness, the building is conceived and arranged to meet perfectly the specialized needs of summer habitation in the White Mountains. Capped by intersecting hipped roofs, punctured by tall brick chimneys and dormers, the house is organized around an asymmetrical floor plan, the principal square portion supplemented by a substantial rectangular wing angled off the northeast corner. By their inclusion of first-floor covered and uncovered piazzas and porches, and second-floor sleeping porches, the architects made every effort to connect the man-made, formalized, human living environment with the realm of nature. In this endeavor, they achieved unqualified success. The interior spaces, particularly the first-floor living room, library, and main stairwell, display rich natural and dark-stained wall siding, paneling (highlighted by beautiful knotty cherry wood), ceiling beams and joists, window and door moldings, fireplace surrounds and mantels, and built-in cabinetry, including window seats, sets of drawers, and book and display shelves. In this exquisitely crafted decor, builder Harriman surpassed in quality and sophistication his other known buildings in Jackson (see Wentworth Hall and Cottages and "Maple Knoll"). George and Elizabeth Saunders and their heirs have been the fortunate beneficiaries of Harriman's productive collaboration with architects Everett and Mead.[42]

∾

The Wilson Cottage

Plan, 1894

(Mrs. C. L. Wilson)

Jackson

South elevation, "Sketch for Mrs. C. L. Wilson, Jackson, N.H.," John Calvin Stevens, Architect, Portland, Maine, 1894. Courtesy of the Maine Historic Preservation Commission, Augusta.

☞ IN PRIVATE HANDS in Maine, there exists a fine set of pen-and-ink design sketches (two perspective elevations; first- and second-story floor schematics) by the noted Portland architect John Calvin Stevens (1855–1940) (see "Peabody Cottage," Gorham). Each sheet is inscribed "Mrs. C. L. Wilson, Jackson, N.H." with the date, "Nov. 22, 1894." The discovery of the plans, however, poses a mystery. A search of available source materials, including old photographs, has turned up no evidence to suggest that a cottage similar to the one depicted in the sketches was ever built in Jackson. Furthermore, none of the surviving summer residences in the town remotely resemble the picturesque Stevens conception, or can be tied historically with the name of Wilson. Nonetheless, had this interesting Shingle/Colonial Revival–style house ever been erected, it surely would have been considered among the most outstanding pre-1930 summer cottages in the White Mountain region.[43]

Conversely, Mrs. C. L. (Caroline F.) Wilson *did* exist, and had every intention of building a house in Jackson, New Hampshire. A brief notice in the 7 July 1894 issue of the *White Mountain Echo* mentions that Wilson, a native of Brookline, Massachusetts, was spending her twelfth summer season at Eagle Mountain House, one of the town's oldest resort hotels. Committed to Jackson for the long term, during the following fall she apparently approached Stevens and commissioned him to prepare the set of design sketches for the cottage of her dreams. At the same time, she negotiated the purchase of five acres of land and water privileges for the house site from the local Meserve family, long associated with the ownership and management of Iron Mountain House. The parcel, for which she paid one thousand dollars, was located on the east side of Thorn Hill Road, probably below Katherine Wormeley's property (see the Wormeley cottages), but commanding the same magnificent views northward of the valley below and the more distant mountains.[44] Here the story ends, for no further information about Wilson and her connection with Jackson has thus far appeared.

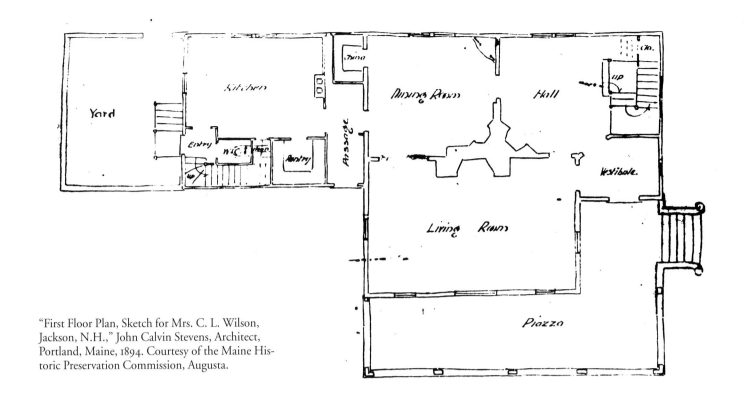

"First Floor Plan, Sketch for Mrs. C. L. Wilson, Jackson, N.H.," John Calvin Stevens, Architect, Portland, Maine, 1894. Courtesy of the Maine Historic Preservation Commission, Augusta.

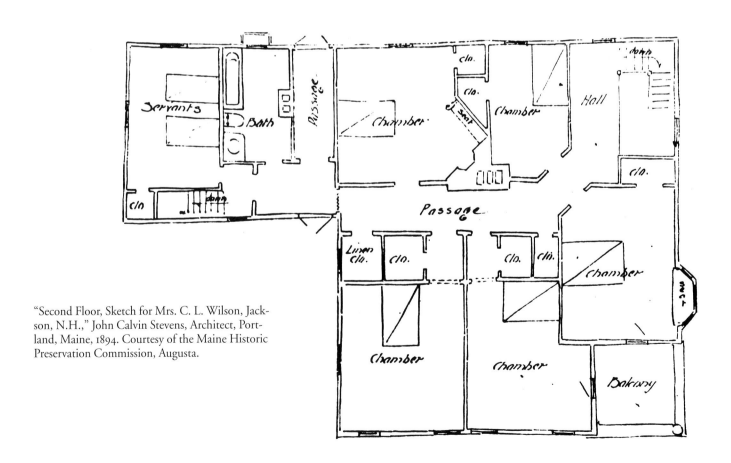

"Second Floor, Sketch for Mrs. C. L. Wilson, Jackson, N.H.," John Calvin Stevens, Architect, Portland, Maine, 1894. Courtesy of the Maine Historic Preservation Commission, Augusta.

We are left, however, with drawings that merit close attention. Intended for a gradually sloping hillside site, the house was to be L-shaped in floor plan, with a vestibule/hall, living room, dining room, kitchen, and pantry on the first floor, and a hallway, five bed chambers, a servant's bedroom, closets, and a single bathroom on the second. An L-shaped, partially enclosed piazza, which doubled as an entrance porch, was to provide ample sitting space for enjoyment of the lovely natural scenery of the Jackson area. The drawings illustrate the asymmetry in form, connected hipped roofs, and square, shingled piazza support piers typical of Shingle-style buildings. Also present are decorative features normally associated with the Colonial Revival—a two-story stairwell window, with a molded semicircular cap; a molded oblong vestibule light with keystones; and a second-story balcony corner support column of the Ionic order. There is a pleasant and refreshing unity to the composition of the house, so common in Stevens' coastal Maine cottages of the same era.[45]

The architect of the Wilson cottage, John Calvin Stevens, was born in Boston and moved with his family to Portland where he later graduated from Portland High School. In 1873, he became office boy in the firm of Portland's Francis H. Fassett, regarded as Maine's leading architect at the time. Stevens advanced quickly in his field, becoming a junior partner to Fassett in 1880, and moving to Boston for a year and a half to head a new branch office of the firm. Returning to Portland in 1884, Stevens left the Fassett office and established his own practice, with particular attention to domestic work in the city and down the coastline in both the Queen Anne and Shingle styles. Albert Winslow Cobb (1858–1941), formerly a draftsman for William Ralph Emerson (see the Fitz cottage and "Maple Knoll," Jackson), joined Stevens as a partner in 1888, imparting to him concepts behind the latest and most fashionable architectural vernaculars. Together they published *Examples of American Domestic Architecture* (New York: W. T. Comstock, 1889), containing many of Stevens' most exemplary Shingle-style designs. Stevens ran an independent office again from 1891 to 1906, during which period he sketched the Wilson cottage plans. His biographers point out that it was in this phase of his career that he began to move away from the Shingle style toward the more formalistic Georgian and Colonial Revival veins. The project for Caroline Wilson in Jackson clearly demonstrates this transition.[46]

∼

"The Boulders"

1895

(Mr. and Mrs. Charles H. Ditson)

Jackson

"The Boulders" (1895), Jackson, N.H. Photograph courtesy of the Jackson Historical Society.

~ BUILT FOR Mr. and Mrs. Charles H. Ditson of Boston in 1895,[47] "The Boulders" was once the finest and most sophisticated example of Colonial Revival–style domestic architecture in northern New Hampshire. Refined yet elaborately detailed, this fascinating reflection of late-Victorian taste clearly displayed the skillful hand of a professional architect, fully versed in the Colonial Revival vernacular. Situated on a knoll overlooking the Wildcat River and Jackson village, "The Boulders" exhibited, in artful combination, numerous qualities and elements commonly associated with the Colonial Revival: a truncated hipped roof; dormers with broken ogee pediments; heavy classical cornices and friezes; fluted corner pilasters; roof, bay, porch, and piazza balustrades; pavilions with closed gables; and varied window sizes and treatments, including the archetypical Palladian. The loss of the house to fire in about 1934 deprived Jackson of one of its most significant buildings, clearly the equal, in terms of scale, grandeur, and articulation, of the Wigglesworth and Fitz cottages on Thorn Hill.

Credited with the design of the house is William A. Bates (1853–1922), a prominent New York City architect, responsible in earlier years for planning the Wentworth Hall and Cottages hotel complex and "The Castle," also in Jackson, for General Marshall C. Wentworth. Bates was highly regarded for his residential and public buildings in and about metropolitan New York, numerous of which were illustrated in national architectural periodicals of the period. Given his background and the location of most of his commissions, it is hardly surprising, therefore, that his work for the Ditsons possessed a suburban character, albeit somewhat tenuously connected with its mountain setting. The Ditsons probably selected Bates as architect as a consequence of their friendship with the Wentworth family, and possible associations with Bates, an occasional summer guest at Wentworth Hall during the 1880s and 1890s. Working with Bates on the construction of the house was contractor Orman S. Spring of Hiram, Maine, the builder of other residences in the Eastern Slope region.[48]

Charles Ditson (1845–1929) was the son of Oliver Ditson, the founder of this country's oldest publishers of sheet music, as well as one of its most successful and widely known before World War II. The senior Ditson, after entering the music business in Boston in the 1830s, established his own firm there, Oliver Ditson & Company, in 1857. In 1864, he set up a branch, Charles H. Ditson & Company, in New York City under his son Charles' management. A third division of the business, headed by another son, James E., was opened in Philadelphia in 1875. Upon Oliver's death in 1888, Charles succeeded his father as president, a position he held until his death. Although he resided in New York City and maintained a country house on Long Island, he spent much time in Boston, where the company continued to be headquartered in its own building in the downtown business district.[49] Charles Ditson and his wife were likely attracted to the White Mountains through social contacts and their ties with the Wentworths. They acquired the land upon which "The Boulders" was erected from neighbors of the Wentworths—two parcels totaling about fourteen acres from George Pinkham in 1894, and a supplementary tract in 1896 from Nelson I. and Jennie E. Trickey, of the family long connected with the operation of Jackson Falls House in the village.[50]

∾

"Maple Knoll"

1896–97

(Mr. and Mrs. Frank H. Shapleigh)

Jackson

∾ "MAPLE KNOLL" IS one of three buildings in Jackson designed by the noted Boston architect William Ralph Emerson (1833–1917), the others being the Fitz cottage (c. 1888) on Thorn Hill, and the Jackson Public Library (1900–1901) in Jackson village.[51] It was built for Mr. and Mrs. Frank H. Shapleigh of Boston in 1896–97, following a land purchase made from the local Trickey family in 1893.[52] The Shapleighs were in all likelihood drawn to Jackson as a consequence of deep associations over many years with the White Mountains and the grand resort hotels. Frank Shapleigh was one of the most prolific and popular of the post–Civil War artists of the region, producing a vast oeuvre, in both oil and watercolor, of the mountains, their most intimate natural features, and the physical evidence of human habitation. The Shapleighs very possibly became acquainted with Emerson through the Fitz family, or at Wentworth Hall and Cottages, where the architect and his future clients were known to have been occasional summer guests during the 1890s.

In his biographical recollections, *Sixty Years' Memories of Art and Artists* (1900), Shapleigh's esteemed professional colleague, Benjamin Champney, recalled "Maple Knoll":

"Maple Knoll" (1896–97), Jackson, N.H. Photograph by the author.

it is situated just back of the Jackson Falls House, but is higher and farther up the road so that the outlook towards the south includes the fine outline of the Moat [mountains] and the lovely valley below. The cottage is unique in architecture, painted in a soft gray tone which harmonizes pleasantly with the near surrounding [predominantly maple] foliage. But the great attraction . . . is the manner in which Mr. Shapleigh has furnished the interior. It is like a great museum of curios brought from most quarters of the world and placed in delightful confusion in every nook and corner of the artistically arranged rooms. He has a natural love for the surroundings, of the furniture of past days, the quaint old bits our grandfather delighted in, and knows how to select what is most artistic and beautiful. But with all this the house is full of comfort and convenience.[53]

During the Shapleighs' years at "Maple Knoll," their attractive cottage, containing the painter's studio, "was the rendezvous for the artists, musicians and writers who made Jackson their summer home,"[54] much like Augustus St. Gaudens' estate, "Aspet," served the summer colony in Cornish, New Hampshire.

"Maple Knoll" is reminiscent of architect Emerson's outstanding Shingle-style country residential work along the shores of Massachusetts and Maine. The floor plan of the house is free-flowing and innovative, with a sensitive treatment of interior space. Two wings (one of two stories, the

Above: Parlor, "Maple Knoll" (1896–97), Jackson, N.H. *Below:* Studio, "Maple Knoll" (1896–97), Jackson, N.H. Photographs courtesy of Mr. George Beal, Bradford, N.H.

other a single story), are angled back from the main block of the building, creating a welcoming, partially enclosed rear entrance area, accessed by a circular gravel drive. Typical intersecting gambrel roofs are broken by a tall central brick chimney, and eyebrow, shed-roof, and truncated gable-roof dormers. Today, the shingle wall sheathing is natural, above latticework and fieldstone masonry foundations. Generous verandas, with heavy, curved-truss supports, grace the cottage, providing the occupants ample opportunity to savor the beauties and natural benefits of nature. The various functional and decorative components of the house effectively blend together into a cohesive, picturesque whole, the clear reflection of a successful collaboration between the owners and the architect.[55]

Frank H. Shapleigh (1842–1906) was born in Boston, attended local public schools, and studied at the Lowell Institute of Drawing. He joined the Union army during the Civil War, was mustered out in 1863, and commenced his career as both a landscape and portrait painter. In 1867, with artist friend John Appleton Brown, he traveled to Europe to study art, visit museum collections, and sketch scenes from nature. Returning to Boston, he exhibited his work, making a painting trip to the western United States

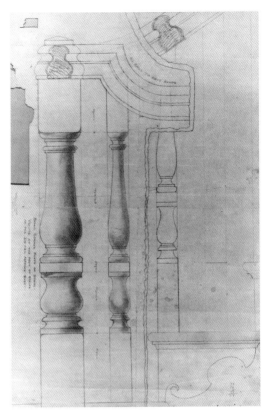

Stairway corner posts detail, "Maple Knoll" (1896–97), Jackson, N.H., William R. Emerson, Boston, Architect. Courtesy of Mr. and Mrs. Bradford Boynton, Jackson and South Conway, N.H.

in 1870. Late in that year, he was married to Mary A. Studley of Cohasset, Massachusetts, who accompanied him on sketching trips throughout New England through the middle of the decade. His growing reputation as a respected New England artist earned him the position of summer artist-in-residence at Crawford House, one of the White Mountains' oldest and most famous grand resort hotels. Alternating between Boston and the North Country, with annual spring stays at Jackson hotels, Shapleigh served in this capacity from 1877 to 1893. During this period he worked occasionally as an illustrator, and produced a large number of oil landscapes for hotel patrons, focusing on such favorite scenes as Mount Washington and the Presidential Range, the Ellis River Valley, Crawford Notch and Elephant's Head, the west side mountains, and the Jackson hills and streams. In the late 1880s, Shapleigh and his wife spent winters in Florida, where he displayed his New England work and painted Florida views. After 1893, the Shapleighs were back in New England, and in 1894–95 went on a two-year tour of Europe. Upon the completion of "Maple Knoll," they moved in for their first full summer in 1898. In a state of poor health after the European sojourn, Shapleigh produced only occasional works of art, and his life centered on a limited social and cultural life in Jackson and Boston.[56] He died, we can conjecture, knowing that "his brush had helped . . . in making better known the wonders of White Mountain scenery."[57]

~

Thorn Mountain Park

1896–98

(Colonel Isaac L. Goff)

Jackson

~ ISAAC L. GOFF of Providence, Rhode Island, played a major role in Jackson's ascendance to the front ranks of the summer resort communities in the White Mountain region. A prominent financier, aggressive real estate developer, and consummate promoter, he offered the following statement about the benefits of vacation time in the mountains in the 1902 edition of *New Hampshire Farms for Summer Homes*:

> I believe business and professional men realize more each year the necessity of taking at least one month's time away from business cares, to get back into the mountains where the air is high, dry, and healthy, and I look forward to the time when it will be as popular to own a summer home in the mountains as it is at present to own one at the seashore.[58]

These few simple words capture the philosophy and motivation that were the driving force behind Goff's highly ambitious Thorn Mountain Park development scheme in Jackson during the 1890s.

Born at Taunton, Massachusetts, Isaac Lewis Goff (1852–1935) spent his youth at local schools and on his father's farm in Rehoboth, attended Bryant & Stratton Business College in Providence, and, after a year of odd

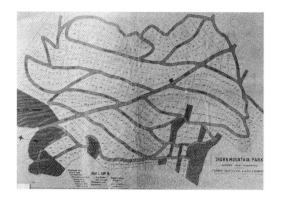

"Thorn Mountain Park, Jackson, New Hampshire,
Thorn Mountain Land Company," map, 1896.
Courtesy of the Jackson Historical Society.

jobs, worked for four years in the real estate office of William D. Pierce. In 1874 he established his own real estate and insurance business in Providence, Isaac L. Goff Co., and was active in several projects that furthered the growth of suburbs of the rapidly expanding metropolitan area. His Washington Park venture was notably successful, an initial sixty-thousand-dollar investment parlayed into assets totaling several million dollars. Goff was also president and treasurer of the Sakonnet Land Company of Rhode Island, and was a director of several banks and insurance companies. Always interested in military affairs, Goff joined the United Train of Artillery in 1880, and eventually was promoted to the rank of colonel. A leading Republican in his home state, he served his party in a number of appointed and volunteer capacities, and for six years was a member of the Providence city committee. He owned several thoroughbred horses, and was often seen at racetracks around the country. He was also a member of yacht and social clubs, the Masons, the Elks, and the Sons of the American Revolution.[59]

Goff had long been interested in the White Mountains and had often visited there with his family during the 1880s and early 1890s. Knowledgeable about the area, and confident in its future, he saw the opportunity to realize real estate investment gains in the expanding tourist economy. Starting in 1894, through a series of separate land purchases, the enterprising entrepreneur systematically acquired most of the west side of Thorn Mountain, a two-thousand-foot ridge above Jackson, looking out on Mount Washington and the entire sweep of the Presidential Range.[60] In 1896, the colonel formed the Thorn Mountain Park Land Company, and commissioned Shedd and Sarle, an engineering firm based in Providence and Worcester, Massachusetts, to draft a subdivision plan for his envisioned Thorn Mountain summer colony. The plan called for the creation of an astounding 327 house lots ranging from one-quarter to one-half acre each, accessed by a web of roads bearing the names of well-known American towns and

"Fern Cliff" (1896), Thorn Mountain Park, Jackson,
N.H. Photograph by the author.

"Tree Tops" (1898), Thorn Mountain Park, Jackson, N.H. Photograph by the author.

cities (Concord, Detroit, Philadelphia, San Francisco, Boston, and so on). At one point, to contend with the steep slope of the mountainside, Goff even considered constructing a cable road for future cottage owners and tourists, and hired Thomas E. Browne, Jr., of New York City, representing the Otis Elevator Company, to prepare a feasibility study. This imaginative transportation solution, however, was never implemented, probably for financial reasons.[61]

Simultaneous with the preparation of the Thorn Mountain Park plan, Goff oversaw the construction of his own family's cottage, "Fern Cliff," at the head of the main road connecting Jackson with the proposed house sites. This very eclectic late-Victorian structure, distinguished by its square and octagonal corner towers, stickwork balustrades, and ample porches, was completed in September 1896. The tourist newspaper *Among the Clouds* praised "the beautiful and sightly new residence," and suggested that it would set a precedent for "the fine class of buildings" that would eventually appear throughout the park development.[62] Among its most impressive features then were its rough-stone foundations, natural wood siding, red roof, and an "artistic and picturesque" rough stone interior fireplace.[63] The architect of "Fern Cliff" was Isaac H. Sisson, a Providence metal patternmaker and dealer in metal ornaments, who may have known Goff as a result of the latter's service as treasurer of the Providence Metal Company. Sisson's experience and expertise as a designer of buildings is unknown, and why he, and not a professional architect, was selected to work for the colonel remains a mystery.[64]

Between 1896 and 1898, Goff induced several other individuals to erect summer houses at Thorn Mountain Park, some of whom were connected with Yale University. In addition to "Fern Cliff," in 1896, he built three others for lot owners close by, one of which, "Thorn Mountain Cabin," was promptly occupied by Dr. W. F. Morrison and his family from Providence. In 1898, Goff added a double residence to the group, "Tree Tops," and "Tin Mine Lodge."[65] Sisson may have been involved with the design of these buildings, but this has not been substantiated. Incorporating elements of the then fashionable Shingle style, each cottage—symmetrical in form and crafted with natural wood and local fieldstone—exhibits charming, indigenous rusticity that irrevocably links it to its still unspoiled, wild mountain environment.

For some inexplicable reason, possibly due to the nature of Goff's conception, Thorn Mountain Park never caught on with prospective buyers, and so far as we know, no additional houses were built during his period of ownership. The Goffs, however, continued to enjoy their unique vacation retreat, perched high on the mountainside, until at least the late 1920s.[66] Despite its apparent failure, Thorn Mountain Park set the stage for the post–World War II cottage and condominium developments that have become such an important part of the White Mountain residential scene today.

≈

"The Studio"

c.1898–99

(Mr. and Mrs. Charles H. Turner)

Jackson

"The Studio" (c. 1898–99), Jackson, N.H. Photograph by the author.

⌁ IN ITS 19 AUGUST 1905 edition, the *White Mountain Echo*, the widely circulated regional tourist newspaper, ran this brief notice in its Jackson column:

> C. H. Turner, the well known Boston artist, was one of the first to establish a home in Jackson, where his picturesque cottage, like a Swiss Alpine chalet, attracts hundreds of visitors during the season. It perches on a hillside [a bluff of Iron Mountain] overlooking the Wentworth Hall [hotel] golf links [and the Ellis River Valley], inviting the wayfarer to stop and rest on its shady gallery.[67]

Although it is no longer the focal point of attention it once was, this provocative and fanciful dwelling, well preserved and maintained, remains one of the White Mountain's most noteworthy small, turn-of-the-century summer residences.

Convinced of Jackson's assets as a result of hotel visits, Turner acquired the land for the house in October 1898 from a local couple, Silas M. and Sophronia S. Thompson.[68] Named "The Studio," and serving Turner's domestic as well as professional needs, the cottage is believed to have been erected starting in late 1898 and completed by the next summer season. The names of its architect (if there was one) and builder have thus far failed to surface. The lack of this information, does not, however, detract from the building's obvious architectural merit. Topped by a moderately pitched gable roof, the two-story rectangular structure rests on massive, mortared, native stone foundations set deep into the slope of the hill. The second story slightly overhangs the first, with an open veranda (the aforementioned "gallery") with light, stick-work balustrades nearly encircling the house on its east and west long sides, and narrower south end. Highly varied, the fenestration includes a large multipaned window in the north end (originally for natural illumination of the artist's studio space); small, square diamond-paned casement windows (single and paired) on the first story; and quadruple, double-sash bay windows on the second. Overall, the house is highly geometric, with crisp horizontal, vertical, and diagonal visual lines accentuated by the white-painted gable molding, exposed second-story floor rafters, and square veranda posts and balustrades.

The creator of "The Studio," Charles Henry Turner (1848–after 1909), though recognized in Boston art circles, is actually credited with no White Mountain landscape scenes in published works treating American art history. He is not listed in Catherine H. Campbell's highly regarded dictionary of nineteenth-century New Hampshire mountain landscape artists (*New Hampshire Scenery*, 1985). Although he is known to have produced landscape paintings, they were of locations in Massachusetts and other areas. Turner was primarily interested in portraiture and figure pictures, a specialty for which he probably found the family mountain retreat extremely conducive. Unlike his Jackson neighbor, Frank H. Shapleigh, whose residence, "Maple Knoll," was primarily a center of regional landscape art, Turner painted a wide spectrum of subjects in his cottage, his work nurtured by the quiet, rural environment of the resort community.

Born in Newburyport, Massachusetts, Turner did not enter the field of art until he was nearly thirty years old. After attending the local public schools and Hampton (New Hampshire) Academy, he served briefly in the Union forces at the end of the Civil War, then from 1866 to 1869 in the Fourth United States Cavalry in Texas. Departing the military at age twenty-one, he was employed for several years as a bookkeeper for the firm of S. Q. Cochran & Company in Boston, and traveled in Europe. From 1877 to 1880, he received his formal art education at Boston's famed Art Museum School, studying with Otto Grundmann. He formally launched his career as an artist in 1881, selling his work throughout the United States. A staunch Mason, Turner was also a member of Unity Art Club and the Boston Art Club, serving at various times as president of both organizations. In addition to his summer studio at Jackson, he resided on Mount Vernon Street, Beacon Hill, in Boston.[69]

❧

"Gray Manor"

1902–3

(Miss Kate C. Baldwin)

Jackson

❧ PARTIALLY SCREENED by trees, on a knoll at the intersection of Thorn Hill Road and Route 16B, stands a substantial gambrel-roofed cottage known historically as "Gray Manor." One of Jackson's most distinctive early-twentieth-century summer homes, it effectively integrates the form, proportions, and surface materials associated with the Shingle style with Colonial Revival design elements. These classical embellishments originally included wide roof and veranda cornice moldings, end gable modified Palladian windows, and regularly spaced and tapered Doric columns supporting verandas that almost completely encircled the building. Today,

"Gray Manor" (1902–3), Jackson, N.H. Photograph, 1972. Courtesy of the Jackson Historical Society.

the front elevation displays perfect symmetry, common in Colonial Revival buildings. Due to alterations in recent years, most notably the enclosing of the verandas, the integrity of the original design has been somewhat compromised, but not with aesthetically detrimental results.

"Gray Manor" was built in 1902–3 for Kate Corrine Baldwin of Brooklyn, New York, on land purchased from her friend Katherine P. Wormeley. For a number of years prior to the purchase, Baldwin had been a regular guest at Wentworth Hall in the village, during which time she probably established her friendship with Wormeley, a previous Jackson summer resident (see the Wormeley cottages). In fact, Baldwin called upon Wormeley to oversee the construction of the house, working with local contractors.[70] In addition, it appears that Wormeley played a role in designing the house, for a set of first- and second-story floor plans, now in private hands, bears her signature. Furthermore, these valuable documents display the same drafting style and penmanship as similar sketch plans that the creative Wormeley prepared about 1892 for "The Satyr," her small cottage higher up Thorn Hill.[71]

For many years, local sources have attributed the design of "Gray Manor" to Stanford White (1853–1906), the world-renowned New York City architect, believed also to have drafted the plans for Wormeley's house, "Brookmead," next door on Thorn Hill Road (see the Wormeley cottages). There are no references to the house in any published materials pertaining to White, however, nor do there exist any drawings or related records in the major McKim, Mead and White collections at the Avery Library, Columbia University, or the New-York Historical Society, New York City. Wormeley was, however, a winter resident of Newport, Rhode Island, where the firm did extensive work, and her house there was designed by one of White's partners, Charles Follen McKim. She may, therefore, have had contact with White there, employed him to draft the plans for "Brookmead," and then referred Baldwin to him for the design of her cottage. Furthermore, it is quite possible that no formal schemes were prepared for either house, and that White sketched basic conceptual plans as a social favor—were this true, it would explain the lack of documentation.

Kate Baldwin and her relations continued to use the cottage until around 1922, when it was sold to Ella S. and Arthur C. Gray (hence its popular name) and operated as a summer inn until 1935. Since then under various owners, it has continued to be used as a hostelry, with such names as Alrich Inn, Jackson Lodge, and, currently, The Inn at Jackson. At some point after 1922, the rear ell was extended, and other modifications undertaken, including the elimination of the open verandas.[72]

3 ～

Gorham/Shelburne

Situated north of Pinkham Notch, Gorham and the adjacent town to the east, Shelburne, were not the locus of major summer cottage colonies, but have made their marks, nonetheless, as tourist centers. The transformation of the economies of these communities from predominantly agricultural to more diverse commenced in 1851 with the arrival from Portland, Maine, of the Atlantic and St. Lawrence Railroad (subsequently the Grand Trunk). Immediately Gorham became a commercial hub for the northeastern White Mountain region, and an array of business enterprises, including hotels, were established by local people as well as outsiders. Primary amongst the hotels was the 250-guest White Mountain Station House (later the Alpine House), opened in 1851, and later supplemented by much smaller Gorham House (1853), and the Eagle Hotel (c. 1870). While it has remained rural and sparsely settled, Shelburne also boasted hostelries, including the Winthrop House, the still operating Philbrook Farm and Cottages, and the Shelburne Spring House. Visitors were attracted to the area by the scenic beauty of the Androscoggin River Valley, flanked by the tall summits of the Mahoosuc Range to the north, and the Moriah and Northern Presidential peaks to the south. During the second half of the nineteenth century, sizable valley land holdings were developed, including the Burbank's famed White Mountain Stock Farm, and the extensive country estates of the Endicott and Aston families. The Peabody family of Portland, Maine, erected the most architecturally captivating of the smaller cottages, high on a hill overlooking the river and Gorham center.

The Peabody Cottage

1903

(Mr. Henry C. Peabody)

Gorham

FRONT ELEVATION
¼" = 1'-0"

COTTAGE AT
GORHAM, NEW HAMPSHIRE.
MR CLARENCE W. PEABODY
John Calvin Stevens, Archt.
Portland, Me.
April 1, 1903
C.F.S.

"Front Elevation, Cottage at Gorham, New Hampshire, Mr. Clarence W. Peabody," John Calvin Stevens, Architect, Portland, Maine, 1903. Courtesy of the Maine Historic Preservation Commission, Augusta.

◇ THIS PLAIN SHINGLE-STYLE cottage was erected during the spring of 1903 from plans prepared by the noted Portland, Maine, architect, John Calvin Stevens (1855–1940) (see the Wilson cottage, Jackson). It was situated on the lower slopes of Sugar Mountain, west of the Grand Truck Railroad and the auto road between Gorham and Berlin, and commanded superb views of the Androscoggin River Valley and the northern White Mountains. Although it burned down around 1970, the house is, fortunately, thoroughly documented by a complete set of the architect's plans, which have survived in the care of family descendants in Maine. These plans clearly convey basic features often associated with the Shingle mode—a gambrel roof pierced by extended and triangular gable dormers, foundation-level latticework screens, and balustraded piazzas, both covered and uncovered, perfectly positioned to take advantage of the mountain sun, fresh breezes, and sweeping vistas.[1]

The early ownership history of the house, on the surface, appears quite complicated, but may be clarified through examination of records filed at the Coos County Courthouse in Lancaster. The title inscription on Stevens' plans indicates that they were commissioned by Clarence W. Peabody on behalf of his father, Henry C. Peabody, both citizens of Portland. The house was subsequently built on land held in the name of Mercy M. Peabody, Henry's mother. Then in July 1903, this tract, with the newly completed building, was conveyed by deed to her son, Henry. He held title to the property until his death in 1911, at which time it passed by will in equal shares to his two sons, Clarence and Henry A.[2] The Portland Peabodys were likely drawn to the Gorham area in part because of the presence of other members of their family. Given common Portland roots, it was logical for them to hire Stevens as their architect.

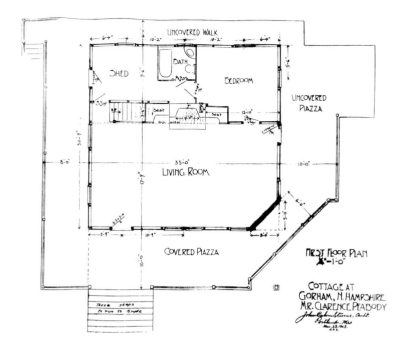

"First Floor Plan, Cottage at Gorham, New Hampshire, Mr. Clarence Peabody," John Calvin Stevens, Architect, Portland, Maine, 1903. Courtesy of the Maine Historic Preservation Commission, Augusta.

Both Henry and Clarence Peabody were distinguished members of the legal profession in Maine. Henry Clay Peabody (1838–1911), a native of Gilead, was educated at Gould Academy, Fryeburg Academy, and Dartmouth College (class of 1859), and received legal training in Portland at the offices of Gen. Samuel Fessenden. Admitted to the Maine bar in 1862, he practiced law in Portland until 1880, at which time he was elected Judge of Probate for Cumberland County, an office he held for the next twenty years. In 1900 he received a gubernatorial appointment as a justice of the Supreme Judicial Court of Maine, where he served until his death. An "all-around good citizen," Henry Peabody was extremely active in public affairs as a conspicuous member of the Knights of Pythias, the Royal Arcanum, and the Odd Fellows, and as a trustee of the Portland Public Library, Frye-

"Drawings of Living Room, Cottage at Gorham, N.H. Mr. C. W. Peabody," John Calvin Stevens, Architect, Portland, Maine, 1903. Courtesy of the Maine Historic Preservation Commission, Augusta.

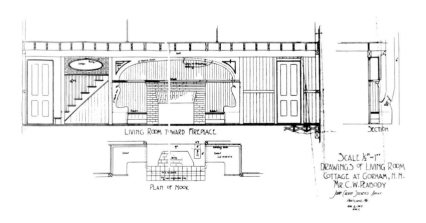

burg Academy, and the Greenleaf Law Library. He also served as a director of the Portland Loan and Building Association and a Fellow of the Maine Academy of Medicine.[3]

His son Clarence Webster Peabody (1871–1940), whose name appears on the cottage plans, was educated at Portland schools, graduated from Bowdoin College in 1893, and from Harvard Law School in 1896. After admission to the Maine bar the following year, he formed a law practice with his brother, Henry, under the name Peabody & Peabody. In 1916 he was appointed a professor at the University of Maine Law School, and during his six-year tenure there became recognized as a specialist in corporation law. Returning to Portland and private practice in 1922, he was soon appointed judge of the Portland Municipal Court where he served for four years. In addition, Clarence Peabody founded the Peabody Law Classics, which was incorporated as the Peabody Law School, with himself as dean, in 1936. During his long career, he also served as secretary of the State Board of Examiners, and was a member of the Portland School Board. His social and recreational interests centered on the Portland Athletic Club.[4] For both him and his father, the family cottage in the White Mountains must have provided a welcome respite from extremely active professional and community lives.

≈

"Wyndham Villa"

1884–85

(Mr. and Mrs. William K. Aston)

Shelburne

"Wyndham Villa" (1884–85), Shelburne, N.H. Photograph courtesy of the Philbrook Farm Inn, Shelburne.

∾ THE STORY OF the magnificent country estate "Wyndham Villa" on the Androscoggin River in Shelburne has long been shrouded in mystery. Little is known about its creator, William K. Aston, and its architect has yet to be identified. Only pieces of the history of the property have surfaced, and in most instances these lack convincing documentation. The principal physical remnant of the Aston legacy, the family cottage, was destroyed by fire over three decades ago, and we know of its appearance only through photographs, a few published references, and the now fading recollections of local citizens. The original house site itself has been unrec-

Parlor, "Wyndham Villa" (1884–85), Shelburne, N.H. Photograph courtesy of the Philbrook Farm Inn, Shelburne.

ognizably transformed by commercial excavation. Although two notable estate outbuildings survive, it is difficult to imagine "Wyndham Villa" as it looked in its heyday. Yet it was at one time the pride of Shelburne, and one of the White Mountain's largest and most important summer vacation farm retreats (see also "The Rocks," Bethlehem, and "Stonehurst," North Conway [Intervale]), attracting notice for the brilliance, uniqueness, and sophistication of its architecture.

Just who was William K. Aston? Sadly, manuscript records, newspapers, genealogies, and other printed works disclose virtually nothing about him.[5] One newspaper source describes him as "a relation of the Vanderbilt family" from New York City.[6] Other sources further identify him as a young German-American lawyer named William Kronberg who traveled to Shelburne on business for a client with the last name of Aston in the early 1870s, and became greatly enamored of the area. Around 1880, he became Aston's heir, with the proviso that he change his name to William Kissam Aston upon the death of his benefactor. Soon thereafter, upon inheriting a substantial fortune, he returned to Shelburne, and in 1883 commenced a series of purchases, mostly on the south side of the river, that by 1900 totaled several hundred acres of fine forest and pasture land.[7] In the first edition (1902) of *New Hampshire Farms for Summer Homes*, Aston made clear the virtues of Shelburne and his rationale for investing there:

> Here in Shelburne fine improved land, as good as any in the state, can still be
> had from $50 to $100 an acre. Shelburne may easily be called the best watered

Stable, "Wyndham Villa" (1884–85), Shelburne, N.H. Photograph by the author.

Barn, "Wyndham Villa" (1884–85), Shelburne, N.H. Photograph by the author.

town in the state, and with its delightful climate, shady road, extensive pine forest, and abundance of trout and game it furnishes the most inviting inducements to the hardy sportsman, tired invalid, easy tourist, or man of affairs. We have no unsightly buildings, saloons, or shops of any kind in the town, and are absolutely free from flies and mosquitoes, while the surrounding hills and scenery are the most picturesque imaginable.[8]

Considering the magnitude of Aston's commitment to the town, we can be sure that these words faithfully conveyed his innermost sentiments. While a resident of Shelburne, he routinely contributed his time and money in support of worthy civic and church projects.

Through citations in the *Gorham Mountaineer*, the local newspaper, we can follow the origins and growth of "Wyndham Villa." In October 1884, Aston bought the farm of A. C. Evans, as well as a nearby church, made plans to build the following spring, let the job to a carpenter, and projected completion for 1 July 1885. By the middle of December the cellar walls for the new house were completed. The next newspaper reference to appear (19 June 1885) informed readers that "Mr. Aston's house is going along quite rapidly, under the supervision of Mr. Smith of Lancaster" [presumed to be the well-known contractor John H. Smith], and that "as soon as the house is finished there is to be a stable, ice house and other buildings put up." Two months later the *Mountaineer* reported that "Mr. Aston and his help . . . are clearing up and beautifying about his magnificent set of buildings . . . [which] pleases our townspeople and causes pleasant remarks." The 25 September issue reported that "Mr. Aston's buildings are nearly completed, and he is grading up his place, removing stones, building fences, etc." During the remainder of the fall, the finishing touches were applied, and the Aston family was able to occupy the estate the following spring.[9]

In its full glory, new and meticulously landscaped, "Wyndham Villa" must have been a sight to behold. In his 1892 book, *Through the Wilds*, Captain Charles A. J. Farrar described the scene as it appeared to onlookers along the road linking Shelburne with Bethel, Maine:

On the high plateau front of Mount Winthrop [Mahoosuc Range] is the picturesque summer cottage of W. K. Aston, a New-York gentleman of wealth and refinement, who tempted by the many beauties of the locality has made it his summer home for several years, and has handsomely and tastily combined art with nature in beautifying his charming estate. The view from the piazza of his palatial cottage [toward the Northern Presidential Peaks] is second to none in New Hampshire.[10]

Displaying asymmetrical elevations and crowned by steep-pitched gable roofs, the cottage was an exotic, highly innovative interpretation of the Shingle style. Most noteworthy of the features on its south-facing main elevation were the closed cylindrical southwest corner sun porch with a conical roof cap, central porte cochere with low hipped roof and finial, and two-storied, cylindrical, southeast corner porch topped by a low conical roof, the second open story accessed by a grand exterior staircase. All wall and roof surfaces were clad in characteristic cedar shingles. The two-and-one-half-story interior contained twelve principal rooms, arranged according to irregular floor plans.[11] Near this main house were a caretaker's cottage, a laundry, an immense horse barn, and a stable/carriage house, all of which still stand. Painted a dark red, and seemingly in immaculate condition, the latter two structures, though much larger in scale, emulate the materials and certain decorative details of the former Aston cottage. An ice house, greenhouses, and other smaller outbuildings also once formed part of the complex, but these no longer exist. On the estate grounds there were stone walls, pathways, bridges, pairs of stone entrance gates, and stone animal figures, including a large fish, fabricated by local stonemason George Emery.[12]

William Aston had not owned "Wyndham Villa" for too many years before his financial fortunes began to turn, and he gradually divested himself of all of his vast property. In 1903 he sold the undivided lands on the south side of the Androscoggin River to the International Paper Company; those lands were then absorbed into the White Mountain National Forest in 1912. As a result of the Panic of 1907, he was forced to mortgage some of his timber holdings on the north side of the river, most of which were eventually acquired by the Brown Paper Company of Berlin. During World War I, he sold off additional portions of the property to supply financial assistance to his native Germany. In 1918, William Rogers Chapman, a musician from Bethel, purchased the rest of the estate, including the buildings, hoping to make it the home of a New England regional music center. When this did not materialize, Chapman sold the property to Dr. Frank H. Gordon for use as a silver fox farm. This risky enterprise, however, collapsed, with considerable loss to local investors. The property then changed hands again, and was further subdivided, the main house becoming a public guest establishment named Shelburne Inn. While owned by Leo Poretta in 1960, this outstanding example of late-Victorian North Country estate architecture was destroyed by a fire of undetermined origins. Despite this unfortunate turn of fate, memories of "Wyndham Villa" and the lavish Aston life-style endure.[13]

≈

"The Stone House"

1884–85

(Mr. Charles Endicott)

Shelburne

⤳ IN HIS POPULAR 1882 fictional work, *Through the Wilds*, Captain Charles A. J. Farrar recounts the details of a trip along the Androscoggin River Valley in Shelburne, and the sighting of an "elegant cottage, built of cobble-stones picked from the land on which it stands." This "charmingly located" house, looking out toward the Mahoosuc Range to the north, and the northern Presidential summits to the west, is identified as the property of one Charles Endicott, of the old and venerable Salem and Boston, Massachusetts, family.[14] This unusual residence, with its adjacent outbuildings, continues today to attract the attention of curious passersby on the main east-west highway connecting Gorham, New Hampshire, and Bethel, Maine.

Despite his deep New England roots, Charles Endicott (1836–96) was a transplant to the Midwest, and a shining example of the American business success story. Born in Beverly, Massachusetts, the young Endicott attended the local public schools, and commenced his business career as a clerk in the dry-goods store of C. F. Hovey in Boston. In the early 1860s, accompanied by his new wife, Caroline Leach, he decided to seek his fortune in the west. In 1865, he purchased an interest in the dry-goods business of T. C. Chapman of Milwaukee, Wisconsin. After just three years, however, Endicott relocated to Detroit where he associated with Cyrenius A. Newcomb to form what would ultimately become the great retail merchandising enterprise of Newcomb, Endicott & Company. Although he devoted the major portion of his time to his business interests, Endicott played an active role in the social, cultural, and intellectual life of Detroit. In 1883, he donated funds toward the purchase of land for the future Museum of Art, of which he became an incorporator and a member of the first executive committee the following year. He was deeply committed to the Unitarian church, and was a generous contributor to its work.[15]

His business career well established, in the early 1880s Endicott decided to satisfy his desire for a "men only" country retreat in the White Mountains. Moved by the beauty, remoteness, and sparse settlement of Shelburne, which he had visited in previous summers, in October 1883 he acquired several contiguous tracts of land on the south side of the Androscoggin River from Joseph Row, Otis Evans, and members of the Philbrook family.[16] Here, in 1884–85, he erected a main residence, an adjacent ice house (with birdhouse cupola), and large barn (with prominent gable-end date marker), all of similar, compatible design and materials. It has been conjectured, though not yet documented, that Endicott served as his own architect as well as construction supervisor, collaborating on the building project with local workmen. This seems extremely likely. The cottage, commonly referred to as "The Stone House," bears a close resemblance to Queen Anne–style plans published in readily accessible American design books of the period. The sophisticated workmanship evident in the structure, particularly the masonry joints and the intricate wood detail (variegated gable siding, eaves barge board, console brackets, porch balustrades and columns, fenestration) strongly suggests the influence of such sources,

"The Stone House" and outbuildings (1884–85), Shelburne, N.H. Photograph by the author.

and is testament to the considerable talents of Endicott and his laborer associates.[17]

The buildings comprising the Endicott estate were constructed to last indefinitely and are models of outstanding Victorian-era structural engineering. For the window sills and eight-foot-wide stone foundation footings of the main residence, granite was quarried in Barre, Vermont, and then shipped by rail to Jefferson, and by oxcart from there to Shelburne. Workers collected fieldstone from the surrounding woods and fields, carefully cleansing it in the nearby river, packing it in protective wrappers, and meticulously assembling it with deep-set mortar joints to form the thick outer walls of the three buildings. To give the fieldstone stability, and for weather resistance and fireproofing, inside liners for the walls were fabricated of bricks believed to have been made at the brickyard that once stood opposite the buildings south of the highway. In the main residence, the original fireplace flues were incorporated into these walls. Looking larger that it is, the Endicott cottage initially contained just four principal spaces (foyer, living room, dining room, library/study) on the first floor and three (bedrooms) on the second. While these spaces have been assigned somewhat different functions by twentieth-century owners, on the interior the house remains much as it was built, with the exception of reconfigured central stairways and bathrooms, the result of remodelings around 1917 and later. Still present inside are cherry door and window frames, fireplace

Barn, "The Stone House" (1884–85), Shelburne, N.H. Photograph by the author.

surrounds, moldings, and paneling, believed to be the work of Endicott himself, who was a cabinetmaker by hobby.[18] "The Stone House" and its outbuildings are a rare North Country example of a construction project in which the financier and first owner was probably involved from its conception to its final physical realization.[19]

4 ～

Randolph/Jefferson

Since the last half of the nineteenth century, Randolph and Jefferson have been important and well-known White Mountain summer vacation communities. With a common boundary, both towns command spectacular, largely unobstructed, panoramic views south across valley farmlands toward the Northern Presidential Range, and the neighboring summits and foothills. They also have enjoyed popularity with summer residents and tourists because of their somewhat isolated location, north of the principal White Mountain massif, pleasantly removed from the heavily urbanized and populated areas of the Northeast. As a consequence, the two towns developed as summer colonies later than their White Mountain counterparts, awaiting the completion of improved rail transportation and the advent of the automobile. They followed the customary regional pattern of evolution, however, with inns and resort hotels preceding, but chronologically overlapping, single-season hotel or privately owned cottages.

In Randolph, the largest cottage groups formed in the vicinity of two hotels, the Ravine House (1877 and after) in the Moose River Valley, and the Mount Crescent House (1883–84) higher up and farther to the east on Randolph Hill. The earliest houses were erected beginning in 1896, with the most active period of construction between 1900 and 1915. Not surprisingly, many of the new property owners were former patrons of the Randolph hotels. While the majority were from the Boston area, others came from farther down the east coast, and as far away as California. The owners included academics, lawyers, writers, physicians, theologians, and businessmen. A sizable number were ardent outdoorspeople, frequent hikers, and often members of the Appalachian Mountain Club. Their cottages, most of which were designed and built by local hotelman and contractor John H. Boothman, are small, plain, and architecturally unsophisticated, even by general White Mountain standards, but are advantageously sited and serve well their intended purposes.

The cottages of Jefferson were concentrated in three locations: at the village center adjacent to the great Waumbek grand resort hotel (1860 and after); on or near Ingerson Road at Starr King; and at the Highlands near the E. A. Crawford House (c. 1870), the Mount Adams House (c. 1864), and other medium-size hostelries. Of the original eleven Waumbek cottages, six have survived, the only buildings remaining from the peak years of the former hotel complex. They show evidence of the creative hand of one or more professional designers, but to date the architect or architects who conceived them remain unidentified. The remaining summer residences on or near Ingerson Road, and at Jefferson Highlands, two of which were moved and remodeled for the Carter family of Boston, are of similar scale, stylistic origins, and overall aesthetic and functional quality.

"Waumbek Cottages," photographs from booklet, *Waumbek Hotel and Cottages, Jefferson, White Mountains* (1916). Courtesy of the New Hampshire Historical Society, Concord

WAUMBEK COTTAGES

Waumbek Hotel Cottages

c. 1890–c.1900

Jefferson

Original west front elevation, The Waumbek Hotel (1860 and after), Jefferson, N.H. Photograph courtesy of Rupert P. Corrigan, Jefferson.

~ THE WAUMBEK HOTEL cottages, referred to as "The Waumbek Colony" in old promotional literature, comprise one of the largest hotel-related groups in the White Mountains. Erected or modified (from older buildings) between 1890 and 1900, they rival in architectural and historical significance similar assemblages constructed for the Profile House in Franconia Notch, the Maplewood Hotel at Bethlehem, and Wentworth Hall at Jackson. At their maximum there were eleven cottages in the vicinity of the hotel, overlooking Jefferson Meadows and the mountains to the west and south. Today, six of the original group remain, independently owned, arranged together, and serviced by a circular drive to the southeast of the former hotel site.[1]

The Waumbek cottages possessed a marvelous array of names that conjure a variety of romantic pictorial and sensory images—"Wyndebrae," "Onaway," "The Maples," "Mountain View," "Swan," "Cherry," "Bashaba," "The Bungalow," "The Wigwam," "The Wayonda," and "Brookside."[2] Most of them were built for private owners on land acquired from the hotel—"Wyndebrae" (c. 1898) for Rev. Harris E. Adriance of Poughkeepsie, New York; "The Maples" (c. 1898) for Dr. William G. Schauffler, hotel house physician, of Cincinnati, Ohio; "The Bungalow" (c. 1898) for Charles L. Raymond of Chicago; "Onaway" (1896) for Charles J. Fisk, a New York City banker from Plainfield, New Jersey, one-time president of the Jefferson Hotel and Land Company, owners of the Waumbek enterprise; and "The Wigwam" (1890) and "The Wayonda" (1896) as personal and rental properties by Samuel R. Davis of Lakewood, New Jersey, the first president of the company. The others were built (or refurbished) and owned by the hotel and leased to socially and professionally prominent clientele who came to Jefferson each summer from all over the United States. Like the other hotels in the region that possessed cottage groups, the

"The Wayonda" (left, 1896) and "Onaway" (right, 1896), The Waumbek Colony, Jefferson, N.H. Photograph by the author.

"Bashaba" (c. 1895), The Waumbek Colony, Jefferson, N.H. Photograph by the author.

Waumbek provided maintenance services and encouraged tenants to take their meals at and participate in the social and recreation life of the resort.[3] As one writer put it in an 1897 article, "cottagers enjoy all the advantages of hotel life with none of its drawbacks"—independence and flexibility were highly prized.[4]

Larger and more substantial than most of the cottages associated with the other White Mountain hotels, those at the Waumbek site feature design elements from both the Shingle and Colonial Revival styles. The most ambitious and perhaps the most attractive of the existing group, "Onaway," displays a dominant fieldstone masonry corner tower with conical roof, drawn from the Shingle vernacular. Portions of the fenestration, the massive hipped roof, and the porch columns and balustrades are clearly Colonial Revival in derivation. The feeling conveyed by this house, as well as the others adjacent to it, is one of enduring permanence within a changing, often harsh, but invariably beautiful natural environment. Stone and wood-shingle building materials are effectively combined in each of the cottages, and link them aesthetically as well as practically to the rocky terrain and abundant forests of the North Country. It is not known who prepared the designs for the Waumbek cottages, but the internationally recognized New York City firm of John M. Carrere (1858–1911) and Thomas Hastings (1860–1929), architects of at least one major addition to the hotel (1889), may have had something to do with their planning. Local builder Eugene C. Gale (1871–after 1953) (see "Buena Vista," Jefferson Highlands), or other contractors who worked on the hotel during the nineties, also may have been involved with cottage projects.[5]

Although virtually all physical evidence has disappeared, the cottages were at one time satellite buildings to a huge grand resort hotel complex, one of America's most famous and sumptuous. Named "Waumbek," mean-

"The Maples" (c. 1898), The Waumbek Colony, Jefferson, N.H. Photograph by the author.

ing "White Hills" in Abenaki, this great hotel originated in 1860 when Benjamin H. Plaisted established a modest hostelry near the center of Jefferson. An immediate success, this early guest facility was expanded in 1865 and around 1879, so that it could accommodate over two hundred patrons. After the acquisition of the property in 1888 by the Jefferson Hotel and Land Company, the hotel building grew dramatically, assuming the appealing decorative trappings of the Colonial Revival style. By 1900, as result of additions, and the absorption of most of the other local hotels, the Waumbek had achieved a capacity of six hundred, and offered a comprehensive list of social, recreational, and cultural opportunities, centering on its scenic eighteen-hole golf course. The hotel flourished until 1928, when on May 9 of that year, a disastrous fire leveled the grand hostelry, along with four of the cottages and other outbuildings. The surviving cottages provide an excellent opportunity for reflection as to what once was.[6]

∾

The Carter Houses

c. 1880–c. 1916–17

(Mr. and Mrs. James R. Carter)

Jefferson (Highlands)

"The Hummocks" (1897–98), Jefferson Highlands, N.H. Photograph courtesy of Ann B. Carter, Milton, Mass.

∾ SINCE THE 1890s, the Carter family of Boston has been a significant presence in the summer life of Jefferson Highlands, renting, owning and occupying houses at the center of the colony, and serving as the dynamic catalyst for much of the social, cultural, and recreational activity there. Family sources indicate that Hubert Lazell Carter was the first family member to visit the Highlands, and that he stayed at the Ethan Allen Crawford House hotel in 1895, or possibly earlier. These records also disclose that Hubert's parents, the James R. Carters, left Cape Cod, their traditional summer retreat, in 1896, and came to the Highlands for the entire season, renting E. A. Crawford's "Siwooganock Cottage." The same year, Henry Carter of Boston arrived, and vacationed at "Dartmouth Cottage," similarly in the Crawford complex. Other family members promptly fol-

Front Elevation (North)
Scale 1·4 inch = 1 foot

Plans of House

"Front Elevation (North), Plans of House for J. R. Carter Esq. at Jefferson Highlands, N.H.," c. 1897. Courtesy of Ann B. Carter, Milton, Mass.

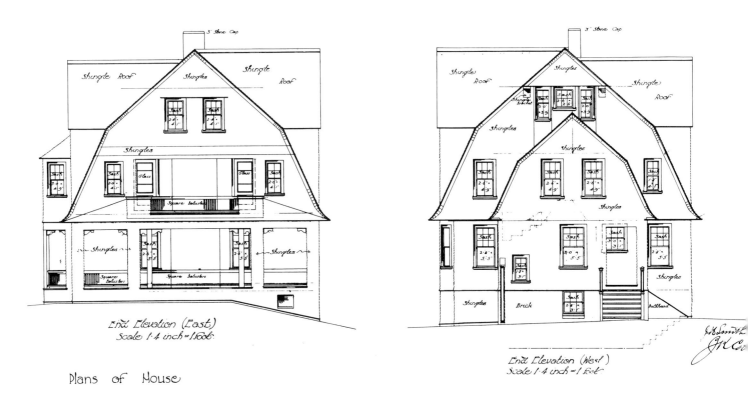

End Elevation (East)
Scale 1·4 inch = 1 foot

Plans of House

End Elevation (West)
Scale 1·4 inch = 1 foot

"End Elevation (East) and End Elevation (West), Plans of House for J. R. Carter Esq. at Jefferson Highlands, N.H.," c. 1897. Courtesy of Ann B. Carter, Milton, Mass.

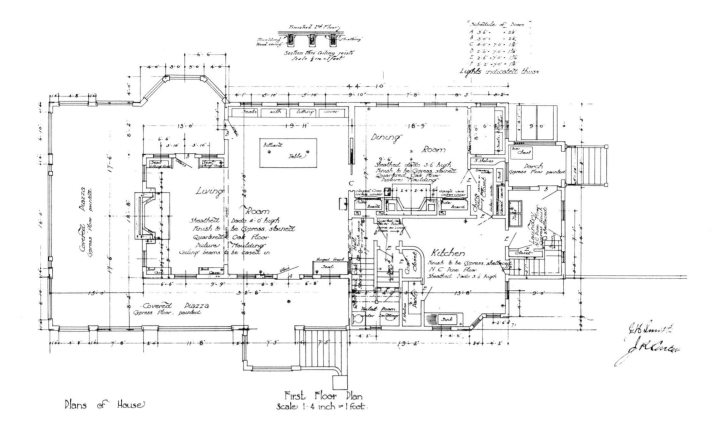

Plans of House

First Floor Plan
Scale 1·4 inch = 1 foot·

"First Floor Plan, Plans of House for J. R. Carter Esq. at Jefferson Highlands, N.H.," c. 1897. Courtesy of Ann B. Carter, Milton, Mass.

lowed, and soon the Carter summer life-style became permanently rooted in the rocky soil of New Hampshire's appealing, but sometimes unforgiving, North Country.[7]

In the 1902 edition of the state promotional publication *New Hampshire Farms for Summer Homes*, James R. Carter, the family progenitor in Jefferson, explained his rationale for coming to the area, "that noble vantage ground":

> For a great many years I have been familiar with the White Mountains, but confining myself of visits of only a week or two.
>
> Six or seven years ago, . . . a friend induced me, by his enthusiastic description of the spot, to hire a cottage in Jefferson Highlands.
>
> The beauties of the situation and the health-giving qualities of the air, and the climate, led me to return the following season.
>
> My enjoyment of the place was fully so great the following season, and finding an old farm on which there was an ideal situation for a summer house, I purchased it and proceeded to spend three times as much as I intended to when I began . . .[8]

The thirty-acre tract to which Carter alluded was acquired in September 1897 in the name of his wife, Carrie G. Carter, from Sophia K. P. Clapp of Woodlawn, Alabama. The purchase price, likely conditioned by the splendor of the mountain vista, was $1,100, a healthy sum for rural land in that day.[9]

It was on this commanding site in 1897–98 that James R. Carter oversaw the construction of one of the great summer houses ever built in the White Mountains. Conceived in the then still popular Colonial Revival style, "The Hummocks," as it was suitably named, was the clear rival of the cottages of the Massachusetts, New Hampshire, and Maine coastlines built in the same idiom, during the same era. The existence in family hands of a labeled set of plans proves without doubt that this exquisitely proportioned and tastefully embellished structure was designed by the noted Boston architectural firm of Hartwell, Richardson and Driver. The senior partner, Henry Walker Hartwell (1833–1919) attended Lawrence Academy in Groton, Massachusetts, and at a young age entered the Boston office of the Billings brothers for his basic architectural training. He opened his own practice in 1885, and functioned independently until 1895 when he entered into partnership with William Cummings Richardson (1854–1935) and James Driver (1859–1923), both of Boston. Born in Concord, New Hampshire, and educated at Lawrence (Massachusetts) High School and MIT, Richardson apprenticed with Boston firms, and ultimately joined with Hartwell and Driver. An Englishman, Driver received his education at London private and technical schools, migrated to the United States in 1883, settled in Boston, and became part of the firm over a decade later. The work produced by Hartwell, Richardson, and Driver included schools, churches, and public buildings in Boston and elsewhere in Massachusetts. After the deaths of both Hartwell and Driver, Richardson carried on under the name Hartwell and Richardson until his retirement in 1930. Exactly how the firm established connections with the Carters is not clear, but it may have been through James Carter's many business associates.[10]

A native Jeffersonian, Henry Stillings, acted as the chief contractor and supervised the grading and laying out of the spacious and lovely grounds. A mountain guide at E. A. Crawford's and previously known to the Carters, Stillings continued to be employed by the family for the seventeen years following the building of the house, caring for the main house, outbuildings, and the gardens, trees, shrubs, lily ponds, fish reserves, and drives that had resulted from his first labors on the property.[11]

A twenty-two-room, wood-framed dwelling, "The Hummocks" contained on its first floor level a large den, hallway, sitting room with fireplace, a large kitchen with butler's pantry, and a substantial dining room with bay windows and half-inch-thick maple paneling. A fieldstone patio looked out on the mountain scenery. The principal space upstairs was a master bedroom with a fireplace and screened, recessed sleeping porch. Altogether there were eight bedrooms on the second floor and a voluminous paneled recreation room in the attic story above. This latter space also served as sleeping quarters for the young boys in the family and was irreverently referred to as the "Steerage." Appropriate to its style, the house was topped by main and secondary gambrel roofs flared at their eaves, their planar surfaces broken by brick chimneys and small hipped and large two-story gable-roof dormers. Sheathed in shingles, the outer walls were penetrated by double-sash windows with pairs of shutters, and several bay windows of varying sizes and configurations. Protected by roofs on three sides of the building on the first-floor level were a series of open porches with balustrades, arched apertures, and square, shingled support posts. The entire visual impression was one of solidity, balance, and cohesiveness. Supplementing the main house, and erected about the same time, were a horse stable with living quarters (later converted to a garage), an ice house, a tool shed, and an electric generator building. Not far from the house, adjacent to the main road, Carter hired a stonemason in 1898 to construct a tall fieldstone tower so that the family could enjoy unobstructed views of the mountains, especially at sunset. A great devotee of tennis, he also had a tennis court installed on the property. From this fascinating estate, only the tower and the stable, currently a residence, stand today. The main house, sold out of the family in 1934, served as a restaurant and small hotel, Tower Inn, after 1953, but tragically burned in February 1969 under suspicious circumstances.[12]

On 17 May 1907, the *Littleton Courier* reported the sad news that the E. A. Crawford House near "The Hummocks" had been destroyed by a disastrous fire.[13] The two cottages, "Siwooganock" and "Dartmouth," and other buildings were spared, however. Beginning two years later, James R. Carter commenced a series of land purchases that ultimately increased the size of his estate to approximately two hundred acres. In 1916, responding to the need for additional family housing, he acquired from Frederick P. Cabot of Boston the former Crawford hotel land north of the road, including the aforementioned cottages. He then proceeded to have these two buildings moved back from the road to their present locations, built a fenced, clay tennis court to the west of them, carried out extensive landscaping, and planted an apple orchard slightly to the east where the E. A. Crawford House had once stood. Family descendants still own and use the houses today, and have preserved them excellently. Originally erected in c. 1880 by E. A. Crawford's sons, Ethan Allen III and Fred, "Siwooganock Cottage" possesses the same late-Victorian eclectic features (half-timbered gables and window bays, patterned brick chimneys, open front porch with turned posts and balustrade components) that are illustrated in early photographs. Although it was enlarged around 1916–17 by the addition of a rear kitchen ell and reconfigured roof, "Dartmouth Cottage" (renamed "Boismont" by Carrie Carter) still displays some of the subtle Queen Anne–style character (particularly the southeast corner octagonal tower with spire roof cap) that it did at the time of its completion in 1894. It was also erected by the two Crawford sons. Hartwell, Richardson, and Driver served as architects for the renovation work. Between the cottages is the former studio of Boston artist, George Hawley Hallowell (he married E. A. Crawford's daughter, Lucy), in recent years used as a recreation facility. The family has maintained many of the trappings, traditions, and prac-

"Boismont" (originally "Dartmouth Cottage") (1894; c. 1916–17), Jefferson Highlands, N.H. Photograph by the author.

"Siwooganock Cottage" (c. 1880 and after), Jefferson Highlands, N.H. Photograph by the author.

tices of summer life as it was carried on by the first generation of Carters in Jefferson.[14]

James Richard Carter (1849–1923), the family member who made the Highlands compound possible, made his mark in the world of business and manufacturing, as well as in his private life. Although he descended from old New England stock, in many respects he was a self-made man. Young Carter attended grade school and the English High School in Boston, spent eighteen months traveling in Europe, and apparently did not go to college. Upon returning home, he took his first job with the firm of Carter Brothers & Company, with which his father, Richard B., was associated. Joining with Frederick Rice, in 1871 they founded Carter, Rice & Company, which was reorganized in 1883 with Carter as half-owner, treasurer, and manager, positions he held until his death. In addition to being head of Carter, Rice & Company Corporation, he served as the president of three affiliated paper companies, and treasurer of Boston's Rice-Kendall Company and Carter's Ink Company, which his brother, John, had started. Active in professional and civic organizations, he was elected president of the Boston Paper Trade Association in 1894, the Boston Merchants Association in 1898, and the Boston Associated Board of Trade in 1901. He took a particular interest in the development of the port of Boston, and committed much time and energy to this endeavor. In religious faith he was a Swedenborgian, and was a leading supporter of the Newtonville Church Society, a director of the New Church Theological School (Cambridge, Massachusetts), president of the Massachusetts New Church Union, and, after 1900, treasurer of the General Convention of the New Jerusalem Church. He was also active in numerous commercial organizations, as well as social and recreational clubs in Boston and Newton, where the family resided. Carter's favorite outside interests were traveling, mountain climbing, tennis, and hunting, which in large part explains why he was initially drawn to the White Mountain region.

Public-spirited and generous with his wealth, Carter made numerous contributions to Jefferson and environs, many of them financial. Along with his summer neighbors, he helped fund the erection of the Jefferson soldiers' monument, and, in partnership with the Bretton Woods Company, helped to develop and fund the Jefferson Notch Road, linking the town with Bretton Woods and Crawford Notch. Opened in 1902, damaged by rainfall, and rebuilt in 1914, this vital artery made Mount Jefferson and the family cabin ("Camp Crawford") there more accessible to hikers. Periodically during the summer, the family sponsored plays and vocal and instrumental musical programs at "The Hummocks" or the cottages. They also hosted social events, and supported the local Highland Chapel, where Sunday services for vacation residents and their friends were conducted.[15] In many notable respects, the Carter family of Jefferson Highlands has represented the best of summer cottage living and local community involvement in the White Mountains since the 1870s.

≈

"Nollis Cottage"

c. 1882

(Rev. Horace W. and Mary A. Wright)

Jefferson (Highlands)

"Nollis Cottage" (c. 1882), Jefferson Highlands, N.H. Photograph by the author.

∼ THE FIRST COTTAGE in the Jefferson Highlands summer colony was erected around 1882 in the name of Mary Angeline Wright (d. 1928) of Abington, Massachusetts, for herself and her brother, Reverend Horace Winslow Wright (d. 1920) of Boston.[16] In the apt words of Jefferson historian George Evans, they "were attracted to build . . . in a place which seemed to them suitable to their tastes, combining remarkable scenery [the Northern Peaks of the Presidential Range], seclusion and a bird paradise."[17] Mary Wright acquired the ten acres of land upon which her new house was built in October 1881 for the modest sum of one hundred dollars from Ethan Allen Crawford, the proprietor of the nearby hotel long known as the E. A. Crawford House (see the Carter houses). This highly desirable sloping tract, originally part of the Crawford family's "Homestead Farm," was situated on the southwest side of the so-called "highway between Jefferson and Randolph," with all-important water rights guaranteed by the Crawfords on the opposite side of the road.[18] Over the subsequent three decades, to 1910, Mary Wright greatly enlarged this initial plot, making five additional land purchases totaling over 125 acres.[19]

Available sources disclose little about Mary Wright, other than the fact that she engaged in oil painting while summering at the Highlands, and, with her brother, shared a passionate interest in the bird life of the area. Principally a theologian by vocation, Horace Wright was perhaps more widely recognized as an ornithologist, and published a volume on bird lore, and several scientific papers on the subject, including articles in *The Auk* and other periodicals.[20] Horace Wright was also highly influential in the enlargement of the Highland Chapel in 1890, and occasionally preached there on Sundays to summer residents and visitors to the area. While at the Highlands, Wright and his sister devoted much of their time to bird watching, taking frequent nature walks across the open fields and pastures, and throughout rolling and more mountainous woodlands.[21]

Called "Nollis Cottage" (later "The Knolls"), the Wright house was considered unusual, in terms of both its architectural character and its landscaping, "with special adornments of trees, scrubs, flowers and berries." The property was intentionally shielded from the road, "with a row of noble birches and spruces leaving fine graveled driveways to . . . [the] cottage."[22] Containing eleven rooms, "Nollis Cottage," while not a strong statement of the Shingle style, does possess certain of its more pronounced features. Asymmetrical in elevations and floor plan, the building is protected by steep-pitched and secondary (east wing) roofs, pierced by brick chimneys and dormers, and with broken planar surfaces on the northeast corner. The walls are covered with cedar shingles, originally uneven, but today arranged in straight rows. To take full advantage of the magnificent mountain panorama, connected verandas (portions were added after the initial building date) extend across the east and south elevations of the house. The windows are traditional double sash, and were at one time framed by shutters. On the principal north elevation are a recessed main entrance doorway, and an off-center, semioctagonal, one-story window bay, often present in Shingle-style residential architecture.[23] The house passed to Mary Wright's nephew, Edmund Wright, in 1928, and eventually out of the family in 1936, but still retains much of its original appearance.[24]

∾

"Buena Vista"

c. 1892

(Mr. William Gordon Hopple)

Jefferson (Highlands)

"Buena Vista" (c. 1892), Jefferson Highlands, N.H. Photograph by the author.

∾ THE COTTAGE DWELLERS of Jefferson Highlands traditionally have sought privacy, solitude and informality in their summer life-styles, and William Gordon Hopple was no exception. A reasonably well-to-do shellac manufacturer and merchant from Brooklyn, New York, Hopple originally came to the White Mountains, as did countless others, because of a hay fever condition. Supposedly, during the summer of 1891, he, his wife, Agnes B., and a daughter vacationed in Bethlehem. While there as guests at the Upland Terrace Hotel, they visited Jefferson in search of a site for a summer cottage, and were so impressed by its unspoiled beauty, rarefied air, and spectacular mountain vistas, they determined to acquire land in the town.[25] Hopple acted quickly, and in September of the same year he purchased a one-and-one-half-acre tract from John W. and Charlotte Crenshaw of the Mt. Adams House Inn. This attractive hillside property was located on the north side of the Jefferson-Randolph road, just east of E. A. Crawford's boarding house.[26] Here, over the next several months, the Hopples built a fine Victorian eclectic house. They gave it the name "Buena Vista," as it overlooked the upper Israel River valley and the Northern Peaks of the Presidential Range to the south.

The Hopple cottage, while it possesses architectural features of some merit, is significant primarily because of its association with the well-known North Country builder Eugene C. Gale (1871–after 1935), originally from Jefferson. In his diary, rewritten excerpts of which were published in the magazine *New Hampshire Profiles* in 1953, he mentions that he was hired by John Crenshaw to construct the house for the Hopples. He likely also served as architect. Over his long and productive career, Gale built or remodeled over three hundred houses and numerous hotels in the mountain region including the Waumbek, the Twin Mountain House, the Mountain View House, the Spalding Inn, and possibly some of the hotels at Jefferson Highlands. He was considered a legendary figure in his field, and his workmanship was not only outstanding, but quite distinctive. The circular porch on the southwest front corner of the Hopple cottage, said to be a Gale trademark, appeared on other buildings for which he was responsible.[27]

Initially buff-colored with dark brown trim, "Buena Vista" was finished with narrow, maple-beaded board in its interior public rooms and six bedrooms. There were no plaster walls due to the lack of heat during the off-season. Just west of the house (and still surviving) are two wooden outbuildings, a garage and a long "carriagehouse" containing quarters for hired help, as well as a bowling alley on the ground floor and a dance hall on the second floor. A tennis court and golf greens, indicative of the family's recreational interests, were located adjacent to the cottage. In its early years, the property was nicely landscaped, with flower gardens, paths, and a boardwalk running down the hill to a stonewall entrance.

Around 1917, after Agnes Hopple's death, the property passed to the Nichols, descendants of the Hopples, then to local owners, and in 1947 to Baroness Hildegard von Rebay von Ehrenwiesen (c. 1890–1967), an accomplished artist and pianist and for over a decade the director of New York City's Solomon R. Guggenheim Foundation Museum of Non-Objective Art, the forerunner of the famed Guggenheim Museum on Fifth Avenue. Renaming the house "Sun Life," Hilla Rebay, as she was commonly known, put an addition on the east side, painted the house and outbuildings white both inside and out, and converted portions of both the house and barn to studios and guest apartments. The buildings have changed little, on their exteriors, since her period of ownership.[28]

~

The McCabe Cottage

1892–93

(Mrs. Gertrude B. McCabe)

Jefferson (Highlands)

The McCabe cottage (1892–93), Jefferson Highlands, N.H. Photograph, c. 1894. Courtesy of Rupert P. Corrigan, Jefferson.

~ IN LATE 1892, Gertrude B. McCabe "of Boston, of Europe, of Asia, or elsewhere as she . . . (chose) to journey,"[29] purchased a hillside tract of land for four hundred dollars from John W. Crenshaw and his wife, Lizzie M., of Jefferson. Located directly across the Jefferson-Randolph road from "Buena Vista," the Hopple cottage, the land was oriented to the south, commanding magnificent sweeping views of the White Mountain massif.[30] In the words of the town historian George Evans, the entire scene seemed "to invite quietude and harmony,"[31] much like the other cottage properties at Jefferson Highlands. Over the next several months, McCabe proceeded to erect one of the most attractive and architecturally provocative houses in the region. Unfortunately no trace of the building remains, as it was destroyed by a mysterious fire around 1927 or 1928. Only the adjacent barn/stable/carriage house has survived to the present day.[32]

Gertrude McCabe was an elusive personality, and information about her is extremely sketchy. Apparently she was quite affluent, was married twice, and had been either widowed or divorced before she joined the Highlands summer colony. It is not known where or how she derived her wealth, or in what professions she or her husbands were engaged. We do know, however, that in 1892 she had a home in Germantown, Pennsylvania, and by 1908 was a resident of Brookline, Massachusetts. She was living in New York City when she passed away in 1935. Not only did McCabe change her place of residence frequently, but she was a great traveler. According to a family story, during the early years of the automobile, she and her chauffeur drove halfway across the Sahara Desert in North Africa. From each of her marriages she had a son; the younger, Thomas, a biologist at the University of California at Berkeley, inherited and sold the Jefferson Highlands property after her death in 1935.[33]

Though it was smaller and less pretentious, the McCabe cottage is reminiscent of similar houses erected about the same time at Bar Harbor, Newport, Manchester-by-the-Sea, and other New England resort communities. Conceived in the then fashionable Shingle style, the cottage "was made with taste, seclusion and comfort, surrounded with trees, shrubs, flowers and fine walks, [and] faced walls on the roadside with iron gates and stone piers."[34] Typically asymmetrical in floor plan and side elevations, the building displayed with eye-catching success numerous features of its style —a variety of main and dormer roof forms (gable, shed, hipped, and Mansard); shingled wall surfaces; extensive porches with slender wooden curved-bracket support posts and classical balustrades; rusticated stone foundations; varied window sizes and types with simple surrounds; and a distinctive octagonal corner tower with a concave bellcast roof cap. To date, available sources have failed to disclose the name of the architect of the McCabe cottage, but in many respects, it recalls the work of the famous New York City firm of McKim, Mead and White, and several of their notable house designs on Long Island and along the New England coast. The construction of the house, however, may be firmly credited to Eugene C. Gale (1871-after 1953), the prolific Jefferson contractor, who also built the neighboring Hopple cottage, and numerous other local buildings.[35]

❧

"Reve-Fonyah"

c. 1917

(Mr. and Mrs. William E. Bird)

The Stockin Cottage

c. 1912–14; c. 1924

(Mr. Edward Stockin)

Jefferson (Starr King)

❧ ALTHOUGH THEY WERE planned and erected by different builders, the Bird and Stockin cottages in the Starr King section of Jefferson possess many common design features. Positioned on the side of the Pliny Range facing south, both houses are fitted with extensive open verandas to take full advantage of the clear, cool air, and the unparalleled mountain panorama highlighted by Mount Washington and the Presidential Range. Displaying low-pitched, flared gable roofs with dormers, wide eaves overhangs with exposed roof rafters, segmental rounded gable windows, and extensive veranda stickwork (decorative as well as functional), these bungalow-type structures accurately illustrate the impact of the California-born Craftsman style on summer residential architecture in the White Mountains during the World War I era.

The older of the two houses, "Reve-Fonyah" (an anagram for "No Hay Fever"), is situated at the center of the Ingerson Road cottage group on the eastern end of the former Isaac Bergin farm, occupied for many years by Charles Ingerson. It was erected in 1917 on the site of the old farmhouse for

"Reve-Fonyah" (c. 1917), Starr King, Jefferson, N.H. Photograph by the author.

The Stockin cottage (c. 1912–14; c. 1924), Starr King, Jefferson, N.H. Photograph by the author.

William E. Bird, Jr. (1862–1936), a New York City businessman who resided in Maplewood, New Jersey. Bird spent his entire working career with the Ward Line, a shipping firm founded by his uncle, James E. Ward. Starting as a messenger at the age of sixteen, he retired in 1906 as vice president and traffic manager. Active in amateur golf circles for many years, he belonged to the Essex County Country Club and Baltusrol Golf Club in New Jersey, and when in Jefferson spent many hours playing the Waumbek Hotel golf course.[36]

A low, wood-frame and shingle structure with native fieldstone foundations, porch posts, and chimneys, "Reve-Fonyah" accommodates spacious interior rooms, including a west wing with six bedrooms, and quarters once used for the full retinue of servants accompanying the Bird family to Jefferson each spring. Writing in the 1920s, town historian George C. Evans was impressed by the plate-glass windows, as well as the "many baths with full-length plate-glass mirrors on the doors." Local sources affirm that Eugene Gale (1871–after 1953), the builder of hotels and other houses in Jefferson (see "Buena Vista," Jefferson Highlands), served as the contractor.[37]

The land upon which the Stockin cottage (today called "The Home Place" by its owners) stands accommodated the farmstead of Moses and Lutheran Ingerson Roberts in the early 1800s. Over the next century, the property changed hands several times, until it was acquired by a Mrs. Millage, otherwise unidentified, who converted the farmhouse to a summer cottage around 1912–14. The property then passed to Ida M. G. Fitzgerald of Stoneham, Massachusetts, who in turn sold it in April 1924 to Edwin Stockin of Watertown in the same state. Stockin, who later lived in Concord, New Hampshire, was the managing owner and editor of the well-known magazine, *The Youth's Companion*. Over the next year or two, he added the broad verandas and "other improvements making it a most inviting cottage." A comparison of a photograph of the house from around 1925 with the building as it appears today shows virtually no change except for roof surface and shingle siding colors. A family source indicates that local contractors, the brothers Allison H., Wilbur, and Roland Nevers, were responsible for the stonework and possibly the wood construction implemented at Stockin's behest. Three years later, Allison Nevers was hired by the Dodge family, owners of the Mountain View House in Whitefield, to build a major addition on their grand resort hotel. Stockin sold the house out of the family in 1944, and, after three additional owners, remarkably it was acquired by Stockin descendants in 1969, who continue to hold title today.[38]

~

"Cara Vita"

1923–24

(Miss Florence W. Fulton)

Jefferson (Starr King)

"Cara Vita" (1923–24), Starr King, Jefferson, N.H. Photograph by the author.

~ ERECTED FOR EDUCATOR Florence W. Fulton in 1923–24, "Cara Vita" is advantageously set on a gradually sloping hillside, underneath the Pliny Range (Mounts Starr King and Waumbeck) in the Starr King section (Ingerson Road colony) of Jefferson.[39] Its broad front elevation faces south toward the grand panorama of the Presidential Range, and the entire White Mountain massif. Although it has been expanded and modified over the years, this long, low, bungalow-type cottage still exhibits many features of the Craftsman style, which so strongly influenced American residential architecture between 1910 and 1930. Native fieldstone foundations, garden walls, and chimneys contrast effectively with the gray-painted, shingle-clad walls of the house in a characteristic Craftsman juxtaposition of building materials. Also present, and typical of this style, are sweeping, low-pitched roofs with deep overhangs, displaying the butt-ends of roof rafters. Casement windows with shutters comprise the fenestration, while triple French doors open out from the living room to the front patio. As a place of summer sojourn, "Cara Vita" presents a gracious and inviting appearance to onlookers.

The creator of the house, Florence Fulton (1865–1957), was the daughter of Rev. John Fulton, an Episcopal clergyman. She was graduated from the New York School of Applied Design for Women, where she later taught book binding, toy making, wood construction, and carving. Later in life, she moved to Bryn Mawr, and subsequently Wayne, Pennsylvania. In Bryn Mawr, she conducted a special program for instructing youth in areas of the fine arts not customarily taught in the public schools. Ultimately, she became the dean of the well-known Philadelphia School of Occupational Therapy.[40]

It is not known what specifically drew Fulton to Jefferson, but she clearly had a great appreciation for its beauty and solitude. Between 1923 and 1926, she purchased three abutting tracts of land totaling about fifteen acres from local residents, above the Starr King Cemetery on Ingerson Road. The open field upon which she erected her cottage was known locally as the Gray farm. With the assistance of a close associate, Virginia W. Garber, she carefully landscaped the property, planting an apple orchard and spruce trees, many of which still stand. Local oral sources suggest that the prolific Jefferson builder Eugene C. Gale (1871–after 1935) (see "Buena Vista") was head contractor for the house. The architect, if there was one, remains unidentified.[41]

5 ～

Bethlehem/Littleton

Situated fifteen hundred feet above sea level and replete with natural advantages, the Town of Bethlehem was at its peak the most extensively developed of the White Mountain summer resorts. Its preeminence in the region resulted from its convenient location north of the major notches, its sweeping mountain vistas, its ample spring water, and its cool, dry, health-promoting climate. In 1857, local politician John H. Sinclair established the first significant hotel enterprise there, "Sinclair House," which later in the century evolved into one of Bethlehem's two grand resort hotels. In the late 1860s and 1870s, spurred by the interest and investments of Henry Howard, a Rhode Island native, Bethlehem arrived as a single-season vacation community. By 1880 there were no fewer than seventeen new hostelries, with Isaac Cruft's Maplewood (1876 and after), ultimately to become the second of the town's grand resort hotels, and the most ambitiously conceived. With the arrival of direct rail service and a national reputation as a haven for hay fever and asthma sufferers, Bethlehem experienced further growth, by the 1920s boasting thirty hotels, with room for well over two thousand patrons.

As it developed as a tourist mecca, Bethlehem gradually amassed what by 1930 was the largest and most diverse concentration of summer residences in the White Mountains. Commencing with Henry Howard's Gothicized "Buckeye Cottage" in 1873, numerous houses were built over the subsequent half century, with great variety in size, style, design sophistication, and location. Most of these buildings were positioned in the center of the town, while others, ranging from modest cottages to country estates, were situated in the surrounding rolling countryside. A high percentage of these have survived in reasonably sound condition. Among the major domestic architectural styles represented in the group are the Stick, Queen Anne, Shingle, Colonial Revival, and Craftsman, some in combination to create curious, compelling, but not always successful amalgams. In those houses that still stand, one may observe the work of area architects Edward Thornton Sanderson and Sylvanus D. Morgan, as well as Hermann V. von Holst of Chicago, Clifford A. Peck of Connecticut, and, subject to future confirmation, the noted Stanford White of New York City. In addition to the Howard cottage, those houses selected for close inspection from Bethlehem's extensive repertoire possess superlative architectural features and have noteworthy historical associations.

West of Bethlehem is Littleton, a substantially larger town that has long been a regional commercial and light manufacturing center, as well as a locus for agriculture and tourism. An early railroad terminus, Littleton boasted several medium-sized hotels, including Thayers (c. 1850), the Oak Hill House (1871 and after), the Chiswick Inn and Cottages (1884–85), The Maples (1888–89), and the Northern Hotel (1898). With the notable exception of the Dickson lodge (1909–10) at "Highland Croft" farm, however, summer cottage development before 1930 was minimal. Two large country estates—"Hill Acres" (c. 1915–16 and after) owned by Mr. and Mrs. John R. Morron (New York City), and "Seven Springs" (c. 1921), the property (now The White Mountain School) of Mr. and Mrs. Eman Beck (Mexico City)—while important historically, hold limited architectural interest, having simply incorporated and expanded on older farmhouses.

"Buckeye Cottage"

1873

(Henry Howard)

Bethlehem

"Buckeye Cottage" (1873), Bethlehem, N.H. Photograph by the author.

⌐ "BUCKEYE COTTAGE" and its first owner, Henry Howard, occupy an important niche in the early development of Bethlehem as a summer resort community. A native of Cranston, Rhode Island, Howard received a secondary level education, studied law, was admitted to the state bar, and in the 1850s was a member of a prominent Providence law firm. Entering business in 1858, he became president of the Harris Manufacturing Company, associated with other entrepreneurial enterprises and developed broad expertise in textiles. In the late 1850s he became involved in local politics, twice winning election to the state general assembly, attending three Republican national conventions as a delegate, and serving two consecutive terms (1873–75) as Governor of Rhode Island. Returning to his business interests, Howard joined a number of corporate boards, and in 1878 was selected by President Rutherford B. Hayes as one of the assistant commissioners to the world industrial exposition in Paris. Known also as a superior lecturer and writer, he often contributed articles, poetry, and travel letters to his hometown newspaper, *The Providence Journal*, and other publications.[1]

Howard's association with Bethlehem began in a most unfortunate manner, which ultimately proved fortuitous for the town. While visiting with family and friends in 1863, he was a victim of a serious runaway coach accident on Mount Agassiz, resulting in a prolonged recuperative stay at the Sinclair House, a large local hotel. While recovering from his injuries, he recognized the potential of Bethlehem as a single-season resort, and determined to devote his time, energy, and financial resources to its future. Immediately he purchased the Carlton and Brooks (Strawberry Hill) farms on Main Street. Over the next decade, Howard returned with his family each summer, adding substantially to his land holdings, and fostering the growth of the local hotel industry through loans and the sale of real estate on credit. His commitment to the town was a major reason that Bethlehem became the primary center for tourism in the White Mountains between 1880 and 1930.[2]

The Howard family house, "Buckeye Cottage," has long been regarded as the oldest summer residence in Bethlehem, and one of the oldest in the entire mountain region.[3] Erected in 1873 by an unidentified builder, the Buckeye is a sterling example of an early, unsophisticated Stick-style cottage, carrying forward several features of the pre–Civil War Carpenter Gothic Revival. From the earlier style, one may observe modest scale and massing, an asymmetrical plan with wings and ell, a one-story full-width porch, roof, and porch finials, and steep-pitched intersecting gambrel roofs, with the principal gable facing forward. Reflecting the influence of the Stick idiom are the decorative trusses at the apex of each major gable, the flat, bracketed hoodmolds (water deflectors) over each window, and the stick-like vertical supports, diagonal braces, and balustrades of the front porch. All these elements are combined to produce a pleasant unified whole.[4]

∾

Maplewood Hotel Cottages

from 1875 to 1895

Bethlehem (Maplewood)

"The Maplewood, White Mountains, Bethlehem, N.H.," colored lithograph by William H. Brett Engraving Co., Boston, c. 1878. Courtesy of the Dartmouth College Library, Hanover, N.H.

∾ ESTABLISHED DURING the 1870s by Isaac S. Cruft, a relocated Boston businessman, the Maplewood Hotel, until it burned in 1963, was one of the largest and most lavish of the White Mountain grand resort hotels. Positioned at the east end of Bethlehem, with spectacular views of the Presidential Range and the mountains to the north, this extraordinary Victorian eclectic complex served a broad guest clientele from the United States (largely eastern seaboard elites), Canada, and abroad. Many of these people, particularly those afflicted with hay fever and other maladies, were attracted to Bethlehem and the Maplewood by the healthful climate. Others came primarily to enjoy hotel social life and the abundant array of recre-

Maplewood Hotel and Cottages Nos. 1–8, Maplewood, Bethlehem, N.H., photographs from booklet, *Maplewood Hotel and Cottages* (1910). Author's collection.

Maplewood Hotel and Cottages Nos. 9–15 and Store, Maplewood, Bethlehem, N.H., photographs from booklet, *Maplewood Hotel and Cottages* (1910). Author's collection.

Cottage No. 12, Maplewood Hotel and Cottages, Maplewood, Bethlehem, N.H. Photograph by the author.

ational and cultural opportunities offered by the Maplewood and other local hostelries.

Cruft, however, had a vision for his new hotel that sharply differentiated his venture from others in the region at the time. Recognizing the wish of some guests to secure greater privacy and independence than was possible in the main hotel building, early in the Maplewood's history he began to build an extensive system of wooden cottages that would eventually total fifteen. These were located within easy distance of the hotel, permitting occupants to take their meals there and to participate in the full range of available activities. Cruft's cottages were among the first to be planned by a hotel enterprise in the White Mountains. Unlike those at the Profile House at Franconia Notch, the Waumbek at Jefferson, and other neighboring guest establishments, they were entirely owned by the hotel corporation.[5]

Photographs, maps, prints, newspapers, and other printed sources comprehensively relate the story of the Maplewood cottages. Cruft erected the first group of five (eventually expanded to six) around 1875 as contiguous units in a single building southeast of the hotel. These were known as the Block Cottages, contained six to seven rooms each, and rented for one hundred dollars or more per month. Over the next decade four separate cottages joined the Block Cottages, forming a row along Cottage Avenue behind the hotel. Subsequently, others were added, including three in 1887 north of the main road running in front of the hotel. By 1888 there were fourteen. The maximum number of fifteen was reached by the early 1890s before most of the cottages associated with the Profile House and the Waumbek Hotel were built.[6] The earliest in the Maplewood group showed the impact of the Gothic Revival, possessing steep-pitched gable main and secondary roofs, roof finials, and barge board gable trim. Those erected in the late 1880s and early 1890s, while displaying the laggard effects of the Gothic, were inspired predominantly by the Stick style. They featured dec-

Cottage No. 14, Maplewood Hotel and Cottages, Maplewood, Bethlehem, N.H. Photograph by the author.

orative gable trusses, overhanging eaves (some with exposed rafter ends), and extensive verandas with delicate supporting posts (some bracketed), balustrades, and foundation latticework. Today, only the three cottages raised in 1887 remain, unfortunately lacking much of their original detail and ambience.[7]

∼

"The Rocks" Estate

1883–1912

(Mr. and Mrs. John J. Glessner)

Bethlehem

"The Big House" (1883), "The Rocks" estate, Bethlehem, N.H. Photograph by George Macbeth Glessner, courtesy of Charles F. Batchelder, III, Rome, N.Y.

∼ IN THE ANNALS of American architectural history, Mr. and Mrs. John J. Glessner's Chicago residence (1885–87), designed by the renowned Boston architect Henry Hobson Richardson (1838–86), has received extensive notice and critical acclaim.[8] Not until recent years, however, has the

Glessner's Bethlehem country estate, "The Rocks," attracted the attention of scholars, popular writers, and the general public. In large part, this is due to three factors: the overshadowing family association through the Chicago house with Richardson's national building repertoire; the status of "The Rocks" as a privately owned and managed property until 1978, when it was donated by family descendants to the Society for the Protection of New Hampshire Forests; and its relatively informal, low-key architecture (of which about twenty buildings remain), several the product of three lesser-known architects. Nonetheless, the family houses and highly specialized main farm structures that constituted the original estate represented a rare, unusually complete, and sophisticated collection of buildings. When it was entirely intact and functioning, "The Rocks," was a model working farm, without equal for its time in northern New Hampshire.[9]

"The Rocks" owes its origins and development to the interest, acumen, and devotion of John Jacob Glessner (1843–1936), the Chicago executive of industrial corporations that were among the leading manufacturers of agricultural equipment in late-nineteenth-century America. Born in Zanesville, Ohio, in 1843, he was educated at local public schools and in the newspaper trade, marrying Frances Macbeth (1848–1932) (see "The Glamis," Bethlehem) of Springfield, Ohio, in 1870. His career in business commenced in 1863 when he was employed by the firm Warder, Brokaw and Childs, manufacturers of mowers, reapers, and army wagons. In 1870, this enterprise was reorganized under the name Warder, Bushnell and Glessner, and Glessner was appointed vice president, with his offices in Chicago. When his company merged with four others to form the International Harvester Company in 1902, he became vice president of the new corporate entity, eventually succeeding to chairman of the executive committee. As a supplement to his business activities, Glessner served as a director of the Chicago Relief and Aid Society, president of the Rush Medical College and the Citizens' Association, and a trustee of the Chicago Orphan Asylum, the Chicago Art Institute, and the Chicago Orchestral Association (see "Felsengarten," Bethlehem).[10] He continued his civic involvements in New Hampshire, committing his time, wisdom, and funds to the town of Bethlehem and the Littleton Hospital.

As Glessner prospered in business in the early 1880s, he became increasingly interested in architecture, the arts, agriculture, and conservation. Searching for an appropriate location for a summer estate, he and his wife decided on Bethlehem, in part because of their son's hay fever condition and the town's reputation for a pollen-free climate. Beginning in 1882 with the acquisition of the Oren Streeter property, Glessner ultimately purchased and consolidated several nineteenth-century hill farms, so that by 1912 "The Rocks" estate incorporated over fifteen hundred acres. In 1883, the Glessners completed a nineteen-room summer home, the "Big House," which served as the focal point and stylistic model for most of the other related residential and farm buildings.[11]

For the designer of this first major building at "The Rocks," the Glessners chose the extraordinarily talented and ingenious craftsman and architect Isaac Elwood Scott (1845–1920). Born in Manayunk, Pennsylvania, he saw service in the Union army during the Civil War, afterward returning to the Philadelphia area where he worked as a wood-carver. Between 1873 and 1883, he resided in Chicago, met and was befriended by the Glessners, and designed furniture for them as early as 1875. They took earlier examples with them to their new Richardson-designed townhouse when they initially moved in in 1887. In the 1882 Chicago directory, Scott is listed both as a designer of interiors and an architect. During his years in Chicago, he teamed with Henry S. Jaffrey and prepared plans for several noteworthy commercial and residential structures. At about the time that he designed the "Big House" in Bethlehem, he apparently left Chicago for New York City, where he spent time from 1883 to 1888. He then relocated to Boston where he taught at the Eliot School in Jamaica Plain, and, according to Boston directories, worked again as a carver. From the 1880s until his death, he spent extensive time as a guest at "The Rocks" during the summer months, designing and carving decorative architectural elements and objects, and instructing the Glessner children in drawing, carving, handicrafts, and nature subjects. Such a close architect-client family relationship is unique among those associated with the planning and construction of summer houses in the White Mountains before 1930.[12]

Perfectly positioned on a rocky promontory, looking down on the Glessner lands, the "Big House," in form, materials, and embellishment, conveyed forcefully the distinguishing qualities of the Queen Anne style. A local fieldstone first story and a shingled second story with overhangs were topped by intersecting roofs broken by gables decorated with latticework and vertical siding. On the north end of the building were connected verandas, providing sweeping views of the mountains in three directions, and overlooking the gardens, farm buildings, animal pens, and rock-filled fields

"The Big House" (1883; c. 1889), "The Rocks" estate, Bethlehem, N.H., photograph from *New Hampshire Farms for Summer Homes* (7th ed., 1909), p. 40. Author's collection.

"Fanny's House" ("Log Cabin," c. 1900), "The Rocks" estate, Bethlehem, N.H. Photograph by George Macbeth Glessner, courtesy of Charles F. Batchelder, III, Rome, N.Y.

"Bluebird Summer House" (c. 1900), "The Rocks" estate, Bethlehem, N.H. Photograph by George Macbeth Glessner, courtesy of Charles F. Batchelder, III, Rome, N.Y.

and pastures below. The roof surfaces were punctured by tall fieldstone chimneys, and single and triple-window shed dormers. Consistent with the Queen Anne mode, all elevations were asymmetrical and the floor plan irregular, with separate cell-like rooms. Over several years, commencing in 1889, a family friend Charles Allerton Coolidge (1858–1936) of the Boston firm, Shepley, Rutan and Coolidge (successors to H. H. Richardson's practice), redesigned the house in the Shingle style, more in keeping with the architecture then in vogue at New England resort communities. In this drastically revised state, the "Big House" was lengthened, the former roof replaced with flared intersecting hipped roofs, the dormers reconstructed with hipped roofs and double windows, new shingle siding installed, a shingled, flared, gable-roofed front porch attached, tall brick chimneys substituted for the originals, and other alterations made. The "Big House" was razed in 1946, but certain architectural elements salvaged from it were installed in "The Cottage" (1888 and later), which still stands adjacent to the farm buildings, and was used as a summer residence by John J. Glessner's granddaughter until her death in 1994.[13]

A second cottage, "The Ledge" (1902–3), and later farm buildings on the estate grounds were designed by another family friend, the architect Hermann Valentin von Holst (1874–1955) of Chicago (see "The Glamis," Bethlehem). Demolished in 1947, "The Ledge" was a Shingle-style house built for John J. Glessner's son, George B. (d. 1926), of Springfield, Ohio. Located near the "Big House," with comparable views, it featured strongly horizontal proportions, and gave the impression of being intimately linked with the rocky, rolling land. Like the "Big House," it possessed shingled wall surfaces (added texture was provided by projecting butts in every third course), and a hipped roof with expansive planes, pierced by hipped-roof dormers and tall chimneys. Hermann von Holst also designed for "The Rocks" a sawmill-pigpen (1906), modifications to the large carriage house and horse barn (originally planned by Isaac Scott in 1884), and a cow barn (1906–7), which burned in 1946. In the words of James L. Garvin, the New Hampshire state architectural historian, the first two structures "utilized a combination of broad roof planes, deeply projecting eaves, cupolas, and exposed decorative braces and trusses to achieve a Richardsonian massiveness that recalls . . . [the Glessner's] employment of H. H. Richardson to design . . . [their] Chicago home." Elevation, section, and floor plans for the cow barn, published in 1909, illustrate a similar composition and selection of elements.[14]

The natural and man-made context—the fields, road system, extensive stone walls, and landscaping—for the architecture of "The Rocks" estate was developed, as Garvin properly notes, "for coherent aesthetic effect . . . achieved gradually through decades of planning and labor." Critical to the creation of this effect was the assistance of the internationally acclaimed Boston landscape design firm of Olmstead Brothers (Frederick Law Olmstead, Jr., and John Charles Olmstead). Under the Olmstead plan of 1904–5, preserved by the family, the hillside between the two houses and the farm

FRONT ELEVATION

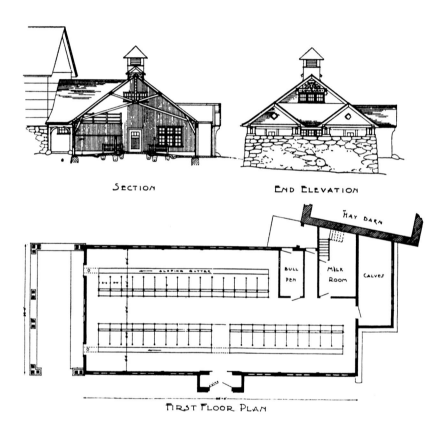

SECTION   END ELEVATION

FIRST FLOOR PLAN

"Cow-Barn on Estate of J. J. Glessner, Esq., Littleton, N.H.," 1906–7. Plan sheet from *Cyclopedia of Architecture, Carpentry and Building*, vol. 6 (1909), op. p. 39. Courtesy of the Hagley Museum and Library, Wilmington, Del.

buildings was developed into a mountain-climate rock garden. Just after 1900, the Glessners terraced the lower slope with surviving fieldstone retaining walls, and planted a garden of perennials and annuals, along with fruit trees and shrubs. An 1898 greenhouse remains at the lower end of this garden. Also at this time, the estate was planted with hundreds of grape vines, clematis and trilliums, accentuating the natural character of the property. The Olmstead contribution augmented earlier landscaping efforts, which included the construction of a system of paths, and a half

Stable (c. 1885), "The Rocks" estate, Bethlehem, N.H. Photograph by the author.

dozen small picturesque gazebos or summer houses at springs, boulders, and scenic vantage points on the Glessner lands. It is believed that most if not all of these structures (a few have survived) were designed by Isaac Scott.[15] The gardens and other plantings, along with the remaining buildings, make "The Rocks" an important document of late-nineteenth and early-twentieth-century American landscape and architectural design.

⌇

The Sayer Cottages

1890–1898

(Mr. William M. Sayer, Jr.)

Bethlehem

"The Outlook" (1890–91), Bethlehem, N.H. Photograph by the author.

⌇ WILLIAM MURRAY SAYER, JR. (1852–1917) of Brooklyn, New York, has long been recognized for the major real estate contribution he made to the Bethlehem summer community. Between 1890 and 1898, he

Sayer Cottage No. 1 (1897), Bethlehem, N.H. Photograph by the author.

Sayer Cottage No. 2 (1897), Bethlehem, N.H. Photograph by the author.

Sayer cottage No. 3 (1897–98), Bethlehem, N.H. Photograph by the author.

financed and oversaw the construction of five wood-frame cottages adjacent to the Arlington House hotel in the west end of the town, one for family use and four as rental properties. A shrewd and successful businessman, Sayer was president of the Rider-Ericson Engine Company in New York City, manufacturers of state-of-the-art, hot-air pumping engines. The origin of his interest in the White Mountains, and specifically in Bethlehem, is not altogether clear. We do know, however, that in the early nineties, he and his family became acquainted with the region as guests at the Highland House hotel, opposite the Arlington. An asthma sufferer, Sayer promptly recognized Bethlehem's rising potential as a health center and single-season resort.[16]

Sayer made his first Bethlehem land purchase in August 1890 from Horace D. Wilder, a local hotelman. Consisting of about two acres, this hillside parcel was situated above South Road, just southwest of "Parva Domus" (1881), the Cleveland family's modest Stick-style cottage, with an outstanding panorama of Vermont's Green Mountain chain to the west.[17] On this advantageous spot, in 1890–91, Sayer erected his elegant residence, "The Outlook," considered by the *White Mountain Echo* to be "the finest place in town, if not in northern New Hampshire." A local builder, William Burges, supervised the construction. Situated on "splendid grounds," in its original form the house was a large, imposing Shingle-style asymmetrical structure, with intersecting steep-pitched gable roofs broken by dormers and tall brick chimneys.[18] The fenestration featured multi-pane over single-pane sash windows, with shutters. Expansive verandas wrapped around the first story providing sitting and promenading areas for enjoyment of the cool air and mountain views. The house has been much modified in recent years, but still possesses the general form and floor plan envisioned by its still unidentified architect.

In 1897, Sayer built the first two of his attractive rental properties on a gradually sloped terrace tract of land fronting on Main Street, just east of the Arlington House.[19] Both are Shingle-style, asymmetrical-plan houses, originally sheathed with cedar shakes, with diamond-pane over single-pane sash windows. The larger cottage (fourteen rooms), closest to the Arlington, is notable for its extensive north- and west-facing porches, the roofs supported by pairs of unusually thin tapered Doric columns. The smaller cottage (ten rooms) to the west of it has much the same exterior appearance as it did when first built, with intersecting gambrel roofs, and porches with arched openings and square, shingle-clad support piers. The two buildings were constructed under the supervision of Ellery D. Dunn, a contractor from Littleton, from plans prepared by Edward Thornton Sanderson (1875–1960), who was not a Littleton native, but maintained architecture offices there during portions of each year in the 1890s. Sanderson designed a number of houses in the Littleton-Bethlehem area, as well as the Maplewood Casino (1888–89), adjacent to the Maplewood Hotel cottages, and the second Oak Hill House hotel (1899) in Littleton, which was never built.[20]

Sayer Cottage No. 4 (1897–98), Bethlehem, N.H.
Photograph by the author.

Sayer waited only a short time before he bought additional land on Main Street, farther east of the first two cottages, toward The Uplands hotel, and began to build two more.[21] Again he employed Sanderson as architect, and, in all probability, Dunn as contractor, though this is yet to be documented. Construction commenced in the fall of 1897, and the houses were ready the following summer. Described by the *Echo* as "handsome structures in the colonial style of architecture," they possess very similar front (north), two-and-one-half-story elevations, with high hipped roofs, shed roof dormers, second-story bay windows, fieldstone foundations, and central porches with Doric columns, flanked by recessed porches with nearly identical column supports. Appended to the west side of each house is a side porch to take full advantage of the western vistas.[22] The completed row of four houses, with "The Outlook" nearby, brings to mind the image of a mid-nineteenth-century New England textile mill community, with the owner/manager's mansion juxtaposed with the rows of factory workers' housing units nearby.[23]

≈

The Knight Cottages

1890–1905

(Mr. Leonard M. Knight)

Bethlehem

"Sunset Lodge" (Knight Cottage No. 2) (1893), Bethlehem, N.H. Photograph by the author.

∾ A BETHLEHEM NATIVE, married to Helen Wilder of the same community, Leonard M. Knight was truly a man for all seasons when it came to his economic pursuits and civic commitments. Early in his working career in the 1880s, he wore several hats as Bethlehem selectman, postmaster, proprietor of the Centennial (later the Arlington) House hotel, and dealer in dry goods, groceries, crockery, and boots and shoes at his store on Main Street.[24] From the late eighties through the first decade of this century, he engaged in real estate investing, acquiring several parcels of land in Bethlehem and elsewhere, building summer homes, and renting them.

Knight Cottage No. 3 (c. 1900–1901), Bethlehem, N.H. Photograph by the author.

In fact he is credited with being the first local person to enter the cottage rental business, preceding William M. Sayer, Jr. (see the Sayer cottages, Bethlehem) by a few years.[25] Volumes of the *White Mountain Directory* published from 1914 to 1929 associate Knight with farming and the auto storage business. He staged these various activities from his home at the corner of Main Street and South Road, directly opposite the Centennial House and his group of desirable rental cottages.[26]

According to county registry of deeds records, in 1887 Knight commenced a period of rapid land acquisition in Bethlehem. Between that year and 1895, he made six separate transactions, acquiring tracts, some with existing buildings, on both the north and south sides of Main Street. Included in these purchases were the South Road lots upon which he erected his cottages.[27] Knight raised his first house ("Cloud View Cottage") on Maple Street in 1890, and his second on the South Road land in 1893. The latter, named "Sunset Lodge," was first tenanted by Rev. Philo W. Sprague and his family from Charlestown, Massachusetts. By 1901, a second South Road cottage ("Knight Cottage No. 3") was constructed between "Sunset Lodge" and Centennial House. A third soon followed next to it. By 1905, Knight owned and managed a total of five summer rental houses in Bethlehem, and they were much in demand among a cultured, accomplished, and well-heeled clientele.[28]

Both "Sunset Lodge" and "Knight Cottage No. 3" exist today in an excellent state of preservation as a result of major restoration projects completed in 1985–87 by the owner at the time. Victorian eclectic in form, they are by far the most architecturally significant of the Knight rental properties. The least altered of the two, "Sunset Lodge" displays features likely inspired by a published design book or serial illustrations of the 1890s. Of particular note are the fish-scale shingling of the gables (contrasted with clapboard siding), heavy roof cornices, and generous connected verandas (on three sides) with thin, turned support posts, and delicate, jigsaw-cut bracketing. Situated to the north on the same sloping hillside, "Knight Cottage No. 3" was probably based on similar visual sources, but is less ornate. Its principal gable end forward, like its neighbors, it also possesses linked verandas on three sides, but with modern balustrades in place of the original clapboarded side walls. It is quite possible that Sylvanus D. Morgan (1857–1940), the Lisbon contractor, built one or both of these houses for Knight. He undertook other construction projects in Bethlehem at the time (see "The Gables"), and the cottages resemble other examples of his work in the town, as well as in Lisbon.[29]

~

"The Bells"

1892

(Rev. Dr. and Mrs. John Rhey Thompson)

Bethlehem

"The Bells" (1892), Bethlehem, N.H. Photograph by the author.

∾ WITH THE "semblance of having been imported from a celestial empire,"[30] "The Bells" (also called "Pagoda Cottage") was erected in 1892 on Strawberry Hill in Bethlehem for Rev. Dr. and Mrs. John Rhey Thompson of Meriden, Connecticut.[31] This whimsical late-Victorian eclectic structure, adorned with Chinese-derived motifs, has long been considered both a curiosity and a paragon among White Mountain summer cottages of its era. Not surprisingly, it has often been misunderstood. During its construction phase, *Among the Clouds* offered the pointed observation that "the comments of average passers-by on this new departure in summer architecture would tend to show that the country of Confucious is a terra incognita to some Americans."[32] About the same time, the rival summer tourist newspaper, *The White Mountain Echo*, in passing editorial judgment, referred to the new Thompson house as a "Flowery Land-like domicile."[33]

Two and one half stories with a square floor plan, "The Bells" is modeled after a Chinese pagoda. Its exterior is embellished with Buddhist-originated style elements such as main and dormer concave corrugated roofs, eaves-suspended metal bells, dragon images, fancy-cut and curved wooden eaves brackets, and a spire atop a square cupola. About the cupola, the *Echo* noted that it contains "an apartment lighted by eight windows, in which the owner expects to be able to penetrate the realms of wisdom defiant of the discomforts of hay fever." The double-sash windows feature the highly unusual thirty-two panes over one pattern. More conventional balustrades encircle the cupola, and the veranda at the first-floor level. Collaborating with John Thompson on the design of the house were local contractors Frank Abbott (the father of Karl P. Abbott, see "Upland Cottage," Bethlehem) and H. L. Phillips, who, much to their credit, were able to interpret successfully the imaginative vision of the owners.[34]

Biographical information about Thompson is meager, but we know enough about him to speculate about the inspiration behind "The Bells." Born in West Virginia around 1854, he was educated at the University of West Virginia, and entered the Methodist Episcopal ministry, holding pastorates in the South and at Jersey City, New Jersey, before moving to the First Methodist Church in Meriden, Connecticut. During the 1890s, he joined the New York East Conference, and over the next decade served as pastor of the Washington Square Church, Manhattan, and Grace, Nostrand Avenue, and Summerfield Churches in Brooklyn. Known to be a man of active and brilliant intellect, Thompson also preached often to appreciative audiences in Bethlehem during the summers, and had a keen interest in Oriental culture and religions. Unfortunately, for much of his life, he was afflicted with hay fever, which initially attracted him to the health-enhancing mountain air of the town. In addition, since childhood, he also suffered severely from neuralgia, was prescribed morphine as an antidote, and was periodically treated for addiction. Local residents have speculated that this unfortunate condition may have caused occasional periods of delusion, which could in part explain the somewhat eccentric character of the house.[35]

Upon Thompson's death at age fifty in 1904, his wife and their family returned to Bethlehem for two additional summers, finally placing the property up for sale in 1906.[36] The new owners, Belle Stowe Sutton and her son J. E. Stowe Sutton, refurbished the interior with polished floors, screens, and other decorations, and introduced numerous technological improvements such as electricity, a telephone, and additional "comforts and conveniences." The *White Mountain Echo* reported that electrical outlets and fixtures "have been installed throughout, so that the place, ablaze with electricity at night," was, perhaps quite fittingly, "like a miniature palace."[37] Only slightly altered today, "The Bells" still conveys a sense of the picturesque and the bizarre.

~

"The Lodge"

1892

(Mr. J. Campbell Harris)

Bethlehem (Maplewood)

~ SITUATED ON MAIN STREET, just east of the three surviving Maplewood Hotel cottages, is "The Lodge," built in 1892 for J. Campbell Harris, originally from Philadelphia.[38] Regarded in *Among the Clouds* as "one of the handsomest villas in [the] vicinity,"[39] this provocative house has long been the focus of curiosity, largely because of its highly unusual exterior form, which seems to have been borrowed from American frontier military architecture of the late 1700s and early 1800s. As in a wooden blockhouse fortress, the upper story overhangs the lower stories, as if to provide some functional advantage to the residents. Clearly designed by a professional architect, to date unidentified, "The Lodge" displays a keen sense of proper proportions, excellent workmanship, and sophisticated knowledge of then fashionable architectural styles. It boasts a pleasant, successfully blended amalgam of details: curved support brackets derived from the Stick style; tall, step-molded brick chimneys associated with the Queen Anne; eyebrow dormers typical of the Shingle; and, a low-pitched hipped roof borrowed from the Colonial Revival. A heavy-appearing porch canopy is cantilevered precariously over the main entrance door at the northwest corner.

Soon after the house was completed, Bethlehem's *White Mountain Echo* published a useful description of the interior layout, demonstrating the careful thought that went into its planning:

> On the first floor are the kitchens and domestic departments while the second is devoted to bed-rooms. The main floor is the third which has in its center a large sitting-room lighted on every side and surrounded by a covered promenade [porch]. Thus a grand view of mountain scenery is obtained in every direction either sitting outside or inside of this spacious room. The edifice is surmounted by a . . . roof containing apartments.[40]

This imaginative building, perfectly suited to its mountain environment, was "calculated to furnish everything that can be desired in the way of coolness and comfort." With design and construction costs rumored to have been $30,000, "The Lodge" was one of the most expensive summer houses built in the White Mountains before 1900.[41]

J. Campbell Harris (1840–1916), the man responsible for the conception and financing of the house, attended Philadelphia public schools, studied law, and was admitted to professional practice. In 1860, he was appointed clerk to the commandant of the United States Marine Corps by his uncle, Colonel John Harris. He served in the Union army throughout the Civil War, achieving the rank of first lieutenant, and remaining in the military until 1869, when he resigned to enter the manufacturing business in his home city. Details are sketchy as to the nature of this business and his role in it, but it is known that he did retire in 1879 at a relatively young age, traveled, and spent increasing amounts of time in New Hampshire.[42] Documents housed at the Grafton County (New Hampshire) Registry of Deeds indicate that between 1883 and 1887, he and his wife, Mary, made a series

"The Lodge" (1892), Maplewood, Bethlehem, N.H. Photograph by the author.

of land investments in Bethlehem. These purchases entailed substantial acreage, mostly on the east side of town in the vicinity of the Maplewood Hotel, along the Maplewood Hill Road leading to Bethlehem Hollow. Included was the house lot.[43] The dates of acquisition correspond perfectly with years when Campbell and his family, according to *White Mountain Tourists' Register* listings, consistently spent their summers at the Maplewood Hotel.[44] Such a pattern was not uncommon for cottage owners in the mountains; visits to hotels in the region often led to commitments to real estate and a permanent stake in the summer community.

≈

"*The Gables*"

1893–94

(Mr. and Mrs. William H. Kellner)

Bethlehem

≈ AFTER SPENDING several seasons in Bethlehem at the Abbott cottage, opposite the Altamonte Hotel, Mr. and Mrs. William H. Kellner of Newark, New Jersey, decided to acquire land in the town and become permanent summer residents. William Kellner (died c. 1931) had spent the bulk of his business career with Hahne & Company, Newark's oldest (established 1858), and, at one time, its largest department store. During the 1880s, he had become an officer of the firm, in part, no doubt, because he was the son-in-law of the founder, Julius Hahne. In July 1893, in the name of Kellner's wife, Clara, the Kellners purchased a house lot from Frank E. Derbyshire, the owner of the Howard House hotel, from Lowell, Massachusetts. With dimensions of one hundred by three hundred feet, this parcel was situated on the north side of Main Street at Park Avenue, conveniently close to the commercial center of Bethlehem, near many of its hotels, rooming houses, and summer cottages.[45]

The Kellners contracted with Sylvanus D. Morgan (1857–1940) of Lisbon as their builder. Construction commenced in August 1893, and was concluded in the fall of the following year. "The Gables," as the Kellners called their new sixteen-room cottage, was one of Morgan's first contracting jobs in Bethlehem, and one of his most innovative and challenging. Drawing much praise from area residents for its "exceedingly handsome" design, the new house was conceived as a late-Victorian eclectic blend of styles, "after the character of a Swiss chalet." In reality, the building is predominantly Queen Anne, possessing asymmetrical elevations, an asymmetrical floor plan, varied fenestration, mixed and patterned wall sheathing, extensive verandas, and complex, intersecting gable roofs. On the rear (north) elevation is a marvelous recessed balcony with semicircular apertures on heavy plinths, balustrades, and roof overhangs. Certain of the decorative detail is classical, especially noticeable in the large triple west side window, at one time fitted with stained-glass panes purchased at the

"The Gables" (1893–94), Bethlehem, N.H. Photograph by the author.

1893 World Columbian Exposition in Chicago. It is highly likely, although it is undocumented, that Morgan himself drafted the plans for the house, employing standardized, prefabricated materials, and drawing inspiration from architectural design books of the period. For example, the exterior of "The Gables" closely resembles in spirit and form several designs that appeared in R. W. Shoppell's *Building Designs* (c. 1890) and *Shoppell's Modern Houses* (1890), published by The Cooperative Building Plan Association, Architects, New York City. Other similar publications of the 1880s and early 1890s could also have served as sources.[46]

≈

"Felsengarten"

1896–1900

(Mr. and Mrs. Theodore Thomas)

Bethlehem

"Felsengarten" (1896–1900), Bethlehem, N.H. Photograph by the author.

≈ SITUATED ON A rocky wooded tract on the eastern slope of what was once called Mount Theodore Thomas (today Garnet Mountain), is the recently restored former cottage of Theodore Thomas, the esteemed American musician and conductor, and his second wife, Rose Fay Thomas, a well-known author, horticulturalist, and member of women's organizations. Named "Felsengarten," meaning "garden of rocks" in German, this rather modest, plain, and functional structure commands attention primarily for its association with the Thomases, and secondarily for its architecture. Its historical value was recognized in 1973 when it was listed on the National Register of Historic Places, administered by the National Park Service. Removed from the center of Bethlehem, with magnificent vistas south toward Mount Lafayette and the Franconia Mountains, the Thomas property in many respects is the epitome of a northern New England rural summer retreat, providing peace and solitude for its owners.[47]

While living in Chicago in the early 1890s, the Thomases became friends of the J. J. Glessners, owners of "The Rocks" estate in Bethlehem,

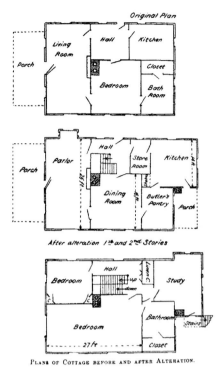

"Plans of Cottage before and after Alteration" ("Felsengarten," 1896–1900), Bethlehem, N.H., from Mrs. Theodore Thomas, *Our Mountain Garden* (1915). Author's collection.

and began their long association with the town. Late in the summer of 1894, during a visit to "The Rocks," the Thomases decided to purchase land in Bethlehem and erect a summer residence. Early in September of that year, they purchased twelve acres of the Whitcomb farm for their house site, including a right-of-way in front of the Whitcomb farmhouse to the road running from the west end of Bethlehem to Franconia.[48] Two years passed before they began to build the house; finally in August 1896, the *White Mountain Echo* reported that "a beginning . . . [had] been made in the drawing of lumber."[49] The building project was entrusted to Rose Thomas, who secured the assistance of an unidentified "architect relative" to draft the plans, and employed "local masons and carpenters . . . to execute them." As on-site superintendent, Mrs. Thomas, with "no professional architect [present] to bother me," improvised as the construction proceeded, altering the floor plans and the placement of doors and windows to suit her specifications. Starting the first year with five rooms on one floor, the cottage was developed in stages in line with the owners' wishes, allowing for complete flexibility. This approach to the project explains why it took four years to finish. The end result, "convenient and practical," was two and a half stories high, set on cellar foundations of twenty-eight by forty feet. Although "not much of the architect's [original] plan was left," the Thomases thought their process "was quite an ideal way to build a house." While "Felsengarten" evolved, they also directed their attention to the surrounding natural setting, converting the rough landscape into a spectacular series of shrub, wildflower, and perennial gardens, linked by broad walkways and meandering paths.[50]

The principal rationale for "Felsengarten" was to provide a place "hidden away from the world" for Theodore Christian Friedrich Thomas (1835–1905), considered by many to be the major catalyst in the origin and early growth of the American symphony orchestra movement in the late nineteenth century. In many ways he was the Arturo Toscanini or Leonard Bernstein of his era, although his name is relatively unknown today outside of music circles. Born in Esens, Germany, the "Meister," as he was called by close family friends, emigrated to the United States with his parents in 1845. A violin prodigy, he commenced his professional career as a soloist, and chamber and symphony orchestra member in New York City and on occasional tour. His first conducting opportunities in the early 1860s impelled him to establish his own orchestra, which he did in 1862. For more than two decades, the Thomas-led group periodically traveled the American continent, stimulating wide interest in symphonic literature and in the formation of other orchestras in major cities such as Boston and Philadelphia. In 1876, Thomas was appointed conductor of the New York Philharmonic Society (he left in 1878, but returned to this post from 1880 to 1885), and also presented concerts at the Philadelphia Centennial Exposition. From 1878 to 1880, he was in Cincinnati as director of the College of Music. He was induced to accept the directorship of the American Opera Company in 1885, but this venture proved financially unstable, and he again committed his talents and energies to his own orchestra until he disbanded it in 1888. From 1891 until his death, he was the founding director/conductor of the Chicago Symphony Orchestra, bringing it broad fame as one of the world's greatest concert ensembles. In 1893 he acted as music director for the World Columbian Exposition in Chicago. Thomas introduced many new orchestral works to America, including compositions by Saint-Saens, Richard Strauss, Bruckner, Wagner, Brahms, and Tchaikovsky. The death of Thomas was mourned throughout the world, numerous cities erected statues and monuments in his honor, and many major newspapers published reminiscences. Although regarded as an able conductor, it was as a musical missionary that Thomas accomplished his most outstanding work, cultivating everywhere a taste for the very best in music.[51]

Thomas' wife, Rose Fay (1853–1929), was extraordinarily accomplished and acclaimed in her own right. Born in St. Albans, Vermont, Rose Thomas spent her young girlhood in Cambridge, Massachusetts, where she was educated. She met Theodore Thomas while living with her brother in Chicago, and was married to him in 1890. Throughout her life, she was committed to the promotion of art and music, the abolition of cruelty to animals, and the conservation of birds and forests. Consistent with these interests, she was the founder and honorary president of the National Federation of Music Clubs and the Chicago Anti-Cruelty Society, and a founder and president of the White Mountain Garden Club. She was not only a demonstrated leader, but also an accomplished author, writing two books at "Felsengarten": *The Memoirs of Theodore Thomas* (1911), and *Our Mountain Garden* (1904), which recounts the making and landscaping of the Bethlehem estate. After her husband's death, Thomas returned to Cambridge, using the Bethlehem house every summer until she passed away. During the nearly twenty-five years she was there alone, "Felsengarten" was the frequent site of social and club events. It also became a veritable mecca, to which many notable guests (including her sister, the New York pianist, Amy Fay) and tourists came to savor the beauty of the gardens and grounds, and the moving panorama of the distant mountains.[52]

~

The Abbe House

1903

(Mr. and Mrs. George E. Abbe)

Bethlehem

~ THIS SOLID AND IMPOSING residence was built for George E. Abbe (Abbey) and his wife, Esther H., in 1903 on a small plot of land behind Frank Abbott's hotel, The Uplands, on Strawberry Hill. Born in 1862 in Enfield, Connecticut, George Abbe graduated from Wesleyan Academy in Wilbraham, Massachusetts, and then became a commercial trader in nearby Springfield. During the 1890s, Abbe, his wife, and their two young children often vacationed in Bethlehem during the summer months, usually staying at the Centennial House (later the Arlington Hotel), after 1895 owned and managed by his brother Fred C. Abbe. It was this experience

The Abbe house (1903), Bethlehem, N.H. Photograph by the author.

that convinced the Abbe family to acquire property in the town and join its already well-established summer community. Evidence suggests that the house may have been winterized, since the Abbes occupied it for much of the first year. Sadly, George Abbe was able to enjoy his new cottage for only a brief period, as he died unexpectedly in December 1904. Esther Abbe and their children returned to Springfield, and the house soon passed to new owners.[53]

According to local tradition, the Abbe house was both designed and built by Sylvanus D. Morgan (1857–1940) of Lisbon, "noted throughout the North Country as an architect and contractor of unusual ability."[54] Numerous houses in Bethlehem have been attributed to this highly talented and productive practitioner. His principal fame, however, rests with his many hotel projects, which he carried out using a variety of architectural styles and building practices. Across the White Mountain region, Morgan was responsible for either entire complexes or additions for The Uplands and the Sinclair Hotel in Bethlehem, Hotel Lookoff at Sugar Hill, the Profile House at Franconia Notch, The Balsams at Dixville Notch, the Mount Washington Hotel at Bretton Woods, the Forest Hills Hotel in Franconia, and the third Summit House on Mount Washington.[55] Like these much larger buildings, and many other Morgan houses, the Abbe cottage possesses a strikingly indigenous quality, particularly evident in the heavy roof joist and gable eaves bracket construction, and the native field-stone foundations supporting the main building mass, side porches and porte cochere. The house also exhibits a combination of styles, as the Colonial Revival idiom (porch and porte cochere classical columns, frieze, and roof balustrades) is successfully juxtaposed with the slightly later Craftsman mode (gable dormers with extended, bracketed roofs; stone exterior chimneys; extended, bracketed main roof). While the proportions are somewhat awkward, the building is aesthetically compelling.

≈

"Edgemont"

c. 1903

(Miss Emily S. Perkins;

Mr. and Mrs. Ruel W. Poor)

Bethlehem

"Edgemont" (c. 1903), Bethlehem, N.H. Photograph by the author.

≈ DURING HIS YOUTH and early adulthood, Ruel W. Poor had a long association with New Hampshire. It comes as little surprise, therefore, that he became a Bethlehem cottage owner once his professional career was firmly established. Born in New London, New Hampshire, in 1860, he was educated at the local public schools and at Wilton Academy in Maine. He launched his successful business career in New Hampshire, first in Concord where he worked at the Page Belting Company from 1877 to 1881, then in Littleton, where he worked at the Littleton Savings Bank and the Littleton National Bank (as chief cashier) from 1881 to 1887. It was during this phase of his career that Poor and his wife, the former Ida M. Sawyer, became acquainted with the White Mountain region. In 1888, Poor resigned his position in Littleton and moved to New York City and the

Garfield National Bank. Advancing up through the administrative ranks, he became president, serving a lengthy tenure from 1902 to 1925. He concluded his active working years as chairman of the board from 1925 to 1928, and also chaired the advisory committee for what became the Garfield Branch of the Chase Manhattan Bank. He passed away in 1941.[56]

Despite Poor's emergence as a national figure in the banking field, he and his wife never forgot the beauty and charm of the White Mountains, and often vacationed there. Late in the summer of 1907, while renting one of William Sayer's cottages on Main Street (see "Sayer Cottages," Bethlehem), they purchased "Edgemont," a handsome Colonial Revival dwelling on Berkley Street belonging to Emily S. Perkins (1866–1941), a composer of hymns and club member from Riverdale-on-Hudson, New York.[57] The history of the building and Perkins' association with it are extremely sketchy. A deed on file at the Grafton County Registry of Deeds verifies that she purchased the house lot in 1902. The earliest known published reference to the house, and Perkins' ownership, appears in the 6 August 1904 issue of Bethlehem's *White Mountain Echo*.[58] It may be assumed, therefore, that she owned the property for only a short period, and that it must have been erected at about that time. For several decades, local residents have suggested that the internationally renowned Stanford White (1853–1906) (see "Wormeley Cottages," Jackson) of New York City was the architect, but such speculation has never been securely documented. The same sources also believed that Sylvanus D. Morgan (1853–1940) (see The Abbe House, Bethlehem), contractor for so many other Bethlehem houses of the period, may well have been the builder. The latter assertion seems quite plausible.[59]

Whether the esteemed White was connected with "Edgemont" or not, it is strikingly apparent, just on the basis of visual inspection, that the house is an outstanding example of the Colonial Revival style. Unusually sophisticated for northern New Hampshire, it resembles many of White's own Colonial Revival residential commissions, and those of his firm, McKim, Mead and White. With a perfectly symmetrical, balanced front facade and rectangular floor plan, the cottage is covered by a truncated, balustraded hipped roof with gable dormers displaying recessed broken arches and partially screening balustrades. The dominant feature of the structure, however, is the massive, recessed front porch with rounded corner projections, which extends across the entire front. Here the classical detailing is most pronounced in the slender Doric columns, plain frieze, and floor-level and flat-roof balustrades. "Edgemont" effectively conveys a feeling of order, intellectuality, and urbanity. In doing so, it reflects well the standards and tastes of the woman who built and briefly owned the house, and the family that then occupied it for almost forty years.

≈

"The Glamis"

1904–5

(Mr. and Mrs. George A. Macbeth)

Bethlehem

"The Glamis" (1904–5), Bethlehem, N.H. Photograph by the author.

FEW IF ANY VISITORS (including students of architectural design) to Bethlehem today are aware of the existence of "The Glamis," perhaps the single most significant example of summer country estate architecture in northern New Hampshire. This is hardly surprising, for to locate it is an exercise in detective work. If one proceeds to the west end of town on Main Street, and follows Prospect Road to the north, within a mile on the left side, one will notice a long fieldstone wall, with two openings, through which nearly overgrown narrow gravel roads plunge into heavy mixed forest growth. At the end of the wall, on the same side of Prospect Road, is another road, leading to a white farmhouse and outbuildings, one of which, built of fieldstone masonry, appears to have been a former horse barn and automobile garage. Passing up the road to the left of this building, one cannot but be struck by the patterned placement and variety of the trees and shrubs, suggesting a formal landscaping scheme of many years past. Moving farther along the road, through heavy undergrowth and long grass, suddenly one sees the shape of a large house, looming up against a backdrop of tall hardwoods. As one draws closer, it is clear that the building has been abandoned, for there is no evidence of life, though efforts have been made to maintain the exterior in stable, weatherproof condition. Its long, strongly horizontal lines, accentuated by expansive overhanging, flared hipped roofs over the main central block and wings, are still impressive. Stylistically, the house combines the shapes, materials, and elements of the Shingle style of the coastal Northeast, with the Prairie style of the Midwest. The mark of a professional architect is evident. Why then was such a house, seemingly out of context for its region, built in the White Mountains? Who was the financier of the project and the first owner? Who served as architect and as contractor and how did they become associated with the owning family?

The answer to these questions begins with George A. Macbeth (b. 1845) of Pittsburgh, Pennsylvania. Born in Urbana, Ohio, he was educated in the public schools, and then apprenticed to the drug and chemical trade. Attracted to the faults and frailties of glass, in 1872 he was one of the organizers of the Keystone Lead Glass Company in Pittsburgh, manufacturers of lamp chimneys. Over the ensuing years he used his scientific knowledge to beautify and improve the heat-resistant qualities of glass, and enhance combustion, perfecting a chimney that was specially adjusted to the flow of heat currents. Demand for the product line increased, and in 1880 Macbeth and his association reorganized the business as George A. Macbeth & Company. Macbeth continued to do glass research, in 1882 introducing the first method of fabricating lamp chimneys from a turned or paste mold. About the same time, he began the manufacture of specialized railroad signal glasses, and placed on the market the first scalloped-top ("pearl-top") lamp chimneys. The creation of the renowned pearl glass was his crowning achievement. The capacity of the plant was again increased in 1891 by the construction of a branch factory in Elwood, Indiana. Here, for the first time in the United States, optical glass was made for scientific purposes. In 1899 the company merged with three other similar concerns to become the Macbeth-Evans Glass Company (with Macbeth as president), the largest lamp glass manufacturer in the world. In Pittsburgh, Macbeth was president of the Art Society for several years, a charter member of the Academy of Science and Art, a member of the Engineers' Society, a director of two banks, the president of one trust company, and a supporter of numerous other institutions in the city.[60]

George Macbeth's first contacts with the White Mountains and Bethlehem were through his sister Frances, the wife of John Jacob Glessner, the Chicago businessman who initiated the development of the neighboring estate, "The Rocks," in the mid-1880s. Over the next two decades, Macbeth and his wife, Kate, often visited there in summer. Finally, in 1904, convinced of the virtues and benefits of the area, they acquired the former Noyes farm on what was then called Cherry Valley Road, and began the planning of their own country house, outbuildings, and grounds.[61] A further outgrowth of their relationship with the Glessners was the Macbeths' selection of Chicagoan Hermann Valentin von Holst (1874–1955) as architect. He was the designer of several buildings or building additions at "The Rocks," starting in 1902. There is no question, therefore, that the Macbeths were familiar with his work, as well as that of Sylvanus D. Morgan (1857–1940) of Lisbon, the builder of so many Bethlehem houses, whom they chose to team with von Holst as contractor.[62] Construction on the property commenced in the fall of 1904, and ended by the following fall.[63]

Hermann V. von Holst was a graduate of the University of Chicago (1893), where his father, who had emigrated from Germany with his family in 1891, was a professor of political science. In 1896, he received his bachelor's in architecture from MIT, then returned to Chicago where he was engaged as a draftsman by the firm Shepley, Rutan and Coolidge. He traveled widely in Europe in 1901, taught architectural design at the Armour Institute of Technology from 1904 to 1906, and worked on four books on architectural orders and Beaux Arts architecture for the American Institute of Correspondence, which was based there. At the same time he established his own architectural practice, inheriting some of Frank Lloyd Wright's

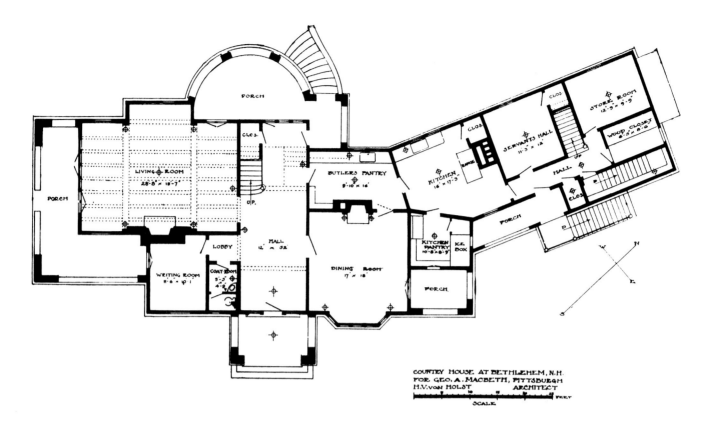

"First-Story Plan of Country House at Bethlehem, N.H.," for George A. Macbeth, Pittsburgh, from the *Cyclopedia of Architecture, Carpentry and Building*, vol. 2 (1909), op. p. 297. Courtesy of the Hagley Museum and Library, Wilmington, Del.

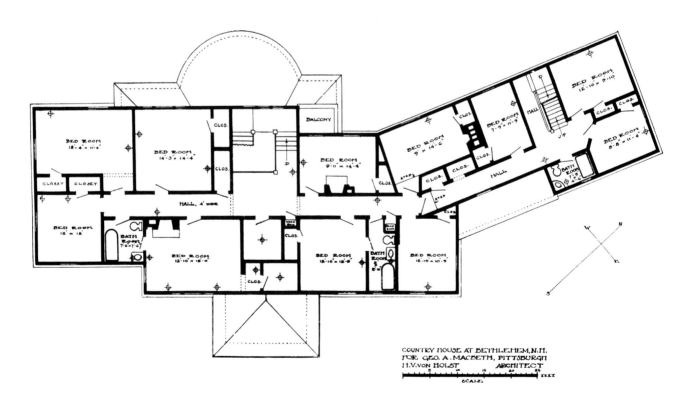

"Second-Story Plan of Country House, Bethlehem, N.H.," for George A. Macbeth, Pittsburgh, from the *Cyclopedia of Architecture, Carpentry and Building*, vol. 2 (1909), op. p. 297. Courtesy of the Hagley Museum and Library, Wilmington, Del.

unfinished jobs when Wright went to Europe in 1909. In 1913, von Holst authored the profusely illustrated book *Modern American Homes* (reprinted in 1982 as *Country and Suburban Homes of the Prairie School Period*). A number of his drawings were exhibited at the Chicago Architectural Club in the early 1900s, including samples of his outstanding academic water-color renderings. Von Holst worked closely with and employed Marion Mahoney, who, with her husband, the architect Walter Burley Griffin, was a widely recognized proponent of the Prairie style. Unfortunately, little is known about von Holst's commissions, and his drawings and office records seem to have been destroyed.[64]

"The Glamis," however, stands out as one shining example of von Holst's abilities, at least in residential architecture. Furthermore, it is believed to be the only example of his work that is at all well documented. Contained in the collections of the Art Institute of Chicago is a 1904 pencil and water-color front (east) elevation perspective sketch (see illustration) that depicts the house as it was intended to look upon its completion. Confirming the architect's vision is a front elevation photograph, along with the first- and second-story plans (see illustrations) published in the 1909 edition of the *Cyclopedia of Architecture, Carpentry and Building* (Chicago, American Technical Society). Located on a rise, formerly with excellent views, particularly to the west, "The Glamis" originally possessed walls of silver-gray-stained shingles, and roofs stained a contrasting deep red brown. The floor plan is asymmetrical, with an unusually spacious living room, dining room, writing room, butlers' pantry, and service facilities on the first floor, and eleven bedrooms and three bathrooms on the second. In the original design, ample space for enjoying outdoor living was provided on the first story by a rear (west) semicircular porch with staircase, and two partially enclosed square side porches.[65] Sometime after 1905, a small cylindrical porch with conical roof was appended to the southeast corner. Three tall brick chimneys provide vertical accents, and seem to anchor the building in the landscape. The varied fenestration, particularly the eyebrow dormer in the front roof plane, underscores the predominantly Shingle-style flavor of the house; but it is the sweeping roof forms, so closely associated with the Prairie style, that give it a singularly individual character.

∽

"Glengarry Cottage"

1908

(Dr. and Mrs. John W. Kenney)

The Ivie Cottage

1908

(Mr. and Mrs. Alvin W. Ivie)

The Beaumont Cottage

1908

(Mr. and Mrs. Charles O. Beaumont)

Bethlehem

"Glengarry Cottage" (1908), Bethlehem, N.H. Photograph by the author.

~ THESE THREE strikingly different cottages were designed and erected during the spring and summer of 1908 by Sylvanus D. Morgan (1857–1940) (see The Abbe House, Bethlehem), the highly esteemed and productive North Country contractor.[66] Morgan was responsible for numerous Bethlehem houses and hotel additions from the 1890s to the 1920s. The fact that he and his assistants were able to construct these cottages simultaneously was quite remarkable, and is evidence of the size, complexity, and efficiency of his business enterprise. Operating from his hometown, Lisbon, New Hampshire, where he maintained centralized shop, storage, and office facilities, Morgan managed extensive contracting projects each year, some using prefabricated materials. It has been conjectured that in the early 1900s, at the height of his business activity, he employed upwards of two hundred workmen on a variety of building ventures throughout the mountain region.[67]

The first of the cottages to be completed and occupied was for the family of John W. Kenney, a dentist from West Roxbury, Massachusetts.[68] Named "Glengarry Cottage" and located just west of the Maplewood section of the town, the house is a subdued, nonetheless interesting example of the late Shingle style. Among its notable features are the long, arcaded front (north) veranda set on stone piers, the main gambrel roof with shed dormers and a central gambreled pavilion, the east-side porte cochere specially constructed to shelter automobiles, and "a large rough stone chimney, built of native granite rocks gathered from the neighboring fields." On the west end, contiguous with the front veranda, is an unusually large sixteen-by-twenty-eight-foot veranda, "indicating that the owner appreciat[ed] that Bethlehem [was], par excellence, a place for out-of-door living."[69]

The second Morgan cottage, a close neighbor to the Kenney house, was completed the middle of the summer of 1908 for Mr. and Mrs. Alvin W.

The Ivie cottage (1908), Bethlehem, N.H. Photograph by the author.

The Beaumont cottage (1908), Bethlehem, N.H. Photograph by the author.

Ivie of Brooklyn, New York.[70] Mr. Ivie (c. 1872–1954) was the manager of the first F. W. Woolworth "5 and 10 cent" store in Manhattan, and retired in 1928 as head buyer for the entire Woolworth retail enterprise. It is hardly surprising that Ivie spent his entire working career with Woolworth's, as Henrietta, his wife, was the sister of Frank W. Woolworth, the founder.[71] Supposedly, the well-known Woolworth heiress, Barbara Hutton, spent time at the house with movie actor Cary Grant, one of her many husbands.[72] Containing a generous eight bedrooms, the Ivie cottage is the only English Tudor–type cottage in Bethlehem, and one of only a few originally steam-heated for year-long use.[73] Today, the building looks quite different than it did in 1908, as the Ivies added two-story wings with enclosed verandas in about 1913. These compromised the effect of the round, broken conical-roofed corner towers.[74]

The third and least interesting of the three cottages was built for Mr. and Mrs. Charles O. Beaumont of Philadelphia. It is situated in the western sector of Bethlehem on Park Avenue, looking out over a portion of the golf course. Only slightly modified since it was raised, the house is difficult to type stylistically, but does clearly display the influence of the Colonial Revival in its columned front entrance porch. Late in the summer of 1908, the *White Mountain Echo* blandly described it as being "of ample size and attractive appearance, . . . finished on the exterior with shingles stained a soft brown, while the roof is green." Extremely well constructed, the Beaumont cottage illustrates particularly well the painstaking care that Sylvanus Morgan and his assistants invested in all his residential structures.[75]

～

"Six Pillars"

1909–10

(Dr. and Mrs. Thorne Shaw)

Bethlehem

～ ONE OF BETHLEHEM'S largest and most pretentious summer residences was "Six Pillars," built in 1909–10 for Dr. and Mrs. Thorne Shaw of New York City. For the previous nine years, the Shaws had summered at the Elm House in the same town. Apparently, Thorne Shaw (d. 1917) carried on a successful medical practice in New York, and had amassed considerable wealth, but available published sources disclose little else about him or his wife. The land upon which the house stood was acquired in June and July 1909 in Julia W. Shaw's name from the Viall and Phillips families, both of Bethlehem.[76] The site the Shaws selected was magnificent—a gradually sloping hillside on the southwest shoulder of Mount Agassiz, commanding a grand prospect of the mountains to the east and south, much the same as that enjoyed by the Thomases from their cottage, "Felsengarten," a half mile away. In her abbreviated history of Bethlehem, Hattie Whitcomb Taylor identified the builder of "Six Pillars" as "Mr. Glover," probably Bert Glover, a general contractor from nearby Franconia, who maintained offices in Littleton. The 14 October 1909 issue of the *Littleton Courier* contradicts this assertion, however, assigning credit to Lewis J.

"Six Pillars" (1909–10), Bethlehem, N.H. Photograph courtesy of Roland Shick, Bethlehem.

Myott and L. Joseph Crane, also from Littleton, and advertised as "general contractors, carpenters and builders." The latter reference is most likely correct. The architect is unknown, though the builder(s) may also have prepared the designs.[77]

Fronting on expansive lawns and a circular drive off the Bethlehem-Franconia road, the Shaw residence was a product of the then fashionable Neoclassical style. The dominant feature, from which the house derived its name, was an impressive front central entry porch, rising two stories to the roof line and supported by six unevenly spaced smooth, rounded, tapered Doric columns. On either side of this porch were one-story verandas which wrapped around the east and west sides of the building and gave inhabitants protected views of the landscape in several directions. Appended to the veranda on the east side was a porte cochere, under which the family's red Pierce-Arrow motor car was often parked. The verandas and the porte cochere displayed Doric columns, one-third the height of those in the grand front porch, but similar in proportions. Other visible features common to the Neoclassical as well as the Colonial Revival styles were the main hipped roof, plain molded friezes under the eaves, flat, molded window caps, and Doric corner pilasters. These various elements were effectively melded together to provide "Six Pillars" with a sophisticated and refined appearance not often seen in North Country residential architecture.

After her husband's death, Julia Shaw continued to use the house into the 1930s, at which time it passed out of her family to other owners. Much mystery is associated with the property during its final years, and it has been the source of rumor and speculation on the part of Bethlehem residents. After standing unoccupied and deteriorating for over a decade, "Six Pillars" was destroyed by fire in July 1980. Many felt that the building had become haunted. Several at the fire scene reported seeing the ghosts of a little boy and his dog silhouetted against the flames in a first-story window. In a photograph of the house taken around 1935–40 (see illustration), what many believe to be the same boy and dog may be seen standing under the canopy roof of the front porch. One of the frequent pleasures as well as the frustrations of local history is the inability to find documentation to support conjecture—this capstone episode in the chronicle of the Shaw estate is likely to remain an integral part of Bethlehem folklore for all time.[78]

≈

"Lone Larch"

c. 1912–17

(Mr. and Mrs. Albert D. Locke)

Bethlehem

"Lone Larch" (c. 1912–17), Bethlehem, N.H. Photograph by the author.

≈ HIGH ON THE SIDE of Lewis Hill in Bethlehem, to the northeast of the summit known as Mount Theodore Thomas (see "Felsengarten," Bethelehm), stands a dominant, solidly built, Craftsman-style residence whose original name was "Lone Larch," for a single larch (tamarack) tree on the property.[79] The house was erected for Albert D. and Minnie I. Locke from the Waban section of Newton, Massachusetts, on land acquired in 1912 by a group called The Five Associates (the Lockes; Albert Locke's sister, Lucy E.; their son, Ellesbree E.; and Dr. Francis M. Morris, all of Waban).[80] A successful businessman, Albert Locke (c. 1871–1958) was for many years the owner of the A. D. Locke stapling machinery company on Lincoln Street in Boston. The Lockes were among the earliest residents of Waban, arriving before 1850. Albert and Lucy Locke's father, William, ran a successful market garden business there until 1899, which indirectly helped make possible the New Hampshire real estate venture.[81]

According to Whitcomb family sources in Bethlehem, "Lone Larch" was erected by Waldo C. Whitcomb (d. 1922), the contractor for the Lemens (see "Dawn Cottage," Bethlehem) as well as other houses, hotel additions, and buildings in the town during the same time period.[82] In the winter and spring of 1917, the *Littleton Courier* cites several business trips that Whitcomb made to Boston, very possibly to consult with Locke and his colleagues about the house plans.[83] On the other hand, in its 16 August

1917 edition, the *Courier* credits the construction of the new "bungalow" to the family firm of Pennock & Son of Littleton, known primarily as electrical contractors, but also expert in carpentry, stone masonry, and painting.[84] A likely scenario is that Whitcomb and the Pennocks worked together on the project, and that Whitcomb, whose farmhouse was near the building site, acted as building superintendent. It is not known if the services of a professional architect were sought, or if Whitcomb and/or the Pennocks drafted the plans, using published Craftsman design sources available at the time.

From its east-facing front porch, looking out over gradually sloping, open, tree-bordered fields, "Lone Larch" (or "Hidden Pastures," its name since 1972) commands one of the finest and most moving panoramic views in the North Country, encompassing the Franconia Mountains, the Presidential Range, and the peaks to the north. Constructed of wood and local mortared fieldstone, the perfectly symmetrical building mass is protected by a medium-pitched gable slate roof, with three large shed-roof dormers on the east roof plane. Small matching gable-roof wings with eaves brackets are attached to the north and south ends. Originally there were fourteen interior rooms, of which a forty-eight-by-twenty-three-foot living room, paneled in western pine, with a great stone fireplace, is the most notable. It is believed that the fieldstone foundations, porch piers, and first-story walls were erected methodically over a five-year period before the upper wooden portion, and its interior framing system and finishing, were completed in 1917.[85]

∽

"Dawn Cottage"

c. 1916

(Mr. and Mrs. William S. Lemen)

Bethlehem

∽ IN MAY AND AUGUST of 1916, William S. and Elizabeth B. Lemen of Brooklyn, New York, acquired two small contiguous parcels of land on the west side of South Road in Bethlehem from the local Knight family.[86] Born in Hastings, Minnesota, William Lemen (1865–after 1929) was regarded as "an artist of superior ability," with a sound education and extensive travel experience throughout the United States. Elizabeth Lemen, his second wife, was also an artist and a native of Brooklyn. It is possible that their common interest in painting, particularly landscapes, may have originally brought them to the White Mountains, although the precise reasons for their coming are not readily apparent.[87]

Soon after they made their land purchases, the Lemens commenced construction on their new summer residence, in all probability in 1916.[88] They gave the house the name "Dawn Cottage" because it faced due east and on pleasant days received the early morning sun.[89] For their builder, they selected the local contractor Waldo C. Whitcomb (d. 1922), who had previously erected houses and hotel additions in Bethlehem, and was highly respected by his fellow townspeople. He was assisted on the project

"Dawn Cottage" (c. 1916), Bethlehem, N.H. Photograph by the author.

Lemen Cottage No. 2 (c. 1940), Bethlehem, N.H. Photograph by the author.

by his brother, Verdie E. Whitcomb, and Hugh E. Lennon, both carpenters. In a winter snapshot photo, contained in a scrapbook compiled by local historian Hattie Whitcomb Taylor, this trio is shown posed in front of the completed house, obviously pleased by their creative and expert handiwork.[90] The identity of the architect of "Dawn Cottage," however, remains a mystery, though it has been speculated that Lemen himself may have drafted the designs in concert with the building crew.[91]

Set on a gradual, sloping hillside, and surrounded by tall hardwoods and conifers, the Lemen house, though modest in size, is a commanding presence. Irregular in shape and floor plan, the building possesses strongly horizontal sight lines, accentuated by its long asymmetrical front elevation, low hipped roof, and front first-story window strips, shielded by shed roofs. Slight hints of the Colonial Revival style are evident in the recessed front entranceway, flanked by round Doric columns, and to its right, a vertical rectangular stained-glass window with a semicircular arch cap. Atop the roof at its center is a small, square observation deck enclosed by a wooden balustrade. White-painted window and door frames and trellises sharply contrast with the brown-stained shingling of the wall surfaces. "Dawn Cottage" seems, in its design and spatial layout, well suited to its function as a summer dwelling.[92]

∾

"Upland Cottage"

1916–17

(Mr. and Mrs. Karl P. Abbott)

Bethlehem

"Upland Cottage" (1916–17), Bethlehem, N.H. Photograph by the author.

⌁ ONE OF THE MOST important and fascinating houses in the White Mountains is "Upland Cottage," built in 1916–17 for hotel impresario Karl P. Abbott and his new bride, Florence Ivie, as a wedding present from her father and mother, Mr. and Mrs. Alvin W. Ivie of Brooklyn, New York. The young couple apparently met in Bethlehem, where he had been raised and she had spent time at her parents' summer house, constructed in 1908 (see The Ivie cottage, Bethlehem). The land upon which the new dwelling was erected originally formed part of the property of The Uplands hotel (more recently, "Upland Terrace"), owned and managed by Karl's father, Frank H. Abbott, from the mid-1880s until after World War I. In October 1918, Frank Abbott conveyed this parcel to his son and daughter-in-law for "$1.00 and other valuable considerations," suggesting that the land also may have been a wedding gift. Sadly, the Abbotts occupied "Upland Cottage" for only a brief time, as Florence died unexpectedly. In 1930, to celebrate her shortened life, her parents erected the Ivie Memorial Episcopal Church, designed by Hanover, New Hampshire, architect Jens Fredrick Larson, on the east end of Main Street.[93]

A native of Bethlehem, Karl Abbott was born around 1891, attended public schools locally, and completed his college preparatory studies at Goddard Seminary in Barre, Vermont. He then attended Tufts College in Massachusetts, later taking a business administration course at the Wharton School of the University of Pennsylvania. After service in the United States Navy during World War I, Abbott returned to Bethlehem and entered the family hotel business at The Uplands. It was at this point in his life that his remarkable career as a hotelman took off, which he describes in detail in his highly successful book, *Open for the Season*, published in 1950. During his apprenticeship at The Uplands, Abbott joined his father in partnership, forming the firm Frank H. Abbott & Son. In 1918, this company was part of a syndicate that acquired the Forest Hills Hotel in nearby

Franconia, and, with Karl as manager, substantially enlarged and improved this facility. His great opportunity in the hotel field, however, came in 1921 when the firm purchased the magnificent New Profile House and Cottages in Franconia Notch from the legendary Colonel Charles H. Greenleaf. Applying personal attention and modern management techniques, Karl substantially increased the hotel's patronage, only to lose the entire resort complex to a disastrous fire in August 1923. Set back by this episode, but undaunted, the Abbotts expanded their business along the entire Atlantic seaboard, first acquiring The Kirkwood Hotel in Camden, South Carolina, also in 1923, and the Vendome in Boston in 1925. Karl's talents as a hotel operator received national validation when the firm was selected to run the Vinoy-Park Hotel in St. Petersburg, Florida. In the 1930s and 1940s, either as owner/manager or manager, Karl was connected with the Sagamore at Bolton Landing, Lake George, New York; the Westbury Hotel in New York City; the Somerset Hotel in Boston; the Dodge in Washington, D.C.; The Towers in Brooklyn, New York; and the Belleview Biltmore and the Flamingo in Florida. Although his association with "Upland Cottage" was all too brief, Karl Abbott provides an historic link between the house and the heyday of the American grand resort hotel industry.[94]

The Abbott house may be properly regarded as an outstanding example of the Craftsman (often-called Arts and Crafts) idiom of the first two decades of this century. University of Virginia professor Richard Guy Wilson, who has extensively studied this period and its domestic architecture, believes that the building could possibly have been designed by Gustav Stickley (1858–1942), a central New York state furniture maker, writer, editor, and architect, who is considered one of the leading lights of the English-originated Arts and Crafts movement in the United States. Furthermore, "Upland Cottage," both in its overall form and specific ornamental features, resembles the residential work of the Pasadena, California, architectural firm of Greene and Greene, nationally recognized at the time for its innovative Craftsman-style conceptions. The house, however, does not appear in Stickley's magazine, *The Craftsman* (1901–16), in which a number of Greene and Greene designs were published, along with many more created and approved by the editor himself. Nor is the house listed in the Greenes' inventory of commissions. It is known conclusively, though, that the Lisbon, New Hampshire, contractor Sylvanus D. Morgan (1857–1940), the builder of additions to The Uplands for the Abbotts, was the contractor for "Upland Cottage." Morgan, who designed as well as built other residences in Bethlehem, may have erected the house based on features of Stickley and other plans, readily available in *The Craftsman* and other publications for public scrutiny and use. It is conceivable also that Morgan received assistance from some heretofore unidentified professional architect.[95]

Whatever the solution to this puzzle, the house speaks eloquently for itself. Characteristic of the Arts and Crafts movement, and the architecture it inspired, "Upland Cottage" is distinguished by its functional simplicity, and, through use of appropriate materials and colors, its effective integration with the surrounding environment. In reaction against the preeminence of the machine age, the various parts of the building, including its interior appointments, appear to be, if they are not in fact, painstakingly hand-fabricated. On the exterior, obvious hallmarks of the Craftsman style are evident, such as the intersecting, low-pitched roofs with deep overhangs, and exposed rafters and purlins; asymmetrical elevations; an irregular, and adeptly configured floor plan; stocky, solid, molded rectangular piers supporting a front veranda and west-side porte cochere (removed in recent years); variegated shingle wall treatments; and mixed double-sash and fixed fenestration. Contrary to the norm in most Craftsman cottages, the building gives the impression of heaviness and permanence, perhaps in response to its harsh, often unpredictable North Country environment. Meticulously selected and crafted features of the interior include: geometrically arranged beveled-edge glass panes in single-hinged doors, windows, double French doors between various rooms, and half-level and wall-to-ceiling bookcases; crystal ball knobs simulating paperweights, infused with air bubbles on doors, cupboards, and drawers; truncated triangular and rectangular wrought-iron ceiling lighting fixtures; heavy oak ceiling beams, ceiling cornice molding, horizontal boarding, and decorated vertical posts; and, in addition to the bookcases, built-in oak furniture such as cabinets, chests of drawers, and sideboards. Instead of functioning like separate units, the interior spaces, differing in texture and light intensity, seem to flow easily together, one to another, much as they do in contemporaneous Prairie-style houses of Frank Lloyd Wright and his disciples. While "Upland Cottage" brought together utility, aesthetics, and economy in the manner of most Craftsman-style houses, it also exuded an up-to-date refinement and sophistication befitting the tastes of its initial owners, Karl and Florence Abbott.[96]

~

The Frank House

1923–24

(Mr. and Mrs. Edgar E. Frank)

Bethlehem

~ ONE OF THE FINEST Colonial Revival–style buildings in northern New Hampshire, the Frank house in Bethlehem has long been shrouded in mystery. Very little is known about the history of "this palatial summer home,"[97] as described in the *White Mountain Echo*. Even less information is available concerning its financiers and first owners. From scattered sources, however, it is possible to partially reconstruct the story of this compelling, almost suburban-style residence, and the people associated with its past.

Originally from Chicago and later from New York City, Mr. and Mrs. Edgar E. Frank initially came to Bethlehem for unknown reasons. In February 1920, they purchased a tract on the south side of Main Street, midway between the center of town and the Maplewood Hotel complex.[98]

The Frank house (1923–24), Bethlehem, N.H. Photograph by the author.

Three years passed before they commenced construction of their house, during which time they visited the community as summer hotel guests. Finally, as reported by the *Echo*, it was "about ready for occupance" in July 1924, "the spacious grounds . . . among the most attractive of any surrounding the many lovely Bethlehem cottages."[99] Supposedly the new house and outbuildings cost the new owners $127,000 to build and furnish, indeed a quite astounding figure for the 1920s. Eager to enjoy their sumptuously appointed new domicile, the Franks immediately moved in. Their stay there, however, was all too brief, for within two months Edgar Frank died unexpectedly. His wife departed promptly thereafter, and though she retained ownership of the property until her death in 1951, neither she nor any other member of her family ever returned. During this twenty-seven-year period, the buildings "stood desolate and neglected, the elegant dwelling boarded up and the grounds allowed to revert to nature." Yet, despite this curious circumstance, the executors of the Frank estate paid an estimated twenty-two thousand dollars in property taxes, before selling to Oscar D. Mann, a Philadelphia businessman, who painstakingly restored the house, adjacent garage/employee living quarters, lawns, and landscaping.[100]

Designed and built by Sylvanus D. Morgan (1857–1940), responsible for numerous other Bethlehem summer residences, the Frank house possesses some of the most pronounced qualities of the Colonial Revival. Covered by a gable roof, framed by stone masonry end chimneys, the main corpus of the building is perfectly symmetrical. The central entranceway is protected by a semicircular open porch supported by four rounded Doric columns. Attached to the east and west ends are non-matching wings with shed-roof dormers, a Morgan trademark. The fenestration is simple six-over-six double sash with finely articulated molding. Cast-iron balustrades, recalling those of Federal-era New England seacoast mansions, may be seen atop the front entrance porch and the flat-roof extension of the west wing.

The wooden tracery of the semielliptical veranda aperture in the east wing also recalls traditional late-eighteenth-and early-nineteenth-century design motifs.[101]

A first-floor plan and detail drawing found in the Morgan house in Lisbon, New Hampshire, provide valuable visual information about the interior, and confirm that Morgan served as architect for the project. Running through the center of the structure in the manner of eighteenth-century Georgian houses, is a wide hallway, high-ceilinged, with a stairway on one side. To the left, facing the rear, is the living room with attached veranda, while to the right are a dining room and card room. Originally, wrought-iron gates were installed on each hallway door frame. The west wing contains a kitchen, serving room, servants' rooms, hallway, and rear porch. On the second floor are bedrooms and baths, with unfinished attic space above. Polished oak paneling and other woodwork, birch floors, facing brick, and stone fireplaces grace these interior spaces. The expensive tastes of the Franks are illustrated by the presence of ornate, imported Czechoslovakian lighting fixtures, and ten thousand dollars worth of Czech beveled-crystal glass panes present in the sun-exposed veranda.[102] Such lavish interior finishing and formal spatial layout are atypical of most summer dwellings in the White Mountain region.

≈

"Adair"

1927–28

(Mr. and Mrs. John W. Guider)

Bethlehem

"Adair" (1927–28), Bethlehem, N.H. Photograph by the author.

≈ IN 1927, THE PROMINENT Washington, D.C., trial lawyer, Frank J. Hogan (1877–1944), in an act of great generosity, acquired land on the west side of Bethlehem, and financed and built a country residence there for his only child, Dorothy Adair Hogan (for whom it was named), and her husband, John W. Guider, also of Washington. The house is maintained in superb condition today as a small inn, its neat, formal appearance

"Front Elevation, Residence Plan for Mr. & Mrs. John Guider, Bethlehem, New Hampshire, C. A. Peck, Archt., April, 1927." Courtesy of Hardy Banfield, Bethlehem.

and quiet pastoral ambience scarcely altered from its early years. Seemingly out of context on its forested, rolling tract, "Adair," however, looks more like an eighteenth-century Connecticut River Valley Georgian mansion than a New Hampshire North Country vacation retreat. Yet, despite its pronounced Colonial Revival design, borrowed from another New England region and era, it maintains a positive and powerful architectural presence, perfectly set on a gradually sloping, partially wooded knoll. This notable aesthetic accomplishment is the product of a collaboration between an obscure engineer/architect, Clifford A. Peck (born c. 1892) of East Haddam and Essex, Connecticut, the world-renowned landscape firm of Olmstead Brothers of Boston, and extremely demanding, but well informed and inventive clients. The story of "Adair," and the distinguished personages associated with it, is one of the most compelling of any of the summer cottages and country estates in the White Mountains.[103]

Although it was Frank Hogan who conceived the idea for this superb rural property, it was John Guider, with significant input from his wife, Dorothy, who determined its ultimate form. Fortunately for modern researchers, there exists comprehensive documentation of both the main house and the surrounding landscaping. In the possession of the current owner is a complete set of blueprint plans, bearing the date, "April, 1927," and the name, "C. A. Peck, Archt."[104] As reflected in these plans, the exterior appearance and interior layout of the house have been little altered since, except for rearrangement in 1963 of the first floor service wing, featuring a new front bay window and sitting room, from designs by New

Hampshire architect Stanley Orcutt.[105] Contained on the interior are sixteen principal rooms: a large basement game room; a first-floor central hallway, spacious living room, sun room, dining room, kitchen, and library; and nine bedrooms on the two floors above. The majority of these rooms are appointed with pine board floors, sheathed beam ceilings, ceiling and baseboard mouldings, and paneled doors. Typical of Georgian-era residences upon which it is modeled, the principal building block is perfectly symmetrical, with a gambrel roof pierced by dormers, matching end chimneys (of stone instead of brick), and a highly articulated classical front double doorway opening into the central hallway extending to a corresponding, but smaller, single rear door. The overall plan is balanced, pleasantly proportioned, and extremely well suited to the purposes of a large family that regularly entertains guests. On clear days, from the east end of the house, there is an outstanding panoramic view toward Mount Washington and the Presidential Range. Near the main house are a swimming pool with cabana, two small ponds, a tennis court, a two-story barn (1953), and a garage with upstairs apartment, recently converted to the owners' cottage.[106]

Housed at the Library of Congress as a part of a large Olmstead Brothers collection of manuscripts, is a valuable group of letters spanning the years 1927 to after 1931 that chronicles the creation of the extensive landscaping gracing the former Guider estate. While the bulk of the correspondence is between John Guider and members of the firm (primarily Percival Gallagher and J. Sloat), there are also letters between the firm and Clifford Peck. These document Peck's continuing close working relationship with Olmstead Brothers, as well as the fact that Peck's initial contact with the Guiders may have originated with the firm's principal partners. According to the letters, the planning of the landscaping commenced in the early fall of 1927, when the house was under construction, and extended into the spring of the following year. During late spring and throughout the summer and fall, the work of planting trees, shrubs, and garden flowers was undertaken in earnest, with the understanding that it would evolve over several years until completed. Simultaneously, the tract was graded, and the roadway and walks laid out, all with Peck's full knowledge and involvement. Curiously, the collection contains no correspondence for 1929, though in earlier letters, the Guiders stated their intention of carrying on the project into the second year. During 1930 and 1931, the Guiders and Olmstead Brothers frequently exchanged letters, which treated the process of continued planting, and the installation of a tennis court, a croquet field, a laundry yard, and a vegetable garden, along with other work items. Peck continued his association with the family and the firm until at least 1931, handling small matters necessitated by the family's distant off-season location in Washington.[107]

Unlike many out-of-state single-season home owners in the White Mountains, John William ("Duke") Guider (1900–1968) had many business and civic interests in New Hampshire, which ultimately led to permanent residence there. Born in Syracuse, New York, Guider received his early education at local parochial schools, and was graduated from the United States Naval Academy in 1922. After a few years as a sales engineer for the Radio Corporation of America in Washington, D.C., he attended Georgetown University Law School, receiving his degree in 1926. Admitted to the District of Columbia bar in that year, he became an associate in the law firm of his father-in-law, Frank J. Hogan, which took the title of Hogan, Donovan, Jones, Hartson, and Guider (later shortened to Hogan and Hartson) when he was promoted to partner. Specializing in communications, libel, and coal law, he remained with the firm until 1942 when he reentered the United States Navy. During World War II, Guider became senior electronics supply officer for both the Bureau of Ships and the Bureau of Supplies and Accounts, departing active service at the rank of captain in 1946.

It was in 1946 that the Guiders committed themselves permanently to New Hampshire, occupying "Adair" much of each year thereafter. John Guider promptly joined the state bar, and launched a second career in the ownership and management of radio and television broadcasting stations in northern New England. From 1952 to 1957 (when he sold the company), he was sole owner, president, and general manager of the White Mountain Broadcasting Company, headquartered in Berlin, New Hampshire. In 1954, he founded stations WMTW-TV and WMTW-FM, with broadcasting towers on the summit of Mount Washington. He served as owner, president, and general manager of the parent Mount Washington Television Company, based at Poland Spring, Maine, from 1954 until the stations were sold in 1966. In addition to his extensive work in communications, he was president of Workshop Cards, designers and manufacturers of greeting cards in Littleton, New Hampshire, from 1946 to 1955. In civic affairs, he was president and trustee of the Littleton Hospital, a trustee of the New Hampshire Catholic Charities, a member of the Rotary Club of Littleton, and a participant in state Republican Party activities. As a consequence of the many personal and professional associations of the Guiders, and Dorothy Guider's parents, the Hogans, "Adair" hosted numerous well-known and highly accomplished guests—national and state political figures; leaders of the legal community; actors and actresses; and sports personalities. The Hogans, often with their cousins, the Byrneses (James F. Byrnes was governor and United States senator from South Carolina, secretary of state under President Franklin D. Roosevelt, and a Supreme Court justice) frequently spent holidays at the estate. The current owners of the house have continued the Guider tradition of regularly hosting friends and acquaintances.[108]

≈

"Highland Croft"

1909–10

(Mr. and Mrs. William B. Dickson)

Littleton

"Highland Croft" (1909–10), Littleton, N.H. Photograph by the author.

∾ IN 1907, WILLIAM DICKSON, a resident of Pittsburgh, Pennsylvania, and Montclair, New Jersey, and first vice president of the United States Steel Company, acquired land in Littleton. This act was regarded as important regional news. In both the *Littleton Courier* and the *White Mountain Echo* (Bethlehem), it was reported that he had purchased the former George Corey Farm on the Waterford Road on the west side of town, "a 100-acre site unusually desirable from a landscape point of view," with a majestic and enchanting prospect of Mount Moosilauke, the Franconia Mountains, and Mount Lafayette.[109] Here, during the fall of 1909 and much of 1910, Dickson and his wife, Mary Bruce, erected "one of the finest bungalows in the White Mountain region, situated on the summit of one of the lofty hills that encompass the village of Littleton." Writing two years after the completion of the cottage, Dickson observed, "We selected this location because of the beautiful scenery and also to escape the enervating heat and humidity of the summer. Our expectations . . . have been fully realized." The Dicksons named their new house "Highland Croft," after the farm upon which it was situated, and took up occupancy in the spring of 1911.[110]

Like many national business leaders of his era, including several with vacation retreats in the White Mountains, William Brown Dickson (1865–1942) was multifaceted in his talents and interests. Born in Pittsburgh, he attended the public schools in Suissvale until 1881 when he went to work as a pulpit boy and crane operator for the Carnegie Steel Company. Over the next fifteen years he served this concern in varying capacities, rose up through the ranks, and in 1897 became a director and assistant to President Charles M. Schwab. When the United States Steel Corporation was organized in 1901, with Schwab as president, Dickson was named second vice president, and in 1909, first vice president. In 1915, due to differences over labor policy with Judge Elbert H. Gary, chairman of the corporation,

Dickson resigned his position, as well as the presidency of a subsidiary firm, Union Steel Company. After four years away from business, he returned to the steel industry in 1915 as one of the organizers, vice president, and treasurer of the Midvale Steel and Ordnance Company, a large manufacturer of munitions for the United States military during World War I. Until he retired in 1923, Dickson was a pioneer among industrial executives in seeking ways to foster better relations between labor and management. In 1911, he was chairman of a new commission in New Jersey which administered one of the first workmen's compensation laws passed by any state in the country. He spoke and wrote on labor and industrial relations, lecturing at Harvard, Wellesley, and elsewhere, and publishing *Democracy in Industry* (1931) and the *History of the Carnegie Veterans Association* (1938). Dickson's outside interests included music, golf, and farming, which he engaged in at "Highland Croft." When in Littleton, he also took an active interest in public affairs, particularly economic development issues, the local Congregational church, as well as singing (he founded the Highland Chorus, which gave concerts in the summers during the 1920s). Although the Dicksons had six children, their Littleton property ultimately passed out of the family after Mary Dickson's death in 1944.[111]

Supposedly costing sixty thousand dollars to build, "Highland Croft" is one of the most interesting of the White Mountains' turn-of-the-century summer cottages. With spacious, free-flowing interior spaces, this efficiently planned and beautifully sited building seems ideally suited for privacy, relaxation, and leisure-time pursuits. The influence of the Craftsman style may be seen in the fieldstone masonry foundation walls and support posts juxtaposed with shingle siding; ample, open piazzas; and deep roof

"Front Elevation, Bungalow for Wm. B. Dickson, Esq., Littleton, N.H., Walker & Chichester, Architects, New York," c. 1909. Courtesy of Joan S. Winton, Littleton.

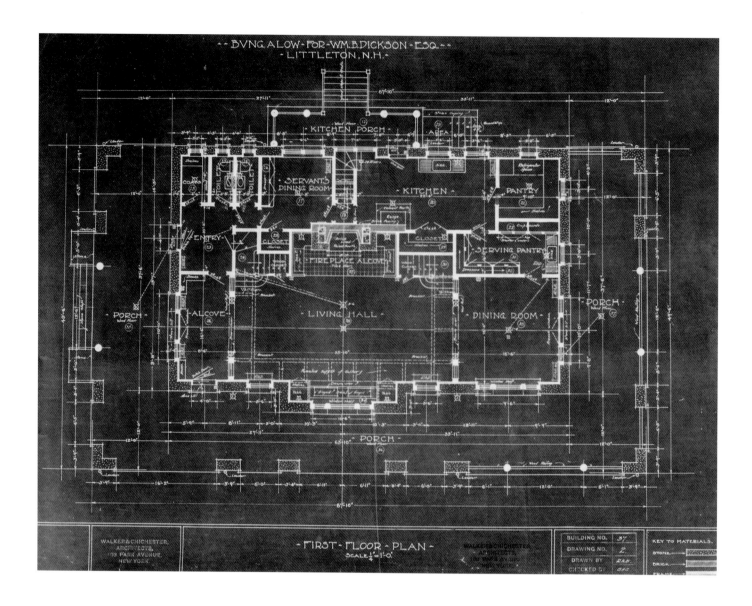

"First Floor Plan, Bungalow for Wm. B. Dickson, Esq., Littleton, N.H., Walker & Chichester, Architects, New York," c. 1909. Courtesy of Joan S. Winton, Littleton.

overhangs with exposed rafter ends. A long, low gambrel roof with large gambrel and flanking shed-roof dormers imitates the forms of the surrounding hill and mountain ridges. The interior is arranged around a voluminous two-story central parlor (see illustration), featuring a large fieldstone fireplace, exposed roof timbers, and a wooden overhanging balcony accessing nine second-floor bedrooms. In addition to the parlor, there are a kitchen, dining room, serving room, pantry, and servants' dining room on the first floor. The articulation of decorative and functional elements is both sophisticated as well as plain and rustic.[112]

"Highland Croft" was the product of a talented architectural team. A set of blueprint drawings in the custody of the current owners bears the inscription "Walker & Chichester," architects at 103 Park Avenue in New York City.[113] The senior of the two men, Harry Leslie Walker (1877–1954), was particularly noted for his ecclesiastical designs, but he also planned other types of buildings and structures, some in Northern New England.

Born in Chicago, he was a student at the Armour Institute of Technology and the Art Institute in his native city, before attending MIT where he received a bachelor's degree in architecture in 1900. After serving two years as a draftsman in architectural offices in Chicago and Atlanta, Georgia, he practiced independently as an architect from 1902 to 1910 in Atlanta, but apparently also maintained a New York City office, and relocated permanently there after 1910. In metropolitan New York, his major commissions included the General Hospital, National Bank, and First Presbyterian Church in Passaic, New Jersey; the Reformed Church, public schools, and the public library in Bronxville; the Christian Herald House in Manhattan; and the Fidelity Title and Trust Company building in Stamford, Connecticut. Walker was active in the American Institute of Architects, the Beaux Arts Institute of Design, the Church Architectural Guild of America, the Architectural League of New York, and in civic affairs in his home town of Bronxville. He had an intellectual interest in his field, authoring articles and lecturing on medieval churches, ecclesiastical symbolism, and early American architecture.[114] It is not readily evident how he became associated with his professional colleague, George H. Chichester (1878–1916), who himself was in independent practice in New York City between around 1909 and 1916. Biographical data on the two men does not indicate that they ever officially formed a firm and it is likely that they simply collaborated on the Dickson house, and possibly other projects.[115]

Interior of "Highland Croft" (1909–10), Littleton, N.H., photograph from *New Hampshire Farms for Summer Homes* (10th ed., 1912), p. 12. Author's collection.

6 ～

Franconia/ Sugar Hill

The town of Franconia in the Gale River Valley, and the neighboring village of Sugar Hill (before 1962 a part of Lisbon), high on the ridge to the south, both saw their economic bases shift from agriculture, iron and charcoal production, and lumbering, to summer tourism and artisanry in the mid- to late-nineteenth century. Between 1852 and 1923, the preeminent grand resort hotel in the western White Mountains, the Profile House, attracted thousands of visitors each summer season to its idyllic Franconia Notch location on the east side of Franconia. It was here in the late 1860s that the hotel cottage concept was first successfully tested in the region, establishing precedent for the privately owned summer residences that would come in subsequent decades. In Franconia village, several miles to the west, several other hotels and boarding houses were erected starting about 1870, with cottages linked directly to the Mount Lafayette House (1882) and the Forest Hills Hotel (1882–83 and after). In the south end of town, oriented more toward the Sugar Hill colony, were the Satchell and Krantz houses, both built for families from Brooklyn, New York.

Impressively situated some sixteen hundred feet above sea level, Sugar Hill profits from its unparalleled sweeping panorama of the mountains from Kinsman Notch to the Northern Peaks of the Presidentials. This lovely elevated community developed slightly later than Franconia as a tourist mecca, but with the arrival of the railroad in nearby Lisbon in the mid-1870s, hotels and summer residences quickly began to appear. Over the next decade, three grand resort hotels—the Goodnow House (later the Franconia Inn) (1875–76 and after), the Sunset Hill House (1879–80 and after), and the Hotel Lookoff (1886–87)—were constructed, followed by several smaller guest establishments, highlighted by the famed Peckett's-on-Sugar-Hill (1906–7 and after). As at other White Mountain resort centers of the era, the presence of the hotels, coupled with improved transportation and changing life-style attitudes, encouraged families, many of whom were former hotel patrons, to invest in their own properties. Along the spine of Sunset Hill, adjacent to the Sunset Hill House, a row of cottages was erected for the Hardens of Boston (1889), the Andrews of New York City (1889–90), the Whites of New Jersey (1891), the Gibbs of Baltimore (1901), and the Wheelers of New York City (1903). Lower down on the east side of the ridge, but enjoying no less spectacular views, are similarly conceived houses built for the Davises of Boston (c. 1891), the Westinghouses of Pittsburgh (c. 1893–94) and the Mallerys of Philadelphia (1916).

"Profile House," engraving from *Summer Saunterings by the B. & L.*, 1st ed. (Boston: Passenger Department, Boston & Lowell Railroad, 1885), p. 82. Author's collection.

Profile House Cottages

1868–1903

Franconia (Franconia Notch)

"Looking Down on the New Profile House and Cottage Colony, Franconia Notch, From Mount Lafayette," photograph from the *White Mountain Echo* 31, no. 5 (8 August 1909): 1. Courtesy of the Appalachian Mountain Club Library, Boston.

◦ UPON VISITING THE Old Man of the Mountain (the Profile) and Franconia Notch State Park today, and viewing the ski area, aerial tramway, recreational buildings, and parking lots, it is difficult to conceive that from the 1850s to the 1920s the valley floor once accommodated one of the oldest and largest grand resort hotel complexes in the United States. Scarcely a trace of this historic and luxurious guest establishment remains. At its height, the Profile House, as the complex was appropriately titled, lodged upwards of six hundred patrons when at full capacity. From its inception in 1852 to the early part of this century, the resort, with the hotel at its center, gradually evolved into a nearly self-sufficient community, constituting a separate world many miles removed from even small village population centers. For visitors to the Profile House, remoteness and close proximity to the mountains and other wild and natural attractions constituted perhaps its principal appeal. For well over half a century, well-heeled and, in many instances, extremely wealthy and socially prominent individuals and families gravitated to the unspoiled, sylvan environment of the Notch, bringing with them a desire for the culture, recreation, cuisine, and social refinements that characterized their lives in American urban centers. In addition, many of these people sought independence, flexibility, and privacy that was not customarily possible in the very public and often quite restrictive existence of the grand resort hotel.[1]

Early in the history of the Profile House, the proprietorship of Taft, Taylor & Greenleaf responded to this need, and began the construction of a series of separate but contiguous guest cottages. From 1868, when the first two were built, to 1904, twenty of these specialized residential buildings appeared in three rows, terraced into the side of Cannon Mountain to the west and south of the main hotel. This cottage group was the largest associated with any hotel in the White Mountains, surpassing in size similar groups at the Maplewood Hotel in Bethlehem, the Waumbek in Jefferson, and Wentworth Hall in Jackson. Unlike those at the other grand resort hotels, the cottages at the Profile House were all privately financed and built

"An Intimate View of the Profile Cottage Colony," photograph from the *White Mountain Echo* 31, no. 7 (22 August 1908): 2. Courtesy of the Appalachian Mountain Club Library, Boston.

Profile House and Cottages floor plans, from booklet, *Profile House* (c. 1890). Author's collection.

on hotel land, with the stipulation that after ten years each must revert by outright sale to the hotel company. The Profile House ownership then had the option to resell or to rent to previous owners or new parties. According to the *White Mountain Echo*, "by this means the cottages . . . kept their exclusive character, . . . [making] them unique in the history of resorts."[2]

The record of the ownership and construction chronology of the Profile House cottages is not well documented, but some salient facts can be substantiated. The initial two, erected for the 1868 season, were owned by William F. Bridge of New York City, and John Kendrick Bangs, the well-known Yonkers, New York, humorist and editor. A third cottage was added in 1882 for David P. Kimball, the Boston philanthropist. By 1890 there were five in the group. In 1896 the sixth was built for J. M. Cornell, the millionaire iron foundryman of New York City. Three more were put up for the summer of 1898, making a total of nine. In 1901 the number reached fourteen, by the addition of three cottages constructed in the spring of that year. The fifteenth was raised in 1901–2, followed by four more in 1902–3. The twentieth and final cottage—the pièce de résistance in the group—was a reduced-scale Colonial Revival interpretation of George Washington's Mount Vernon in Virginia, built in 1903 for Mrs. A. H. Alexander of New York City, the mother of Mrs. Theodore Roosevelt, Jr.[3] Containing ten rooms and "furnished with antique furniture throughout," "Mount

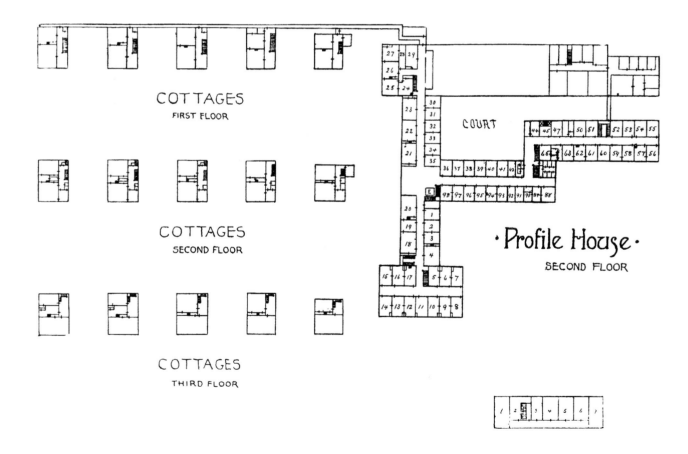

COTTAGES
FIRST FLOOR

COTTAGES
SECOND FLOOR

COTTAGES
THIRD FLOOR

COURT

· Profile House ·
SECOND FLOOR

Vernon Cottage," as it was quite properly termed, was a fitting capstone to the full assemblage.[4] Some of the other cottages were named—"Asyoulikeit," "Rock Ledge," "Trealone," and "Profile"—but most were simply numbered. In 1908, a New Hampshire state publication reported that all twenty cottages were privately owned and regularly occupied every year— "fifteen belong to New Yorkers, three to Bostonians, and the other two to businessmen in Columbus, Ohio, and New Haven, Connecticut."[5]

The Profile House cottages were conceived in varying mid- and late-Victorian eclectic styles, with the Stick and the Colonial Revival influence most in evidence. Most of them were probably not architect-designed, though in a few instances the first owners may have contracted the service of architects from the cities of their origin. It may be safely assumed, however, that all of them were erected by local contractors, with Sylvanus D. Morgan (1857–1940) of Lisbon, the designer and builder of the second or "New" Profile House in 1905 6, the most obvious possibility. Old photographs (see illustrations) of the complex show several cottages of nearly identical appearance in each of the three rows, suggesting that architectural plans were reused. Variation in exterior form occurred in circumstances where owners made alterations (new wings, ells, porches, decorative elements, and so on) in their domiciles, individually tailoring them to meet their tastes and requirements. To protect the residents from the elements, the cottages were connected to each other and to the hotel by covered walkways with red carpeting. These proved to be their fatal flaw, for when the great fire destroyed the second Profile House on 2 August 1923, the flames spread from house to house along the walkway roofs. Not one building in the Profile House complex was left standing after that fateful day in White Mountain history.[6]

⌒

"The Lodge" ("Tudor Cottage")

1889–90 and 1925–26

(Forest Hills Hotel)

Franconia

⌒ FORMERLY CONNECTED WITH the Forest Hills Hotel in Franconia, "The Lodge" enjoys the unique distinction of being the only pre–World War I cottage in the White Mountains to undergo both a nearly total rebuilding and a complete stylistic transformation. Erected in 1889–90 in the Shingle style as a single-family or small-group guest house, it was converted thirty-five years later to an English Tudor Revival-style, single-family residence. It survives today as small inn, the only significant building remaining from the once extensive Forest Hills complex.[7]

Opened for the 1883 summer season by owners Harry W. Priest and James W. Dudley, the Forest Hills Hotel was situated on Pine Hill overlooking Franconia village, with magnificent vistas across the Gale River Valley onto the Franconia Mountains. In its initial Victorian eclectic incarnation, the main hostelry achieved instant popularity; it featured the latest technological advances, beautifully maintained grounds, and a full range of

"Forest Hills House, Franconia, N.H.," cabinet view no. 48 by C. P. Hibbard, photographer, Lisbon, N.H. Reproduced courtesy of the photograph's owner, the Sugar Hill Historical Museum, Sugar Hill, N.H.

recreational and social options. At first the hotel accommodated 150 patrons. In recognition of the growing demand, as well as the competition posed by other regional resort hotels, by 1910 the Forest Hills also boasted several guest cottages. In addition to "The Lodge," the first of these, Priest and Dudley built two more in 1891, one of which, "The Log Cabin," was constructed of six-inch spruce logs in order to simulate early American frontier vernacular architecture. Under a new owner, Herbert Hunt, "Herbert Cottage," a simple rustic bungalow, appeared in 1902, followed by the "Farm-House" cottage, a remodeled older dwelling, in 1908. Although the hotel was later enlarged to 250 guest spaces, the cottage-building phase essentially ended with the Hunt proprietorship.[8]

Of the Forest Hills Hotel cottage group, "The Lodge" is the most important architecturally and historically. Opened for the 1890 summer season, it was built for year-round use, a departure for hotel-related cottages in the White Mountains. The 1894 guidebook, *The Great Resorts of America*, contains an advertisement promoting the building for the winter season:

> ["The Lodge"] . . . is the best appointed house in the White Mountains. Rooms are heated by open fire and furnace, and can be made comfortable in any weather. The piazza is enclosed in glass in winter. One finds here large, comfortable sleighs built expressly for "The Lodge," an abundance of fur and wool robes, toboggan suits, leather and duck jackets, wool leggings, arctics, snow shoes, skates, toboggans, double runners, fire-arms, fox-hounds, guides and game. . . . Victims of the grip and protracted colds, find relief and cure in the dry and bracing atmosphere of our Northern winter.[9]

"The Lodge, Forest Hills Hotel, Franconia, In Winter," photograph from *White Mountain Life* 1, no. 10 (2 September 1897). Courtesy of the Dartmouth College Library, Hanover.

"The Lodge" (1925–26), Forest Hills Hotel, Franconia, N.H. Photograph by the author.

Evidence of the "off-season" orientation of "The Lodge" could be seen in the unusually tall brick chimneys, rising high above the steep-pitched gambrel roof and servicing the fireplaces and furnace inside. Typical of the Shingle style, the cottage was snugly wrapped in natural-wood shingles, flared at the foundation and first-story levels, and encasing the front veranda piers. Ample sun exposure, and, consequently, daytime warmth, was provided on the main south-facing elevation with its veranda, two-story corner bay, and hipped-roof dormers. Neat and compact in appearance, "The Lodge" was a fine representative example of its style, consistent with the plain, functional design tradition of its region.[10]

The metamorphosis of "The Lodge" to its modern form came at the instigation of Bethlehem hotelman Karl P. Abbott (see "Upland Cottage," Bethlehem), who formed a syndicate and bought the entire Forest Hills Hotel property in 1918. For several years, he continued to live in Bethlehem, until the tragic death of his wife, Florence, prompted him to relocate closer to his place of work. Desiring a new summer house near the hotel, and a residence for his children and a new bride, Abbott decided to adapt "The Lodge" to fit his needs. Possibly employing Sylvanus D. Morgan (1857–1940), the builder of his Bethlehem cottage, as contractor in 1925–26, Abbott had the structure disassembled down to its foundation level, and rebuilt on the same site along the lines of "The Lodge," but smaller in scale and markedly different in style.[11] At the time of its completion, the *White Mountain Echo* succinctly characterized the new building as "the most delightful of half timber and stucco houses in Elizabethan style." Though smaller than its predecessor, "Tudor Cottage," as the house has since been called, is larger than it seems, containing generous public spaces on the first floor, and six bedrooms, baths, and closets on the two attic floors above. Repeated from "The Lodge" on the front elevation are the veranda with steep-sloping roof, and the dormers, the southwest one reproducing the upper portion of the former two-story bay. Of a "modern" design for the 1920s, "Tudor Cottage" met the needs of the young Abbott family, and provided the White Mountain region with a provocative addition to its twentieth-century residential repertoire.[12]

❧

"Gale Cottage"

1890

(Dr. William C. Prime)

Franconia

❧ THE 12 JULY 1890 ISSUE of the tourist newspaper the *White Mountain Echo* contains a superb, detailed description of "Gale Cottage," which was then under construction for William C. Prime, the esteemed author, journalist, art historian, and world traveler from New York City:

a beautiful cottage on the banks of the Gale River, northwest of the Mt. Lafayette House [hotel], Franconia, is now nearing completion. It is particularly remarkable for its massiveness and solidity. The [two] big [end] chimneys have

"Gale Cottage" (1890), Franconia, N.H. Photograph by the author.

consumed in their erection 21,000 bricks. Its piazzas encircling the [two-and-one-half-story, gable-roof] house are twelve feet deep and have their roofs supported by heavy pillars through which run iron rods, firmly connecting the plates and sills. The walls are twelve inches thick and finished inside with ornamental panels. The floors are equally solid, while the stairs besides, being durable, are handsome in appearance. Two spacious fire-places down stairs, and two upstairs, some of them decorated with ornamental tiling, are strong reminders of the hearths of old so much referred to in song and story. A covered walk two hundred feet long connecting the cottage with the Mt. Lafayette House, and a *porte-cochere* are among the external arrangements.[13]

While it lacked distinctive stylistic traits, this "quaint rustic structure" was for its time one of the most imaginatively planned and substantially built summer residences in the White Mountain region. Subject to only minor alterations in over a century of use, "Gale Cottage" is owned and maintained today by Prime's descendants.[14]

Born at Cambridge, New York, William Cowper Prime (1825–1905) was a man of remarkable accomplishment and versatility, with an honored place in the literary history of the White Mountains. Receiving his early education under the direction of his father, a secondary school headmaster, young Prime was graduated from the College of New Jersey (Princeton University) in 1843. He then studied law, gained admission to the New York bar in 1846, and practiced his profession in New York City until 1861. In that year, he turned from law to journalism, becoming part owner and editor in chief of the *New York Journal of Commerce* and president of the Associated Press. Stepping down from these positions in 1869, he turned his attention to numismatics, art collecting, and the history of book illustration, amassing a significant library of early illustrated books and medieval woodcuts. Prime and his wife, Mary Trumbull (whom he married in

1851), shared a passion for old porcelain and assembled a fine collection documenting the history of pottery. He possessed an active interest in the Metropolitan Museum of Art from its founding in 1870, holding for many years the positions of trustee and vice president. Through his efforts, the governing board at Princeton established an art history department, and in 1884 Prime was summoned as professor and chair. Over a period of fifty years, he published numerous books, including *Owl Creek Letters* (1848); *The Old House by the River* (1853); *Later Years* (1854); *The Holy Cross* (1877) after a visit to the Near East; *Boat Life in Egypt and Nubia* (1857) and *Tent Life in the Holy Land* (1855), reflecting his interest in biblical studies; *Coins, Medals and Seals, Ancient and Modern* (1860); *Pottery and Porcelain of All Times and Nations* (1878); and *McClellan's Own Story* (1886), which he edited and for which he wrote a short accompanying biography. Prime also wrote three vacation books pertaining to New England: *I Go A-Fishing* (1873), based on his fishing experiences at Lonesome Lake and other favorite haunts in or near Franconia Notch; *Along New England Roads* (1892); and *Among the Northern Hills* (1895).[15]

Prime's long connection with the White Mountains dates from his first visit in the early 1850s. Blessed with the resources necessary to spend time as a man of leisure, he and his wife came to the Profile House in Franconia Notch in the 1860s, occupying a suite of rooms, and actively participating in the social and recreational life of the resort hotel. Prime's favorite outdoor pursuit was trout fishing, which he carried on in the lakes and streams of the Notch, and, beginning in 1876, high up the side of Cannon Mountain, at Lonesome Lake. In that year, Prime and his fishing companion William Bridges purchased the lake and surrounding land, built a cabin there, and established a remote retreat. After his wife's death in 1877, he continued to come to the Notch each summer, and ultimately was joined there regularly by his sister-in-law, Annie Trumbull Slossen, the author and entomologist, after her husband passed away.[16] Between 1876 and 1895, Prime made a series of land purchases in Franconia, including the acquisition of the land for "Gale Cottage" in 1889.[17] The next year (or soon thereafter), as the house was under construction, Slossen purchased the Mt. Lafayette House, which explains the covered walkway link with "Gale Cottage" alluded to in the 1890 *White Mountain Echo* quotation above. During this period, she, Prime, and their mutual friend, the noted naturalist Bradford Torrey, often shared the cottage, taking excursions in the nearby forests and open fields.[18] Prime maintained his lengthy love affair with the White Mountains until 1904, when, discouraged over man's increasingly damaging impact on the environment, he declared that it would be his last summer. This proved to be a prophetic statement, for he died during the winter of 1905, leaving as his legacy his many literary creations, his collections, his influence as a teacher, and his unusual North Country vacation abode.[19]

≈

Sunset Hill House Cottages

1889–99

Sugar Hill

Sunset Hill House, Sugar Hill, N.H. Photograph, 1973, by the author.

~ ARRANGED IN A north-south line along the sixteen-hundred-foot crest of Sunset Hill in Sugar Hill is a row of four year-round houses, commanding unparalleled views of the Franconia Mountains, the Presidential Range, and Mount Washington to the east and north. Early in this century, three of these formed the major portion of the small summer cottage colony associated with the Sunset Hill House, formerly one of Sugar Hill's three grand resort hotels. The fourth cottage was destroyed by fire around 1980, but its modern replacement does not detract unduly from the fine overall aesthetic impression created by the group. Until the 1950s, when it was demolished, "The Bungalow," originally owned by the Andrews family, extended the row to the north along the full backbone of the ridge. Certainly, no surviving collection of cottages in the White Mountains possesses the natural advantages of the magnificent Sunset Hill site.[20]

Until it was torn down in 1973–74, the massive Sunset Hill House was the physical, social, and recreational raison d'être for the cottages. Erected in 1879, with space for 125 guests, it opened the following season under the managing ownership of Henry H. Bowles and Seth F. Hoskins of Lisbon. Over the next two decades, the new hotel experienced financial success, calling for numerous expansions or new auxiliary buildings, so that by 1903, it was able to accommodate 325 patrons. In the late 1880s, Bowles and Hoskins responded to the desire by some guests for more spacious and independent quarters. They began to sell off small parcels of land to the north and rear of the complex for the construction of several privately owned, single-family summer cottages. In doing so, they presumed that

"Glamorgan" (1889), Sunset Hill House, Sugar Hill, N.H. Cabinet view by Bessie F. Nickerson, Sugar Hill, 1889. Author's collection.

the new owners, in most cases former visitors to the hotel, would continue to participate actively in resort life.[21]

The first of these cottages, at the north end of the row, was erected in 1889 for Mr. and Mrs. Joseph Bradford Harden of Jamaica Plain, Boston. Joseph Harden was a businessman, associated with the Boston firm of C. A. Browning and Company. Christened "Glamorgan" by the family, this tall, pitched-roof, wood-frame and clapboard house is set back from the road, with a broad lawn in front. Initially painted red (it is now white), the building presents a perfectly symmetrical front facade, dominated by a large central pitched-roof dormer, and a wraparound veranda supported by paired square posts and encircled by a balustrade.[22] Nineteenth-century views of "Glamorgan" show a central front stairway rising to a pitched-roof, oblong entrance aperture, but these features no longer exist. Also absent are certain small window openings, and the original stepped caps of the brick chimneys. Soon after the cottage's completion, the *White Mountain Echo* quite accurately regarded the Harden cottage to be "an ornament to the vicinity, . . . the forerunner of many similar summer residences in that delightful district."[23]

The cottage built next was "Lindhurst," for Mr. and Mrs. Hugh White Adams of Elizabeth, New Jersey, and later of Yonkers, New York.[24] Hugh Adams was considered to be "one of the largest iron dealers in the country."[25] The house was erected in 1891 just to the south of "Glamorgan," on land acquired from Bowles and Hoskins the previous fall.[26] Attempting to top the compliments paid the Harden house, the editors of the *Echo* characterized "Lindhurst" as "the handsomest summer residence anywhere in the neighborhood."[27] Unlike "Glamorgan," which was stylistically rather bland, the Adams cottage, as it originally appeared, displayed a fertile and well-integrated combination of Shingle and Colonial Revival elements, drawn from a variety of sources. Although the house has been modernized and slightly enlarged in recent years, it still possesses a few of these first fea-

"Lindhurst" (1891), Sunset Hill House, Sugar Hill, N.H. Photograph by Rev. Samuel Stickney Nickerson. Reproduced courtesy of the photograph's owner, the Sugar Hill Historical Museum, Sugar Hill, N.H.

tures. Certainly there is no mistaking the sweeping gable roof planes, triangular dormers, and shingle wall sheathing of the Shingle. Most of the Colonial Revival adornment is gone, but old photographs reveal a building rich in classical ornament from that vernacular. Most notable were heavy eaves molding and entablatures; rounded, tapered Doric porch columns; rounded and flat pilasters flanking the three front dormer windows; and balustrades with molded balusters and rounded Doric column posts (topped by urns) atop the one-story wings, ell, and two of the three front dormers. The house was probably designed by a professional architect, but no sources have yet surfaced upon which to base an attribution. Sylvanus D. Morgan (1857–1940) of Lisbon is identified as the builder in newspaper sources.[28]

The next cottage in the group, "The Pavilion," was originally in perfect alignment with the others, but in recent years has been moved forward toward the road, enlarged, and modernized. It is closest to the site of the Sunset Hill House, and its former tennis courts. Built in 1895 by the hotel as a small recreation and social facility, it was converted to a six-room cottage in 1899, and may have been sold to private owners after 1905.[29] It is believed that the first to hold title after the hotel could have been Mrs. A. E. F. White of Detroit, who, with members of the Stoepel family from Albion, Michigan, was the first to rent it after the conversion.[30] Still quaint and well-kept, "The Pavilion" does not look markedly different today than in hotel photographs dating from around 1900 to 1910. A south side entrance porch has replaced paired front (east) stairways, square columns have supplanted turned porch columns, and a wooden balustrade has superseded iron cresting on the truncated, concave hipped roof. Otherwise, the little building is wholly intact, still conveying an Oriental flavor.[31]

The last cottage built was "Allbreeze," like "Lindhurst" an effective, though very different amalgam of the Shingle and Colonial Revival styles,

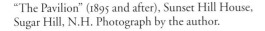

"The Pavilion" (1895 and after), Sunset Hill House, Sugar Hill, N.H. Photograph by the author.

"Allbreeze" (1903), Sunset Hill House, Sugar Hill, N.H. Photograph by Rev. Samuel Stickney Nickerson. Reproduced courtesy of the photograph's owner, the Sugar Hill Historical Museum, Sugar Hill, N.H.

so much in vogue around the turn of the century. It was erected in spring 1903 for Mr. and Mrs. Albert H. Wheeler of New York City, and Mamaroneck, West Chester County, New York. Albert Wheeler was a successful stockbroker in the city and a member of the New York Stock Exchange.[32] In the words of the *White Mountain Echo*, the Wheeler cottage had "all the earmarks of a very comfortable country club building," surely a "new and modern structure." The *Echo* went on to say:

> The house is a symphony in gray [shingle siding] and with its low French windows, stone work and big gable in the center is a model in harmony. The ground floor [interior] is done in Flemish oak finishings, while the upper story is in white enamel.[33]

Unlike the somewhat older cottages on either side, "Allbreeze" perfectly melded with the landscape. A strong sense of horizontality was conveyed by its low sweeping main and secondary roofs, its roof cornices, and its front (east) veranda, enclosed by a balustrade, regularly broken by round, tapered Doric support columns. This house also was more than likely the creation of a professional architect, possibly from the New York City area.

~

"The Bungalow"

1889–90

(Mr. and Mrs. James F. Andrews)

"The Bungalette"

1901

(Mr. and Mrs. Rufus M. Gibbs)

Sugar Hill

"The Bungalow" (1889–90), Sugar Hill, N.H. Photograph by Rev. Samuel Stickney Nickerson. Reproduced courtesy of the photograph's owner, the Sugar Hill Historical Museum, Sugar Hill, N.H.

~ ERECTED IN 1889–90 on Sunset Hill, slightly north of the Sunset Hill House cottages, "The Bungalow" was long regarded as Sugar Hill's most unusual cottage (it was torn down in the 1950s).[34] Two stories high, with double-tiered encircling porches and a dual-pitched hipped roof, it closely resembled French Colonial houses built in rural Louisiana in the late eighteenth and early nineteenth centuries. While the southern influence in the design of "The Bungalow" was pronounced, the house func-

"The Bungalette" (1901), Sugar Hill, N.H. Photograph by the author.

tioned extremely well in its northern mountain setting. On all four sides, large doors and windows were focused outward to take full advantage of the magnificent surrounding vistas. The ample porches encouraged outdoor leisure and recreation. A curious vestige of the then fashionable Shingle style was present in the eyebrow dormer windows centered on the front and rear roof planes. Otherwise the house was as pure an example of French Colonial Revival architecture as could be found anywhere in the United States at the time.

"The Bungalow" was built for Mr. and Mrs. James Frederic Andrews of New York City. Until his retirement in 1907, James Andrews (c. 1847–1915) was a member of the New York Stock Exchange, and a successful stockbroker with the firm of J. M. Noyes & Company in the city. His outside activities included memberships in the Masons, the Bridgeport (Connecticut) Country Club, and the Lotus, New York Athletic, Manhattan, and Colonial clubs. The Andrews had three children, a son and two daughters. It was for one of the daughters, Cornelia, that James Andrews financed and constructed "The Bungalette" in 1901 soon after her marriage to Rufus MacQueen Gibbs (1871–1916) of Baltimore, a native of New Orleans.[35]

A graduate of St. Paul's School (Concord, New Hampshire) and Yale (class of 1893), Gibbs succeeded his father, Major John Sears Gibbs, in 1902 as the president of the Gibbs Preserving Company, one of the largest business enterprises in Baltimore. Professionally prominent in the city, he served as president of both the Baltimore Canned Goods Exchange and the Board of Trade, a director of the Maryland Trust Company and the Maryland Casualty Company, a trustee of the Maryland School for Boys, and a member of the Maryland League for National Defense when it was formed in 1914. Like his father-in-law, he was a club man, belonging to the Baltimore, the Maryland, and the Baltimore Country clubs. He also found time to contribute to his church, Christ Protestant and Episcopal, where he was a vestryman, and organized a young men's group. After his premature death, his wife and children continued to occupy the Sugar Hill cottage during the summers until the 1940s.[36]

Positioned a hundred feet to the north of "The Bungalow," "The Bungalette" is an exact duplicate of the upper half of its predecessor. It almost appears as if the top section of the Andrews house were simply sliced from the main body of the building to create the Gibbs cottage. Only the placement of the chimneys differs. Documents preserved at the Grafton County Registry of Deeds indicate that in 1907, James Andrews, soon after the death of his wife, Harriet, transferred ownership of "The Bungalette," adjacent lands, and water rights to Rufus Gibbs and his young family.[37]

~

"Wayside Lodge"

c. 1891

(Mr. Isaac H. Davis)

"Westinghouse"

c. 1893–94

(Mr. and Mrs. Henry H. Westinghouse)

Sugar Hill

"Wayside Lodge" (c. 1891 and after), Sugar Hill, N.H. Photograph by the author.

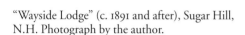

∽ BUILT ABOUT the same time and situated opposite each other on Birches (formerly Davis) Road, the Davis and Westinghouse cottages are linked historically, and are the product of the same regional naturalistic building tradition. Their origins date from 1890 when Isaac H. Davis of Boston, otherwise unidentified, made his initial Sugar Hill (then part of Lisbon) land acquisition from Anson Whipple, a local resident. Simultaneously, he secured water rights from David Hildreth, whose land abutted the Whipple tract and farmstead. In 1892–93, Davis significantly augmented these purchases, buying a half dozen other pieces of land nearby, as well as elsewhere in Sugar Hill. About 1891, on the former Whipple farm, Davis constructed a summer cottage, which exists today, in only slightly altered form, as part of a somewhat larger year-round house.[38]

Commanding one of the best area views of the Franconia and Presidential ranges, "Wayside Lodge," as Davis named his new house, was (and still is) attractive and well proportioned, but plain and functional. What it may have lacked in high architectural styling, however, it more than compensated for with its provocative asymmetrical elevations, combining wall and roof shingle sheathing, and fieldstone foundations, wall piers, and chimneys. This aesthetically compelling use of building materials indigenous to the region ultimately caught the attention of editors of the nationally circulated *Ladies Home Journal*, which designated the house a prize winner for design in the May 1899 issue. A decade later in 1909, "Wayside Lodge" was illustrated in one of the volumes of the *Cyclopedia of Architecture, Carpentry and Building*, undoubtedly because of the presence of Hermann Valentin von Holst, architect for the Glessners and Macbeths in neighboring Bethlehem (see "The Rocks" estate" and "The Glamis"), on its editorial board. A friend of the Glessners, von Holst was a guest at their country estate, likely knew of and saw the Davis cottage, and incorporated into his building plans for "The Rocks" (1902–7) and the Macbeth residence (1904–5) materials and features similar to those of "Wayside Lodge."[39]

While the Davis cottage has received recognition for its siting and planning, the nature of its construction and the random arrangement of the interior rooms suggest that it was not designed by a professional architect. Nonetheless, the still unknown contractor (the probable designer) deserves credit for creatively borrowing general qualities and specific elements from several architectural styles and melding them into a coherent whole. From the Shingle style vocabulary one may observe sweeping, low-pitched roofs, latticework, and the liberal use of shingles on all surfaces. The unfinished tree-trunk porch and veranda posts, and the fieldstone masonry chimneys, foundations, and wall piers are reminiscent of the rusticated version of the Craftsman vernacular. Oblong and modified Palladian windows and a classical veranda balustrade add a Colonial Revival flavor to the irregular-shaped building mass. The second owners, Eben M. and Mary Alice Taylor, enlarged the house, but preserved its original visual integrity after purchasing it around 1900. In 1984–86, the owners razed, but sympathetically and meticulously reconstructed the south end so that it appears much as it did seventy-five years ago.[40]

Whereas Isaac Davis was a relative unknown, and little if anything has been published about him, his neighbor Henry H. Westinghouse (1853–1933) possessed a last name that is synonymous with the history of American mechanical invention and electrical technology. The little brother of the inventor and manufacturer George Westinghouse, an American icon, he had an established reputation in his own right. Born in Central Bridge, New York, Henry Westinghouse graduated from high school in Schenectady, and studied mechanical engineering at Cornell University in 1871–72. He then joined the Westinghouse Air Brake Company, with which he was associated his entire working career. He eventually became chairman of the board of this corporation as well as Canadian Westinghouse, Ltd., and was

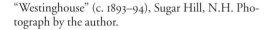
"Westinghouse" (c. 1893–94), Sugar Hill, N.H. Photograph by the author.

a director of Westinghouse Electric and Manufacturing Company, Westinghouse Brake and Saxby Company, Ltd., in London, and Compagnie des Freins Westinghouse in Paris. In 1883, he invented the famed Westinghouse single-acting steam engine. Two years later he founded the New York City engineering firm of Westinghouse, Church, Kerr & Company, though he maintained residence in Pittsburgh. During his life he was a member of the American Society of Mechanical Engineers and the American Academy of Political and Social Science, a fellow of the American Academy of Arts and Sciences, and a trustee of Cornell University. Westinghouse may have become attracted to New Hampshire through his wife, Clara Saltmarsh, who had relatives in the state.[41]

Between April 1893 and May 1894, the Westinghouses made a series of land purchases from Isaac Davis, most of which were opposite "Wayside Lodge" on or near Davis Road. Here, on a grassy knoll with outstanding vistas, they erected their new cottage, and, using their last name to suitable advantage, christened it "Westinghouse."[42] "Westinghouse" uses the same building materials and possesses many of the same design features as "Wayside Lodge," except that it has a much heavier and bulkier appearance. This is the result of the square floor plan, high gambrel main roof, cumbersome front three-window dormer, and southwest corner half-octagonal, two-story bay. In particular, the selection and arrangement of materials, closely mimicking "Wayside Lodge," strongly suggests the possibility that the two cottages may have had the same builder. The Westinghouses vacationed at Sugar Hill for only a few years, ultimately departing for Lenox, Massachusetts, where George Westinghouse was a prominent member of the summer colony. In 1908 the house passed to the Wintherbothams of Chicago, who married into the Poole family, still part of the Sugar Hill summer colony.[43]

~

"Funfield"

1916

(Mr. Otto T. Mallery)

Sugar Hill

~ WHILE A STUDENT at Princeton University, Philadelphian Otto T. Mallery, later to become a distinguished economist, met Ernest Poole, a fellow member of the class of 1902. Poole and his family were regular Sugar Hill summer residents; he had a great affection for the White Mountain region, which he shared with Mallery, and ultimately expressed in his writings, most notably his widely popular *The Great White Hills of New Hampshire* (1946). Responding to his classmate's urgings, Mallery visited Sugar Hill on several occasions over a number of years, staying at the Sunset Hill House hotel, and possibly with the Poole family.[44] Ultimately, in 1915 and 1916, Mallery purchased two parcels of land, totaling forty acres and water rights, from Bowles and Hoskins Company, the proprietors of the Sunset Hill House, and other local property owners. Bounded by Aldrich (later Carpenter) and Birches roads, and tracts owned by William E. Satchel and

"Funfield" (1916), Sugar Hill, N.H. Photograph by the author.

the Bowles family, this mixture of pasture and wood lots commanded a magnificent panorama of the Franconia Mountains and the Lafayette Range. This fact had been recognized some years before when a small hotel, the Old Mountain House, had occupied the site, only to be destroyed by fire. Seeing the same potential as the former hotel owners, Mallery laid plans to construct his new vacation retreat on the foundations of the old historic structure. Endowed with the name "Funfield," the Mallery house was constructed in 1916, and was first occupied by family members the following summer.[45]

For his architect, Mr. Mallery selected John Graham, Jr. (1888–1957), also a Philadelphia native, and a personal friend through membership in the Franklin Inn Club and other common interests. Born in Camden, New Jersey, Graham graduated from Chestnut Hill Academy in Philadelphia, and received his bachelor's degree in architecture in 1911 from the University of Pennsylvania. From 1911 to 1916, he worked for two Philadelphia firms, launching a brief independent practice in 1916, during which period he apparently prepared the plans for "Funfield." This phase in his professional life, however, was interrupted by World War I, in which he served the United States Army as Captain of Engineers from 1917 to 1919. Upon returning home he became part of the firm of Thomas, Martin, Kirkpatrick & Graham for two years, moving to the firm of Folsom, Stanton & Graham in 1921. Records indicate that by 1930 Graham had returned to independent practice. In 1938 he relocated to Washington, D.C., to join the staff of the United States Housing Authority as a project planner for new public housing. During World War II he served as a technical advisor for defense and war housing, but retired from public service in 1945 to return to private practice. At the time of his death, he was associated with James M. McHugh of Arlington, Virginia. An occasional foreign traveler, he devoted one of his trips to studying residential architecture, which resulted in his 1940 book, *Housing in Scandinavia*. Virtually all of Graham's independent work between 1911 and 1930 consisted of designs for houses, garages, and other related outbuildings in or near Philadelphia. While residing in the city, he also belonged to The Athenaeum, the Franklin Institute, the T-Square Club, the Philadelphia Cricket Club, and the University of Pennsylvania Architectural Society. During his career he maintained ties with Otto Mallery, and periodically visited the family at Sugar Hill.[46]

Graham's imaginative house design for the Mallerys integrates features of the then still fashionable Craftsman style with elements of his own conception. Consequently, "Funfield" is like no other summer residence in the White Mountain region. Particularly striking and unusual are the bowed, steep-pitched, intersecting roofs, with their truncated gable ends, and their recessed second-story balconies. According to the family sources, Mallery convinced Graham of the aesthetic virtues of the curved-roof configura-

Stable and garage, "Funfield" (1916), Sugar Hill, N.H. Photograph by the author.

"Music Box" (1919), "Funfield" (1916), Sugar Hill, N.H. Photograph by the author.

tions, intended to echo the silhouetted forms of the nearby mountains. Present from the Craftsman idiom are native mortared fieldstone walls and chimneys (contrasting with second-story clapboard siding), exposed and ornamented second-story floor joists, variegated window glazing, and square recessed balcony support posts linked by flat, saw-cut balustrade sections. The interior rooms are spacious, handsomely appointed, and well lit by natural illumination. Both inside and outside are excellent examples of panel tile work, installed by Joseph Allen of the famed Enfield Pottery Works of Whitemarsh, Pennsylvania.[47] Although it is flamboyant in style and rich in embellishment, "Funfield" seems quite in harmony with the surrounding wooded, rolling countryside.

Adjacent to the main house are four other dependent, but important outbuildings. The oldest and largest of these, also designed by Graham, was built in 1916 as a garage/stable/carriage house. Viewed from the entrance drive, one is immediately impressed by its perfect symmetry, paneled entrance doors, and ponderous bellcast roof topped at its center by an octagonal cupola, the bellcast cap repeating the main roof form. To the southwest of the house, a couple of hundred yards down the hillside, is the "Music Box," a quaint, one-room music and social facility constructed in 1919 from plans by the internationally renowned French-American architect Paul Philippe Cret (1876–1945) of Philadelphia. In 1926, the New York City architectural firm of (Charles) Rich and (Frederick) Mathesius designed a small writing retreat on the estate for Mallery, which the family called the "Log Cabin." Rich (1855–1943) was well known in New Hampshire, serving as the official architect for Dartmouth College, and drafting plans for twenty campus buildings. The fourth outbuilding, named "The Flower Pot," is a "kit" house, built in 1930 from standardized plans by E. F. Hodgson Company of Boston and New York City. Intended as an artist's studio for Mallery's daughter, Rosemary J., it was blown down in the great hurricane of 1938, only to have the pieces picked up and reassembled on another site nearer the main house.[48]

The man behind the creation of "Funfield," Otto Todd Mallery (1881–1956), was remarkably accomplished professionally, and extremely active in a variety of organizations and endeavors. Upon reviewing his biographical sketches, it is difficult to conceive how he had time to plan the Sugar Hill estate, and spend generous amounts of summer time there. Born at Willets Point, New York, he prepared for college at The Hill School before attending Princeton. After receiving his undergraduate degree, he did postgraduate work in economics and sociology at the University of Pennsylvania and Columbia University. He commenced his career in 1903 as a bond broker, but finding social and political science more to his liking, in 1908 he assumed the position of field secretary for the former Philadelphia Playgrounds Association, continuing with this organization as treasurer (1918–25) and president (1925–48). In this capacity, Mallery fostered the development of municipal playgrounds in the city, and served as an officer of both the Philadelphia Public Playgrounds Commission and the Philadelphia

Board of Recreation. A national figure in the field of parks, playgrounds, and recreation, he was a director of the Playground and Recreation Association of America (later the National Recreation Association), president after 1937, and chairman of the board from after 1950 until his death. Mallery had a related concern for the elderly, and helped to establish the Golden Age Clubs in Philadelphia. The Otto Mallery Recreation Center in Germantown, Philadelphia, was dedicated in his honor in 1946.

Mallery's civic and governmental activities comprise a list so extensive that they pose a challenge even to summarize briefly. During the 1920s and 1930s, he was a member of conferences on unemployment under three presidents, promoting the idea of federal, state, and local public works projects. In the pre-Depression years, his many positions included the presidency of the Public Education Association of Philadelphia (1911–14), staff member in the secretary of war's office as chief of the federal aid and works section (1919), executive secretary of the Pennsylvania Emergency Public Works Commission (1917–23), and other assignments with offices of the United States government. During the Depression, Mallery continued his sterling record of public service, both in the state of Pennsylvania and on the national level, which included work for the National Resources Planning Board, the National Youth Administration, and the Pennsylvania State Planning Board. From 1953 to 1956 he was the chair of the Interdependence Council, of which he was the founder and the major supporter. An authority on stabilization of unemployment through planned public works, he published a number of works on the subject, and cosponsored federal legislation in 1931. He was a trustee of American University, Washington, D.C., and the American Academy of Political and Social Sciences. His outside interests numbered music, forestry, tennis, and golf. In New Hampshire, he belonged to the Profile Golf Club in Franconia (formerly the Profile House course) along with many of his Sugar Hill neighbors. His first wife, Rosamond R., whom he married in 1910, died in 1915, leaving him to supervise the "Funfield" project on his own. He married his second wife, Louise M., in 1918. He had two children by each marriage, and his descendants continue to enjoy and care for "Funfield" today.[49]

7 ∾

Campton/Waterville

Despite its scenic beauty and accessibility from Boston and other eastern seaboard cities, the Pemigewassett River Valley on the west side of the White Mountains did not experience summer resort development to the same degree as the communities north of Franconia Notch, or in the Eastern Slope region. The primary tourist center, North Woodstock, boasted two major hotels—the Deer Park (1886–87) and Alpine House (1890–91 and after)—but much smaller hotels, inns, and boarding houses originated in the valley communities of Woodstock, Thornton, Campton, and Plymouth to the south. The few single-season cottages that were built in these towns were for the most part privately financed and owned, and were modest in size and architecturally undistinguished. Notable exceptions were the intriguing residences designed by artist F. Schuyler Mathews for his family and relatives at Blair's in West Campton.

In Waterville Valley, at the headwaters of the Mad River tributary of the Pemigewassett, the most extensive cottage assemblage in the region formed in the vicinity of the Waterville Inn (1867–68). Certain of these structures combine late-Victorian eclectic styling with rustic simplicity in a manner characteristic of so many White Mountain cottages built before the turn of the century.

Blair's Colony Cottages

c. 1884–c. 1903

West Campton

"El Fureidis" (first, c. 1883–84), Blair's Colony, West Campton, N.H. Photograph courtesy of Carol Newcomb, West Campton, N.H.

∾ ON THE WEST SIDE of the White Mountains, the Pemigewasset River Valley featured a small number of modest summer cottages constructed prior to 1930. By far the most aesthetically appealing as well as historically important of the group were those designed by the talented author and illustrator F. Schuyler Mathews at "Blair's Colony" in the vicinity of Blair's Hotel (c. 1840) in West Campton, for himself, his immediate family, and others. Simple in form, but well built and creatively embellished, these three single-season wood-frame, shingle and clapboard residences were fine examples of turn-of-the-century eclecticism. Advantageously sited and painstakingly landscaped, they sat atop the bluff forming the west bank of the river, commanding moving views of the Franconia Range, Franconia Notch, and the Lafayette Range to the north, and the Waterville mountains and the Sandwich Range to the northeast. Sadly, only one of the three houses stands today; the others were torn down in 1961 to make way for Interstate 93, which links Boston with northern New Hampshire and Vermont.[1]

Truly a man for all seasons, Ferdinand Schuyler Mathews (1854–1938) was one of the White Mountain region's most distinguished and accomplished artistic as well as literary summer personages. Born at New Brighton on Staten Island, New York, he was educated at local schools, the Cooper

"El Fureidis" (second, c. 1892–93), Blair's Colony, West Campton, N.H. Photograph courtesy of Carol Newcomb, West Campton, N.H.

The Reuter cottage (c. 1902–5), Blair's Colony, West Campton, N.H. Photograph by the author.

Institute in New York City, and other institutions, and traveled extensively in Italy to augment his art education. Settling in Cambridge, Massachusetts, for many years Mathews worked for Louis Prang & Company, the well-known lithographic art publishers of Boston, as a special artist, concentrating on decorative design. He was known particularly for his splendid colored and black-line renderings of birds, flowers, animals, and landscape scenes, which decorated Prang cards, pamphlets, and book publications. He was also a productive independent author, writing and illustrating several notable books, including *Familiar Flowers of Field and Garden*; *Familiar Trees and Their Leaves*; *Familiar Features of the Roadside*; *Familiar Life in Field and Forest*; *The Golden Flower*; *The Writing Table of the 20th Century* (1900); *The Fieldbook of American Wildflowers* (1902); *Fieldbook of Wild Birds and Their Music* (1904); *Fieldbook of Trees and Scrubs* (1914); *Book of Birds for Young People* (1921); and *Book of Wild Flowers for Young People* (1923). In addition, he illustrated and contributed poems to Prang's "White Mountain Vistas" series of booklets, published around 1889 under the titles *The Crystal Hills*, *The Saco Valley*, and *The Pemigewassett Valley*. Many of the volumes listed above, as well as his magazine articles, though not specifically focused on the White Mountains, contained images and scenes of this region, particularly the Pemigewassett Valley where the Mathews family spent so many summers. In addition to his art work and writing, and in recognition of his expertise as a naturalist, Mathews served as a botanical illustrator on the staff of the Gray Herbarium at Harvard University.[2]

The cottages at Blair's for which Mathews prepared plans were erected between about 1884 and 1903. Each of these buildings possessed the same precise, imaginative detail found in his paper art work. He erected the first of these houses for himself and his wife, Caroline Maynard Mathews, on land that he acquired from the Blair family in November 1883.[3] Entitled "El Fureidis" ("Paradise" in Arabic), this quaint, two-and-one-half-story dwelling combined features associated with the English Tudor (casement fenestration, patterned shingle roofing, roof finials, dormer gable half-timbering) and the American Shingle (latticework, varied wall surfacing) styles. The roof configuration was reminiscent of a seventeenth-century eastern Massachusetts "saltbox" house. Within a few years after the cottage was built, Mathews added a small second-story bedroom in a larger dormer projection set on turned support posts over the front porch stairway. The name "El Fureidis" appeared on a rectangular plaque mounted under the front dormer window. Fire destroyed the cottage around 1892, but during the next year it was replaced on the same site by the second "El Fureidis," nearly identical in size and appearance (see illustration), and also built from designs by Mathews. The necessity of replacing the first house provided him with the opportunity to make subtle changes and refinements, apparent on the exterior in altered fenestration, paint colors, porch details and latticework.[4]

In November 1902, Mathews sold a tract of hillside land adjacent to "El

"Gladstone" (c. 1909–10), Blair's Colony, West Campton, N.H. Photograph courtesy of Carol Newcomb, West Campton, N.H.

Fureidis" (previously part of the Blair homestead) to Mary F. Reuter of New York City.[5] The basis of her association with the Mathews family is unknown, but present-day local sources affirm that Mathews also designed the Reuter cottage. Erected sometime between 1902 and 1905, this small but highly provocative building possesses many of the features and materials once present in "El Fureidis," further confirming Mathews' role as architect. We are lucky still to be able to admire the yellow-and-red-patterned front gable facade, geometric porch balustrades, and foundation screening of the Reuter cottage, as it is the sole survivor of the original Blair's summer colony.[6]

The third cottage in the group, called "Gladstone" by its first owners, was designed by Mathews for his second cousin, Edith Stebbins Elphinstone, and her husband, Reginald H., of South Orange, New Jersey. It was built around 1909–10 on a three-acre parcel of land, purchased from the Werden family and located near the other houses on the east side of the Plymouth-Franconia road overlooking the river.[7] A larger and more conventional residence than its neighbors, "Gladstone" exhibited signs of the Colonial Revival influence in its gable end cornice molding, roof and rear (west) screen finials, and south wing hipped roof. The architect's penchant for fanciful, geometric embellishment could be observed in the balustrades of the east- and north-facing porches, the varied latticework of the rear screen, the stickwork of the foundation screening, and the low, curved, parapet-like strips atop each gable end of the main pitched roof. This house, like the others, bore the unmistakable stamp of its creator, markedly distinguishing it from other summer cottages of its era in the mountains.[8]

∾

Waterville Inn Cottages

c. 1870–1952

Waterville Valley

∼ THE WATERVILLE VALLEY summer colony, one of the oldest in the White Mountains, has managed to retain its historic character despite the development there of a major ski resort in the 1960s. More self-contained and isolated than other vacation communities in the region, it is ringed by imposing four-thousand-foot peaks—Mount Tecumseh to the west, the Osceolas to the north, the Tripyramids to the north and east, and Sandwich Dome to the southeast. Much of the surrounding land falls within the protective boundaries of the White Mountain National Forest. The town's growth has therefore been limited to the valley floor and, for the most part, has been controlled and discrete. Most important, the older surviving architecture has not been overwhelmed or compromised by the proliferation of modern condominiums, inns, private residences, recreational facilities, and commercial and service buildings.

The traditional center of leisure-time activity and tourism in the valley was the Waterville Inn, which burned in 1967. Opened in 1868 in Nathaniel Greeley's 1840s expanded farmhouse, it was acquired from the Greeleys by Silas B. Elliott in 1885. Over the next decade, Elliott twice enlarged the hotel to its peak capacity of 175 guests.[9] Soon after the inn opened, guests began to build their own cottages, preferring privacy and flexibility to the customary regimen and public nature of hotel life. The first of these was "Osceola Cottage," put up by Moody Elliott sometime before 1870, rebuilt in 1887, and employed as an annex to the inn. Perhaps symbolically, "paths to all of [the cottages] radiated out from the inn like bent spokes of a wheel." Each of them possessed only a rudimentary kitchen, as most of the residents ate their meals and took part in other activities at the inn, during the daytime and the evening.[10] Unlike the cottages at the Maplewood Hotel at Bethlehem, and the Waumbek Hotel at Jefferson, virtually all of those cottages associated with the Waterville Inn were privately owned, some situated on former hotel land, and others on land acquired from citizens of the town. Many of them still stand, albeit with alterations, and, in a few cases, on new sites.

The Davis/Briggs cottage (1880), Waterville Inn, Waterville Valley, N.H. Photograph by the author.

The Peloubet/Norton/Wilke cottage (1883), Waterville Inn, Waterville Valley, N.H. Photograph by the author.

The Elliott cottage (1911), Waterville Inn, Waterville Valley, N.H. Photograph by the author.

Spanning over three decades of Waterville history, three of these cottages comprise a representative group. Conspicuously visible from the Valley Road, they are perhaps architecturally the most interesting. The oldest of these (see page 175), built for Mr. J. W. Davis and Dr. Frederick C. Briggs in 1880, is a fine modified Stick-style chalet, and features patterned shingle wall sheathing, prominent eaves and porch support brackets, decorative gable roof trusses, varied and irregularly placed fenestration, and an asymmetrical floor plan. The second, known as the Peloubet-Norton-Wilke cottage (above) was erected for Rev. Dr. Francis N. Peloubet and his family in 1883. It was also conceived in the Stick style, but, unlike its predecessor, displays an almost perfectly symmetrical front facade, and light, fragile-appearing porch construction, particularly the roof and deck balustrades, and the foundation latticework screening. The third house (left), raised in 1911 for Mrs. Carrie H. Elliott, the wife of the late Silas Elliott, is more ponderous and plainer in appearance, with the horizontality and overhanging low-pitched roofs associated with certain Craftsman-style bungalows of the World War I era. It provides a note of contrast in a group of cottages that are decidedly Victorian in character.[11]

8 ～

Holderness/
Sandwich/
Moultonborough

The southern edge of the White Mountains is defined by the Lakes Region of central New Hampshire. Here, in the foothills overlooking Squam Lake and Lake Winnipesaukee, are several summer residences with architectural attributes as well as significant historical associations. On the southeast side of the Squam Range bordering Squam Lake are the Webster and Coolidge family cottages, designed by Boston-based architects for business and professional clients. In the Ossipee Mountains north of Lake Winnipesaukee is Thomas Plant's "Lucknow," one of New England's most outstanding country estates, built on the site of Benjamin F. Shaw's earlier estate, "Ossipee Mountain Park." Farther east in the Ossipee Mountains, high above the Winnipesaukee basin, is Roland Park on Dan Hole Pond. Dating from the 1880s to World War I, this small hilltop summer cottage colony is of interest less for the design of its quite modest individual buildings, than for its planning and social organization.

Webster Estate Cottages

1896–1911

(Mr. Frank G. Webster and sons)

Holderness

"The Homestead" (1896), Webster estate, Holderness, N.H., photograph from *New Hampshire Farms for Summer Homes* (11th ed., 1913), op. p. 24. Author's collection.

∼ SINCE THE LATE 1890s, the Webster estate has been the summer home of Frank G. Webster, the prominent Boston financier, his two sons, Laurence J. and Edwin S., and their descendants. One of the largest turn-of-the-century country vacation properties in New Hampshire, it was rivaled in the White Mountain region only by John J. Glessner's "The Rocks" in Bethlehem and Thomas G. Plant's "Lucknow" in Moultonborough. At its height, it consisted of five thousand acres, primarily in the town of Holderness, but also extending into nearby Ashland, Sandwich, Plymouth, and Campton. The site where the Webster cottages and other associated buildings are located, three miles north of Holderness Bridge, is bordered by the Squam Mountain Range to the west (incorporating Mount Webster, named after Frank G. Webster), and on the east by Squam Lake, still one of the most beautiful and unspoiled inland bodies of water in New England. With the impressive views across the lake toward Red Hill and the mountains to the north, the family houses are advantageously positioned on open, former pasture land, gently sloping down to the wooded shoreline. Architecturally noteworthy and evoking a working agrarian tradition, the Webster estate buildings fit unobtrusively and harmoniously into uncommonly lovely natural surroundings.[1]

The progenitor of the family property holdings in Holderness, Frank G. Webster, was born in 1841 in Canton, Massachusetts. Entering the world of finance at a young age, he rose through the ranks, and in 1886 became a member of the highly regarded Boston banking and investment firm Kidder, Peabody and Company. Known as the Dean of State Street, Webster eventually became president of the firm, securing a prominent place in Boston's financial and social communities. Exercising broad leadership in business, he served on the boards of directors of numerous New

West elevation, "The Homestead" (1896), Webster estate, Holderness, N.H. Photograph by the author.

England companies, including the Boston Safe Deposit and Trust Company, the National Shawmut Bank, the Boston Steamship Company, and the Bigelow-Hartford Carpet Corporation. He also found time to engage in philanthropy, supporting Boston hospitals and other charities, and provided financial assistance and business advice to many young men initiating professional careers. As testament to his influence and success, notices of Webster's death in 1930 appeared in virtually every major newspaper in the United States, as well as the Paris edition of the *New York Herald Tribune*.[2]

An ardent conservation advocate, Webster first visited the Squam Lake area in 1881. While a guest at the Asquam House, on Shepard Hill at the south end of the lake, he met and went fishing with Captain William Carnes. Upon Carnes' death, Webster purchased Carnes' former summer camp on Carnes Island. Concerned about the preservation of the lake and excessive timber cutting on adjacent lands, in 1891 he purchased from Willy Sleep a large lakeside parcel in Holderness, commencing the development of the family estate. To design his summer cottage, Webster turned to the new, inexperienced, and obscure Boston architecture firm of Wales and Holt, again demonstrating his interest in advancing the professional fortunes of young, aspiring men. The selection of Wales and Holt to design

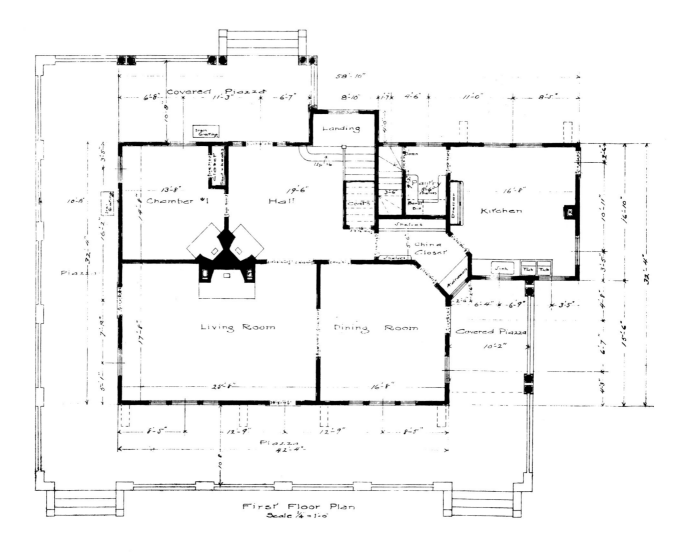

First Floor Plan
Scale ¼ = 1'-0'

"First Floor Plan, House for F. G. Webster, Esq.,
Holderness, N.H., Wales and Holt, Archts., Boston,
Mass.," c. 1896. Courtesy of Mr. and Mrs. Laurence
J. Webster III, Holderness.

the house may have been influenced by the fact that Edwin Webster and
George Canning Wales (1869–1940) attended MIT at the same time and
probably knew each other. Soon after their work for the Websters, the
architects dissolved their partnership, and thenceforth neither was conspicuously active in architecture. Wales, however, later distinguished himself
as an etcher and lithographer, specializing in old square-rigged ships, and
his prints are in the collections of many major libraries.[3]

Erected in 1896, Frank G. Webster's house, "The Homestead," is an outstanding inland rural example of the Shingle style, generally popular primarily on the New England seacoast. The strikingly similar cottage of
Laurence J. Webster, also designed by Wales and Holt, and built slightly
to the south in 1903, deserves the same accolade. Clad in characteristic
unpainted wood shingle siding and asymmetrical in form, both houses
contain all the major features of the Shingle style. On the exterior, these elements include Colonial-derived gambrel roofs pierced by bellcast hipped-
roof dormers, exposed roof rafters, multiple brick chimneys, second-level

The Laurence J. Webster cottage (1903), Webster estate, Holderness, N.H. Photograph by the author.

West elevation, the Laurence J. Webster cottage, Webster estate, Holderness, N.H., Wales and Holt, Architects, Boston, Mass., c. 1903. Courtesy of Mr. and Mrs. Laurence J. Webster III, Holderness.

shed-roof extensions protecting open verandas, classical veranda columns set on shingled plinths, and multipaned, grouped, double-sash windows. Both buildings possess wings, to which are attached small ice houses topped by quaint cupolas. Each is two-and-one-half stories tall and is supported by on-site granite block foundations enclosing a partial basement. Adjacent to the two houses are tennis courts and formal gardens (c. 1907), a shingled potting shed with greenhouse wing (c. 1910), and a shingled five-portal automobile garage (c. 1910).[4]

Typical of the Shingle style, the irregular interior plans of both cottages are simple and unpretentious. Each possess first-floor entry halls, enlarged

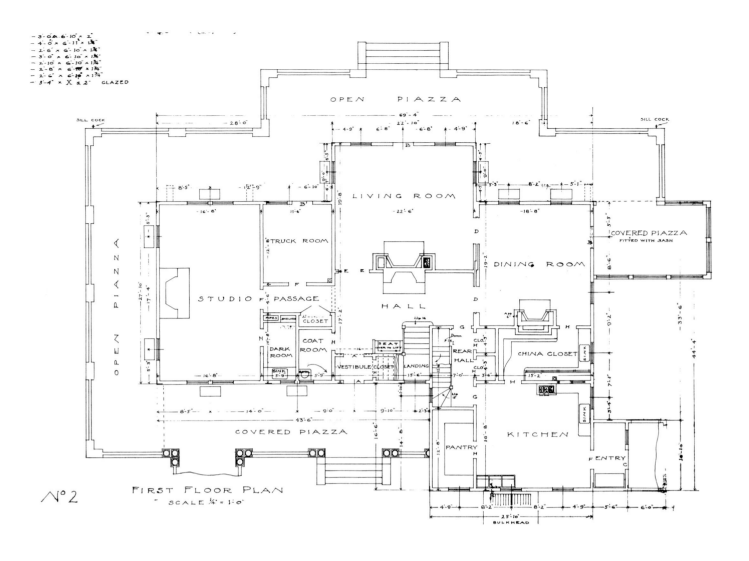

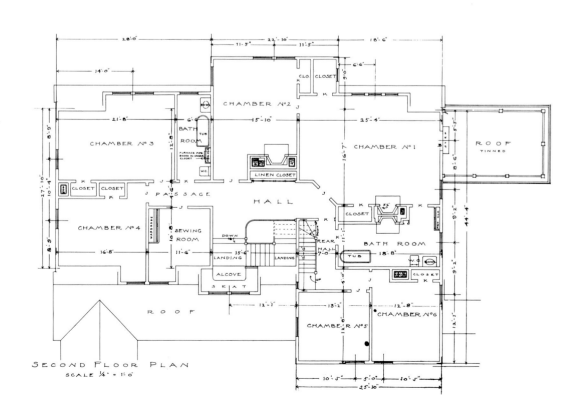

Above, first floor plan, and *right,* second floor plan for the Laurence J. Webster cottage, Webster estate, Holderness, N.H., Wales and Holt, Architects, Boston, Mass., c. 1903. Courtesy of Mr. and Mrs. Laurence J. Webster III, Holderness.

N° 2

FIRST FLOOR PLAN
SCALE ¼" = 1'·0"

SECOND FLOOR PLAN
SCALE ¼" = 1'·0"

South end, "Burleigh Brae" (1910–11), Webster estate, Holderness, N.H. Photograph by the author.

to create sizable rooms fitted with fireplaces and built-in seating. The open verandas appear as outside first-story extensions of the rooms inside, accentuating the horizontality of the two structures. All the major rooms of each house, including the bedrooms and the master bath, feature fireplaces, for heating as well as decoration. In addition to the entry hall, "The Homestead" contains a living room, dining room, kitchen, and service areas on the first floor, with bedrooms, baths, and storage spaces upstairs. The Laurence Webster house accommodates the hallway, a dining room, living room, studio, kitchen, pantry, and service areas on the first floor, and six bed chambers, plus bathrooms and storage spaces above. Present in both are Colonial Revival-inspired door and window molding, built-in bookcases and cabinets, wainscoting, corner cupboards, banquettes, cornice moldings, and fireplace surrounds.[5]

Webster's sons, Edwin and Laurence, were both trained as engineers, graduating from MIT in the 1880s. In 1889, Edwin Webster (1867–1950) joined with Charles A. Stone, a college friend, and, contrary to the advice of colleagues, established one of the nation's first electrical engineering firms. Initially Laurence Webster was a partner, but was forced into early retirement due to poor health. Over the years, the Stone and Webster Corporation evolved into an internationally renowned, multimillion-dollar consulting, investment, and construction business, and today remains highly visible and active in the electrical engineering and public utilities fields. When the firm was incorporated in Massachusetts in 1920, Edwin Webster became its president, and he served in this capacity for ten years. From 1941 until his retirement in 1946 he was chairman of the board. During the years of his association with the firm, subsidiaries were split off from the parent company in the areas of engineering construction activities, securities sales and investment management, public utilities properties, real estate, and general building. Over the course of his career, Edwin Webster was a director of numerous corporations, and was a trustee of MIT, the Massachusetts General Hospital, and the Museum of Fine Arts in Boston, and the American School of Classical Studies in Athens, Greece. Among his hobbies were horticulture, photography, fishing, and golf, all of which he could pursue at his Holderness house.[6]

Named "Burleigh Brae," the Edwin Webster house is the largest and most grandiose of the three Webster family summer homes. Built in 1910–11 under the supervision of Stone and Webster contractors, this elongated, two-and-a-half-story, roughly L-shaped structure is set on granite foundations, matching fieldstone walls on the front east- and northeast-facing elevations. An octagonal tower with a pyramidal roof joins the two major components of the house on the front facade. Characteristic of its style, the then fashionable Craftsman, this overgrown chalet-type building possesses an asymmetrical plan and wall elevations, intersecting gable roofs with exposed rafter overhangs, brick chimneys rising above fieldstone flues, dark shingled wall surfaces, projecting second-story gabled windows, fragile-appearing verandas and balconies, a variety of multipane window sashes, and shed-roof dormers and door and window protectors. The primary feature of the interior is a cavernous central living room, rising up two stories.

East front elevation, "Burleigh Brae" (1910–11), Webster estate, Holderness, N.H. Photograph by the author.

"House for Mr. Edwin S. Webster at Holderness, N.H.," front elevation perspective by Horace S. Frazer, Architect, Boston, c. 1910. Courtesy of Elizabeth H. Valentine, Holderness.

While "Burleigh Brae" may appear to some to lack the cohesion and unity of the Frank G. and Laurence J. Webster cottages, in fact it successfully combines powerful, contrasting horizontal and vertical visual forces in a highly picturesque, well-articulated building mass.[7]

For the architect of his magnificent vacation retreat, Edwin Webster selected Horace S. Frazer (1862–1931) of Boston. Born in Crosswicks, New Jersey, Frazer received his secondary education at Philips Academy, Andover, Massachusetts, and graduated from the Sheffield Scientific School at Yale University in 1883. He then went on to receive a bachelor's degree from MIT in 1885, the same year that he was employed as an apprentice draftsman with the firm of Cabot and Chandler in Boston. At other times before 1890 he was an associate in the Boston architectural firms of Peabody and Stearns, and of Longfellow, Alden and Harlow. In 1890–91, Frazer maintained an independent practice, forming a partnership with J. H. Chapman (d. 1895) around 1892. During the few years they worked together, Chapman and Frazer designed several residences in the Boston area, as well as the Merchants' Bank Building in New Bedford, Massachusetts, the Concord (Massachusetts) High School, and the State Armory in Nashua, New Hampshire. Continuing the firm name after Chapman's death, Frazer further established his reputation in domestic architecture, drafting plans for houses in Boston and environs, as well as along the coast of Maine. One of his commissions there was "Rock Ledge" (1902–3) for George H. Walker at Walker's Point, Kennebunkport. The summer cottage of President and Mrs. George H. W. Bush, this rambling wood and stone dwelling resembles in plan Edwin Webster's "Burleigh Brae." Both follow a formula Chapman and Frazer (Frazer alone after 1895) employed for large summer residences—the public and living spaces of the owners were located in a single rectangular block, while the service spaces were situated in an attached, but separate wing, set at an angle to the principal portion of the building.[8]

≈

"Far Pastures"

1919–27

(Mr. Archibald Cary Coolidge)

Sandwich

◦ SITUATED ATOP A HILL overlooking the northern end of Squam Lake is "Far Pastures" (also known as "Stone House") built for Archibald Cary Coolidge, with his brother J. Randolph Coolidge, Jr., as architect. According to local legend, the house derives its primary name from its location on the farther pasture of the former Smith farm, near maple trees "which won renown at the Chicago World Fair of 1893 when Samuel B. Smith was awarded a medal for his maple products."[9] Work commenced on the house in the summer of 1919, with Larkin D. Weed, the accomplished local contractor of numerous Sandwich-Tamworth area residences, in charge of building operations. Unlike most houses of its region and era, "Far Pastures" was constructed almost entirely of materials from the surrounding land—red oak and white pine wood, and granite fieldstone, painstakingly cut by Weed and his assistants on the building site. Due to the owner's frequent trips to Europe after World War I, the builders were blessed with the unusual luxury of time, and hence the opportunity to create a superbly crafted structure. Eight years passed before the house was completed and first occupied in 1927.[10]

One of five brothers instrumental in the development of the family properties at Squam Lake, Archibald Cary Coolidge was a remarkably ver-

satile and talented man. Born in 1866, he graduated from Harvard University summa cum laude in history in 1887, and continued his formal studies in the same field at European universities. World traveler, diplomat, writer, editor, and academic, Coolidge was for thirty-five years associated with Harvard, serving as professor of history and as the first director of the Harry E. Widener Memorial Library. Upon his death in 1929, the property passed to his nephew, Joseph R. Coolidge, the son of the architect, and after his death in 1936 was used for over thirty years by Joseph Coolidge's widow, Anna C. Coolidge. The house was sold outside the family around 1980.[11]

Architect J. Randolph Coolidge (1862–1928) also graduated from Harvard (bachelor's degree in 1883, master's degree 1884), and after a brief banking career, completed his architectural training at MIT, the Ecole des Beaux Arts in Paris, and at Dresden and Berlin, Germany. Upon his return to Boston in 1898, Coolidge first worked independently before establishing a partnership with Henry J. Carlson, operating under the firm name of Coolidge and Carlson from 1903 to 1922. Designer of residential buildings, libraries, churches, and commercial structures, Coolidge was perhaps best known for his dormitory and other commissions at Harvard, and Wellesley, Bates, and Hamilton colleges. In Sandwich, where he took up residency after his retirement, he is known to have designed the town hall, the Samuel Wentworth Library, and the Sabine house, and to have rebuilt and expanded his own "Hodge House" on Squam Lake. He also prepared plans of the caretaker's residence (c. 1926–27) for "Far Pastures." Located at the base of the hill below the main house, this pleasant Colonial Revival wood-frame and clapboard structure was initially known as the "Red House," but after a paint color change in the late 1930s has since been known as the "Yellow Cottage."[12]

Inspired by English country house architecture, particularly Norman stone buildings, "Far Pastures" is the epitome of solidity and permanence. With walls of meticulously finished and fitted granite blocks, the building sits comfortably on its lofty site, its rooms arranged on different levels instead of conventional stories. Intersecting truncated pitched roofs provide distinctive form to the building. Occupying the center of the house with a sweeping view of the lake, is the great living room, featuring a cathedral ceiling, brass light fixtures, a tile floor, hand-hewn oak beams and paneling, and a massive stone fireplace, flanked by bookshelves and reading nooks. Surrounding the ample space is an upstairs balcony, with doors leading to the bedrooms. The original furniture was "of [the] heavy English type," many of the chairs being high-backed, elaborately carved settles. Of the many cottages and camps erected by the Coolidges at Squam Lake, "Far Pastures" is unquestionably the most sophisticated and significant architecturally.[13]

~

"Ossipee Mountain Park"

c. 1880–81

(Mr. Benjamin F. Shaw)

Moultonborough

"Ossipee Mountain Park" (Shaw estate), Moultonborough, N.H., engraving from *Summer Saunterings by the B. & L.*, 1st ed. (Boston: Passenger Department of the Boston & Lowell Railroad, 1885), p. 69. Author's collection.

∽ BETWEEN 1879 AND 1886, Benjamin Franklin Shaw, a Lowell, Massachusetts, textile magnate, acquired lands totaling over 350 acres in the Moultonborough sector of the Ossipee Mountains north of Lake Winnipesaukee.[14] It was here, at an elevation of over 1,000 feet, that he created "Ossipee Mountain Park," one of the most beautiful, unusual, and intriguing rural estates in northern New England. At the center of this huge tract, on open former farmlands, Shaw erected a group of buildings as a tranquil summer mountain retreat for himself, his family, and friends. To provide comfortable access to the property, he constructed a road up the mountainside, over a mile long, with magnificent outlooks of the Lakes Region below. Public-spirited and aware of the merits of the natural environment, Shaw next opened the property to interested visitors. Work crews cut a five-mile system of paths along the Wehlaka Brook, through glens and groves, and across the rolling terrain, and to the summit of the highest neighboring peak (2,975 feet), later christened "Mount Shaw." They also built twelve attractive rustic bridges over the brook, wooden benches, shelters, and an observation pavilion on the crest of the "Crow's Nest," a rocky promontory affording superb views in all directions. Such lovely natural features as the Falls of Song, Emerald Pool, Veil Falls, the Cascades, Pewee's Pool, the Ravine, the Crags, and Echo Vale enthralled onlookers and were depicted in commercially produced stereo and cabinet photographs of the 1880s. The park attracted large numbers of people, including such literary notables as John Greenleaf Whittier and Lucy Larcom, and artist Irene Jerome, who arrived in horse-drawn buggies, carryalls, and wagons. Ultimately, to protect the "weird and the wild," as one writer characterized the property, Shaw found it necessary to require reservations and charge an admission fee. Even after his death in 1890, the next owner, Mrs. E. F. Pettingill, kept the park open, while using the buildings as a small resort facility.[15]

Erected around 1880–81, Shaw's vacation complex consisted of the main dwelling, "Wehlaka Hall," a guest house, "The Lodge," substantial barns, and other outbuildings. By far the largest and most imposing structure in the group was "The Hall," a fine, rectangular-plan Stick-style mansion that resembled a modest hotel of the era as much as it did a residence. Intended to accommodate the Shaws as well as ample numbers of guests, this building possessed a steep-pitched roof, tall brick chimneys, hipped-roof dormers, prominent eaves brackets, expansive first- and second-story verandas, delicate stickwork balustrades, bracketed vertical support posts, and other features typical of its style. Directly adjacent was "The Lodge," a single-story, pavilion-like annex, with roof form, porch, and post-and-bracket detail similar to that of the main house. In nineteenth-century photographs and engraved views, the complex conveys a feeling of openness and hospitality, consistent with Shaw's democratic and enlightened philosophy of land use.[16] The buildings were either demolished or burned in 1913 after the park was acquired by Thomas G. Plant and he developed his grand five-thousand-acre estate, "Lucknow," on the original Shaw lands and contiguous parcels.[17]

Benjamin Shaw, the man who conceived the vision of Ossipee Park, was born in 1832 in Monmouth, Maine. He attended the common schools and Topsham Academy, but his family's straitened financial circumstances prevented him from proceeding to college. After working odd jobs in Maine, he married Harriet Nowell Howard in 1853, and they moved to Philadelphia, where he joined the well-known publishing firm of J. B. Lippincott and & Co. Here he experienced his first career success, becoming head of clerical work, earning a generous salary, and building a handsome villa in Germantown, Pennsylvania. Increasingly restless in his job, and seeing the need for the improvement of geography textbooks, he committed nights and weekends for three years to compiling his highly successful *Primary Geography* (1862) and *Comprehensive Geography* (1864). Finally, by 1865, as a result of his heavy work schedule, he was forced to alter his life-style, departed Philadelphia, secured a government claims position, and attempted cattle ranching in Kansas. When the ranching venture failed, he returned home to his young family, which had relocated to Danvers, Massachusetts; he did so "not so well off in purse, though much better in health."

It was at this point in his life that the enterprising and versatile Shaw made his mark in the New England textile industry, and began the rise to financial eminence that would make his idyllic "Ossipee Mountain Park" possible. From 1865 to 1868 he was general manager of outside operations and investments for Dr. J. C. Ayer & Co. in Lowell, and on his own time invented the seamless stocking and the automatic loom for its production. During the eight years following his departure from Ayer & Co., he focused on other inventions, devising processes for making glue, gelatine, and superphosphate, and also wrote more, particularly poetry. In 1877 he further perfected the seamless stocking, and a year later founded the Shaw Stocking Company in Lowell, later manufacturer of the famous "Shawknit Stocking." Here he remained as president until his death, advancing the company to worldwide renown, and further enhancing his fame as an inventor with the Shaw-woven loom and stocking in the late 1880s.[18] Largely self-educated and self-made, Benjamin Shaw was in many respects the personification of the American dream, and, in gratitude for career success, he made "Ossipee Mountain Park" his gift to the American people.

≈

"Lucknow"

1911–14

(Mr. Thomas G. Plant)

Moultonborough

"Lucknow" (1911–14), Moultonborough, N.H., photograph from booklet, *Lucknow* (c. 1925). Author's collection.

≈ UPON A VISIT to "Ossipee Mountain Park," the spectacular rural retreat of the Shaw family, in about 1900, the writer Lucy Larcom commented: "Is there really and truly such a place as Fairyland? Yes . . . It is hidden away in the woodlands at the foot of the Ossipees [mountains] near the lovely shores of Lake Winnipesaukee." This magnificent property was later acquired, much of it sight-unseen, by the complex, eccentric, multimillionaire inventor and shoe manufacturing mogul, Thomas G. Plant, who created his own lavish estate, incorporating the lands formerly occupied by the Shaws (see "Ossipee Mountain Park"). Here, between 1911 and 1913, he acquired over six thousand acres of woodlands, meadows, and pasture in a series of separate real estate transactions. On a rocky outcrop, known as "The Crow's Nest" (Lee Mountain), offering an unparalleled panorama of Lake Winnipesaukee and the Belknap Mountains to the south, he erected a highly unusual, majestic, sixteen-room mansion, supplemented by an immense stable/garage, two gate houses, a greenhouse, farm outbuildings, and an eighteen-hole golf course. Short in stature, with great personal drive and a sense of his own destiny, Plant much admired and strongly identified with Napoleon Bonaparte; in tribute to his idol, he titled his estate "Lucknow," supposedly after one of Napoleon's country retreats. Under later owners, open as a popular tourist attraction, it has been known by its more popular name "Castle in the Clouds."[19]

Born in Bath, Maine, in 1859, Thomas Gustave Plant left his very large and relatively poor family at the age of thirteen, moving to Boston where he found work as a lacer in a shoe factory. Though he lacked a formal education, he possessed a shrewd and enterprising business mind and excellent technical ability, and quickly progressed in the shoe industry. As a young man he developed and patented several machines for the manufacture of shoes. In 1891, he founded his own business in Lynn, Massachusetts, which two years later was incorporated as Thomas G. Plant Company. Over the next three decades, this concern attained an international reputation for its outstanding women's footwear (under the trade names of Queen Quality and Dorothy Dodd), ultimately relocating to the Jamaica Plain district of Boston in 1927. Over the years, Plant sold several patents and acquired other shoe factories, creating a group of industrial interests that were said to be worth at least twenty-one million dollars when he sold out to the United Shoe Machinery Corporation in 1910. Retiring at the relatively young age of fifty, he traveled extensively in North America and in Europe, where he met his second wife, Olive Dewey, a Wellesley College graduate, whom he married in 1913. Besides his mountain estate, Plant left two other notable legacies: the Plant Memorial Home for the elderly, which he endowed and had built in Bath in 1917; and, on the nearby shores of Lake Winnipesaukee, Bald Peak Colony Club, a private, living/recreational complex consisting of numerous buildings (clubhouse, cottages, dormitories, dining hall, stables, and boat house) and an eighteen-hole golf course completed between 1919 and 1921. A victim of bad investments in Russian and German bonds and currency, Cuban sugar, and other unsuccessful business ventures, Plant lost his entire vast fortune during the 1920s and 1930s, and was forced to mortgage most of "Lucknow" to the banks in order to pay back taxes. He and his wife, however, were permitted to remain in residence until his death in 1941. He was buried in his hometown, Bath, where a simple stone marks his grave.[20]

Plant's decision to develop a peaceful retirement retreat in the Ossipee Mountains was largely influenced by his brother, William, a business associate and Manchester shoe factory owner, who owned a house in Wolfeboro on Lake Winnipesaukee. Plant had undoubtedly visited there and knew the area. Much of the land that comprised "Lucknow" was purchased with William acting as his agent. The plans for the main house and dependent structures were drafted during the winter of 1912 and 1913, with construction commencing the following spring. Anxious to complete the project as soon as possible, Plant employed approximately one thousand laborers, most of them Italian-American stonemasons from Boston, who lived in camps on the site. Also included in this group were teamsters and carpenters, the majority from the surrounding countryside. In addition to the buildings, the work crews also erected miles of stone walls, and, guided by Plant and a chief engineer, laid out the golf course, over thirty miles of single-lane roads, a five-acre lake, and an extensive system of paths and hiking trails, many with rusticated bridges and shelters. The particolored

South front, "Lucknow" (1911–14), Moultonborough, N.H. Photograph by the author.

Library, "Lucknow" (1911–14), Moultonborough, N.H., photograph from booklet, *Lucknow* (c. 1925). Author's collection.

granite stone used in buildings was quarried from the estate, precisely cut into pentagonal shapes, and fitted together with a minimum of mortar to produce beautifully executed, almost seamless, construction. All of the heavy oaken structural members and elm interior finishing were supposedly crafted by shipyard workers in Bath, arrived at the contracting site by rail to Laconia, then by boat across the lake to Moultonborough, and by horse-drawn vehicles the remainder of the trip. Oaken dowels, instead of nails, were used to assemble the wood components of the buildings. The terra-cotta roofing materials were imported from Spain, and the fireplace marble from Italy. When the project was completed in 1914, total costs, including all land parcels, were said to have exceeded one million dollars. During the period of construction, Plant lived close by at "Westwynde," a farmhouse located below on the main road.[21]

Designed to harmonize with the irregular contours of the landscape, the mansion at "Lucknow" is a curious, highly naturalistic, and ruggedly picturesque eclectic blend of styles, incorporating elements of Swiss Alpine, Norwegian, Japanese, and English Norman architecture. These were said to symbolize several diverse cultural heritages of the United States, which Plant had experienced throughout his work life. Set on a ledge-rock plateau with carpet-like lawns and gardens, the house combines long, broken, horizontal sight lines with the upward vertical thrusts of the four tall chimneys, and two bellcast-roof octagonal towers. One of its most outstanding features is "the massive, low broken-lined roof of Spanish tile multi-colored in softly blended shades of brown, red and yellow." Arrayed across the exterior walls are balconies, tall French doors, and varied leaded casement window groupings framed by hand-hewn oak timbers. Extending beyond the wide, overhanging eaves are many rafters, their unfinished ends suggesting gargoyle faces. A covered walkway connects with a pergola at the

Hall, "Lucknow" (1911–14), Moultonborough, N.H., photograph from booklet, *Lucknow* (c. 1925). Author's collection.

Library and alcove, "Lucknow" (1911–14), Moultonborough, N.H., photograph from booklet, *Lucknow* (c. 1925). Author's collection.

west end, from which additional mountains and the incomparably beautiful Squam Lakes basin can be seen. While the building conveys a feeling of light fantasy, it simultaneously exudes a sense of solidity and permanence like the surrounding granite New Hampshire hills of which it is an integral part.[22]

Fortunately for present-day scholars, the interior of the main house is thoroughly documented, thanks to photographs and descriptions published when Plant first put the property up for sale in the mid-1920s. The entire inside is exquisitely appointed with beamed ceilings, intricate moldings and paneling, hardwood floors, and, in certain of the casement windows, hand-painted scenes of the estate and the superb views one can enjoy from it. On the first floor, the principal rooms are introduced by a magnificent oak-paneled lobby (originally a game room) with a grand fireplace, stairway, and large built-in organ designed by the Aeolian Organ Company. Under Plant's ownership, this space contained two bear rugs, a Siberian tiger rug, and two mounted deer heads, intended to reflect his skill as a hunter. Off the hall is the living room (formerly the library for nature, horticulture, and Napoleonic books, and memorabilia), finished in the same refined manner, with bookcases, a fireplace flue incorporating a picture window, an alcove with window seat, a pair of hand-carved mahogany griffins, and French doors opening out to a garden. On the other side of the hall, paneled in Cambridge elm, is the dining room, octagonal in shape, with a star-patterned hardwood floor, hand-carved mantel, built-in china cabinets, and a canvas-over-plaster ceiling embellished with raised wisteria clusters. Seating twelve people, this space also possesses French doors to the outside. In addition, the first floor contains a spacious entrance hall with quarry tile floor, an adjoining small office and coat room, a guest bedroom with bath, a kitchen complex (kitchen, servants' hall, cook's pantry, and butler's pantry), and large east-facing sun parlor. On the second floor are two master suites (with bedrooms, baths, and dressing rooms), and an octagonal guest bedroom, two staff bedrooms, and a hallway illuminated by a large skylight. The basement formerly accommodated the staff quarters, a laundry room, an "air conditioned" safe for painting storage, a furnace room, pet quarters, and drying chambers. The house boasted such innovative amenities as central vacuum, incinerator, and intercom systems; needle, "wrap-around" shower-baths; retractable window shades; a self-cleaning oven; brine-cooled refrigerators; a brine-cooled wine cellar; a forced-hot-water radiator heating system; hydro-powered electric generators; and interior fire hydrants for fire suppression, fed by a special reservoir above the mansion on neighboring Mount Roberts. The presence of modern technology is hardly surprising in view of Plant's record as an inventor, and may well have been the product of his own genius.[23]

According to local lore, Plant was extremely demanding and stubborn as a client, attempted to work with three architects, fired them all, and designed the buildings of "Lucknow" himself. The sophistication of their design and engineering, however, suggests at least a collaborative working

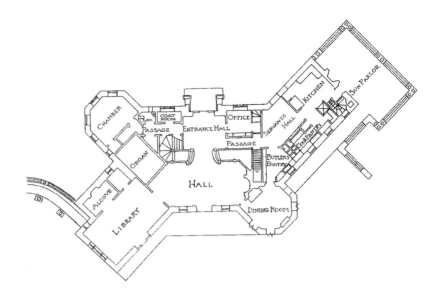

First floor plan, "Lucknow" (1911–14), Moultonborough, N.H., from booklet, *Lucknow* (c. 1925). Author's collection.

Gatekeeper's lodge, "Lucknow" (1911–14), Moultonborough, N.H. Photograph by the author.

relationship between property owner and professional architect. Barry Rodrique, a Plant descendant and his recent biographer, has asserted that the Boston architectural firm of Coolidge and Carlson (see "Far Pastures," Sandwich) acted as the "ghost" planners of "Lucknow," succeeding other architects whom Plant had deemed unsatisfactory. The same partners also designed the Plant Memorial Home in Bath, Maine, in 1917, and it is unlikely that Plant would have hired them a second time had he not been pleased with their efforts in Moultonborough.[24] The logic of a Coolidge and Carlson commission is further confirmed by the fact that the partners, particularly Joseph Randolph Coolidge, Jr. (1862–1928), were known for their proficiency in planning rural and country houses and estates, and had served as architects of other houses in New Hampshire's Lakes Region. As a consequence of his extensive architectural training and travel in Europe, Coolidge was well schooled in European national styles and building practices, and he often imbued his buildings with a strong international eclecticism. Of the White Mountain country estates and residences erected before 1930, "Lucknow" expresses such eclecticism more emphatically and effectively than any other.

Tamworth/ Chocorua

9 ∼

The Town of Tamworth, including the summer colony in the vicinity of Chocorua Lake, is the most southerly of the White Mountains' major single-season vacation communities. Despite this advantageous location, within reasonable distance of Boston and other metropolitan areas of the Northeast, it did not undergo transformation from a predominantly agricultural to a tourist economy until the 1890s and more recently. Unlike North Conway and Bethlehem, Tamworth lacked direct rail transportation (the closest rail stops were over six miles away in Madison to the east and Ossipee to the south), and hence failed to develop as a significant hotel center. Access was limited to gravel wagon and coach roads until after 1900, when the automobile and improved roadways encouraged more frequent visitation to the area. Tamworth, however, possessed other distinct and compelling assets—an abundance of farm properties suitable for conversion to summer use; lovely, scenic rolling countryside crossed by sparkling streams and an excellent system of local roads; and numerous spectacular potential house sites, with awe-inspiring prospects of the imposing granite cone of Mount Chocorua and the Chocorua mountain range to its west.

Like many White Mountain inns and hotels in attractive natural settings, John Henry Nickerson's Chocorua Inn (1863 and after) overlooking Chocorua Lake, spawned a number of local land purchasers and summer cottage builders from its guest list. The Scudders and Bowditches from Boston were among the first of Chocorua's summer residents. From the 1870s through the first decade of this century, the colony gradually formed, its members representing academe, the clergy, the literati, the professional ranks, and the business realm. East of the lake and the main road, on the ridge formed by Washington and Heavenly hills, substantial summer residences were erected for the Scudder, Chadwick, Hammer, Bowditch, Page, James, Salter, Hutchinson, Grant/Stone, and Reynolds families. South and west of the lake, newly constructed residences or adapted farmhouses accommodated the Lorings, the Sherwins, the Bolles, the Maynadiers, the Runnells, the Wainwrights, the Thayers, the Balches, and the Walkers. A member of the colony, Boston architect C. Howard Walker, planned his own as well as several other houses there. Also present in Chocorua were residential commissions by the architects Peabody and Stearns of Boston, their former draftsman Edwin J. Lewis, Jr., also of Boston, Ernest M. A.

Machado of Boston and Salem, and Charles A. Platt of New York City. The legacy of this noted group of designers was a collection of houses sporting qualities of the Shingle, Colonial Revival, and Craftsman styles, and, through the use of native building materials, exhibiting a rusticity suited to the rural forested and mountainous environment in which these houses were situated.

Elsewhere in Tamworth, other summer cottages were scattered, primarily in the south end of town, in the northwest sector on or adjacent to Great Hill and Cleveland Hill, and at the Wonalancet colony. Foremost among these are architect-designed residences built for Mrs. A. C. B. Wells, Dr. and Mrs. John H. Finley ("Kilmarnock"), and Mr. and Mrs. Elliot C. Clarke ("Great Hill Farm"), and houses designed and erected by local builders for Mr. and Mrs. Edgar J. Rich, and sisters Marjory and Gertrude Gane ("Seven Hearths").

"Great Hill Farm"

c. 1895–c. 1915

(Mr. and Mrs. Elliott C. Clarke)

Tamworth

"Great Hill Farm" (c. 1895-c. 1901), Tamworth, N.H. Photograph by the author.

"Perspective Sketch, Cottage of Mr. E. C. Clarke at Tamworth Village, N.H.," Albert C. Fernald, Architect, Boston, c. 1901. Courtesy of the Society for the Preservation of New England Antiquities, Boston.

∾ IN 1892, ELLIOTT CHANNING CLARKE (1845–1921), of old Boston lineage, began to acquire and consolidate several small farms to form a single large country estate in the vicinity of Great Hill in the northwest district of Tamworth. Transacted over a six-year period, and later supplemented by other parcels, these purchases were made from several of Tamworth's most established families—Cooley, Thornton, Marston, Edgell, Rollins, and others.[1] What brought Clarke to Tamworth is unknown, though it may have been his wife, Alice Sohier, who had family connections in New Hampshire. An 1867 graduate of Harvard College, with additional courses in engineering at MIT, Clark served as a civil engineer in var-

PERSPECTIVE·SKETCH·⊕·
COTTAGE OF MR.E.C.CLARK.
AT TAMWORTH VILLAGE, N.H.

Albert C. Fernald, Archt.
186 Devonshire St. Boston

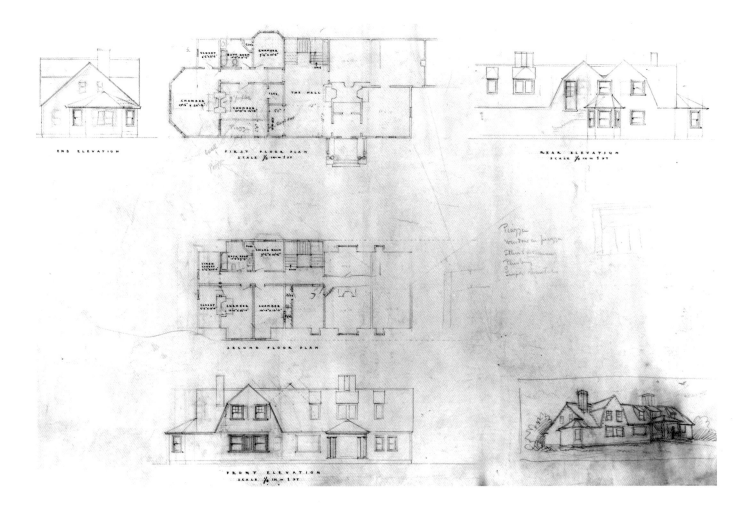

Elevation sketches, "Great Hill Farm," Tamworth, N.H., by Peabody and Stearns, Architects, Boston, c. 1897. Peabody and Stearns Collection, Boston Public Library. Reproduced courtesy of the Trustees of the Boston Public Library.

ious parts of the country, participating in the design and construction of railroad bridges and tunnels, water works, and sewerage systems. In the mid-1880s, he was a member of a special commission to develop a system of drainage for the Mystic, Blackstone, and Charles River valleys of Massachusetts, and wrote the summary report for the state. He was a fellow and treasurer of the American Academy of Arts and Sciences in Boston for thirteen years, and contributed his fiscal expertise to the textiles business, and as a director of the State Street Safe Deposit and Trust Company in Boston.[2] Clarke was a highly motivated man of many talents, who possessed the vision, organizational skills, and energy to create the network of tracts and farm buildings to which he ultimately gave the highly appropriate name, "Great Hill Farm."

The core portion of the main residence on the Clarke property is believed to have been built as early as 1785, possibly by Samuel Moulton. Originally one and a half stories, with a central brick chimney, this modest, traditional, wood-frame and clapboard structure is notable for its interior twelve-inch-square, hand-hewn ceiling beams, paneling, and pine board floors.[3] Between around 1895 and around 1915, the Clarkes progressively expanded their house, also adding outbuildings to accommodate social/

Front pavilion entrance, "Great Hill Farm" (c. 1895–c. 1901), Tamworth, N.H. Photograph by the author.

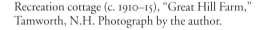

Recreation cottage (c. 1910–15), "Great Hill Farm," Tamworth, N.H. Photograph by the author.

recreational activities, vehicles, and the functions of a working farm. Sometime around 1897, or possibly later, a large two-story wing was appended to the southwest end of the house from plans by the highly regarded Boston architectural firm Peabody and Stearns, the designers of other Tamworth domestic and associated buildings about the same time (see "Conni Sauti" and "Willowgate"). Intended primarily as sleeping space (there were six bedroom "chambers," a stairwell, closets, and baths), this low, pitched-roof extension, distinctly Colonial Revival in spirit, visually complemented the much older farmhouse, maintaining an excellent sense of massing and proportions. Except for a recent change in paint colors (from yellow to dark red), and the addition of a one-story sun room on the end, this wing is virtually unchanged from the time that it was built. Its most pronounced features include a large gambrel-roof dormer over a double window and small piazza (later expanded to form a large open porch), and a similarly scaled double dormer above a first-story bay window on the rear elevation. At the time that the wing was constructed, a one-story porch supported by Doric columns was placed before the front central entrance to the farmhouse. Concurrent with the Peabody and Stearns project, Clark also built a caretaker's cottage, a large barn, and a carriage house on the property.[4]

A set of architectural plans in the possession of the current owners indicate that about 1901, additional modifications were made to the main residence under the direction of architect Albert C. Fernald of Boston. These alterations included a first-story bay window and a second-story gable incorporating a Palladian window directly above the porch, both on the front elevation. The floor plan remained essentially unchanged, but for the slight enlargement of one second-floor chamber and the first-floor dining room.[5] Fernald did further work for the Clarkes around 1910–15, when he designed a fine recreation cottage for the use of the family. Positioned a couple of

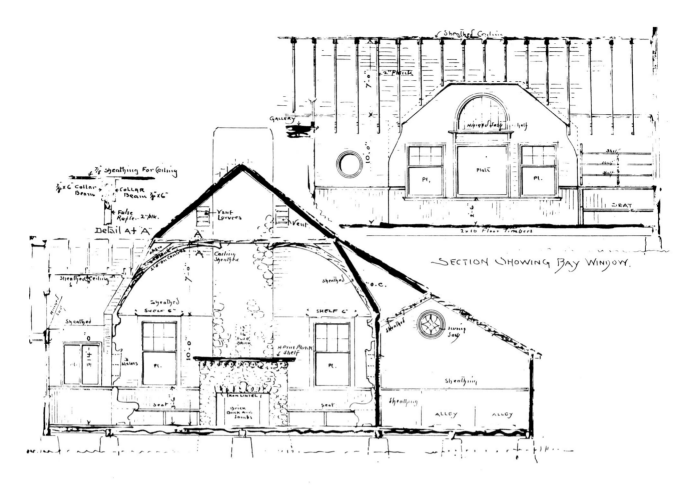

SECTION SHOWING BAY WINDOW.

CROSS SECTION

Detail at A

For MR. E. C. CLARKE,
TAMWORTH, N.H.

Albert C. Fernald, Archt.
Boston, Mass.

FRONT ELEVATION

Facing page, "Cross Sections and Front Elevation, Recreation Cottage for Mr. E. C. Clarke, Tamworth, N.H., Albert C. Fernald, Archt., Boston," c. 1910. Courtesy of Anne S. Mock, Tamworth.

hundred yards behind the main house, this quaint, Colonial Revival–style building incorporates a spacious, two-story hall, with a large fieldstone fireplace on one end facing a gallery. Still present in this attractive, wood-paneled space are original gaming tables, built-in seating furniture, and animal trophies from Clark's worldwide hunting expeditions. Attached to the north rear side of the cottage is an ell containing a two-lane bowling alley. Blending effectively with the nearby pine and hardwood forest, the building displays natural shingle sheathing, white wood trim, and a fieldstone chimney, rising above a medium-pitched gambrel roof. A heavy framed Palladian window in the northeast end gable illuminates the interior gallery. Plain and domestic in appearance, the building echoes the form and principal features of the main house.[6] Fernald's designs for "Great Hill Farm" are a compatible supplement to the older architecture of the farmhouse, as well as the addition by Peabody and Stearns.

≈

"Kilmarnock"

1906

(Dr. and Mrs. John H. Finley)

Tamworth

"Kilmarnock" (1906), Cleveland Hill, Tamworth, N.H., Photograph by the author.

≈ IN 1905–6, STEVENSON HILL in Tamworth became the summer home of two good friends—Dr. John H. Finley, the president of the College of the City of New York, and Grover Cleveland, the former two-term president of the United States.[7] Upon discovering the location, President Cleveland enthusiastically proclaimed its advantages in a letter to the secretary of the New Hampshire State Board of Agriculture:

> The beautiful mountain views on every side, the deliciously cool atmosphere, the pleasant rambles and rides, and the charming lakes and streams within easy reach make a complete list of attractions, while a fair measure of remoteness from the distractions of crowds and business and social activities fittingly emphasize them all.[8]

Cleveland, who had leased a summer house in neighboring Sandwich the previous two seasons, wasted little time: acting decisively, he purchased two hill-top farms, one for himself and the other for the Finley family. In October 1905, Finley and his wife, Martha, took formal possession of their farm, paying Cleveland and his wife, Frances, one thousand dollars for the property. Immediately they began laying plans for the construction of their new summer cottage, which they named "Kilmarnock," in celebration of John Finley's Scotch-Irish lineage.[9]

As architects for their vacation houses, both the Clevelands and the Finleys selected the partnership of Walter H. Kilham (1868–1948) and James C. Hopkins (1873–1938) of Boston. The connection with the firm was apparently through Kilham, who himself had a country farm nearby, which he had refurbished and called "The Clearing."[10] Kilham and Hopkins formed the firm in 1900, a relationship which they maintained until 1925, when Roger Greeley became the third partner. During the period before 1920, Kilham and Hopkins developed a large architectural practice, designing numerous educational buildings, public structures, and private homes, largely in Boston and around Massachusetts. Included on their list of major commissions were buildings for Radcliffe College in Cambridge, Massachusetts, the Dedham High School, the Lincoln School in Framingham, Salem High School, Waltham City Hall, Dover Town Hall, and the Andrew Jackson School and Students' Houses in Boston. After 1920 the firm was responsible for the offices of the Atlantic Monthly Magazine, the auditorium of the Wentworth Institute, the Massachusetts Institute of Pharmacy, and the Faneuil Branch of the Boston Public Library, all in Boston. The partnership was also known for its suburban and rural residential architecture, particularly after World War I. Kilham gained recognition as an architectural historian, publishing a highly regarded book, *Boston after Bulfinch*, in 1946.[11]

For Grover and Frances Cleveland, Kilham and Hopkins conceived and orchestrated the renovation of nineteenth-century farm buildings in 1905 to create the vacation estate "Intermont." For the Finleys, however, the firm designed an entirely new cottage, commanding perhaps the most spectacular vista in Tamworth of Mount Chocorua and the Sandwich Range. With long, low lines, and expansive, low-pitched gabled surfaces, "Kilmarnock" is without question the best turn-of-the-century example of a Craftsman-style rusticated bungalow in the White Mountains. Particularly noteworthy are its tall native fieldstone chimneys, triangular gable brackets, unenclosed eaves overhangs, and natural wood porch posts and balustrades. The interior is distinguished by several large unfinished spaces, and an overall feeling of unrestrained spaciousness. A comparison of recent and old photographs of the house reveals that only minor alterations have been made since it was completed in the spring of 1906.[12]

In the planning of "Kilmarnock," John Finley (1863–1940) sought the ideal leisure-time retreat from an unusually active life as educator, editor, and author. For his era, he was the consummate Renaissance man. His

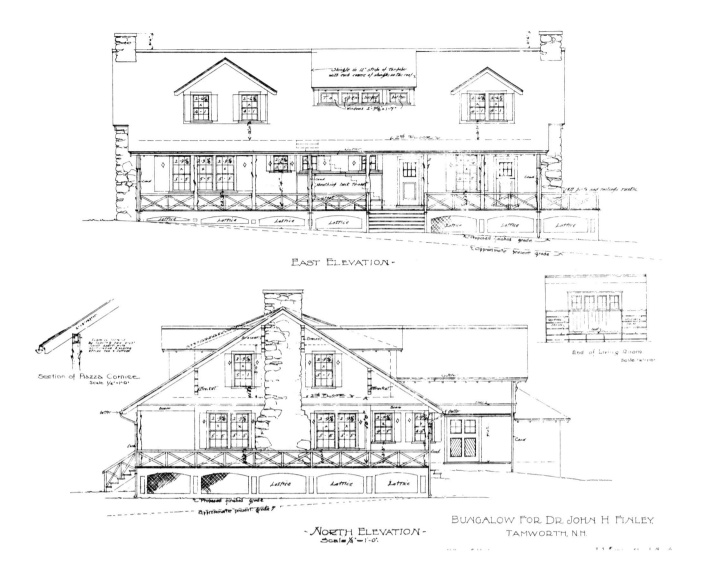

EAST ELEVATION-

Section of Piazza Cornice
Scale 1/2"=1'-0"

2nd FLOOR

-NORTH ELEVATION-
Scale 1/8"=1'-0".

End of Living Room
Scale 1/4"=1'-0'

BUNGALOW FOR DR. JOHN H. FINLEY.
TAMWORTH, N.H.

"East and North Elevations, Bungalow for Dr. John H. Finley, Tamworth, N.H.," Kilham & Hopkins, Architects, Boston, c. 1906. Courtesy of the Walter H. Kilham Collection, Brookline Historical Society, Bookline, Mass.

career was mercurial. Born in Grand Ridge, Illinois, he graduated from nearby Knox College in 1887 and spent the following two years as a graduate student in history, politics, and economics at Johns Hopkins University. His first major position came in 1892, when he was just twenty-eight years old, as president of his alma mater. He left Knox in 1899, however, to become the editor of *Harper's Weekly* in New York City. He accepted the newly established chair of politics at Princeton University a year later, only to return to New York in 1903 as the president of the College of the City of New York (today part of the City University of New York). He remained in this post for ten years, resigning in 1913 to become commissioner of education of the state of New York. He arrived at his final place of employ, where he would work twenty years, in 1921, when he was made associate editor of the *New York Times*, succeeding to editor in chief in 1937. Finley had an incredible range of interests, including the classics, walking and trail hiking (he once walked seventy-two miles in a day), and such organizations as the

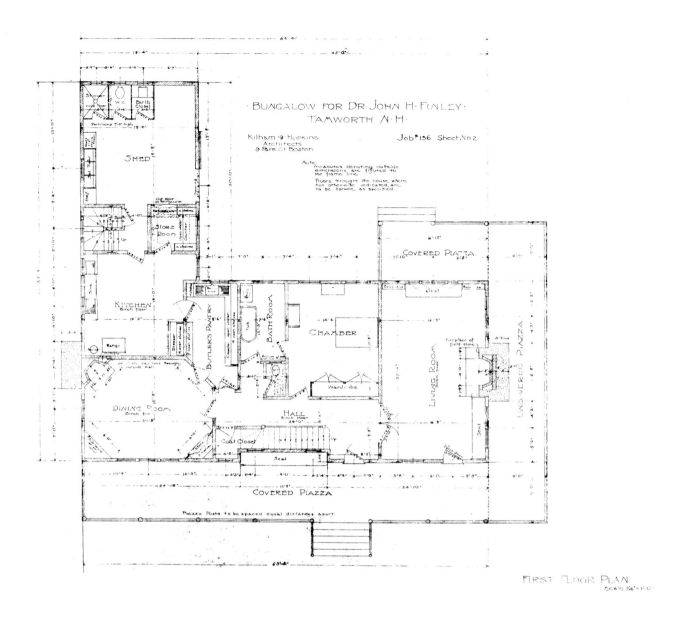

"First Floor Plan, Bungalow for Dr. John H. Finley, Tamworth, N.H.," Kilham & Hopkins, Architects, Boston, c. 1906. Courtesy of the Walter H. Kilham Collection, Brookline Historical Society, Brookline, Mass.

Boy Scouts of America, the New York Commission for the Blind, Phi Beta Kappa, and the New York Adult Education Council. He was the author of numerous books and articles, and was constantly in demand as a public speaker during his accomplished career. Finley's list of honors was truly astounding—offices and honorary memberships in national and international learned and philosophical societies, honorary degrees from thirty-two American and Canadian institutions of higher education, and decorations from thirteen foreign governments. The presence of the Finleys and the Clevelands on Stevenson Hill added much luster to an already remarkably talented Tamworth summer community.[13]

⁓

"Seven Hearths"

1912–1913

(Mrs. Frank E. Harkness)

Tamworth (Wonalancet)

"Seven Hearths" (1912–13), Wonalancet, Tamworth, N.H. Photograph by the author.

⌇ OF THE SEVERAL seasonal cottages and hotel structures once comprising the Wonalancet community in Tamworth and Albany, "Seven Hearths," the home for many years of the writer Marjory Gane Harkness, is perhaps the most imposing and aesthetically provocative. According to oral as well as documentary sources, the house was erected in 1912–13 on a tract of over fifty wooded acres. Prior to her marriage, Harkness and her sister, Gertrude, then both of Chicago, Illinois, acquired this land in 1912 from Ira B. and Alice L. Tilton, Arthur T. and Katherine Sleeper Walden, and Julia P. Lombard.[14] Initially the two sisters shared the house, but it ultimately passed to Harkness, who owned it and used it as a year-round residence until 1942.[15] The property has had several owners since.

Set on an open rise slightly north of the Wonalancet Highway, "Seven Hearths" is a curious amalgam of features from three architectural styles current in the eastern United States early in this century. Evidence of the Colonial Revival may be observed in the rectangular floor plan with central stairhall; tall matching brick end chimneys; steep-pitched roof; front, central doorway with transom and side lights; double-sash windows with shutters; and square porch columns and balusters. Although seemingly out of character for New Hampshire's White Mountains, the Spanish Colonial Revival left its mark in the stucco exterior wall surfaces and the orange tile roof. Signs of the Craftsman vernacular, which like the Spanish Colonial Revival originated outside of New England, may be seen in the open roof cornices with exposed rafters, and the long shed dormers piercing expansive roof planes. Typical of summer residences in the region, particularly in the Chocorua district of Tamworth, are the many open porches, with sleeping balconies above (a rear porch was removed some years ago).

The rather plain, functional, and logically arranged interior of the house contrasts with the more actively articulated exterior. Unbalanced principal floor plans, while highly workable, depart completely from the perfect symmetry of the front facade. The major rooms on the first floor include a large west living room, and an east side dining room and music room/ library. There are ten bedrooms, and, consistent with the name of the house, seven brick fireplaces. There is virtually no interior detail, with cypress wood employed for plain flat and slightly rounded door, window, and fireplace molding strips. Despite the simplicity and conservatism of the interior decor, evidence of quality workmanship is everywhere present.

Local sources suggest that the accomplished Sandwich contractor Larkin D. Weed (1855–after 1932), responsible for so many other summer dwellings in the area, was the designer and builder, but this assertion is thus far unsubstantiated. Moreover, conflicting evidence exists in the inscribed name of Edgar Goss, Jr., also of Sandwich, present on an unexposed surface of a first-floor window frame, along with the date "March 10, 1913," which, at the least, further documents the dating of the house. It is conceivable that Goss, though lacking a reputation as a general contractor, may have planned and erected the house himself, or have been a member of Weed's construction crew. Throughout her life, Harkness always affirmed that there was no professional architect, and the inventive, improvised character of the design all but confirms the hand of a local builder.[16]

Marjory Gane Harkness (1880–1974), the person with whom "Seven Hearths" has been primarily associated, was, like so many of her neighbors, extremely versatile and talented. Born in Yonkers, New York, she later moved to the Midwest with her family, returning east to graduate from Smith College with a bachelor's degree in 1901, and then do graduate work at the University of Chicago and the Sorbonne. She, her mother, and her sister traveled around the world. In 1918, she married Frank E. Harkness, a Chicago attorney, and resided in Washington, D.C., and Lake Forest, Illinois. After his death in 1934, Marjory Harkness demonstrated her innate, heretofore latent abilities. Launching into the real estate business, she became the secretary and later the director of the New Hampshire Board of Realtors, and sold properties throughout the southern White Mountain region. An outstanding musician, she further perfected her skills as a violinist. It was, however, as a reporter for the Laconia, New Hampshire, newspaper, and as an independent writer and editor that she made her principal mark. She was the author of *"A Brook of Our Own": A Few Notes from the File of a Mountain Real Estate Office* (1945), and *The Tamworth Narrative* (1958), an informal history of the town. Her editorial projects included the *Percy Lubbock Reader* (1957) and *The Fishbasket Papers: The Diaries, 1768–1823, of Bradbury Jewell, Esq., of Tamworth* (1963). In addition, she had articles published in the *Atlantic Monthly*, *Scribner's*, and the *New Yorker* magazines.[17] The environment of Wonalancet village and "Seven Hearths" proved the ideal place for her to practice her literary skills and pursue her other interests, including volunteer service to local organizations. While in the manner of other North Country summer residents, she complained, tongue in cheek, about the disadvantages of house ownership ("always consuming large tax and maintenance funds, too big to rent conveniently, too remote to sell"),[18] she was deeply attached to her adopted home and its scenic surroundings, and generously contributed her time and expertise to its betterment.

≈

"Birchentower"

1875–1932

(Mr. and Mrs. Marshall S. Scudder)

Tamworth (Chocorua)

"Birchentower" (1875–1932), Chocorua, Tamworth, N.H. Photograph by the author.

≈ LIKE MANY FAMILIES who built summer houses in the White Mountains before the turn of the century, the Scudders of Boston were initially introduced to the region as hotel patrons. In the early 1870s, Mr. and Mrs. Marshall Scudder were guests at the Chocorua House, owned and operated by John Henry Nickerson. Captivated by the serenity and scenic beauty of the area, they decided to buy land there and establish a summer domicile. In September 1874, with the help of their friend Nickerson, they purchased two tracts totaling about twenty-five acres on either side of the Chocorua Village–Conway road, just down the hill to the north of the hotel. While their tangible investment was in land, they also acquired what would later be regarded by many as "the most photographed view in New England."[19]

The Scudders set to work immediately to create their ideal single-season cottage. Within the next year, they had the former Emery farmhouse (c. 1845), situated just east of the road, moved by oxen back up the hillside, amongst birch trees, onto new foundations. At the same time they added a kitchen ell, front porch, and distinctive central Victorian eclectic tower to the original building block.[20] In an 1895 article, published in the *Granite Monthly*, Franklin Ware Davis alluded to the relocated house and its magnificent surroundings:

the Scudder place is the oldest of those of the neighborhood owned by summer visitors. Its brown gothic-gable stands a few yards above the carriage road. From its very door stone, the land slopes to the [Chocorua] lake side, and the view is over the near field, the pretty wind-kissed water, the little rustic [Fowler's Mill Road] bridge, and the wooded shores, up to [Mount] Chocorua's horn of silence, lone, bare, and bleak. It is not to be excelled for picturesqueness all the hills over.[21]

Most appropriately, the house has traditionally been known as "Birchentower."

Marshall Scudder retained ownership of his Chocorua property for only a few years before he died. His half-brother, Horace E. Scudder, the noted writer and editor, was the next owner, purchasing "Birchentower" and the adjacent land from Marshall Scudder's estate. Born in Boston in 1838, Horace Scudder completed preparatory studies at Roxbury and Boston Latin schools before entering Williams College, from which he graduated in 1858. Soon afterward he went to New York City where he was a teacher of private students and a writer of children's stories. In 1864 he returned to Boston to take the position as a reader of manuscripts and general editorial assistant at the recently organized firm of Hurd and Houghton. He remained with this firm, later to evolve into Houghton, Mifflin & Company, the remainder of his working life. Always interested in children and their social and intellectual growth, in 1867 he launched a juvenile monthly, *Riverside Magazine for Young People*. He became a member of the firm in 1872, but after just three years retired from the partnership to devote his full energies to editorial tasks. He reached the pinnacle of his literary career when he served as editor of the *Atlantic Monthly* from 1890 to 1898. His writings touched on a number of fields for varied audiences: *The Life and Letters of David Coit Scudder* (1864); eight juvenile "Bodley Books" of travel (1876–84); *The Dwellers of Five-Sisters Court* (1876); *Stories and Romances* (1880); *Noah Webster* (1882); *Life and Letters of Bayard Taylor* (2 vols., 1884), with Marie Hansen-Taylor; *A History of the United States* (1884) for schools; *George Washington: An Historical Biography* (1890); *Childhood in Literature and Art* (1894); and *James Russell Lowell, a Biography* (2 vols., 1901). In addition to his many literary contributions, he served higher education as a trustee of Williams and Wellesley colleges, and of the Episcopal Theological Seminary of Cambridge.[22]

After Horace Scudder's death in 1902, "Birchentower" passed to his only living daughter (he and his wife, Grace Owen, had twin girls, one of whom predeceased him), Sylvia Church Scudder, who married Ingersoll Bowditch of Boston. During their long period of ownership, which lasted well into this century, the house underwent near total transformation to the building that one may view today. In 1903, the Bowditches added a bedroom and extra bathroom. It was in 1917, however, that the major expansion occurred with the construction of the large south wing, its longitudinal axis set at an obtuse angle to the main axis of the house to encompass the superb vista of Mount Chocorua. Topped by intersecting truncated gable roofs, suggesting the impact of the then-popular Craftsman style, the wing contains a large first-floor living room, with bedrooms and bathrooms above. It is of particular interest that this wing was designed by a friend of the family, Lois Lilley Howe (1864–1964) of Boston, the first woman to receive an architectural degree from MIT, and the cofounder of one of the first architectural firms (Howe, Manning and Almy) to be established by women in the United States. This addition was the only portion of the house thus far linked with a professional architect; later the Bowditches modified the original connected farmhouse in 1932, creating a new dining room from a former hallway on the first floor, altering the bedrooms above and removing the Victorian tower. The bulk of the house, therefore, is a product of new construction since Marshall Scudder made his initial real estate purchases in 1874. Painted a naturalistic grey-green color, "Birchentower," its several parts spontaneously generated under the same family ownership, seems to blend unobtrusively into its sylvan environment. In our frenetic modern era, it has remained a comfortable refuge and a place for relaxing social, recreational, and cultural pursuits.[23]

~

The Sherwin Cottage

c. 1885–86

(General and Mrs. Thomas Sherwin)

"Greycroft"

c. 1896

(Mr. and Mrs. Charles G. Loring)

"Masquemoosic"

c. 1896–97

(Mr. and Mrs. Wilton P. Wainwright)

Tamworth (Chocorua)

~ THREE COTTAGES LOCATED within a short distance of each other on the west side of Chocorua Lake are believed to have been designed by the prolific Boston architect C. Howard Walker (1857–1936), himself a resident of the Chocorua summer colony and the planner of several other houses there (see "Pine Cone"). While none of these buildings has yet been securely documented as a Walker commission, visual evidence and local oral tradition quite convincingly connect them with Walker's architectural repertoire. Not only are they strikingly similar in size, proportions, and materials, but they share characteristics with other known examples of Walker's work in the White Mountain region. Each was built during the decade when Walker was most active in Chocorua and this area of Tamworth experienced its most active period of residential growth.[24]

The first of the three cottages was constructed for General Thomas Sherwin and his wife, Isabel Fisk Sherwin, of Jamaica Plain, Boston, on one hundred acres of prime land with Chocorua Lake shore frontage. They acquired this substantial tract, known historically as "the Hatch place," from Tamworth resident Charles E. Beck and the estate of Moses C. Varney in May 1885. Based on the date and location of this purchase, and a published reference to the house, a construction date of around 1885–86 seems reasonable.[25] Typical of others of Walker's residential designs, the Sherwin cottage is characterized by low, horizontal lines, with medium-pitched principal and secondary gable roofs broken by single and multiple window dormers. Several of the roofs, including the dormers, possess trun-

The Sherwin cottage (c. 1885–86), Chocorua, Tamworth, N.H. Photograph by the author.

"Greycroft" (c. 1896), Chocorua, Tamworth, N.H. Photograph by the author.

cated ends. A common Walker trademark is the local fieldstone masonry in the porch walls and square support columns, which contrasts so effectively with the dark-toned shingled wall surfaces. The long rear (west) ell, at least its final two sections, is believed to be a later addition, and may incorporate one or more older farm buildings.

A friend of Charles P. Bowditch (see "Connie Sauti"), who apparently enticed him to come to Chocorua, Sherwin (1839–1914) was born in Boston and, like many of his Chocorua neighbors, graduated from Harvard College (class of 1860). For a brief time he taught high school, but in 1861 joined the Union army in the Civil War, in which he served until 1864. For gallantry at the Battle of Gettysburg and meritorious service during the war, Sherwin was commissioned as colonel and brigadier general of the United States volunteers. He then resumed his teaching at the Boston English High School, and between 1866 and 1883 held administrative posts for the city of Boston. In 1883 he commenced a career in the telephone business that was to span over a quarter of a century, during much of which he was president of the New England Telephone and Telegraph Company. Subsequently, he was chairman of the board of directors until his death, and was an officer or director of other corporations, several in the telephone industry. In all probability, Sherwin met Bowditch through their common involvement in the telephone communications field.[26]

Styled "Greycroft" by its owners, the Lorings of Boston, the second of the Walker-associated cottages is, like the others, a fairly modest-sized structure, featuring dark natural roof and wall shingling, contrasting with fieldstone porch walls, support columns, and plain pilasters. Exhibiting a rusticated look, characteristic of most of Walker's other regional houses, and displaying traits of the Shingle style, "Greycroft" is distinguished by its intersecting gambrel roofs, broken by brick chimneys and flat and hipped-roof dormers. Dating the cottage at around 1896 is based on the year of the Lorings' initial land purchase in Chocorua, as well as the deed description, placing the house and subsequent abutting land acquisitions on Philbrick Hill.[27]

Charles Greely Loring (1828–1902) was most likely also introduced to the Chocorua colony by Charles P. Bowditch. Loring and Bowditch had common Boston and Harvard social ties, and shared an interest in historical archaeology and book collecting. Born in Boston, Loring received a bachelor's degree from Harvard in 1848, and a master's in 1851. Over the next few years he was a member of Louis Agassiz's scientific expedition to the Lake Superior district, attended scientific school at Harvard, and traveled with his father in Europe and the Near East. During the Civil War, Loring rose to the rank of brigadier general; in 1865, he was breveted major general of volunteers in recognition of his "gallant and meritorious service." Returning to civilian life, he resumed his travels to the Near East, committing himself to the study of Egyptology. In 1872, when the new Museum of Fine Arts in Boston was forming, he installed the Way Collection of Egyptology, was made a trustee, and was appointed a member of the

"Masquemoosic" (c. 1896–97), Chocorua, Tamworth, N.H. Photograph by the author.

collections committee. Four years later, Loring became curator of the museum, a position which he held with distinction until just before his death. His extensive private library, treating Egyptian history, culture, and artifacts, was left to the museum. His cottage in Chocorua has passed to subsequent generations of the Loring family.[28]

"Masquemoosic" (called "Stonecrop" by its current owners), the third Walker-attributed cottage, was erected in around 1896–97 for Mr. and Mrs. Wilton P. Wainwright of Boston. Unfortunately, to date Wainwright has been an elusive personage, and little is known about him, his profession, or why he and his wife chose Chocorua for the family summer residence. County deeds records show, however, that the Wainwrights acquired a single thirty-two-acre parcel of land from the Sherwin family in December 1895,[29] after summer visits to the Chocorua House hotel with their children. The Wainwrights built in around 1896–97.[30] The result of their collaboration with Walker was a small house, with broad low-pitched roof planes, juxtaposing native mortared fieldstone (end chimney, porch walls, and square column supports) with dark weathered shingle walls. Like the Sherwin cottage and so many other Chocorua residences, "Masquemoosic" commands a striking view of the cone of Mount Chocorua across Chocorua Lake. This dominant feature of the local landscape was the primary visual ordering point influencing the placement and planning of "Masquemoosic" and virtually all of the other houses in the community around the lake.

~

The Chadwick Cottage

c. 1890–91

(Dr. and Mrs. James R. Chadwick)

Tamworth (Chocorua)

The Chadwick cottage (c. 1890–91), Chocorua, Tamworth, N.H. Photograph courtesy of Scott Paul, Chocorua.

∾ SEEMINGLY CLINGING TO the steep western side of Washington Hill, with a split view of Mounts Whiteface and Chocorua, is the rustic Shingle-style cottage originally built for Dr. and Mrs. James R. Chadwick of Boston. According to local oral history sources, the house was but another of Boston architect C. Howard Walker's ingenious designs for the Chocorua summer colony (see "Pine Cone"). Collaborating with Walker on its construction in about 1890–91 was the talented contracting team led by Larkin D. Weed (1855–after 1932) of nearby Whiteface (Sandwich) (see "Far Fastures," Sandwich, and "Juniper," Tamworth). The Chadwick residence bears many of the hallmarks of Walker's other commissions in Chocorua, with its irregular floor plan and asymmetrical elevations, fine interior wood paneling and other detail, and native fieldstone foundations and square porch piers juxtaposed with natural shingle-sheathed outer walls. Dark, green-painted molding strips define the eaves and frame the window and door apertures. The presence of the first-floor sitting porch and two second-floor open sleeping porches accentuates the primary purpose of the cottage—to provide optimal vacation rest, relaxation, and leisure.[31]

Drawn to Tamworth as a result of his Harvard ties, James Chadwick (1844–1905) was born in Boston, where he received his secondary education at E. S. Dixwell's School. He then proceeded on to Harvard College, from which he was granted his bachelor's degree in 1865. After two years in Europe, he returned home, entered the Harvard Medical School, and graduated with master's and medical degrees in 1871. Following additional study of medicine, emphasizing gynecology, in Europe, he returned to Boston, was appointed lecturer at the Harvard Medical School in 1873, and commenced the formal practice of medicine in his native city. During the next year he assisted in the establishment of the gynecological department at Boston City Hospital. In 1876, in conjunction with his father-in-law,

Dr. George H. Lyman, he played an important role in the organization of the American Gynecological Society, later serving as its secretary and president. Versatile, as were so many accomplished people of his generation, Chadwick had a variety of interests, one of which was books. One of the founders of the Boston Medical Library, he was its librarian for three decades, helping to build and diversify its outstanding collections. He was also the founder and first president of the Harvard Medical Alumni Association, and in 1892 helped to reorganize the New England Cremation Society. A productive scholar, his bibliography contains over sixty citations largely treating gynecology, medical libraries, and cremation. As a pioneer in his field of specialization, Chadwick enjoyed a national reputation, and circulated in appropriate company with the distinguished group of leaders comprising the community around Chocorua Lake.[32]

Like many of their neighbors, the Chadwicks first became acquainted with Chocorua and its real estate possibilities through summer hotel stays in the late 1880s, in all probability at John Nickerson's Chocorua House. Convinced of the advantages of the area, in August 1890, Chadwick acquired approximately seven acres of land to the east of the main road, north of the hotel, between parcels owned by Charles P. Bowditch and Samuel Scudder. Three months later he added ten acres to this initial purchase. Over the next year, on this beautifully situated tract, his family erected their vacation home, for more than a decade, a primary locus of cultural life in Chocorua.[33]

~

"Pine Cone"

c. 1891–92

(Mr. and Mrs. C. Howard Walker)

Tamworth (Chocorua)

West elevation, "Pine Cone" (c. 1891–92), Chocorua, Tamworth, N.H. Photograph by the author.

~ C. HOWARD WALKER's position in the Chocorua summer community was comparable to that held by New York architect Charles A. Platt (see "Heavenly Hill" and "The Clearing") at the famed Cornish colony in the Connecticut River Valley of central New Hampshire. Like Platt at Cornish, Walker, an internationally known Boston architect and educator, was both a designer of houses as well as a summer resident, forging fruitful client relationships through his network of friends over a nearly twenty-year period. Furthermore, both Platt and Walker prepared the plans and supervised the construction of their own houses at their respective places of summer sojourn. Walker's professional career, however, developed in a different direction than Platt's, as biographical data and memorial statements by his professional colleagues attest.

C. Howard Walker (1857–1936) was born in Boston, educated at Boston public schools, and received his architectural training in the office of Sturgis and Brigham. In 1879 he entered professional practice in New York City, but in 1881 he traveled to Europe, where he spent the next three years participating in an archaeological expedition to Asia Minor, traveling, and studying famous architectural monuments. Returning to Boston in 1884, Walker resumed practice as an architect, and over the next five years (under several firm names) was responsible for the design of apartment houses, schools, private residences, and public buildings in the city and environs. Subsequently, he joined with Thomas R. Kimball to form a partnership in Omaha, Nebraska, and the two men promptly gained wide recognition as official architects for the Trans Mississippi Exposition, held in Omaha in 1898. This led to Walker's selection to head the Board of Architects, formed to execute plans for buildings comprising the Louisiana Purchase Exposition, which opened in St. Louis in 1903.[34]

After the partnership with Kimball ended by mutual consent, Mr. Walker once again returned to his native city, reestablishing an office there and carrying on architectural practice from 1919 until his death, independently and with his son, Harold D., as a partner. Among his best known works in Boston were the Oliver Ditson Building (see "The Boulders," Jackson), the Washington Irving High School, the British Consulate, the Longfellow School, the Franklin Bank building, and the Mount Vernon Church, along with other public and educational buildings in the city and its suburbs.[35]

Although his record as an architect was certainly not undistinguished, it was as a lecturer, writer, and servant to the field of architecture that Walker was best known. While still a relatively young professional, he was appointed to the Boston Art Commission in 1898. Later on he became director of the Department of Design at the Boston Museum of Art. During his career he lectured often at the Museum, Harvard, MIT, the Lowell Institute, the New England Conservatory of Music, and the Child-Walker School of Fine Arts, of which he was one of the founders. He made perhaps his most indelible impression on his profession as an editor of the Boston-based *Architectural Review*, and the author of superb articles on building design and decoration, published in the *Review* and other journals. In recognition of his broad accomplishments, the Royal Institute of British Architects confirmed his international reputation by making him an honorary member. In 1921, the University of Pennsylvania conferred on him the honorary degree of Doctor of Fine Arts. Walker was also a member and officer of the American Institute of Architects, the National Fine Arts Commission, the Boston Institute of Architects, the Copley Society, the American Academy of Arts and Sciences, the St. Botolph and Economic clubs of Boston, and the National Arts Club of New York. After his death, his friends and his colleagues in architecture extolled his talents "as a teacher and as an exponent of architectural history and principles."[36]

Walker and his wife, Mary Louise, were first attracted to the White Mountains as summer residents during the late 1880s. As early as 1878 and 1879, however, prior to his marriage, he had made sketching trips to the region, and his sketchbooks from these years contain lovely, detailed panoramas of Franconia Notch, the Sandwich Range, Mount Osceola, Mount Moosilauke, the Pemigewassett Valley, the Presidential Range, and other natural features.[37] Walker's first two land acquisitions in Chocorua were in 1891 and 1893, and comprised a thirty-acre parcel with driveway right-of-way facing Chocorua Lake and the mountains to the north.[38] It was on the 1891 purchase that he erected the plain and functional late-Shingle-style house that has survived, essentially unaltered to this day. Two stories and L-shaped, with slightly flared intersecting hipped roofs, "Pine Cone," as it was titled, contains impressive interior public spaces, distinguished by their finely detailed natural dark-wood paneling, ceiling beams, and staircase motifs, all executed in the classical idiom.[39] The house, with its pleasant surrounding woods, conveys a sense of reassuring serenity and peace.

South end, "Pine Cone" (c. 1891–92), Chocorua, Tamworth, N.H. Photograph by the author.

"Kalarama"

c. 1891–92

(Mr. Gustavus Browne Maynadier)

Tamworth (Chocorua)

⌁ "KALARAMA," SUGGESTING the words "kalo orama," meaning "pleasant view" in Greek, was the realized dream of Gustavus Browne Maynadier, a railroad engineer from Roxbury, Massachusetts. According to family tradition, Maynadier discovered the open, north-facing hillside site of this distinctive Shingle-style house while canoeing on nearby Chocorua Lake in the 1880s. The first recorded documentation of any Tamworth real estate acquisitions in the Maynadier name, however, was not until 1891, when a sixteen-acre tract of land with right-of-way access was sold for $700 by the Gilman family to Gustavus' son, Gustavus Howard Maynadier. The family cottage was erected on this parcel around 1891–92. It is believed that the elder Maynadier designed "Kalarama" without the assistance of an architect. In doing so, he was said to have applied expertise in structural design acquired while planning railroad bridges in Peru. The substantial wooden frame of the house is testament to the skills and knowledge of both the designer and builder.[40]

Collaborating with Maynadier on the construction of "Kalarama" was Larkin D. Weed (1855–after 1932), from the Whiteface section of the neigh-

"Kalarama" (c. 1891–92), Chocorua, Tamworth, N.H. Photograph by the author.

boring town of Sandwich. Over a period of fifty years, Weed established a broad reputation as a builder and remodeler of public buildings, summer cottages, and other types of structures in Sandwich, around Squam Lake, and in Chocorua and other portions of Tamworth (see "Far Pastures," Sandwich). "Kalarama" was one of his earliest commissions. Weed and Maynadier crafted a building most notable for its huge wooden beams (shipped from Maine) which span the width of the attic, the second-floor rooms, and the large first-floor parlor, built to resemble a captain's cabin in the stern of a sailing ship. Y-shaped in form, with fragile-appearing side verandas, the house possesses an impressive total of twenty-three windows, many of which provide a lovely panorama of the Sandwich Range, with the dominant rocky cone of Mount Chocorua at its east end. The presence of shingled wall surfaces, diamond-shaped and round-arched windows, and non-matching roof dormers are convincing evidence of the Shingle style.[41]

The house remained essentially in its original form until the 1920s, when, under the direction of Gustavus Howard Maynadier, a Harvard English professor, the verandas were replaced, and a new two-story ell containing two bedrooms over a kitchen was appended to the rear.[42] Today, it continues to be used and enjoyed by the descendants of the first owner, one of only a few pre-1930 summer cottages in the White Mountains to have this distinction.

≈

"Cairncroft"

1892

(Mr. and Mrs. Emil C. Hammer)

Tamworth (Chocorua)

"Cairncroft" (1892), Chocorua, Tamworth, N.H.
Photograph by the author.

~ IN JULY 1892, *Among the Clouds*, the tourist weekly published on the summit of Mount Washington, offered this encapsulated assessment and description of "Cairncroft," one of the new cottages in the Chocorua vacation colony:

> One of the prettiest and best summer residences in all of the White Mountain region is Mr. E. C. Hammer's beautiful stone residence situated just below the Chocorua House [hotel]. The lower story is built of rough stones artistically set, above it is shingled and rough stone pillars around the broad piazzas give it a very rustic appearance. The lawn is beautifully laid out with huge pyramids of curiously shaped stones piled here and there. The mammoth stone walls, fully 10 feet wide, for fences add much to the beauty of the lawn.[43]

Except for the addition of dormers and a second-floor sleeping porch in the 1930s, the house, its adjacent barn, and other outbuildings, look much as they did when they were erected during the spring and summer of 1892, on land acquired two years earlier.[44] Unlike other cottages in Chocorua whose mountain and lake vistas have become obscured by forest growth, "Cairncroft" has retained its superlative view of Chocorua Lake and the mountains to the north, its expansive and open front lawn appearing almost as exactly it did in nineteenth-century photographs.[45] Descendants of the original owners continue to hold title to the property, strongly committed to the preservation of its buildings, as well as the visual and documentary record that forms the basis of its story.

Given the lack of published materials about him, Emil Christian Hammer (c. 1820–1894) would appear to be somewhat of an enigma, but his remarkable life accomplishments belie such a characterization. Born in

Ice house (left), stable (center), and well house (right), "Cairncroft" (1892), Chocorua, Tamworth, N.H. Photograph by the author.

Copenhagen, Denmark, from a "family of noble extraction," he came to the United States about 1840, first engaging in several business enterprises in Boston. Chief among these was the Waltham Manufacturing Company, of which he became the treasurer in the 1880s, and a director and principal stockholder. He also had interests in two Boston banks and several manufacturing corporations outside of the Boston area. In 1864, with his brother Thorvel F. Hammer, he acquired the Branford (Connecticut) Malleable Iron and Fittings Company, which grew to become one of the most successful industrial concerns of its kind in the world. Twenty years later, he single-handedly established the United States Watch Company of Waltham, Massachusetts, and is reputed to have spent about six hundred thousand dollars developing the business. He was sole owner, treasurer, and a director at the time of his death. In 1864, President Abraham Lincoln appointed him to the post of Danish vice consul for Massachusetts, based in Boston. Hammer was also recognized as an accomplished artist, was a consistent benefactor to the Boston Art Club, and was regarded as one of the most knowledgeable art critics in Massachusetts. His estate was said to have been worth ten million dollars, a fabulous sum for the time, and he left behind numerous as well as "unostentatious" charities, and "a host of dependents in this country and in Europe."[46]

Local residents have long speculated that the architect of "Cairncroft" was C. Howard Walker (see "Pine Cone"), the designer of at least three other Chocorua cottages about the same time. Based on visual comparisons with other known Walker commissions, such an assumption is quite plausible. A full set of plans in the possession of the present owners, however, proves without question that the architect was not Walker, but Edwin James Lewis, Jr. (1859–1937) of Boston, a graduate of MIT and a former draftsman with the firm of Peabody and Stearns, who later designed two houses of their own in Tamworth (see "Great Hill Farm" and "Willowgate"). After 1887, Lewis practiced alone from his offices at 9 Park Street, specializing in rural dwellings and church buildings. From his plans, more than thirty-five churches in the United States and Canada were erected. His best known work in Boston was the Second Unitarian Church. Highly regarded by his professional colleagues, Lewis was elected to the American Institute of Architects early in his career, became an AIA Fellow in 1891, and was an active member and secretary of the Boston Society of Architects. He frequently lectured on historical and ecclesiastical topics, and devoted time to municipal reform. Lewis' work for the Hammers at Chocorua reflects a skilled sophistication in the handling of site relationship, materials, massing, proportions, floor-plan configurations, fenestration, and other subdued but defining details. In all respects, "Cairncroft" is both a successful product of and a contributor to its still largely unspoiled mountain and lake country environment.[47]

≈

"Conni Sauti"

1892–93

(Mr. and Mrs. Charles P. Bowditch)

Tamworth (Chocorua)

"Conni Sauti" (1892–93), Chocorua, Tamworth, N.H. Photograph by the author.

꙳ THE BOWDITCHES FROM Jamaica Plain, Boston, were among the founders and first members of the Chocorua summer colony. Their long association with Chocorua began about 1880 when a friend, Henshaw B. Walley, attracted Charles P. Bowditch to the locale. He immediately became captivated by the beautiful natural setting, tranquility, and agreeable climate. Over the next several summers, Bowditch, his wife, Cornelia, and their children spent time at the Chocorua House, run by John Henry and Clarinda Nickerson.[48]

Around 1890, according to local sources, a tragic episode occurred, which, eventually proved fortuitous, not only for the Bowditches, but also for the Chocorua community. Just east of Chocorua Lake, on the main road north to Conway, was a red farm house, today known as "Red Gables," which was then owned by the Cone family. Included in the property was a beach area on the lake. Here young boys from the neighborhood often swam naked, inspiring warnings from the very short-tempered man of the house, Sylvester Cone, not to do so. Finally, after repeated words with the boys, there was a confrontation, Cone overreacted, and shot and killed one of them. A trial ensued, and Cone was sent to jail. Soon thereafter, his farm was offered for sale, and Charles Bowditch hastened up from Boston, and purchased the entire property. This was the first of many subsequent Bowditch land acquisitions in Chocorua.[49]

The Bowditch cottage, "Conni Sauti" ("pleasant view" in Abenaki), was erected in 1892–93 from plans by Boston architect C. Howard Walker (1857–1936) (see "Pine Cone," Tamworth). The builder was Wyatt Bryant, possibly of the Sandwich family.[50] During the 1890s and early 1900s, Walker became an integral part of the Chocorua colony, building his own house and designing others there for friends and new clients. Facing west and set back from the road on a gradual rise, "Conni Sauti" commands a "splendid view of [both] lake and mountain." Conceived in the then fashionable Shingle style, this large and imposing house has a frontage of approximately one hundred feet, with two wings, sixty and ninety feet in length, set at right angles to the central block.[51] Completely sheathed in red-brown natural shingles, the building is marked by its matching gable-roof wing pavilions with their two-story, semioctagonal bays; tall brick end chimneys; long front veranda; and shed and gable-roof dormers piercing the expansive front roof planes. The interior, particularly the central hall and dining room, displays fine wood paneling and other detailing characteristic of architect Walker's best work. Attached to the rear of the house is a service ell (c. 1896) with a drive-through porte cochere surmounted by a second story with cantilevered porches and a steep-pitched roof. This later addition was designed by the nationally renowned Boston architectural firm of Robert Swain Peabody (1845–1917) and John Goddard Stearns, Jr. (1843–1917) (see "Willowgate," Tamworth)—their complete set of drawings is contained in a larger collection of their work at the Boston Public Library.[52] Upon viewing "Conni Sauti" today, one is immediately struck by its indigenous quality, as it is seemingly rooted in the land, in perfect harmony with its natural surroundings. It is difficult to fault the superlative joint effort of Walker, Peabody, and Stearns.

Charles Pickering Bowditch (1842–1921), the grandson of the mathematician and navigational expert Nathaniel Bowditch, was blessed with two simultaneous, highly successful careers. In his native city, Boston, he established himself as a businessman, financier, and corporate trustee, serving over the years as president of the Pepperell Manufacturing Company and the Massachusetts Hospital Life Insurance Company, and as a director of the American Bell Telephone Company and the Providence Railroad

Court side elevation, rear ell, "Conni Sauti" (1892–93), Peabody and Stearns, Architects, Boston, c. 1896. Peabody and Stearns Collection, Boston Public Library. Reproduced courtesy of the Trustees of the Boston Public Library.

COURT SIDE ELEVATION

Corporation. His interests, however, were remarkably eclectic, as evidenced by his membership, and in some cases offices held in organizations and learned societies connected with the fields of art, the sciences, anthropology, history, geography, genealogy, and archaeology. He had particularly close associations with the American Academy of Arts and Sciences, and Harvard University, from which he had received bachelor's (1863) and master's (1866) degrees. At Harvard, he served as a trustee of the Hopkins Fund, and as a member of the faculty at the Peabody Museum of Archaeology and Ethnology, for which he was the major benefactor before World War I. Over the years he assumed a "commanding position in American archaeology," becoming the greatest scholar of Maya hieroglyphic writings, in large part due to his 1910 book, *The Numeration, Calendar Systems and Astronomical Knowledge of the Mayas.* For the Peabody Museum he funded expeditions to Central America, helped plan exhibition galleries for the objects collected, and donated a library which he had built in Maya studies as well as photographic reproductions of manuscripts and rare books treating the languages of Mexico and Central America. He also founded and funded instructorships and fellowships at the museum in Central American archaeology. In addition to his appointment at Harvard, he was a member of the archaeology department at the University of Pennsylvania. His deep involvement in archaeology resulted in a strong commitment to preserving the natural environment; at Chocorua, he and his friend John Sumner Runnells (see "Willowgate") acquired large timber tracts adjacent to Chocorua Lake, which led to the creation by the state of New Hampshire of the Bowditch-Runnells State Forest. His legacy was thus preserved, not just by "Conni Sauti," but by these magnificent, protected stands of white pines and other trees, which the public continues to enjoy today.[53]

~

"Heavenly Hill"

1898–99

(Mr. and Mrs. George H. Page)

Tamworth (Chocorua)

~ IN 1899, TWO distinguished Episcopal clergyman, the Reverends Percy Stickney Grant and Joseph Hutchinson, both of New York City, George H. and Mary H. Page of Brookline, Massachusetts, and Lilias Page of Boston formed a syndicate and purchased approximately twenty-five acres of land in Chocorua from Robert T. Hay of Boston. Situated on a pronounced hilltop, a mile north of Tamworth Iron Works on the road to Conway, the tract overlooked the Chocorua House inn, and the Hammer and Scudder properties, with awe-inspiring views of Chocorua Lake and Mount Chocorua in the distance. To this beautiful elevated site, they assigned the name, "The Heavenly Hill," and over the next few years built four summer cottages there. Three of the houses are worthy of notice because of their association with the New York City architect Charles Adams Platt (1861–1933). Platt was one of the leading designers and landscape

"Heavenly Hill" (1898–99), Chocorua, Tamworth, N.H. Photograph by the author.

planners of the American country house during its prominence at the beginning of the twentieth century.[54]

Charles Platt was born in New York, was educated at private schools, and briefly attended the National Academy of Design and the Art Students League in the city, studying both architecture and art. In 1882 he went to Europe to continue his studies, and after five years returned to New York, joined the Society of American Artists, and engaged professionally in painting and etching. He also spent time with a group of artists at the Cornish, New Hampshire, workshop of the famous sculptor Augustus Saint-Gaudens, making valuable contacts that would later lead to architectural commissions. In 1892 Platt returned to Europe, sketched and painted, and traveled to Italy with his brother William, where he collected material for his only book, *Italian Gardens*, published in 1894. According to his biographers, he rather drifted into the practice of architecture, working with his first client in 1889–91. His career launched, he proceeded to receive numerous commissions for gardens in the Italian Manner, as well as urban and rural houses. While he concentrated largely on residential buildings, he also designed apartment houses, commercial edifices, educational structures, and campus schemes. Among his most noted works before World War I were the Winston Churchill house and garden, the Herbert Croly house and garden, the Misses Lawrence house, and his own house and garden, all in Cornish; the Frank Cheney, Jr., house, South Manchester, Connecticut; the Frank T. Maxwell house, Rockville, Connecticut; the Theodore H. Dunham house, Northeast Harbor, Maine; the John T. Pratt house and garden, Glen Cove, New York; the William G. Mather house, Cleveland, Ohio; the Robert H. Schutz house, Hartford, Connecticut; the Studio Building and Astor Court Apartments, New York City; and the Leader-News Building in Cleveland. After 1916, when he established an architectural office in New York City, Platt turned more to museum and education designs: the Freer Gallery and an addition to the Corcoran Gallery, Washington, D.C.; the Lyman Allyn Museum, New London, Connecticut; and buildings and campus plans for the University of Illinois (Urbana), Connecticut College (New London), Deerfield (Massachusetts) Academy, and Phillips Academy (Andover, Massachusetts). He also served as consulting architect on projects for Dartmouth College (Hanover, New Hampshire), Johns Hopkins University (Baltimore, Maryland), and the University of Rochester (New York). In 1928, he retired from active practice to Cornish, and became president of the American Academy in Rome.[55] Throughout his career, Platt worked consistently in the classical tradition, and "his buildings reveal a sureness and a mastery of style which placed him in the forefront of the American Renaissance."[56]

Charles Platt's foremost commission for "The Heavenly Hill" consortium in Chocorua was for George H. Page, a Boston schoolteacher, and his wife, Mary H., the sister of Reverend Joseph Hutchinson. Erected in 1898–99, "Heavenly Hill," as the new owners christened their house, was one of the architect's earliest buildings.[57] Fortuitously, it is fully documented by a set of plans at the Avery Library, Columbia University, New York City.

"East Elevation, House for George H. Page, Esq., Chocorua, N.H.," Charles A. Platt, Architect, New York City, c. 1898. Courtesy of the Avery Architectural and Fine Arts Library, Columbia University in the City of New York.

·· EAST·· ELEVATION·· ·

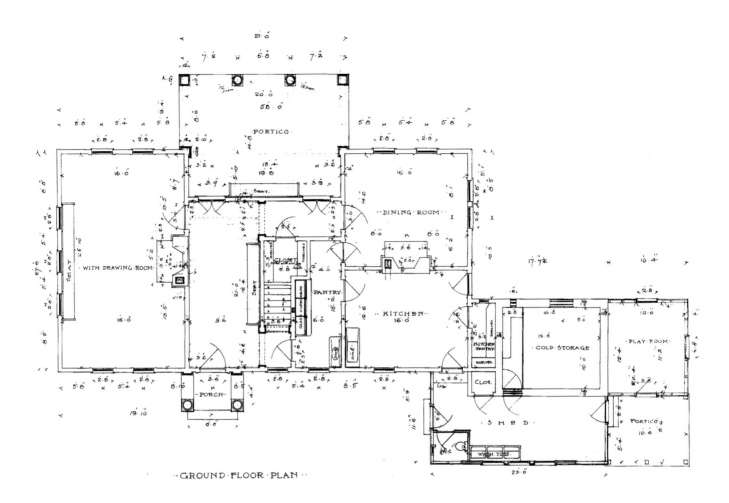

· GROUND · FLOOR · PLAN ·

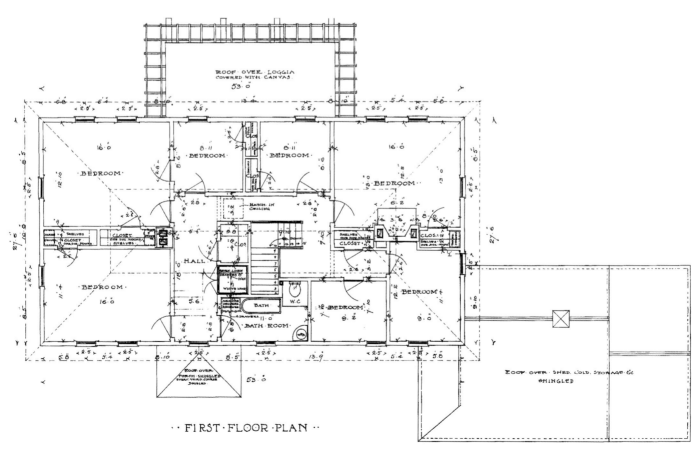

· FIRST · FLOOR · PLAN ·

"Weatherledge" (Grant/Stone House, 1907), Chocorua, Tamworth, N.H. Photograph by the author.

According to Platt's most recent and principal biographer, Keith N. Morgan, in this dwelling, and in other residences in Chocorua, Dublin, New Hampshire, and other New England rural communities, the architect "developed a variable model that he considered appropriate for the informal summer life of sophisticated, but not ostentatious, urbanites." In all these houses, in various combinations, one may observe balanced floor plans; low, emphatically horizontal massing; low hipped main and secondary roofs; deep overhanging eaves with exposed rafter ends; roughly textured flush wall boarding with deep channels separating the boards; tall brick chimneys with molded, perforated flue caps; and entrance porches and loggias supported by classical round or square columns. Deceptively larger than it looks, "Heavenly Hill" contains a drawing room, hallway, dining room, kitchen, pantry, and service wing on the first floor, and three large and four small bedrooms and just one bathroom on the second. "Invariably painted white and carefully set in their site, these houses [speak] with proper proportions and great charm of New England and the Renaissance, fresh air and recreation."[58]

Positioned two hundred yards east of "Heavenly Hill," also on the crest of the hilltop, is a second, strikingly similar house, that is equally pleasant-looking and functional. It is, however, an architectural curiosity. Erected in 1907 by Rev. Percy Grant (1860–1927) for his sister Margaret and her husband, Dr. Eugene Stone (1861–1916), of New York City, this handsome dwelling is a nearly exact reverse mirror image of the Page house except that it possesses two-foot longer dimensions in its principal exterior walls, and an adjacent rather than connected ice house. The interior layout closely resembles that of "Heavenly Hill." It has been conjectured that the Grant/Stone house, today known as "Weatherledge," was built from the original Platt plans for "Heavenly Hill," employing the services of a talented local contractor and assistants. Surrounded by stately conifers and hardwoods, the house looks out on an open lawn, its main longitudinal axis directly facing and parallel to that of the Page residence. Such a conscious pairing of domestic buildings is unique in the White Mountain region.[59]

～

"Willowgate"

1899–1900

(Mr. and Mrs. John S. Runnells)

Tamworth (Chocorua)

～ THE STORY OF John Sumner Runnells (1844–1928) is one of a local boy who made good, and, as he was inclined to say, a Chocorua summer resident "born, not made."[60] Originally from Effingham, New Hampshire, at a young age he moved to Tamworth, where his father, the elder John Runnells, served as pastor of the Free Will Baptist Church for thirty-five years. The younger Runnells received his early education in the Tamworth public schools, then studied at New Hampton (New Hampshire) Academy and Amherst College, from which he graduated in 1865. During the next couple of years he taught school in Rochester and Dover, New Hampshire, while studying law. Typical of many New Englanders of his generation, he decided to go west, settling in Iowa in 1868. Quickly he made his mark there, joining the Iowa bar the following year and becoming the private secretary to the governor of the state. He then spent two years in England as United States consul at Tunstall, returning to Iowa in 1871, practicing law for the next sixteen years, participating in Republican Party politics, acting as reporter for the state supreme court, and serving as United States district attorney for Iowa from 1881 to 1885.

It was in Chicago, however, that Runnells achieved national stature. Relocating there in 1887 with his wife, the former Helen R. Baker (d. 1918), he founded the law firm of Runnells, Burry & Johnstone, with which he continued as senior partner until his retirement in 1913. In 1888 he accepted the position of general counsel for the Pullman Palace Car Company, the world's foremost railroad car building concern, advancing to vice president in 1911. He then succeeded Robert Todd Lincoln, the son of Abraham Lincoln, as president, serving in that capacity until 1922, and as chairman of the board until his death. Over the course of his legal and business career in Chicago, he was a member of several bank and industrial corporation boards, and organizations such as the Chicago Historical Society, the Saddle and Cycle Club, the Chicago Club, and the University clubs of Chicago and New York. Runnells was regarded by his peers as an eloquent speaker and gifted writer. His hobbies included book collecting and automobiling, which he frequently engaged in while in Great Britain, Europe, as well as the White Mountains of New Hampshire.[61]

While living in Chicago, the Runnells family often made summer visits to Chocorua, staying with family, friends, and at the Chocorua House inn. In 1892, Runnells and his wife made their first land purchase in the summer colony, a fifty-acre tract on Fowler's Mill Road from Mary J. Gilman.[62] Seven years passed before they built. In the spring and summer of 1899, they erected a grand summer residence on a rise commanding superb views of Chocorua Lake and the spectacular granite cone of Mount Chocorua beyond. Just before the completion and total furnishing of the house, however, disaster struck in early August: despite the best efforts of local firefighters, the house was completely destroyed by fire in a few hours. The *White Mountain Echo* poignantly reported, "the only thing that remained of the magnificent estate was one chimney which was left standing." The resilient Runnells determined to rebuild on the same site, and, within days of their misfortune, they contracted with architects and carpenters to perform this task.[63]

Commenced in late fall, 1899, the new house was ready for occupancy the following summer. Acting as architects was the prestigious Boston partnership of (Robert S.) Peabody (1845–1917) and (John Goddard) Stearns, Jr. (1843–1917), responsible for other work in Chocorua about the same time (see "Conni Sauti" and "Great Hill Farm"). In fact, it is a reasonably safe conjecture that the same firm prepared the designs for the first cottage, and that these were simply reused. Fortunately, a complete set of plan

"Willowgate" (1899–1900), Chocorua, Tamworth, N.H. Photograph from *New Hampshire Farms for Summer Homes* (7th ed., 1909), p. 44. Author's collection.

sheets for the main house and outbuildings exists at the Boston Public Library. Among these are elevation and floor sketches for a stable, carriage barn, and service wing, enlarged from an older Gilman family farm structure; this drawing closely resembles a stable building that survived the 1899 fire, and still stands on the property today.[64]

The firm of Peabody and Stearns was regarded as the most important architectural office in Boston from 1886, when Henry Hobson Richardson died, to World War I. Its position there was comparable to that of McKim, Mead and White in New York City during the same era. The influence of the firm was extraordinarily widespread, in part because of the number, variety, and significance of its commissions, but also because it served as a virtual school of postgraduate study for rising architects, many of whom later became leaders in the profession. During their long association, Peabody (a graduate of Harvard and the Ecole des Beaux Arts), Stearns (a product of the Lawrence Scientific School at Harvard), and their associates designed a broad array of buildings, mostly in New England, but also elsewhere in the United States. The firm's list of over one thousand commissions includes educational buildings (for Harvard, Smith College, Simmons College, Lawrenceville School, Groton School, Worcester Academy); commercial structures (India Building, Boston; U.S. Customhouse tower, Boston; Security Building, St. Louis; Exchange Building, Boston; United Bank Building, New York City); hotels (The Antlers and Glen Eyrie Lodge, Colorado Springs; The Brunswick, Boston); churches (Church of the Messiah, St. Louis; Union Church, Northeast Harbor, Maine); town and city halls

"North and East Elevations, House for J. S. Runnells, Esq., Chocorua, N.H.," Peabody and Stearns, Architects, Boston, c. 1899. Peabody and Stearns Collection, Boston Public Library. Reproduced courtesy of the Trustees of the Boston Public Library.

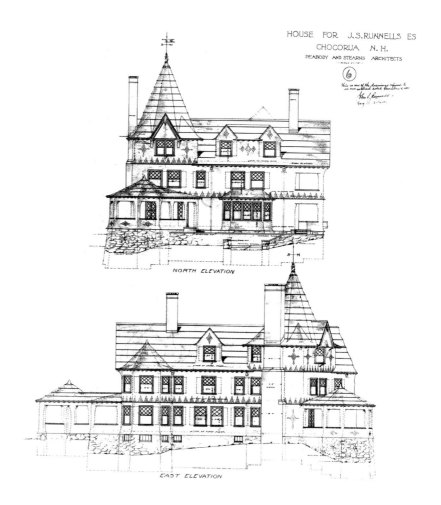

HOUSE FOR J.S.RUNNELLS ES
CHOCORUA N.H.
PEABODY AND STEARNS ARCHITECTS

NORTH ELEVATION

EAST ELEVATION

"Side Elevation and First Floor Plan, Alterations in Stable for J. S. Runnells, Esq., Chocorua, N.H.," c. 1899. Peabody and Stearns Collection, Boston Public Library. Reproduced courtesy of the Trustees of the Boston Public Library.

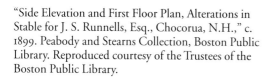

SIDE ELEVATION

FRONT ELEVATION

(Clinton, Chelsea, and Worcester, Massachusetts); World's Columbian Exposition buildings, Chicago (1892–93); other public buildings; and great numbers of well-conceived and well-executed houses and large estates in urban, suburban, and rural locations. Peabody and Stearns' work at Chocorua, a summer community dominated by Boston-area people, no doubt resulted from the firm's many professional contacts in and around the Bay State capital city.[65]

Pioneers of the American Shingle style, Peabody and Stearns created numerous vacation retreats in this idiom between 1880 and 1905, particularly along the New England coast. "Willowgate" rivaled some of the firm's most outstanding cottages in Maine on the islands of Islesboro and Mount Desert. Like these cottages, the Runnells house suggested "the rustic style of life, removed from the world of commerce and industry."[66] Similarly, "Willowgate" featured complex and sculptured massing, an asymmetrical floor plan and elevations (see illustrations of drawings), steep-pitched gable roofs penetrated by pronounced gable dormers, tall brick chimneys, natural stone foundations, piazzas, enclosed porches, and a porte cochere. Tudor-style trim, characteristic of the firm's late-Shingle-style residential architecture, was evident everywhere on the exterior, most notably in the

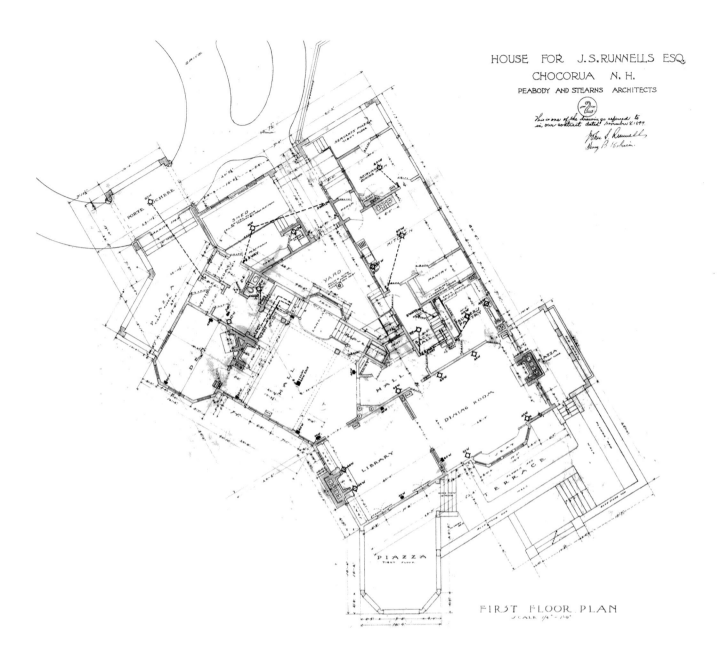

HOUSE FOR J.S.RUNNELLS ESQ
CHOCORUA N.H.
PEABODY AND STEARNS ARCHITECTS

FIRST FLOOR PLAN

"First Floor Plan, House for J. S. Runnells, Esq., Chocorua, N.H.," Peabody and Stearns, Architects, Boston, c. 1899. Peabody and Stearns Collection, Boston Public Library. Reproduced courtesy of the Trustees of the Boston Public Library.

patterned shingle siding, diamond-pane over single-pane sash windows, steep-pitched tower and dormer gable roofs, and roof finials. The ponderous but picturesque corner tower, present in so many Peabody and Stearns houses, gives "Willowgate" an air of permanence, rooting the entire unified building in the ground. The interior, fully electrified and containing an elevator, was spacious and free-flowing, with seven major rooms on the first floor, eight on the second, and six in the attic story, all enclosing an open, central trapezoidal courtyard. In its prime, the Runnells cottage was one of the preeminent summer residences in the White Mountains, and its demolition in the mid-1940s was regrettable.[67]

≈

"The Clearing"

1901–2

(Miss Lilias Page)

Tamworth (Chocorua)

"The Clearing" (1901–2), Chocorua, Tamworth, N.H. Photograph by the author.

of "The Heavenly Hill," a hundred yards east of the main road north to Conway, is "The Clearing," a modest but nonetheless impressive summer cottage erected in 1901–2 for Lilias Page of Boston. Sister of George H. Page, the first owner of "Heavenly Hill," farther up the hillside, Page was a partner in the syndicate that jointly acquired land in the vicinity in 1899 (see "Heavenly Hill"). Her portion of the original twenty-five-acre tract consisted of about seven acres, today heavily forested, but at the time relatively open, permitting outstanding views of Chocorua Lake and the White Mountain panorama to the north and northwest. Only occasionally in residence herself, Page financed and built the house largely as an investment, often renting it to the owners of Chocorua House hotel next door as an annex for their guests.[68]

Like her brother's house, Page's cottage was designed by the accomplished New York City artist and architect Charles A. Platt (1861–1933). It is believed that the Pages' connection with Platt was through their sister Annie, who was a friend and model for the sculptor Augustus Saint-Gaudens at his Cornish, New Hampshire, studio. Beginning in the late 1890s, Platt was a member of the famed Cornish summer artists colony and knew Saint-Gaudens and his colleagues, so such an association is quite possible. Platt likely found Chocorua a very appealing and appropriate setting for his country residential architecture, for in many respects it resembled Cornish, with its distinguished array of artists, intellectuals, and literati.[69]

Overlooking a small grassy open area surrounded by tall trees, "The Clearing" is a hipped-roof, two-story, wood-frame structure sheathed in

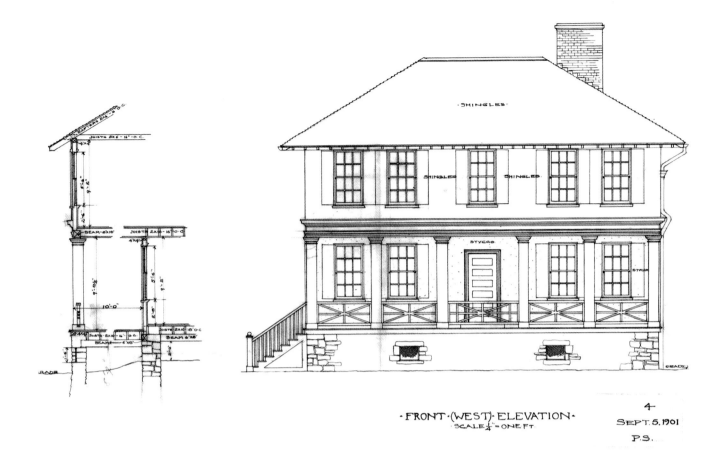

· FRONT · (WEST) · ELEVATION ·
SCALE ¼" = ONE FT.

4
SEPT. 5. 1901
P.S.

"Front (West) Elevation, House for Miss Lilias Page, Chocorua, N.H.," Peabody and Stearns, Architects, Boston, c. 1899. Courtesy of the Avery Architectural and Fine Arts Library, Columbia University in the City of New York.

FOLLOWING PAGE: "Plan of Ground Floor, House for Miss Lilias Page, Chocorua, N.H.," Peabody and Stearns, Architects, Boston, c. 1899. Courtesy of the Avery Architectural and Fine Arts Library, Columbia University in the City of New York.

natural-colored cedar shingles. In much the same fashion as "Heavenly Hill," the roof is marked by overhanging eaves with exposed rafter ends. On the front (west) facade of the house is its primary feature, a perfectly proportioned classical veranda, recessed under the second story. Six load-bearing square Doric columns, bound together by balustrade sections, rise up to a plain frieze, and support the rooms above. The frieze extends completely around the building, creating a distinct line of demarcation between the stories, and contrasting with the shingled wall surfaces. All components of the veranda, in addition to the frieze and inside wall, are painted white, consistent with the classical idiom that Platt applied in virtually all of his residential commissions. The floor plan of the main block of the house is nearly square, with a central hall, sitting room, parlor, dining room, kitchen, and pantry on the first level, and, on the larger second level, eight bedrooms serviced by just one bathroom, a hallway, and closets. Appended to the southeast rear is a small ell, originally accommodating a woodshed and laundry. Typical of the architect's early country summer houses, the interior layout is efficiently arranged, with no wasted spaces. With its effective siting, functional plan, and aesthetically pleasing embellishment, "The Clearing" is a highly successful example, albeit small and understated, of Platt's residential repertoire.[70]

~

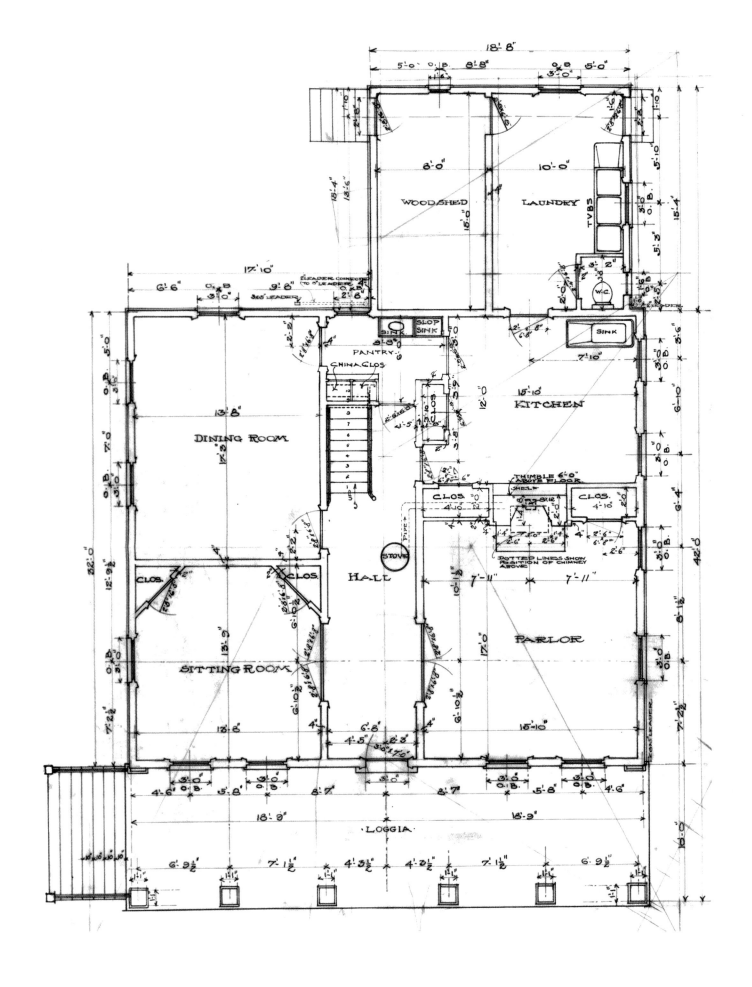

"Avoca"

c. 1905–6

(Miss Margaret J. Thayer)

Tamworth (Chocorua)

North front elevation, "Avoca" (c. 1905–6), Chocorua, Tamworth, N.H. Photograph by the author.

∾ ONE OF THE White Mountain region's most outstanding summer cottages, and its best example of the rusticated version of the Shingle style is in many respects a research enigma. What little is known about "Avoca," its origins, and its history, has been derived from personal interviews, inspection of the house and grounds, and deed references.[71] The earliest deeds for the property suggest that construction occurred in 1905 and 1906, and that the first owner and financier was a single woman, Margaret J. ("Annie") Thayer from Brooklyn, Kings County (subsequently Nassau County), New York. Extensive searches of genealogical and family history sources have failed to turn up any additional information about her. Despite the high quality and sophistication of the design, the house is not illustrated or discussed in the professional architectural literature of its day, and its designer remains a mystery. Local residents have conjectured that Boston and Chocorua architect C. Howard Walker (1857–1936) (see "Pine Cone," Tamworth) might have conceived the plans, but no evidence has yet surfaced to prove this, and the house does not resemble any other with which Walker is associated in Chocorua. It is more likely the product of a New York City–area architect or architectural firm.

The eleven-acre tract upon which Thayer built her house was purchased in July 1905 from Henshaw B. Walley, who had acquired it from Charles P. Bowditch (see "Connie Sauti," Tamworth) in 1883.[72] Also in 1905, by legal agreement with Walley, Thayer secured the right of access to and the use of shoreline on Chocorua Lake, which permitted her to erect a boathouse, bathhouse, and wharf, with the provision that she remove them "if requested."[73] It is not altogether clear exactly how long Thayer owned "Avoca," but it is documented that upon her death sometime after 1910, the property passed by bequest to Mary (Dannat) Thayer Scudder, also from Brooklyn and believed to be her sister. When Mary Scudder died in 1924, all land, buildings, and contents were transferred to her husband,

West end, "Avoca" (c. 1905–6), Chocorua, Tamworth, N.H. Photograph by the author.

Townsend Scudder, under her will.[74] A native of Northport, New York, Townsend Scudder (1865–1960) received a bachelor of laws from Columbia University in 1888, filled two separate terms as a justice of the supreme court of the state of New York, and was twice elected to the United States Congress from the First District of New York (Queens, Nassau, and Suffolk counties) in 1898 and 1902. He was a horticulturist by avocation, and one of the country's foremost breeders and exhibitors of cocker spaniels.[75] For nearly half a century, the house in Chocorua served as a welcome and restful retreat, far removed from the demands of a busy professional career and an active social and religious life.

Surrounded by majestic tall white pine trees, "Avoca" is positioned on a slight rise, set back a couple of hundred feet from the gravel road in front. Protected by a medium-pitched gable roof, broken by large gable and small shed-roof dormers, the main mass of the house possesses strong horizontal sight lines, juxtaposed against the vertical thrusts of two field-stone chimneys. Encircling the building on three sides is a shed-roofed porch, with plain support posts and balustrades, and latticework screens concealing the framing supports underneath. Attached to the rear of "Avoca" is a former ice house, covered by a secondary canopy roof, added several years after initial construction. Inscribed on one of the roof rafters is the name "Weed," suggesting that the prolific Sandwich, New Hampshire, contractor, Larkin D. Weed (1855–after 1932) and his assistants (see "Juniper Lodge," Tamworth), erected the secondary roof, and very possibly the entire house. A hundred yards behind this ell is an imposing carriage house/garage, of materials and style elements compatible with the much larger residence. While it is a formidable architectural statement, "Avoca," in the manner of other Chocorua cottages, seems in perfect harmony with its sylvan environment. To achieve this was an exemplary accomplishment for the thus-far unidentified architect.[76]

Carriage house, "Avoca" (c. 1905–6), Chocorua, Tamworth, N.H. Photograph by the author.

"Juniper Lodge"

1910–11

(Mr. and Mrs. James B. Reynolds)

Tamworth (Chocorua)

~ IT WAS THROUGH Salome Machado Warren, a Smith College friend of Mrs. (Florence Dike) Reynolds from Cambridge, Massachusetts, that Mr. and Mrs. James B. Reynolds of New York City discovered Chocorua and decided to establish a summer residence there.[77] Quoted in the 1913 edition of *New Hampshire Farms for Summer Homes*, James Reynolds expressed his personal sentiments about their plans:

> My reason for choosing New Hampshire as my vacation state is simple. The quality of the air, the beauty of the country, with its charming combination of mountains, lakes and fine trees, the great variety of unusually attractive drives, and the agreeable people, all combined to make the temptation to build at Chocorua irresistible.[78]

For the location of their dream vacation retreat, the Reynoldses decided on the crest of Washington Hill, facing westward toward jewel-like Chocorua Lake and the sublime mountain backdrop extending from Mount White-face on the west to Mount Chocorua on the east. In September 1906, they acquired thirty acres of land at this superb site from Frederick LeRoy Sargent, also of Cambridge, and commenced preparations for the construction of their new house and outbuildings.[79]

In their choice of architect, the Reynoldses were again influenced by Salome Warren. Their selection was Warren's brother, the young Ernest M. A. Machado of Salem, Massachusetts.[80] Born in 1868, Machado was educated at the Salem schools and the Massachusetts Institute of Technology. At the time of his commissioning by the Reynoldses, he maintained an office in Salem, as well as in Boston where he was in partnership with Arthur L. Weeks of St. John, New Brunswick. With his professional peers and clients, "he enjoyed a first class reputation as an architect, and furnished plans for several magnificent dwellings in Salem, Boston and vicinity, and along the whole North Shore."[81] In Salem, he served as the restoration architect in 1899 for the Essex Bank Building (1811), and drafted the designs for the Harlan P. Kelsey house (c. 1902–3), the Blake Memorial Chapel (1904–5) in Harmony Grove Cemetery, and the William M. Jelley house (1905–6).[82] Tragically, on 22 September 1907, Machado was drowned in a canoeing accident while traveling from his camp on Ossipee Lake to visit his sister, Salome Warren, in Chocorua.[83] It is not known definitively if he completed the plans for the Reynolds residence, as the original drawings and related records and correspondence appear no longer to exist. For unexplained reasons, the Reynoldses waited until 1910 before beginning the building of their house. Over the ensuing year, Florence Reynolds worked with "an able woman architect" (identified only as "Miss Cotton," or the "she-architect" in Chocorua) of New York City, in finalizing the details of the interior, the color schemes, and the furnishings.[84] More than likely, the original Machado plans, possibly in altered form, guided the construction. Inspired by local plant life and the related natural color

Mrs. James B. Reynolds, Larkin Weed (with his dog) and work crew, "Juniper Lodge," Chocorua, Tamworth, N.H., c. 1911. Photograph, courtesy of Susan R. Peter, Chocorua, N.H.

scheme, the Reynoldses named the new house "Juniper Lodge," first occupying it for the 1911 summer season.

A rare and rather charming old photograph arranged by Florence Reynolds and discovered when "Juniper Lodge" changed hands in 1980, provides unmistakable evidence as to the identification of the builder and his crew. The photograph (see illustration) shows a group of eighteen people seated near the main (east) entrance of the house when it was nearing completion in 1911. In the center of the front row are Florence Reynolds, and to her left, the chief contractor, Larkin D. Weed (1855–after 1932), of Sandwich, New Hampshire, and his pet dog. Present with them in the picture are Weed's sons, Chester and Cleveland, and his other assistants. A renowned local builder, Weed was responsible for the construction of nu-

Parlor, "Juniper Lodge" (1910–11), Chocorua, Tamworth, N.H. Photograph courtesy of the Smith College Archives, Smith College, Mass.

Hallway, looking toward the dining room, "Juniper Lodge" (1910–11), Chocorua, Tamworth, N.H. Photograph courtesy of the Smith College Archives, Smith College, Mass.

merous summer residences and other buildings in Sandwich, Tamworth (see "Kalarama," Chocorua) and adjacent towns over a thirty-year period.[85]

Although it has undergone some alteration over time, "Juniper Lodge" (retitled "Juniper" in 1980) possesses many of the qualities of a classic, rambling Craftsman-style bungalow of the early twentieth century. Long and low to the ground, with strong horizontal lines, the house is perfectly suited to its site. The broad front elevation, with swept-back wings on the north and south ends, takes full advantage of the rounded backbone of the ridge, and the grand prospect to the west. The low-pitched gable roof with

Stairwell and hallway, "Juniper Lodge," (1910–11), Chocorua, Tamworth, N.H. Photograph courtesy of the Smith College Archives, Smith College, Mass.

"Juniper Lodge" (1910–11), Chocorua, Tamworth, N.H. Photograph by the author.

truncated ends is broken by tall fieldstone chimneys, and, in the center back and front, by matching eyebrow dormer windows. Deep roof overhangs display signs of the inner structural system with their exposed rafter heads. Typical of the Craftsman vein, the fenestration is highly variable, with plate glass and French windows of several shapes and sizes (some with diamond-pane glass) arrayed across the walls. The walls are further accented by second-story window bays and doorway lintel hood roofs, each supported by curved brackets. Recessed open east and open canopy west porches (the latter has been replaced by a modern "Florida"-type porch) with curved-bracket support columns provided welcoming places of refuge and relaxation, as well as protective shielding for the main and secondary entrance doors. The overall design is singularly successful, with all these diverse elements combined effectively into one coherent architectural statement.

In a memorial essay published after Florence Reynolds' death in 1919, Salome Warren commented about "Juniper Lodge" and its principal on-site originator:

> she created such a harmonious house externally and within as is seen hardly once in a lifetime. She cared much for greens and blues and the mysterious shade in which these two colors blend; so that the juniper, which grew about the place in profusion, appealed to her particularly, and the entire house was created on this

East front entrance porch, "Juniper Lodge" (1910–11), Chocorua, Tamworth, N.H. Photograph by the author.

color scheme. . . . Every beam and rafter, every tile and dish, every rug and curtain, every floor is saturated in the various tones of the juniper plant and berry. . . . There is something uplifting about the house, like her own atmosphere. . . . I never saw a home which so completely expressed the rare personality of its author. I like to regard it as her monument.[86]

Although the original color scheme has been somewhat modified, and the Reynolds era furnishings are gone, the spacious interiors of the house, with their Craftsman-inspired exposed raftered ceilings and paneling, continue to express the fruitful collaboration of the architects, the builders, and Florence Reynolds.[87]

James Bronson Reynolds (1861–1924) was one of the Chocorua summer colony's most highly acclaimed members. Born at Kiantone, Chautauqua County, New York, he was prepared for college at the village school, and at the Hopkins Grammar School in New Haven, Connecticut, before graduating from Yale in 1884. After a year of travel abroad, he returned to the Yale Divinity School, completed a bachelor's degree in divinity in 1888, but was not ordained. He commenced his career as a noted social reformer with the College Young Men's Christian Association of America, traveling most of the European continent for over two years, and striving to improve relations among Protestant Christian university students. Returning to the United States in 1893, Reynolds was inactive due to illness for the next two years, but recovered sufficiently by 1894 to become the head worker at the University Settlement and fellow in sociology at Columbia University in New York City. Here he became immersed in the labor movement for political reform, and committed to an active role in municipal and state politics. He was made chairman of the executive committee of the Citizen's Union in the campaign of 1897, and in 1900 was appointed by Governor Theodore Roosevelt to the State Tenement House Committee. He subsequently became a friend and confidant of Roosevelt, and during the latter's presidency, served as special advisor on the municipal affairs of the District of Columbia, a member of the 1906 special commission to investigate the Chicago Stock Yards, and chairman of a commission to study and report on industrial conditions in Panama. From 1910 to 1913, he was assistant district attorney for New York County, and from 1913 to 1916 was counsel to the American Hygiene Association. While in New York, he was a member of the Century Association, the Social Reform and City clubs, the National Municipal Reform League, and the Underwriters' Club. He retired to New Haven, his ancestral home, where he died.[88]

Upon his death in 1924, Reynolds left "Juniper Lodge" to Smith College as a memorial to his wife. Included in the bequest were beautiful custom oak furnishings, fine antique objects, many pieces from the Reynoldses' collection of Oriental art, Victorian colored glass, pattern glass, brasses, pottery, rare china, and much of the family sterling silver. The will specifically stipulated that the estate should be used as a vacation or rest retreat for Smith graduate students, Smith alumnae, women faculty members, women administrators, visiting foreign students, and, in deference to James Reynolds' alma mater, Yale women graduate students. For fifty-four years, with the exception of three years during World War II, Smith operated the property for the purposes intended, until a succession of annual operating losses persuaded college officials to sell in 1980. Since then, under two private owners, this magnificent property has been returned to residential use, and has reassumed some of the special aura it possessed when under the caring stewardship of James B. and Florence Dike Reynolds.[89]

~

"Birch Knoll"

1913

(Dr. and Mrs. Franklin G. Balch)

Tamworth (Chocorua)

South front elevation, "Birch Knoll" (1913), Chocorua, Tamworth, N.H. Photograph by the author.

~ DR. FRANKLIN GREENE BALCH (1864–1958), whose descendants still claim Chocorua as their place of summer sojourn, became a property owner by virtue of his 1894 marriage to Lucy R. Bowditch, the daughter of Mr. and Mrs. Charles P. Bowditch (see "Conni Sauti," Tamworth). He was yet another of the talented group of old-stock Bostonians who have, for over a century, made Chocorua an intellectually live and socially active community. Born in Jamaica Plain, Boston, he received his bachelor's degree from Harvard in 1888, a master's from Harvard in 1892, and a medical degree from the Harvard Medical School, also in 1892. After that year, Balch carried on a practice in Boston, serving as an honorary surgeon at the Massachusetts General Hospital, a consulting surgeon at the Faulkner Hospital and the Lawrence (Massachusetts) Memorial Hospital, and as a surgeon to outpatients at the Carney Hospital. Extremely involved in professional medical organizations, Balch was a member of the Massachusetts Medical Society, the New England Medical Society, and the American Medical Association, and was a diplomat to the American Board

North rear elevation with sleeping porches, "Birch Knoll" (1913), Chocorua, Tamworth, N.H. Photograph by the author.

of Surgery and fellow of the American College of Surgeons and American Surgical Association. In Boston, he joined the Harvard and Tavern clubs, and participated in Unitarian church affairs.[90]

The Balch residence, to which the family gave the name "Birch Knoll," is the youngest of the several houses in Chocorua designed by Boston architect C. Howard Walker (1857–1936) (see "Pine Cone," Tamworth). Erected in 1913, it is completely documented by a set of blueprint plans still in the possession of owning family members.[91] A close examination of these plans attests to the fact that the building, both inside and out, is virtually unchanged from the time of its construction. Displaying signs of the Colonial Revival style (truncated, intersecting hipped roofs; channeled window moldings; a broken semicircular front doorway pediment with side lights and base paneling), "Birch Knoll" is a highly successful statement of suburban cultural refinement in a beautiful sylvan, lake and mountain setting. Sheathed in dark-toned shingles, with white door and window trim and dark green shutters, the house has a highly natural look, and seems an integral part of its environment. While the dominant visual lines are horizontal, the roofs are surmounted by tall, brick, capped chimneys that echo the strong verticality of the surrounding towering white pine trees. On the front (northeasterly) elevation, a long, covered, first-story piazza and matching sleeping "balconies," positioned on opposite ends of the roof above, permit residents sterling views of Chocorua Lake and Mount Chocorua's dominant pyramidal rock summit. The interior—practical and plain, with a minimum of wood finishing adornment—features a large living room, central hall, dining room, den and kitchen wing (kitchen, pantry, china closet, laundry, service hall) on the first floor; and six family bedrooms, a hall, and servants' wing (three small bedrooms, hall, linen closet, bathrooms) on the second floor. There is a spacious attic story above. Just to the northwest of the house, and topped by a ventilating cupola, is a combined ice and wood storage building, aesthetically compatible with its much larger neighbor. Efficiently arranged to suit the relaxed patterns of vacation life, "Birch Knoll" has served well the needs of four successive generations of Balch family members.[92]

10 ~

Outlying Locations

The Bemis Cottage

1856–1868

(Dr. Samuel A. Bemis)

Hart's Location

~ IN 1880, SAMUEL ADAMS DRAKE, the popular author of books about New England, visited Crawford Notch, and in a lovely glen under the shadow of Mount Crawford, spotted "a solidly built English country residence with gables," set on a natural terrace on the west side of the valley floor. Knocking at the door, he and his traveling companions were ushered in by a servant and were introduced to the elderly and bearded Dr. Samuel A. Bemis, one of the most enigmatic, compelling, and versatile personalities the White Mountain region has ever seen. Drake's impressions of Bemis are worthy of note, and help set the stage for further consideration of the man, his unusual residence, and his vast wilderness domain: "We had an excusable curiosity to see a man who, in the prime of life, had forsaken the city, its pleasures, its opportunities, and had come to pass the rest of his life among these mountains; one, too, whose enormous possessions procured for him the title of Lord of the Valley."[1] Who, then, was Bemis, what prompted him to settle in the North Country, and what was his legacy?

Born in Vermont in 1793, Samuel A. Bemis moved to Cambridge, Massachusetts, at an early age, and in 1810 was apprenticed by his father to the watch trade. At the conclusion of his apprenticeship, he became a clerk in a watchmaker's shop in Boston, in time purchasing the business and running it on his own. Encountering trying economic times after the War of 1812, he turned to the profession of dentistry, for which his sharp mind and excellent manipulative skills made him most suitable. He was self-trained as there were no dental schools in the United States at the time. Bemis gradually established a large practice amongst the first families of Boston, and made a fortune in the specialty of dental surgery, further refining the fabrication of false teeth. Apparently he perfected them to such a degree that they were not only cosmetic, but actually could be used by his patients for eating purposes![2]

The Bemis cottage (1856–58), Hart's Location, N.H. Photograph by the author.

Bemis' first contact with New Hampshire and the mountains was in the summer of 1826, when he visited Bartlett for reasons relating to his health and an unhappy love affair. His trips became frequent and he returned annually for the next thirty years (he retired about 1840), often staying with the family of Abel Crawford at his well-known Mount Crawford House at the southern end of Crawford Notch. Close friendships between Bemis and members of the Crawford family developed, and over time, when their fortunes were down, he lent them substantial sums of money. There is no record that these loans were ever repaid, or that Bemis attempted to recoup them. Finally, in the early 1850s, after the deaths of Abel Crawford and his wife, Hannah, Bemis foreclosed on a mortgage he had received on their property, and took possession. With this real estate acquisition Bemis commenced a series of land purchases extending over twenty years, until he amassed an estate of several thousand acres, extending for miles up and down the Notch. He bought the parcel upon which he erected his house in 1855.[3]

In devising plans for his mountain abode, he relied on his own talents and inclinations instead of turning to a professional architect. A former owner of the house after Bemis believed that he employed English published sources to create his ideal twenty-room rural cottage; in fact, it is known that he owned volumes containing English design plates of villas and houses, as well as farm layouts, one of which closely resembles the building as it appears today. For the fitted ashlar granite building stone used in the foundations and the first story, laborers accessed a quarry beside the Sawyer's River, three miles from the construction site, and cut and dragged the blocks into place. They then dug a basement, approximately sixty by ninety feet, in which twenty-one slender pillars of granite were placed to support the middle of the house, and eleven brick chimneys. The second attic story, protected by steep-pitched, Gothic-inspired gable roofs, and the superstructure were built from timber harvested, hauled, and milled on the Bemis lands. Under the recessed, first-story porch there is a so-called "ghostwalk," thirty feet long and five feet wide, with a ceiling of granite slabs. The adjacent farm buildings were similarly constructed, with painted clapboard siding. Begun in 1856, the Bemis complex took eight years to complete, and was intended to be as permanent as the mountains surrounding it. During this period, the doctor resided in the former Crawford family farmhouse. Directing the entire project was Leander Nute, of the North Conway family, who was credited with building the covered bridge over scenic Goodrich Falls in Jackson about the same time. The existence of such a complex, many miles from the nearest town, not surprisingly was controversial and attracted criticism—Bemis himself was typed by many as an overly wealthy, eccentric, hardy mountaineer hermit. In fact, such a characterization is only partially accurate.[4]

Bemis' interests were amazingly eclectic, and went far beyond dentistry, rural farm architecture, and animal husbandry. His forty-year retirement, lasting until his death in 1881, was not uneventful, or without considerable accomplishment. Through Boston intellectual Josiah Hawes, he became absorbed with the daguerreotype process, and made a series of pictures in Crawford Notch that are among the earliest photographic images of the White Mountains. Experts regard him as a pioneer in American landscape photography. Nurtured by a friend, the botanist William Oakes, Bemis also developed a passion for horticulture, and successfully experimented with the cultivation of various apple types on his property. Like the writer William C. Prime (see "Gale Cottage," Franconia), he was an ardent fisherman, tying his own flies and experimenting with fish stocking of ponds and streams. He was an early member of the Boston Natural History Society, and collected numerous mineral specimens while trail hiking throughout the mountains. He is credited with naming more peaks in the White Mountains than any other person, and hiked well into his seventies. Bemis often befriended artists, among them Godfrey Frankenstein, who came to sketch in the Notch. Public-spirited and concerned with the education of youth, he had a schoolhouse erected on his property, and occasionally gave instruction to the children of Hart's Location.[5] The Bemis place, today used as an inn, is literally and figuratively a monument to the tenacity, creativity, and enterprise of a most unusual man.[6]

∾

The Dutton Camp

c. 1898–99

(Mr. and Mrs. Harry Dutton)

Errol

The Dutton camp (c. 1898–99), Umbagog Lake, Errol, N.H., photograph from *New Hampshire Farms for Summer Homes* (5th ed., 1907), p. 44. Author's collection.

∾ CERTAIN PEOPLE who purchased and developed summer vacation properties in the White Mountain region before 1930 preferred direct access to the outside realm of nature and its recreational offerings, the opportunity to exercise independent thought and action, and relative isolation, removed from the busy, more confining hotel or cottage community environments. Boston businessman Harry Dutton was just this kind of individual. Originally a New Hampshire native, he was born in Hillsborough Bridge in 1854, the grandson of Ephraim, and the son of Benjamin Frank, the builders of the magnificent Greek Revival Dutton twin houses in the center of Hillsborough. In 1859, the family relocated to Boston, where Harry's father established a small domestic wares and millinery jobbing house. Over the years the business grew and prospered, taking the name Houghton and Dutton in 1874 when Benjamin F. and Samuel S. Houghton of Melrose, Massachusetts, joined in partnership. Upon completion of his education in the local schools and at the Highland Military Academy in Worcester, Massachusetts, Harry Dutton joined the firm, eventually becoming one of its partners and officers. Soon thereafter he married Alice, Samuel Houghton's daughter, and they made their home in Medford, where they raised three children. During Harry's association with Houghton and Dutton, it became one of the largest, most popular, and most successful department stores in Boston, with a wide reputation throughout New England. In doing so, it generated considerable income for Harry Dutton and other members of the Dutton family who had an interest in the business.[7]

In the late 1890s, seeking a peaceful retreat from the pressures of urban life and his active mercantile career, Harry Dutton conducted an extensive search of the lake country of northern Maine and New Hampshire for the ideal summer home site. He discovered the spot of his dreams while on a fishing vacation at Umbagog Lake in Errol, a sparsely settled farming and lumbering community well north of the principal cottage colonies in the mountains.[8] In 1897, the enterprising Dutton negotiated the purchase of Moll's Rock or Metallak Island (later known as Dutton's, and Million Dollar Island), flat, partially wooded, approximately three acres in size, and situated near "The Narrows" in Umbagog Lake.[9] Immediately he set about transforming the island into a palatial wilderness estate for his family and as a location for the entertainment of their circle of wealthy and distinguished guests. Commencing about 1898, blocks of granite were shipped north from Massachusetts, and moved by boat across water to the island for the construction of shore retaining walls and parts of the building foundations. Then, with the help of local labor and Harvard University students employed for the summer months, Dutton supervised the construction of the main camp and several auxiliary structures, including servants' quarters, a utility shack, a boathouse, and an observation tower. As the automobile and improved roads made the North Country more accessible, within a brief period of time the Dutton island estate became a chief point of interest, "the finest . . . of its kind in the country." The final price tag was said to be fifty thousand dollars, an astounding amount of money at the time for the creation of a single-season, rural residence.[10]

Positioned at the center of the island, but within easy reach of the lake shore, was the main camp. It was truly an extraordinary building by any standard of measure, but particularly so because of its remote location. The sophistication of the strongly horizontal design, blending perfectly with the natural beauty of the island and the surrounding water, suggests that the camp must have been planned by a professional architect (likely from Boston), but to date no name has surfaced. From old photographs, it is clear that his structure possessed a U-shaped floor plan, with the tapered, cylindrical, shingled observation tower (with concave conical roof) connected to the primary block by a covered walkway set on a picturesque semielliptical arch. Supported by mortared indigenous stone foundations, the building was one story tall with the principal section and two ells covered by intersecting red-shingled, dual-pitched, hipped roofs resembling expansive circus tents. The planes of the roofs sloped down to cover wide columned verandas, which encircled the entire complex, providing easy outdoor access from most of the interior rooms. At several points along the verandas, wooden stairways with balustrades dropped down from the viewing and promenade decks to ground level. In both visual and functional respects, the main camp was like a great pleasure pavilion, its primary purpose to give total satisfaction to its occupants and users. Stylistically, it was modeled after a late-eighteenth- or early-nineteenth-century French Colonial plantation house, raised off the ground to be free of moisture, yet opened up as much as possible to promote exposure to the healthy natural climate.[11]

Seemingly out of context in its sylvan lake setting, the Dutton camp offered the very best in elegant and gracious living. It was the perfect meeting place of wilderness and domesticity. On the inside were seven large bedrooms, a great parlor, a kitchen, a formal dining room, service spaces, and a trophy room containing specimens of New Hampshire birds and animals, and expertly mounted trout from the nearby waters. Particularly noteworthy was the dining room, with its parqueted floors, rich, dark, wood-paneled walls, and sixteen-foot-high cathedral ceiling of parqueted solid wood sections broken by heavy criss-crossing support beams. When the camp was torn down in the early 1940s, this fascinating interior was saved (along with three other rooms and a veranda section). A portion of the camp was literally sawed away from the rest of the building and moved across the winter ice of Umbagog Lake to form part of a residence in Upton, Maine. Today only the massive stone walls and observation tower remain on Metallak Island to remind us of the luxurious, urbane, leisurely summer life-style that Harry Dutton and his family brought to the North Country at the turn of this century.[12]

≈

The Caretaker's Cottage

1903

(Mount Washington Hotel)

Carroll (Bretton Woods)

Caretaker's cottage (1903), Mount Washington Hotel, Bretton Woods, Carroll, N.H. Photograph by the author.

THE MOUNT WASHINGTON HOTEL at Bretton Woods has long enjoyed the distinction of being the most impressively situated, grandiose, and lavish of the thirty grand resort hotels erected in the White Mountains between 1850 and 1930. Planned and built as a single homogeneous complex between 1901 and 1906, the Mount Washington was the product of the most ambitious hotel construction project ever undertaken in the region. Upon its formal opening, this significant North Country business enter-

Mount Washington Hotel (1901–3 and after), Bretton Woods, Carroll, N.H. Photograph by the author.

prise quickly became the centerpiece of the White Mountain hotel industry as well as the area economy, a status that it has retained to this day. Beautifully sited on a rocky rise, with the Presidential Range as a backdrop, the great six-hundred-guest hostelry is a paragon of Edwardian-era eclecticism, its most dominant features executed in the conspicuous, yet tasteful, Spanish Renaissance Revival style.

Responsible for conceiving and financing the new hotel venture was Joseph Stickney (1840–1903), the well-to-do, New York City–based owner of the nearby Mount Pleasant House, who had made his money in Pennsylvania coal and railroads. Following the advice of a friend and business associate, the Florida hotel and railroad entrepreneur Henry Flagler, Stickney selected a relative unknown from New York City, Charles Alling Gifford (1861–1937), as his architect. Respected for his residential designs in the New York metropolitan area, Gifford also came to the project with experience in resort hotel planning, and had worked in the Mediterranean eclectic styles. Representing Gifford at the contracting site was superintendent of construction William G. Phillips of New York City. Contracts were negotiated with E. F. Getchell of Concord, New Hampshire, for the stonework, and the well-known firm of C. M. Russell & Company of Newark, New Jersey, for the balance of the construction. Through the collaboration of this talented team, and a large corps of skilled Italian laborers, Stickney was able to realize his dream of a hotel complex that would match, if not eclipse, all others of its era in the United States.[13]

Adjacent to the main hotel, several outbuildings were erected before

1906 as support facilities. These included an immense carriage house and stable, male and female employee dormitories, a kitchen, a boiler and power plant, a gas house, a water-powered print shop, a large farmhouse, other maintenance buildings, and a site manager's cottage. The latter structure was replaced in the fall of 1903 by a new caretaker's cottage, which in many respects mimics the form and embellishment of the hotel. Block-shaped and modest in size, this pleasantly proportioned residence possesses a two-and-one-half-story southeast corner tower with pyramidal roof that repeats the form of the much taller, paired, corner towers on each end of the hotel. Present in the plain architrave on the tower front are three port-hole windows ringed by decorative wood-carved wreaths and other plant motifs similar to those in the emblems adorning the hotel towers. Penetrating the rear hipped roof plane is a nicely scaled eyebrow monitor window. Correspondence contained in hotel records at the New Hampshire Historical Society confirms that Gifford also designed this cottage. The contractors associated with the hotel construction very likely also worked with Gifford on this smaller project. Phillips was the initial occupant of the cottage, which has continued in use for hotel staff and occasional guests to the present time.[14]

≈

The Balsams Cottages

1906–c. 1916

Dixville Notch

The Balsams Grand Resort Hotel (1874–1918 and after), Dixville Notch, N.H. Photograph by the author.

∾ SITUATED IN BEAUTIFUL and sublime Dixville Notch, on the northern edge of the White Mountains, is The Balsams Grand Resort Hotel, one of America's most historic and illustrious guest establishments. It owes its origins to Colebrook, New Hampshire, native George Parsons, who in 1874 erected a small fifty-guest inn there. Named Dix House in memory of General John A. Dix, the first local landholder, this hostelry has survived as the core of the extensive complex that occupies the site today.

The man who made such growth possible was Henry S. Hale of Philadelphia, who, with his wife, was a guest at Dix House during the 1880s. In 1895, after Parsons' death, he acquired the property from Parsons' widow under the aegis of the newly formed Dixville Improvement Company. Renaming the hotel The Balsams, Hale launched an ambitious development scheme, transforming it into a substantial enterprise, capable of accommodating up to 150 patrons. Over the next two years, Hale added several new outbuildings, paths and roads, recreational facilities, and the artificial Lake Gloriette to the property, pursuing his dream of transforming the Notch into the "Switzerland of America." During the first decade and a half of this century, he carried out his master plan, expanding the main hotel, adding more outbuildings, laying out an eighteen-hole golf course on Keyser Mountain, and creating two more lakes for aesthetic benefit, recreation, and water power. Hale's efforts culminated in 1916–18 with the construction of the great Rhenish eclectic south wing, "Hampshire House," which increased the capacity of The Balsams to approximately 400 guests. The addition of "Hampshire House" all but completed The Balsams complex as we know it today, despite a succession of owners after the property left the ownership of the Hale family in 1922.[15]

While The Balsams, unlike other regional hotels, has never been committed to the guest cottage concept on a broad scale, there were four associated, but detached, residences built on the grounds during the dynamic and magical Hale era. The first and oldest of these is "The Wind Whistle," erected in 1906 as the "new and sumptuous summer home" of the Hales, "beneath giant white birches but a few paces . . . [to the northwest] of the hotel." Widely acclaimed as "one of the most comfortable and attractive"[16] summer houses in the North Country, this solid, hipped-roof stucco (first

"The Wind Whistle" (left, 1906), "The Stone Cottage" (center, c. 1915), and "The Captain's Cottage" (right, c. 1916), The Balsams Grand Resort Hotel, Dixville Notch, N.H. Photographs from booklet, *The Balsams, Dixville Notch, N.H.* (c. 1931). Author's collection.

Three of the attractive cottages which may be rented either with hotel service or housekeeping facilities.

"Beaver Lodge" (c. 1912), The Balsams Grand Resort Hotel, Dixville Notch, N.H. Photograph by the author.

story) and shingle-sheathed (second story) building reflects, albeit it in a low-key manner, the influence of the then popular Colonial Revival style. After the Hales moved to a new residence, "The Wind Whistle" was used for hotel patrons. From the 1920s to the 1940s, it was known as "The Children's Hotel," housing the young offspring of guests, along with their nurses or nannies.[17]

Perhaps the most interesting, and surely the largest of the cottages at The Balsams is "Beaver Lodge," erected around 1912 on the east shore of Lake Gloriette by Henry Hale for himself and his family. Positioned on a gradually sloping hillside overlooking the water and the Dixville Mountains, this handsome, distinctly Craftsman-style cottage is shielded from the road behind by a rough castellated stone masonry wall terminating on its northeast end with a tall, arched gateway at the head of the entrance drive. The exterior of the wood-frame and clapboard house is marked by long, horizontal lines, low-pitched main and dormer roofs with bracketed overhangs, and an ample front porch. The interior rooms, particularly the spacious first-floor parlor and dining room, possess marvelous dark-wood paneling, moulding strips, and other decorative accents. Also present throughout the house is an unusually fine and varied collection of Craftsman ceiling and wall electric light fixtures of dark-toned hammered metal and glass. It is highly likely that "Beaver Lodge" was designed and built by Sylvanus D. Morgan (1857–1940), the productive contractor from Lisbon,

Contracting crew, "Beaver Lodge," The Balsams
Grand Resort Hotel, Dixville Notch, N.H., c. 1912.
Courtesy of The Balsams Grand Resort Hotel.

New Hampshire, to whom so many hotels, hotel additions, and residences in the White Mountains have been attributed. In certain obvious respects, the Hale cottage bears a striking resemblance to a number of Morgan's other residential commissions. Furthermore, Morgan is believed to have served as builder of the 1910 extension to the west wing of the hotel complex, bringing him into direct contact with the owning family.[18]

The third separate residence at The Balsams, and the only one that has not survived, is "The Stone Cottage," put up around 1915. Based on stylistic similarities to his other houses, particularly the cottage (1903) for the Abbe family in Bethlehem (see the Abbe House), it is very possible that this quite fetching Craftsman-style building may also have been designed and constructed by Morgan. Originally located on a raised plateau east of and adjacent to the hotel, "The Stone Cottage" was distinguished by low-pitched main and dormer roofs, triangular stick eaves brackets, and a long, front, wraparound, open porch supported by square shingled posts. For much of its history, this structure was rented to hotel guests, the principal being Broadway, New York City actor and dancer Frederick Stone, for whom it was named. While serving as the residence of Neil Tillotson, the current owner of The Balsams, it was swept off its foundations in the great flood of March 1960 (which inundated the present hotel entrance parlor and grounds), and was demolished.

Set on the hillside behind and to the northeast of the hotel is "The Captain's Cottage," a modest, small-scale rusticated Craftsman-style dwelling erected around 1916. During its first decade, it quartered guests, but from 1927 to around 1940, it was employed as a private residence by Captain Frank Doudera, the multifaceted owner of The Balsams after the Hales. Though scarcely evident today, originally this wood-frame building possessed wide, unfinished exterior siding, and an open front porch supported by tree trunk posts. Inside is a large central living room with a great stone fireplace, watched over by animal trophies from Doudera's hunting expeditions; this intriguing space rises the full height of the house, with the second-floor bedrooms reached from a balustraded balcony accessed by a stairway. Since 1970, "The Captain's Cottage" has been used as a residence by one of the current managing partners and his family.[19]

～

"Mount Prospect Lodge"

1912–13

(Mr. and Mrs. John W. Weeks)

Lancaster

～ THE WEEKS FAMILY ESTATE, with the main house, "The Lodge," at its center, was planned and developed at the direction of Lancaster native John Wingate Weeks, congressman and senator from Massachusetts, secretary of war under Presidents Harding and Coolidge, and a leading conservationist of his era. Spectacularly situated on 2,058-foot Mount Prospect, two miles south of Lancaster village, the house, outbuildings, and grounds offer an unparalleled 360-degree panorama of mountain vistas, including the entire massif of the White Mountains to the east and south, the Green Mountains of Vermont to the west, and the Kilkenney range, the Percy Peaks, and the upper Connecticut River Valley to the north and northeast. No other residence in New Hampshire's North Country possesses such a highly unusual and truly moving site.[20]

Created "as a summer retreat and a testament to Week's affection for the locale of his ancestry and birth, the estate also typifies a spirit of private land conservation often seen in New Hampshire at the turn of the twentieth century." At that time, many of state's unprofitable private farms were being abandoned and offered for sale to be acquired by private investors (many of whom were summer vacationers), with an interest in preserving, maintaining, and creatively using the land. Driven by this same mission, Weeks bought several farms on Mount Prospect in 1910, including the wooded summit tract. Taking advantage of the freedom and flexibility offered by the new automobile, he first laid out a new auto road to the summit, replacing an older carriageway servicing a former thirty-five-guest hotel. With easy access provided, he then erected the house and outbuildings in 1912–13, completing the mountaintop estate that over the years has hosted numerous dignitaries, including President Warren G. Harding. Accommodating one of the best preserved and most significant of New Hampshire's pre–World War I grand summer homes, the Mount Prospect

"Mount Prospect Lodge" (1912–13), Mount Prospect, Lancaster, N.H. Photograph by the author.

lands (comprising 420 acres) were donated to the state of New Hampshire in 1941 by John W. Weeks' two children, Sinclair Weeks and Katherine Weeks Davidge. Today, they are maintained as a memorial historic site and conservation museum by the New Hampshire Division of Parks and Recreation.[21]

The main house of the Weeks estate, "Mount Prospect Lodge," is an excellent example of the then-popular Craftsman-style bungalow, "enlarged to an unusually ambitious scale and embellished with elements of old English half timbering," Spanish red terra-cotta roofing tile, and rusticated exposed roof joists and rafters. Linking the symmetrical, rectangular bungalow form to native materials are the split fieldstone terraces, retaining walls, chimneys, and porch piers of the cottage. In the stuccoed walls of the house the builders employed "a material then prized for its natural quality, its durability, and its resistance to fire." The inverted two-story interior plan, with the functional rooms (formerly a dining room, kitchen, and six bedrooms) on the first floor, and a grand thirty-by-seventy-foot hall (living room) with picture window balconies on the second, is calculated to maximize the advantages of the elevated location, and the breathtaking views it affords of the surrounding scenery. Protecting the building is a truncated gable roof with gentle undulations above each of the front facade (south-facing) picture windows and the central balustraded deck doorway (over the entrance portico) on the second floor. This pleasant roof shape is repeated in the rear elevation. Accompanying the house on the summit are a four-stall garage (mimicking the style and materials of the house), a pump house, a small servants' cottage, and an eighty-seven-foot-tall water and lookout tower, converted to a fire observation tower.[22]

Weeks' decision to transform the summit of Mount Prospect into a private vacation estate was strongly conditioned by his deep family roots in the Lancaster area. Born in 1860 on a local farm, he attended local primary and secondary schools. In 1877, he entered the Naval Academy at Annapolis, graduated four years later, and continued in the navy until 1883, when a general cutback in personnel necessitated his discharge. He next went to Florida, worked as a land surveyor for several years, and met Mary A. Sinclair (the daughter of hotelman John Sinclair of Bethlehem), whom he married in 1885. Returning to New England in 1888, he accepted an offer to enter the banking and brokerage business in Boston. There, in collaboration with Henry Hornblower, he established the firm of Hornblower & Weeks, which quickly became one of the most respected financial houses in the United States. As a consequence of this success, Weeks amassed a fortune, becoming a high-profile leader in the business world. His first political office was in 1900 as alderman-at-large in his home city of Newton, Massachusetts. Three years later he was elected mayor. In 1904, his friends convinced him to run for Congress. He was elected, severed his business

Garage, "Mount Prospect Lodge" (1912–13), Mount Prospect, Lancaster, N.H. Photograph by the author.

connections, and served four terms in the House of Representatives until 1913 when the Massachusetts legislature named him to succeed retiring Winthrop Murray Crane as United States senator. One of the high points of his years in the House was his sponsorship in 1909 of the Weeks bill (it passed in 1911), which authorized federal-state cooperation "for the protection of watersheds and navigable streams"; the net effect of this conservation legislation for New Hampshire was the federal acquisition of additional lands for the expansion and establishment of national forests. Weeks' tenure in the Senate was limited to one term, as he was defeated for reelection in 1918. At the Republican convention of 1916, however, his name was placed in nomination as a possible presidential candidate, and he was runner-up to the final choice, Charles E. Hughes. After leaving the Senate, he came to the attention of Warren G. Harding during the national presidential campaign of 1920. Upon his election to the presidency, Harding named him secretary of war, and he held this appointment into the Coolidge administration, until ill health compelled him to retire in 1925. He then returned to the peace and natural splendor of his beloved "Mount Prospect Lodge," spending his final days there until he died in July 1926.[23]

Epilogue

The Cottage Phenomenon Takes New Form

The summer cottage phenomenon in the White Mountains has persisted to this day, but has undergone considerable transformation. A decrease in cottage construction was first evident between 1910 and 1930 as a result of the dampening effects of the federal income tax amendment (1913), the institution of state income taxes, and World War I. The Great Depression and World War II further hastened the decline in the regional cottage movement. Reinforcing this historical trend over the same years was the long, downhill slide of the hotels and the railroads, which had initially fostered the growth of the resorts and attracted cottage financiers and builders to the mountains.

After World War II, and a return to national prosperity during the 1950s, summer cottages were built in greater numbers than during the preceding three decades. They were, however, less ambitiously conceived than their pre–World War I forerunners, and often were erected on smaller pieces of land and/or concentrated in groups. The cottage ideal continued to be eroded as the practice of long summer stays was gradually undermined by new economic pressures and altered family life-styles. The advent of the modern, two-career family, as well as competing uses of peoples' money and time, have curtailed the vacation experience, and made ownership of a single-season house less desirable and practical. Today most people simply lack the requisite disposable income to erect and sustain the kind of summer residences so enjoyed by the more affluent members of previous generations.

Other factors have also affected the summer cottage phenomenon in the White Mountains since World War II. With the availability of high-speed automobiles and expanded road systems, increasingly people have tended to travel rather than spend their limited vacation time in a single place. The resulting patronage has sustained the remaining hotels, cabins, campgrounds, motels, and bed and breakfast establishments, offering other lodging options to summer vacationers. Competition for cottages has also been posed by improved, worldwide airplane transportation links, which have promoted foreign travel and deterred people from making a real estate commitment to a single summer community. In recent years, single-family cottage construction has also been discouraged by the fast growth and great popularity of condominiums, which are attractive because of their reasonable cost, efficient size and operation, easier maintenance, and year-round use potential. Most larger single-family houses have proven impractical for short-term use, and as focal points for both summer and winter sporting and social activity. Made more economical and feasible by modern design theories, building materials, and practices, the condominium unit and the small, year-round dwelling have become the predominant expressions of residential architecture in the White Mountains. Thus, the cottage concept lives on, albeit altered from the markedly different, halcyon era preceding World War I. In the future we can expect the architecture of leisure and recreation to undergo further change, but the legacy of the region's first summer cottages will be lasting.

Appendix

Architects, Commissions, Building Dates, and Client Names

All commissions are documented, with the exception of attributed buildings, which are asterisked.

William A. Bates (New York City) (1853–1922)
Wentworth Hall and Cottages, Jackson, 1881–c. 1915
"The Castle" ("The Towers") (Wentworth), Jackson, 1891–92
"The Boulders" (Ditson), Jackson, 1895
*The Hurlin cottage, Jackson, 1896

J. Randolph Coolidge (Coolidge & Carlson) (Boston) (1862–1928)
*"Lucknow" (mansion, stable, gatehouses) (Plant), Moultonborough, 1911–14
"Far Pastures" ("Stone House") (Coolidge), Sandwich, 1919–27

Charles A. Coolidge (Shepley, Rutan and Coolidge) (Boston) (1858–1956)
"The Big House" reconstruction at "The Rocks" estate (Glessner), Bethlehem, 1889

Paul Philippe Cret (Philadelphia) (1876–1945)
"Music Box" at "Funfield" (Mallery), Sugar Hill, 1919

Stephen C. Earle (Boston and Worcester, Mass.) (1839–1913)
*"Bergenheim" (Fette), North Conway (Intervale), c. 1880
"Kilbarchan" (Schouler), North Conway (Intervale), 1879
"Stonehurst" reconstruction and expansion (Merriman), North Conway, 1895

William R. Emerson (Boston) (1832–1917)
The Fitz cottage, Jackson, c. 1888
"Maple Knoll" (Shapleigh), Jackson, 1896–97

(Arthur Greene) Everett (1855–1925) and *(Samuel W.) Mead* (18??–19??) (Boston)
"Hilldrift" (Saunders), Jackson, 1904–6

Albert C. Fernald (Boston) (18??–19??)
"Great Hill Farm" modifications (Clarke), Tamworth, c. 1901
"Great Hill Farm" recreation building (Clarke), Tamworth, c. 1910–15

Horace S. Frazer (Boston) (1862–1931)
"Burleigh Brae" (Webster), Holderness, 1910–11

Eugene C. Gale (Jefferson, N.H.) (1871–after 1935)
*"Buena Vista" (Hoople), Jefferson Highlands, c. 1892
*The McCabe cottage, Jefferson Highlands, 1892–93

Charles Alling Gifford (New York City) (1861–1937)
Caretaker's cottage (Mount Washington Hotel), Bretton Woods, 1903

John Graham, Jr. (Philadelphia) (1888–1957)
  "Funfield" (Mallery), Sugar Hill, 1916

Anne Grant (New York City) (18??–19??)
  "Sylva-of-the-Pines" (Cottle/Cox), Bartlett (Intervale), c. 1902

Bradford Hamilton (Boston) (18??–19??)
  "The Manor House" (Carruth), North Conway (Kearsarge), c. 1911

(Henry W.) Hartwell (1833–1919), *(William C.) Richardson* (1854–1935), and *(James) Driver*
  (1859–1923) (Boston)
    "The Hummocks" (Carter), Jefferson Highlands, 1897–98
    "Siwooganock Cottage" and "Dartmouth Cottage" ("Boismont") modifications
      (Carter), Jefferson Highlands, 1916

Lois L. Howe (Boston) (1864–1964)
  "Birchentower" addition (Scudder), Tamworth (Chocorua), 1917

(Walter H.) Kilham (1868–1948) and *(James C.) Hopkins* (1873–1938) (Boston)
  "Intermont" (Cleveland), Tamworth, 1905
  "Kilmarnock" (Finley), Tamworth, 1906

Edwin J. Lewis, Jr. (Boston) (1859–1937)
  "Cairncroft" (Hammer), Tamworth (Chocorua), 1892

Ernest M. A. Machado (Salem, Mass.) (1868–1907)
  "Juniper Lodge" (Reynolds), Sugar Hill, 1910–11

F. Schuyler Mathews (Boston) (1854–1938)
  "El Fureidis" (Mathews), West Campton, c. 1884 and 1893
  "Gladswood" (Elphinstone), West Campton, c. 1909–10
  The Reuter cottage, West Campton, c. 1902–5

Charles Follen McKim (New York City) (1847–1909)
  "The Satyr" (Wormeley), Jackson, 1892

Sylvanus D. Morgan (Lisbon, N.H.) (1857–1940)
  *"The Gables" (Kellner), Bethlehem, 1893–94
  *"Lindhurst" (Adams), Sugar Hill, 1891
  *The Abbe house, Bethlehem, 1903
  The Beaumont cottage, Bethlehem, 1908
  The Ivie cottage, Bethlehem, 1908
  "Glengarry Cottage" (Kenney), Bethlehem, 1908
  *"Beaver Lodge" (The Balsams), Dixville Notch, c. 1912
  *"The Stone Cottage" (The Balsams), Dixville Notch, c. 1915
  The Frank house, Bethlehem, 1923–24
  *"Tudor Cottage" (Forest Hills Hotel), Franconia, 1925–26

(Robert S.) Peabody (1845–1917) and *(John G.) Stearns* (1843–1917) (Boston)
  "Conni Sauti" addition (Bowditch), Tamworth (Chocorua), c. 1896
  "Great Hill Farm" addition (Clark), Tamworth, c. 1897
  "Willowgate" (Runnells), Tamworth (Chocorua), 1899–1900

Clifford A. Peck (Essex, Conn.) (c. 1892–19??)
  "Adair" (Hogan/Guider), Bethlehem, 1927–28

Charles A. Platt (New York City) (1861–1933)
  "Heavenly Hill" (George H. Page), Tamworth (Chocorua), 1898–99

"The Clearing" (Lilias Page), Tamworth (Chocorua), 1901–2
*The Grant/Stone house (after Platt plan), Tamworth (Chocorua), 1907

Frederick Pope (Boston) (1838–c. 1915)
The Pratt house, North Conway (Kearsarge), 1894

John Pickering Putnam (Boston) (1847–1917)
The Wigglesworth cottage, Jackson, c. 1888

Charles Rich (Rich and Mathesius) (New York City) (1855–1943)
"Log Cabin" at "Funfield" (Mallery), Sugar Hill, 1926

(Arthur) Rotch (1850–94) and *(George Thomas) Tilden* (1845–1919) (Boston)
"Concordia Hut" (Nichols), North Conway (Intervale), 1888–89

Edward Thornton Sanderson (Littleton, N.H.) (1875–1960)
*"The Outlook" (Sayer), Bethlehem, 1890–91
Sayer Cottages Nos. 1 and 2, Bethlehem, 1897
Sayer Cottages Nos. 3 and 4, Bethlehem, 1897–98

Isaac E. Scott (Chicago) (1845–1920)
"The Big House" at "The Rocks" estate (Glessner), Bethlehem, 1883
Horse barn at "The Rocks" estate (Glessner), Bethlehem, 1884

Isaac Sisson (Providence, R.I.) (18??–19??)
"Fern Cliff" (Goff), Jackson, 1896

(George) Snell (Snell and Gregson) (Boston) (1820–92)
"Stonehurst" (Bigelow), North Conway, 1871–72; 1875–76

John Calvin Stevens (Portland, Maine) (1855–1940)
Observatory for "Birchmont" (Tucker), North Conway, c. 1889
The Wilson cottage, Jackson, 1894
The Peabody cottage, Gorham, 1903

Gustav Stickley (New York State) (1858–1942)
*"Upland Cottage," Bethlehem, 1916–17

Hermann Valentin von Holst (Chicago) (1874–1905)
"The Lodge" at "The Rocks" estate (Glessner), Bethlehem, 1902–3
"The Glamis" (Macbeth), Bethlehem, 1904–5
Sawmill-pigpen (1906), cow barn (1906–1907), and remodeled carriage house and
horse barn (1907) at "The Rocks" estate, Bethlehem

(George C.) Wales (1869–1940) and *(Henry C.) Holt* (18??–19??) (Boston)
"The Homestead" (Frank G. Webster), Holderness, 1896
Laurence J. Webster house, Holderness, 1903

C. Howard Walker (Boston) (1857–1936)
"The Knoll" (Hurd), North Conway (Intervale), c. 1885–86
*The Sherwin cottage, Tamworth (Chocorua), c. 1885–86
*The Chadwick cottage, Tamworth (Chocorua), c. 1890–91
"Pine Cone" (Walker), Tamworth (Chocorua), c. 1891–92
"Connie Sauti" (Bowditch), Tamworth (Chocorua), 1892–93
*"Greycroft" (Loring), Tamworth (Chocorua), c. 1896
*"Masquemoosic" (Wainwright), Tamworth (Chocorua), c. 1896–97
"Birch Knoll" (Balch), Tamworth (Chocorua), 1913

(Harry Leslie) Walker (1877–1954) and *(George H.) Chichester* (1878–1916) (New York City)
 "Highland Croft" (Dickson), Littleton, 1909–10

Stanford White (New York City) (1853–1906)
 *"Brookmead" (Wormeley), Jackson, 1894–95
 *"Gray Manor" (Baldwin), Jackson, 1902–3
 *"Edgemont" (Perkins), Bethlehem, c. 1903

Notes

Key to Abbreviations (Periodicals, Reference Works, and Books)

AABN   *American Architect and Building News*

ACAB   *Appleton's Cyclopedia of American Biography*

ATC   *Among the Clouds*

BDAA(D)   *Biographical Dictionary of American Architects (Deceased)*

DAB   *Dictionary of American Biography*

GM   *Granite Monthly*

GRHWM   Tolles, *The Grand Resort Hotels of the White Mountains*

GRM   *Gorham Mountaineer*

LC   *Littleton Courier*

MEA   *Macmillan Encyclopedia of Architects*

NCAB   *The National Cyclopaedia of American Biography*

NHFSH   *New Hampshire Farms for Summer Homes*

NHP   *New Hampshire Profiles*

NYT   *New York Times*

WMD   *The White Mountain Directory*

WME   *White Mountain Echo*

WML   *White Mountain Life*

WWA   *Who's Who in America*

WWNE   *Who's Who in New England*

WWWA   *Who Was Who in America*

1. *DAB* 1, pp. 254–55; *NCAB* 3, p. 20; Stone, *History of Massachusetts Industries*, vol. 2, pp. 1884–99.

2. Deed, Erastus B. Bigelow from Stephen Mudgett, Carroll County Registry of Deeds, book 56, p. 525, 6 November 1870. The sale price was $15,000, an astounding figure for the time. Bigelow made subsequent purchases from John A. and Mary E. Barnes (book 59, p. 197, 23 January 1871); John A. Barnes, Mary D. Pendexter, and William C. Seavey (Conway) (book 58, pp. 470, 471, and 480, 11 October 1871); Richard S. and Mary E. Storrs (Brooklyn, N.Y.) (book 59, p. 229, 23 January 1872); Mary D. Pendexter (book 60, p. 288, 17 October 1872); and Lewis Gray (Bartlett) (book 60, p. 389, 18 November 1872). Other acquisitions followed in 1877, 1879, and 1880.

3. Daniel Merriman, "Annals of Stonehurst," 1871, 1872 and 1875 entries, Massachusetts Historical Society, Boston; Withey, *BDAA(D)*, p. 563; Lynne Emerson Monroe, "Intervale Historic District," New Hampshire Division of Historic Resources Area Form, Concord, N.H., 1992. The 1875 fire supposedly was caused when the superintendent, Allen, kindled a fire in the wood furnace and kept the coal air duct closed.

4. *NCAB* 18, p. 173; biographical clipping file, Worcester (Mass.) Historical Museum.

5. Monroe, "Intervale Historic District."

6. *WME* 18, no. 1 (6 July 1895): 6; Merriman, "Annals of Stonehurst," 1895 entry; Monroe, "Intervale Historic District"; Steven Caming, "Flavor of the English Countryside," *The Irregular* (North Conway), Section B, 17 September 1976; Phil Bertiaume, "A Country Inn to the Manor Born," *Country Almanac*, Fall 1984, pp. 71–74.

7. Monroe, "Intervale Historic District"; "Annals of Stonehurst," 1871 entries; Monroe, New Hampshire State Historic Preservation Office Inventory Forms for the "Stonehurst" farm buildings (1988), the "Brown Cottage" (1987), and the "Red Cottage" (1987).

Today, the "Red Cottage" and the "Brown Cottage" are privately owned, while the farm buildings accommodate tourism-related business enterprises. The farm continued in operation until the time of Helen Merriman's death in 1933.

8. *WME* 30, no. 1 (13 July 1907): 13, and no. 5 (10 August 1907): 1; *WME* 31, no. 5 (11 July 1908): 14; Monroe, "Intervale Historic District"; *NHFSH*, 6th ed. (1908), p. 40, and 8th ed. (1910), p. 10; "James Bryce in the White Mountains," *Appalachia* 42, no. 3 (15 June 1979): 97–100; John Ranlett, "James Bryce: Pioneer Conservationist," *Appalachia* 43, no. 4 (15 December 1981): 70–74; *AMC White Mountain Guide*, 25th ed. (Boston: Appalachian Mountain Club, 1992), p. 246.

9. Monroe, "Intervale Historic District." The current name of the inn is "Stonehurst Manor."

10. *AABN* 5 (8 March 1879): 7, no. 166. Unfortunately, little is known about the builder, A. Thurber, but it is likely that he completed work for other clients in the North Conway area at the time.

11. Deed, James Schouler from Mary D. Pendexter, Carroll County Registry of Deeds, book 70, p. 22, 22 September 1877. The purchase was made for $500.

The parcel was bound by the North Conway–Bartlett road and lands owned by Erastas B. Bigelow (see "Stonehurst") and Charles R. Dinsmore. Schouler added two acres to the original tract in 1878 by purchase for $375 from the Dinsmore family (book 72, p. 107, 5 October 1878).

12. Withey, *BDAA(D)*, pp. 186–7; *NCAB* 11, p. 147.

13. *DAB* 8, pp. 459–60; *NCAB* 11, p. 181; *ACAB* 5, p. 427.

14. *WME* 9, no. 8 (21 August 1886): 7; *ATC* 17, no. 28 (17 August 1893): 1; inscription, North Conway (N.H.) Public Library.

15. Monroe, "Intervale Historic District"; *WME* 13, no. 1 (5 July 1890): 5; date marker, "1880," on front gable of house; deed, William E. Fette from Henry A. Chase (Salem, Mass.), Carroll County Registry of Deeds, book 74, p. 1, 27 October 1879. The sale was made for "$1.00 and other valuable considerations." The tract was bordered by Dinsmore family lands. In 1887 (22 December, book 81, p. 331), the line between the Fette and Dinsmore lands was straightened.

16. Monroe, "Intervale Historic District"; Monroe, New Hampshire Reconnaissance Survey Form for the Fette Cottage, New Hampshire Division of Historical Resources, Concord, 1987.

17. Monroe, "Intervale Historic District."

18. *WML* 1, no. 2 (8 July 1897); obituary, *Boston Transcript*, 12 January 1899; obituary, *Boston Journal*, 12 January 1899; alumni biographical files, Harvard University Archives, Cambridge, Mass.; *Class of 1858 40th Anniversary Report* (Cambridge, Mass.: Harvard University, 1898), pp. 37–38.

19. Deed, Melancthon M. Hurd from Mary D. Pendexter, Carroll County Registry of Deeds, book 84, p. 451, 28 September 1886. The lot is situated on the east side of North Conway–Intervale highway, northwest of the Currie property, bordering on Neighbor's Row. The purchase price was $600 and the lot size in excess of one acre. Hurd added a small piece of land to this initial purchase the next year (see deed, Melancthon M. Hurd from Mary D. Pendexter, book 86, p. 8, 16 June 1886). On 5 September 1888, he further expanded his real estate holdings, again from Pendexter (see deed, book 90, p. 60), by "76 square rods" for the sale price of $400.

20. *The Sanitary Engineer and Construction Record*, 11 February 1886, p. 248. The cost was estimated not to exceed $5,000 in this source. The first floor plan consisted of a parlor, entrance hall, library, dining room, and service ell (kitchen, storeroom, china closet and storage rooms). The second floor, illuminated by gable end windows and dormers, contained four or five large bedrooms in the main block, and additional smaller bedrooms for children and servants in the ell.

21. *The Sanitary Engineer and Construction Record*, 11 February 1886, p. 248. Members of the Intervale community with Boston associations (Bigelow/Merriman, Schouler, Fette, Nichols) had ties with Boston-originated members of the Chocorua summer colony. It is as a result of this connection that Walker probably secured the commission to design "The Knoll."

22. New Hampshire State Historic Preservation Officer (Concord) Survey Form—State Historical Resources Survey, 1987.

23. W. J. Burke and Will D. Horne, *American Authors and Books, 1640 to the Present*, rev. ed. (New York: Crown Publishers, Inc., 1972), p. 318; *A History and Genealogy of the Family of Hurd in the United States* (New York: privately printed, 1910), pp. 130, 182; Monroe, "Intervale Historic District." In about 1920, Hurd's sister, Alice G., built a "rustic Shingle-style" cottage between "The Knoll" and "Nirvana," the Currie house, on Neighbor's Row. It also still stands. In 1924 "The Knoll" was sold by the heirs of Melancthon Hurd to Myrtie Eastman, of New York City (deed, Carroll County Registry of Deeds, book 167, p. 395). Today, the house is used as a recreation lodge, and is owned by the White Mountain Ski Runners Club.

24. *WML* 1, no. 2 (8 July 1897); *WME* 16, no. 1 (1 July 1893): 1; *WME* 17, no. 1 (7 July 1894): 15; *WME* 20, no. 1 (3 July 1897): 16; *WME* 30, no. 5 (10 August 1907): 20; *WME* 31, no. 1 (11 July 1908): 14; *WME* 31, no. 1 (16 July 1910): 7.

25. Reconnaissance Survey Form, New Hampshire State Historic Preservation Office, Concord, 1987; deed, Sarah C. Currie (wife of C. George) from Adeline Dinsmore, et al., Carroll County Registry of Deeds, book 84, p. 179, 5 June 1885; deed, Sarah C. Currie from Abbie P. and Elijah J. Dinsmore, book 84, p. 179, 5 June 1885; deed, Sarah C. Currie from C. Royal and Fred W. Dinsmore, book 84, p. 179, 5 June 1885. This tract was bordered by land owned by Mrs. S. D. Pendexter and John A. Barnes, and Neighbors Row. Subsequently, the Curries supplemented this initial acquisition with one acre plus in 1886 (Sarah C. Currie from Mary D. Pendexter, book 86, p. 203, 15 September 1886), and two small parcels in 1894 (Sarah C. Currie from Caroline M. Eastman, book 98, p. 572, 8 December 1894; Sarah C. Currie from William M. Wyman, book 102, p. 429, 14 September 1894).

26. Monroe, "Intervale Historic District," sheet 5. East of the main residence is a small one-and-one-half-story carriage house, sheathed in clapboards, with shingles on the upper attic story gable ends and shed roof dormer.

27. Tatman and Moss, *Biographical Dictionary of Philadelphia Architects: 1700–1930*, pp. 266 and 268; *WWWA*, vol. 1 (1897–1942), p. 396; Withey, *BDAA(D)*, pp. 209–10. Fielding graduated from Germantown Academy (Penn.) in 1883. Plans for the house have yet to be discovered.

28. Clipping files, University Archives and Records Center, University of Pennsylvania, Philadelphia, Pa.; *Lloyd's Clerical Directory for 1888 . . .* (Hamilton, Ohio: News and Telegraph Publishing Co., 1898), p. 193; letter from Rev. F. Lee Richards (Historiographer, Episcopal Diocese of Philadelphia) to author, 9 January 1995; "The Reverend C. George Currie, D.D.," unpublished manuscript, 3 pp., Kenyon College Archives, Olin and Chalmers Libraries, Gambier, Ohio; letter from Aaron B. Webber (Student Archivist, Kenyon College) to author, February 1995. Philip Zantzinger used "Nirvana" as his summer house until the 1920s, and was the architect of the North Conway Public Library around 1905. The house then passed from Zantzinger to Molly Lenox and Gladys Remick, who worked for Bloomingdale's department store in New York City.

29. Deed, Harry Peirce Nichols from Mary D. Pendexter, Carroll County Registry of Deeds, book 90, p. 51, 5 September 1888. The purchase price was $400. See also New Hampshire State Historic Preservation Office Survey Form 196 (November 1987), Conway, Carroll County, "End, Neighbors Row," NHSHPO, Concord; Dethier, *A Chronicle of Concordia by the Decade, 1888–1988*, pp. 3–4.

30. *WWWA*, vol. 1 (1897–1942), p. 897; "In Memoriam—Doctor Harry Peirce Nichols, 1859–1940," *Appalachia* 23, no. 3 (June 1941): 390–91; Susan Nichols Pulsifer, *Witch's Breed; The Peirce-Nichols Family of Salem* (Cambridge, Mass.: Dresser, Chapman & Grimes, 1967), p. 432; *ATC* 20, no. 20 (10 August 1897), p. 4, 21, no. 33 (25 August 1897), p. 4, 23, no. 52 (13 September 1899), p. 4, 37, no. 46 (13 September 1915), p. 1, and 38, no. 23 (9 August 1916), p. 1; Tolles, *GRHWM*, p. 147. Rev. Nichols had climbed Mt. Washington over one hundred times by 1915, and likely added impressively to the total over subsequent years.

31. New Hampshire State Historic Preservation Office Survey Form 196; Dethier, *A Chronicle of Concordia*, p. 13, and photographs. According to a family cost sheet, the house was estimated at just over $3,000.

32. Withey, *BDAA(D)* pp. 529, 600; Dethier, *A Chronicle of Concordia*, p. 4.

33. Letter, Rotch and Tilden, architects, to Mrs. Harry P. Nichols, Boston, Mass., 1 September 1888, family papers, "Concordia Hut," Intervale, N.H.

34. *ATC* 14, no. 9 (21 July 1890): 1.

35. *The Valley Visitor* (North Conway, N.H.), 15 September 1988, p. 5; *ATC* 18, no. 41 (30 August 1894): 1; *WME* 32, no. 11 (18 September 1909): 2; Catherine H. Campbell, *New Hampshire Scenery: A Dictionary of Nineteenth-Century Artists of New Hampshire Mountain Landscapes* (Canaan, N.H.: Phoenix Publishing for the New Hampshire Historical Society, 1985), p. 104; engraving, "Mount Washington from the Valley of Conway," by John Smillie after John F. Kensett, 17.9 × 26.5 cms., American Art Union, New York, 1851.

36. Kilbourne, *Chronicles of the White Mountains*, p. 228; deed, Payson Tucker from Elizabeth J. Plummer (wife of I. Frank Plummer), Carroll County Registry of Deeds, book 92, p.373, 14 December 1889. The land was part of the former McMillan farm, and was across the main Conway–North Conway road from the McMillan House, one of the village's oldest hostelries. Tucker added to this initial purchase on 25 November 1891, when he acquired several tracts from Joseph W. Symonds (book 96, p. 316), including the former Artist's Falls House property.

37. *ATC* 14, no. 9 (21 July 1890): 1; *WME* 13, no. 1 (5 July 1890): 5, no. 4 (26 July 1890): 7, and no. 10 (6 September 1890): 7; *WME* 14, no. 2 (11 July 1891), p. 5. Apparently, the house was suitable for winter as well as summer use. A cottage was built on the northern side of "Birchmont" in 1891 (*WME* 14, no. 5 [August 1891]: 7).

38. *ATC* 18, no. 41 (30 August 1894): 1.

39. *WME* 16, no. 2 (8 July 1893): 2.

40. Tolles, *GRHWM*, pp. 118–21; "Observatory at North Conway for Mr. Payson Tucker," rendered elevation, pen and ink on tracing cloth, n.d., John Calvin Stevens Collection, Avery Library, Columbia University, New York City.

41. *ATC* 17, no. 2 (18 July 1893): 1.

42. Sale advertisement, *ATC* 25, no. 21 (5 August 1901): 5; *WME* 27, no. 4 (30 July 1904): 4; *The Valley Visitor*, 15 December 1988, p. 6; *WME* 33, no. 1 (16 July 1910): 4; booklet, "Birchmont for Year 'Round Vacation Joy" (New York: Manufacturers Trust Company, c. 1948); *The Emteeco* (magazine of the Manufacturers Trust Company, New York City) 1, no. 2 (April 1945); advertisement, "New Hampshire Summer Guide" insert, *NHP* 7, no. 4 (April 1958): 60. Perhaps the most impressive legacy of Payson Tucker is the elaborate granite watering trough that he presented to the town, containing a large basin for horses and two small side bowls for dogs and other small animals. It is located on the west side of the main road (Route 16), opposite "Birchmont." Today the two-hundred-room Red Jacket Motor Inn occupies the house site.

43. Ephraim Tucker, *Genealogy of the Tucker Family . . .* (Worcester, Mass.: By the Author, 1895), pp. 183–84; Philip W. McIntyre and William F. Blanding, eds., *Men of Progress . . . State of Maine* (Boston: New England Magazine, 1897), pp. 94–95; *Portland* (Maine) *Board of Trade Journal* 1, no. 4 (August 1888): 121, and vol. 9, no. 9 (January 1897): 263; newspaper obituary notices for Payson Tucker, 1890, biography files, Maine Historical Society, Portland; *The Valley Visitor*, 15 December 1988, p. 5.

44. Mortgage deed, Fred I. Pratt from Albert Barnes, Carroll County Registry of Deeds, book 104, p. 299, 12 December 1893; advertisement for house sale, *WME* 28, no. 5 (August 1905): 8, vol. 31, no. 1 (11 July 1908): 7, and vol. 32, no. 1 (10 July 1909): 12.

45. *WME* 1, no. 1 (7 July 1894): 15. The property acquisition was confirmed by a mortgage deed dated over a year after the house was finished and occupied. Such a practice was not unusual.

46. *ATC* 17, no. 6 (22 July 1893): 1.

47. Charles H. Pope, *A History of the Dorchester Pope Family, 1634–1888* (Boston: By the Author, 1888), p. 210; *Boston City Directory* for 1895, 1900, 1904, 1910 and 1914; Bainbridge Bunting, *Houses of Boston's Back Bay: An Architectural History, 1840–1917* (Cambridge, Mass.: The Belknap Press of Harvard University Press, 1967), p. 157.

48. *ATC* 18, no. 41 (30 August 1894): 11. Here Pope is identified as architect of the Pratt cottage. Such a designer attribution is rare in White Mountain region newspapers of the late nineteenth and early twentieth centuries.

49. *ATC* 29, no. 9 (22 July 1905): 1. Apparently, the house did not sell, and the Pratts retained ownership for several more years.

50. *WME* 21, no. 3 (16 July 1898): 16.

51. *ATC* 29, no. 9 (22 July 1905): 1.

52. *WME* 22, no. 4 (29 July 1899): 16.

53. *WME* 22, no. 2 (15 July 1899): 5.

54. *WME* 28, no. 5 (5 August 1905): 8.

55. Harold B. Carruth, *Carruth Family: Brief Background and Genealogical Data of Twenty Branches in America* (Ascutney, Vt.: By the Author, 1952), p. 79; telephone interview, Dr. Thomas J. McDonough, North Conway, N.H., 4 September 1994; deed, Ellen Carruth from Clara E. and Hiram H. Dow, and Almira H. and Lester C. Barnes, Carroll County Registry of Deeds, book 138, p. 515, 21 December 1910. The sale was officially made "for $1.00 and other valuable considerations," with unstated payment made later. The lot was approximately two acres and was bounded by land owned by A. B. Dow, Eliza J. Bouton and L. F. Bunker. Apparently, upon Carruth's death in 1923, her nephew Henry Pope Carruth (b. 1884) inherited the property. He and his wife, Leona M., sold to N. C. Cates of North Conway on 31 July 1925 (deed, book 171, p. 453), likely because they were unable to access it easily from their home in Chillicothe, Ohio.

56. Carruth, *Carruth Family*, pp. 79 and 106.

57. Carruth, *Carruth Family*, pp. 79 and 106; Schrock, *Directory of Boston Architects, 1846–1970*, p. 32; Boston Building Inspector Reports and Boston Architects File, Department of Fine Arts, Boston Public Library.

During his years in architectural practice in Boston, Hamilton had offices at 178 Devonshire Street, 163 Olive Street, and 236 Summer Street. In addition to listing these addresses, Boston city directories locate him at his house in Milton to 1924, after which there is no further mention of him.

58. Floor plans (cellar; first floor; second floor) for the Ellen Carruth House, Kearsarge, N.H., by Bradford Hamilton, 163 Oliver Street, Boston, Dr. and Mrs. Thomas J. McDonough, North Conway, N.H. An extensive veranda running across the entire west elevation was removed some years ago.

59. *WME* 25, no. 6 (9 August 1902): 17; *NHFSH*, 2nd ed. (1904), p. 17.

60. *Women's Who's Who of America*, 1914 ed., p. 208; *ATC* 32, no. 5 (11 July 1910): 3.

61. *Women's Who's Who of America*, 1914 ed., p. 210.

62. *NHFSH*, 2nd ed. (1904), p. 19.

63. Merrill, *History of Carroll County*, p. 931; *ATC* 30, no. 23 (7 August 1906): 4; *WME* 41, no. 11 (21 September 1918): 13.

64. *WME* 28, No. 7 (19 August 1905), p. 8.

65. *WME* 25, no. 6 (9 August 1902): 17. The land upon which the cottage was built was acquired by Misses Cottle and Cox from Jonathan and George E. Gale of Bartlett for $450 on 16 September 1901 (Carroll County Registry of Deeds, book 116, p. 477). They expanded their land holdings in 1903 (purchase from George E. Gale, book 20, p. 598, 29 June) and 1906 (purchases from George E. Gale, book 127, p. 253, 5 January, and Carrie F. Wheeler, book 127, p. 386, 25 January).

2. JACKSON

1. Tolles, *New Hampshire Architecture*, p. 268; Tolles, *GRHWM*, pp. 84–90; New Hampshire Historical Society *Newsletter* 20, no. 4 (July 1983): 7.

2. Withey, *BDAA(D)*, p. 42; *WME* 17, no. 5 (4 August 1894): 16, and vol. 18, no. 12 (21 September 1895): 2. William Bates began his career as an architect with the firm of Herter Brothers. Ultimately, he organized his own firm under the name of Bates and How.

Many of Bates' residential designs in the metropolitan New York City area were published as plates in nationally circulated architectural periodicals.

3. Merrill, *History of Carroll County*, p. 961; *ATC* 5, no. 25 (13 August 1881): 3, and vol. 6, no. 14 (1 August 1882): 8.

4. Merrill, *History of Carroll County*, p. 961; *WME* 8, no. 1 (27 June 1885): 8, and no. 12 (12 September 1885): 8; *ATC* 9, no. 1 (11 July 1885): 8. See front elevation view and floor plans for the entire complex in *AABN* 18, no. 520 (12 December 1885), supplement, op. p. 3. A highly inaccurate, lyrical birds-eye view, supposedly from Bates' New York office, was also published in vol. 20, no. 13 (13 March 1894) of *Architecture and Building*.

5. *WME* 38, no. 1 (17 July 1915): 1; *ATC* 38, no. 32 (22 August 1916): 1; *The Reporter* (North Conway, N.H.), 3 November 1982, p. 1. The casino was enlarged in 1892. About 350 guests could be accommodated in the complex in 1930.

6. Personal interview with Mrs. Roland E. (Merideth) Christie, Jackson, N.H., 22 March 1994; interview with Mrs. Arthur (Rachel) Doucette, Jackson, 22 June 1993; interview with Mrs. Delmar F. (Charlotte) Haskell, Jackson, 12 April 1994; *ATC* 18, no. 4 (18 July 1894): 4; *WME* 19, no. 1 (4 July 1896): 2.

7. Deed, Esther Strahan (wife of Thomas F. Strahan), Carroll County Registry of Deeds, book 88, p. 43, 2 September 1887. The land faced on the Five-Mile Circuit Road, and was bordered by parcels owned by George Pinkham, George P. Meserve, and George M. Davis. Originally there was an old farmhouse on the home site, but it was burned by the Strahans to make way for their new cottage. The current owners of the property demolished the house in 1997, leaving the older outbuildings intact.

8. Interview and visit with Dr. Ashton Emerson, Jackson, N.H., 3 August 1994. Blueprint plans may possibly exist in the hands of the current owners. In 1894, the Strahans added "a very picturesque bowling alley" with walls of "fine old logs" (*WME* 17, no. 1 [7 July 1894]: 16).

9. Walter M. Pratt, *Seven Generations: A Story of Prattville and Chelsea* (Chelsea, Mass.: privately printed, 1930), pp. 116, 154, 160, and 168; *Massachusetts of To-Day* (Boston: Columbia Printing Co., 1892), p. 382; Stone, *History of Massachusetts Industries*, vol. 2, p. 1635; *WME* 31, no. 1 (11 July 1908): 13. The Strahans had six children, four of whom had died by 1892.

10. Stone, *History of Massachusetts Industries*, vol. 2, p. 1635.

11. *Concise Dictionary of American Biography*, 4th ed. (New York: Charles Scribner's Sons, 1990), p. 1297.

12. Deed, Edward Wigglesworth and Walter Scott Fitz from Adeline Wentworth, Carroll County Registry of Deeds, book 88, p. 148, 19 October 1887.

13. Deeds, Carroll County Registry of Deeds. Edward Wigglesworth from Alonzo and C. B. Chesley, book 90, p. 45, 5 September 1888; Edward Wigglesworth and Walter Scott Fitz from Charles W. and Mary A. Gray, book 90, p. 297, 7 May 1889; Edward Wigglesworth and Walter Scott Fitz from Charles W. and Mary A. Gray, book 93, p. 430, 15 July 1890;

Edward Wigglesworth and Walter Scott Fitz from Warren C. Gray, book 96, p. 514, 2 January 1892; Edward Wigglesworth from Alonzo Chesley, book 99, p. 189, 24 January 1893; Edward Wigglesworth from Christy B. Farmer, Melissa J. Langley, and Samantha A. Willey, book 99, pg. 169, 24 January 1893; Edward Wigglesworth from Lewis W. Hanson, book 99, p. 188, 24 June 1893; Edward Wigglesworth and Walter Scott Fitz from Warren C. and Abbie E. Gray, book 100, p. 237, 21 July 1893.

14. *WME* 43, no. 6 (14 August 1920): 9.

15. *WWWA*, vol. 1 (1897–1942), p. 1002; Oscar F. Adams, *A Dictionary of American Authors*, 5th ed., rev. and enl. (Boston and New York: Houghton, Mifflin Co., 1904), p. 545.

16. *AABN* 24, 15 September 1888, plate no. 664.

17. Illustrated description of the Wigglesworth cottage, ms., n.d., Jackson (N.H.) Historical Society.

18. Telephone interview with Miss Helen Kerr (Lexington, Mass.), 19 January 1994.

19. *WME* 19 (1 August 1896): 14.

20. See Zaitzevsky and Miller, *The Architecture of William Ralph Emerson*, pp. 75–87; Reed, *A Delight to All Who Knew It*, pp. 138–44.

21. Placzek, *MEA*, vol. 2, pp. 24–25; Zaitzevsky and Miller, *The Architecture of William Ralph Emerson*, pp. 2–3; Reed, *A Delight to All Who Knew It*, pp. 11–15; Withey, *BDAA(D)*, p. 198. Little is known about the life of William R. Emerson, and no office records have survived.

22. Sylvia Fitts Getchell, *Fitts Families (Fitts-Fitz-Fittz): A Genealogy* (Newmarket, N.H.: By the Author, 1989), p. 265. Both Henrietta and Walter Fitz had ties with the Museum of Fine Arts. Henrietta Fitz's son, Edward Jackson Holmes, by her first marriage, was director of the museum.

23. Deeds, Carroll County Registry of Deeds, Walter Scott Fitz and Edward Wigglesworth from Adeline Wentworth, book 88, p. 148, 10 October 1887; Walter Scott Fitz and Edward Wigglesworth from Charles W. and Mary A. Gray, book 91, p. 297, 7 May 1889; Walter Scott Fitz and Edward Wigglesworth from Charles W. and Mary A. Gray, book 93, p. 430, 15 July 1890; Walter Scott Fitz and Edward Wigglesworth from Warren G. and Abbie E. Gray, book 96, p. 514, 2 January 1892; Walter Scott Fitz from Edward and Sarah W. Wigglesworth, book 98, p. 209, 16 September 1892; Walter Scott Fitz and Edward Wigglesworth from Warren G. and Abbie E. Gray, book 100, p. 237, 21 July 1893. To the south of the Fitz cottage, serving both it and the Wigglesworth house, a large barn once stood. It was demolished in the late 1950s.

24. *NHFSH* (1902 ed.), p. 30; deeds, Carroll County Registry of Deeds: Katherine P. Wormeley from Warren G. and Abbie E. Gray, book 92, p. 202, 12 October 1889; book 92, p. 224, 31 October 1889; book 97, p. 482, 18 June 1892; book 100, p. 223, 13 July 1893; book 100, pp. 253–54, 15 August 1893; book 102, p. 473, 20 September 1894. See also, Katherine P. Wormeley from George and Lorinda Meserve, book 103, p. 231, 19 December 1894; Wormeley from G. P., W. W., and A. P. Meserve, book 104, p. 587, 11 November 1895; Wormeley from George Meserve, book 106, p. 479, 29 September 1896 (water access); Wormeley

from George Meserve, book 106, p. 480, 29 September 1896 (water access); and Wormeley from Mary E. Gray, book 115, p. 49, 8 November 1900. These parcels were located both on the east and west of Thorn Hill Road. Certain of these transactions were for water access and/or the right to lay water pipes.

25. Garland, *Yesterdays*, pp. 67–68; *WME* 14, no. 5 (1 August 1891): 5. "The Poplars" was later renamed "Thorn Hill Cottage."

26. *WME* 15, no. 6 (6 August 1892): 17; date marker "1892" over parlor fireplace, "The Satyr"; *NHFSH* (1902 ed.), p. 30. In this booklet Wormeley is quoted as saying, "the house, stable, laundry, etc, (from designs by my friend, C. F. McKim), cost about $8,000." One may conjecture, therefore, that McKim may well have been involved with "The Poplars" renovations, as well as the new cottage.

27. *WME* 15, no. 6 (6 August 1892): 17; Rhoda Garrison, "Waldweben, 1891–1991: The History of a House in Jackson, New Hampshire" (Jackson: Unpublished typescript and manuscript in family hands, 1991), pp. 3, 4, and 11. A Dutch door connecting the front porch and the living room contains a stained glass window in the design of Wormeley's coat-of-arms. In addition to the house, the property formerly contained a small laundry structure, a barn (which burned in 1907) and an ice house. In 1912, the Ritchie family purchased the property from the estate of Katherine P. Wormeley, and renamed the house "Waldweben," meaning "forest murmurs," in German. The basic architectural plan of the house has remained intact, except for the addition in 1913 of a small room off the kitchen.

28. Garland, *Yesterdays*, pp. 69–70; "Miss Wormeley's Houses on Thorn Hill Road, Jackson," photocopied typescript (Thorn Hill Lodge letterhead), n.d., Jackson Historical Society; *WME* 18, no. 1 (6 July 1895): 4, 18, no. 11 (14 September 1895): 14, and 19, no. 1 (4 July 1896): 2; Suki Casanave, "Romance in the White Mountains," *NHP* 40, no. 3 (May/June 1991): 13 and 18.

29. *DAB* 10, p. 534; *NCAB* 8, p. 367; Edward T. James, ed., *Notable American Women, 1907–1950: A Biographical Dictionary* (Cambridge, Mass.: The Belknap Press of Harvard University Press, 1971), vol. 3, pp. 674–75; John F. Kirk, *A Supplement to Allibone's Dictionary of English Literature and British and American Authors* (Philadelphia: J. B. Lippincott & Co., 1896), vol. 1, p. 1549; obituary, *WME* 31, no. 6 (15 August 1908): 16, *WME* 19, no. 1 (4 July 1896): 2. For full information on Charles Follen McKim and Stanford White, consult Withey, *BDAA(D)*, pp. 409–12, and 652–53; Van Vynckt, *International Dictionary of Architects and Architecture*, vol. 1, pp. 563–65, and 983–84; and Placzek, *MEA*, vol. 3, pp. 140–51, and vol. 4, pp. 390–94.

30. Blithe Damour, "The Wentworth Castle," *NHP* 33, no. 8 (August 1984): 53; Merrill, *History of Carroll County*, p. 969.

31. *WME* 17, no. 5 (4 August 1894): 16; promotional booklet, *Wentworth Hall and Cottages* (Jackson, N.H.: By the Hotel, c. 1910); "Thorncastle, Jackson, N.H.," for Gen. M. C. Wentworth, *Building* 3, no. 15 (December 1885), design plate 242.

32. *WME* 14, no. 1 (4 July 1891): 2. The date of construction is recorded in a mosaic of white stones on the fronts of the corner towers.

33. *WME* 18, no. 1 (6 July 1895): 15 and vol. 16, no. 3 (15 July 1893): 8.

34. *WME* 14, no. 1 (4 July 1891): 2.

35. Ibid.; "Wentworth Castle, Jackson, New Hampshire," Sotheby Parke Bernet International Realty Corporation (New York City and Boston) sales prospectus, 1982; letter, Dave E. Arata to George B. Gilman, New Hampshire Department of Resources and Economic Development, Concord, 18 July 1984.

36. Merrill, *History of Carroll County*, pp. 869–71; *NCAB* 16, pp. 186–87; H. M. Poole, "Wentworth Towers," 1894 *Boston Globe* typescript article, Jackson Historical Society; obituary, "Gen. M. C. Wentworth," *The Reporter* (North Conway, N.H.), 8 July 1915, p. 3; obituary, "General M. C. Wentworth," *ATC* 37, no. 2 (13 July 1915): 2; obituary, "General Marshall C. Wentworth," *GM* 47, no. 8 (August 1915); obituary, "General M. C. Wentworth," *WME* 38, no. 1 (17 July 1915): 1. After Georgia Wentworth's death, "The Castle" was unoccupied for nearly thirty years, but was largely restored under the ownerships of Countess Mathilde Mara de Brinska of Bavaria from 1959 to 1982, and David E. Arata of San Francisco from 1982 to 1988. See Robert Newman, "Ninety-Seven-Year-Old Jackson Landmark Seeks Fourth Owner," *Magnetic North* 6, no. 3 (Winter 1988): 52–53, 55.

37. Deed, Isaac Y. Chubbuck from Nelson I. and Jennie E. Trickey, Carroll County Registry of Deeds, book 94, p. 194, 8 August 1890; interview, Mrs. Roland E. (Merideth) Christie, Jackson, N.H., 22 March 1994. While the dating of "Thorn Lodge" is imprecise, the house appears on the Jackson town map in the *Town and City Atlas of the State of New Hampshire* (Boston: D. H. Hurd & Company, 1892). This is the basis for the construction date of around 1891.

38. Isaac Chubbuck's son, George T., inherited the property about 1896. In 1950, the property passed to another descendant, Marion L. Waterman, and then to the current owners, Mr. and Mrs. Roland E. Christie, in 1970.

39. Deed, George E. Saunders from Nelson I., Jennie E., and George I. Trickey, Carroll County Registry of Deeds, book 116, p. 206, 2 July 1901. This parcel was also bordered by lands owned by Charles B. Perkins and Wilham W. Trickey.

40. Interview with Mrs. Roland E. Christie, Jackson, 22 March 1994; letter, Alta M. Gale to the author, 23 January 1994; *Mr. William Saunders and Mrs. Sarah Flagg Saunders, Late of Cambridge . . .* (Cambridge, Mass.: privately printed, 1872), p. 27; Minutes of the Harvard College Faculty Meeting, 27 June 1870, Harvard University Archives, Cambridge, Mass. Harriman cleverly constructed the fireplace and chimney of the house before doing the interior finishing so that he could work in warm circumstances during the winter months.

41. Withey, *BDAA(D)*, pp. 101–2, 202, 414; Placzek, *MEA*, vol. 1, pp. 363–64. Cabot, Everett and Mead entered into partnership in 1885 and remained together until Cabot's retirement in 1896. Everett and Mead maintained the partnership into the first decade of this century.

42. Interview with Alta M. Gale, Jackson, N.H., 4 August 1994; undated blueprint plans (16 sheets) for a "House for George E. Saunders, Jackson, N.H.," Alta M. Gale; interview with Charlotte Haskell, Jackson, N.H., 12 April 1994. "Hilldrift" contains a storage and utility cellar; a living room, library, kitchen, pantry, and bedroom on the first floor; and four bedrooms (one substantially larger than the others) on the second floor. A photograph of the builder, Andrew C. Harriman, hangs by the traditional Colonial Revival front entrance door on the first floor.

Andrew Harriman also is believed to have been the contractor for the small Stick-style G. C. Hayes (later Fernald) cottage (c. 1889), opposite "Maple Knoll" further down the hill toward Jackson village.

43. Design sketches (two perspective elevations; first and second story floor plans) for Mrs. C. L. Wilson, Jackson, N.H., by John Calvin Stevens, Portland, Maine, xeroxes of sheets in private hands, Maine Historic Preservation Commission, Augusta.

44. *WME* 17, no. 1 (7 July 1894): 16; deed, Caroline F. Wilson (Brookline, Mass.) from Jennie E. Meserve (wife of Jonathan E.), Carroll County Registry of Deeds, book 102, p. 442, 12 September 1894; deed, Caroline F. Wilson from George and Lorinda Meserve, book 102, p. 470, 12 September 1894 (water access privileges, and the right to lay aqueduct to "premises located on Thorn Hill Road").

45. Design sketches for Mrs. C. L. Wilson, Jackson, N.H., by John Calvin Stevens. For information and photographs of Stevens' Maine houses, see Stevens and Shettleworth, *John Calvin Stevens: Domestic Architecture*.

46. Placzek, *MEA*, vol. 4, p. 130; Withey, *BDAA(D)*, pp. 572–73; Wodehouse, *American Architects*, pp. 182–83; Damie Stillman, et al., *Architecture and Ornament in Late 19th-Century America* (Newark, Del.: Department of Art History and the University Gallery, University of Delaware, 1981), pp. 66–69; Scully, *The Shingle Style and the Stick Style*, p. 113. Stevens was in partnership with his son, John Howard Stevens, from 1906 to 1940, during which time they designed buildings of all types.

47. *WME* 19, no. 1 (4 July, 1896): 2.

48. Withey, *BDAA(D)*, p. 42; *WME* 17, no. 5 (4 August 1894): 16; *WME* 18, no. 1 (6 July 1895): 15, no. 2 (13 July 1895): 15, no. 4 (27 July 1895): 15, no. 12 (21 September 1895): 2; *WME* 49, no. 1 (10 July 1926): 14. The 6 July 1895 *WME* commented, "The design is of a colonial nature and exhibits throughout that artistic vein that has won for . . . Bates . . . the highest commendation." The newspaper also correctly speculated that the costly and elegant house "will occupy a leading position in the cottage colony of Jackson." The Ditsons owned the house until Charles Ditson's death in 1930. Apparently, from then until it burned, the house was owned by Spruce Mountain Lodge and Bungalows in Jackson. Under its original name, it was operated year round as a small inn, "ideal for rest and relaxation, also for winter sports," and "catering to refined people" (*Winter in New England* [Boston: Boston and Maine Railroad, c. 1931], advertisement, p. 21).

49. *DAB* 3, p. 321; *WWWA*, vol. 1 (1897–1942), p. 326; *NCAB* 7, p. 358; Stone, *History of Massachusetts Industries*, vol. 2, pp. 1292–94; *ATC* 35, no. 5 (16 July 1913): 1.

50. Deeds, Carroll County Registry of Deeds. Charles M. Ditson from George Pinkham, book 102, p. 529, 4 October 1894; Charles H. Ditson from George Pinkham, book 103, p. 87, 17 November 1894; Charles M. Ditson from Nelson I. and Jennie E. Trickey, book 106, p. 98, 27 May 1896. See also "A Plan of Charles M. Ditson's Land," surveyed by G. W. M. Pitman, 20 May 1896, plan book 2, pp. 104–5, Carroll County Registry of Deeds. The price of the two parcels acquired from George Pinkham totaled $2,050. The purchase price of the Trickey land was $2,000.

51. Reed, *A Delight to All Who Knew It*, p. 144; Placzek, *MEA*, vol. 2, p. 24.

52. Deed, Frank H. Shapleigh from George P. and William W. Trickey (co-owners of the Jackson Falls House), Carroll County Registry of Deeds, book 101, p. 47, 9 November 1903. The Shapleighs added to their initial land acquisition in 1900 (Frank H. Shapleigh from Jacob and Josephine Payton, book 114, p. 523, 9 October) and 1903 (Frank H. Shapleigh from George W. and William W. Trickey, book 121, p. 522, 9 November), their total holdings amounting to seven acres. See also *WME* 19, no. 1 (4 July 1896): 1, and vol. 20, no. 1 (3 July 1897): 11; *ATC* 22, no. 2 (19 July 1898): 4, and vol. 28, no. 28 (9 August 1904): 1. Local contractor Andrew C. Harriman may have built "Maple Knoll," but to date, this is pure conjecture.

53. Benjamin Champney, *Sixty Years' Memories of Art and Artists* (Woburn, Mass.: By the Author, 1900), pp. 168–69.

54. *WME* 29, no. 3 (21 July 1906): 4. Obituary notice for Frank H. Shapleigh.

55. Interior detail drawings for the Shapleigh cottage, Mr. and Mrs. Bradford L. Boynton, Jackson and South Conway, N.H.; Placzek, *MEA*, vol. 2, pp. 24–25; Zaitzevsky and Miller, *The Architecture of William Ralph Emerson*, pp. 8–28; Reed, *A Delight to All Who Knew It*, pp. 11–20.

56. *NCAB* 25, p. 428; Charles O. Vogel, ed., *Full of Facts and Sentiment: The Art of Frank Shapleigh* (Concord: New Hampshire Historical Society, 1982), pp. 7–18. Shapleigh had a separate studio building at the Crawford House, which the Appalachian Mountain Club owns and uses as a hikers' hostel today. Mary Shapleigh continued to own and use "Maple Knoll" well into the 1920s.

57. *ATC* 30, no. 51 (8 September 1906): 1.

58. *NHFSH*, 1st ed., 1902, pp. 30–31.

59. *WWNE*, 1909 ed., p. 413; *NCAB* 8, p. 167.

60. Deeds, Carroll County Registry of Deeds. Isaac L. Goff from Simon Fernald, book 102, p. 376, 21 August 1894; from Edgar A. Perkins, book 104, p. 265, 20 August 1895; from Harrison P. Dearborn, book 105, p. 116, 17 December 1895, and book 105, p. 344, 13 February 1896; from Simon Fernald, book 105, p. 345, 13 February 1896; from Edgar A. Perkins, book 110, p. 295, 4 August 1898; and, from Perkins and Trickey, book 114, p. 302, 4 August 1900. This first collection of purchases totaled well over one thousand acres. After a hiatus of seven years, from 1902 to 1909 Goff continued to amass real estate holdings on or near Thorn Mountain in Jackson. From 1911 to 1914,

he made several land transfers to his four children—Josephine A., William D., Lillian L., and Isaac L., Jr. Their mother was Anne Janette Richards of Providence, whom the colonel married in 1875.

61. "Thorn Mountain Park," plan for Thorn Mountain Land Company (linked with Isaac L. Goff Co., Providence and Pawtucket, Rhode Island), Shedd and Sarle, Engineers (Worcester and Providence), 1896, Jackson (N.H.) Historical Society; *ATC* 20, no. 51 (6 September 1896): 4. Goff also provided for the installation of electricity in the Thorn Mountain Park cottages, one of the first instances of residential use in the White Mountain district.

62. *ATC* 20, no. 51 (6 September 1896): 4.

63. Ibid.; *WME* 19, no. 11 (12 September 1896): 14.

64. *ATC* 20, no. 51 (6 September 1896): 4; *WME* 19, no. 11 (12 September 1896): 14; *The Providence Directory* (Providence, R.I.: Sampson & Murdock Co., 1901), p. 194. See also 1906 edition, p. 711. The contractors for "Fern Cliff" are identified in the *WME* (12 September 1896, p. 14) as "Messrs. Abbott and Stuart," but no other information about them is given in this or other available sources. It is likely that they were both local artisans.

65. Interview with Charlotte Haskell, Jackson, N.H., 12 April 1994; *WME* 19, no. 1 (4 July 1896): 2, and no. 11 (12 September 1896): 14; *WME* 21, no. 1 (2 July 1898): 21, and vol. 32, no. 5 (7 August 1909). The five cottages erected between 1896 and 1898 still stand, though two of them are in deteriorating condition.

66. *WME* 49, no. 1 (10 July 1926): 14.

67. *WME* 28, no. 7 (19 August 1905): 8.

68. Deed, Charles H. Turner from Sophronia S. Thompson (wife of Silas M. Thompson), Carroll County Registry of Deeds, book 110, p. 453, 10 October 1898. The sale price was $400 for approximately 124 square rods of land on the west side of the Ellis River and the highway, "near the covered bridge."

69. *WWNE*, 1909 ed., p. 942; Peter Hastings Falk, ed., *Who Was Who in American Art* (Madison, Conn.: Sound View Press, 1985), p. 633.

70. *ATC* 27, no. 8 (21 July 1903): 4; Garland, *Yesterdays*, p. 51; deed, Kate C. Baldwin from Katherine P. Wormeley, Carroll County Registry of Deeds, book 119, p. 289, 3 October 1902. The purchase was made for "$1.00 and other considerations." The tract was a part of the so-called "Lucy Field," sold by members of the Trickey family to Miss Wormeley in 1895 (book 104, p. 587, 11 November 1895). Over the years Baldwin often occupied the house with her sister Mary, and her niece, Miss Corinne Waldron (see *WME* 29, no. 1 [7 July 1906]: 14; *WME* 30, no. 1 [13 July 1907]: 16; *WME* 33, no. 1 [16 July 1910]: 15).

71. Sketch floor plans (photocopies) for "Gray Manor," Jackson, c. 1902, Jackson Historical Society; sketch floor plans for "The Satyr," Jackson, c. 1901, Garrison family, Jackson, N.H.

72. Garland, *Yesterdays*, p. 51.

3. GORHAM/SHELBURNE

1. Withey, *BDAA(D)*, pp. 572–73; interview with Francis Peabody, Gorham, N.H., 18 July 1993; plans, "Cottage at Gorham, New Hampshire, Mr. Clarence W. Peabody," 1 April 1903, private collection through the Maine Historic Preservation Commission, Augusta, Maine. The seven plan sheets include a front elevation, a rear elevation, north and south end elevations, first and second floor schematics, and a living room detail.

2. Deed, Mercy M. Peabody (Gorham) to Henry C. Peabody, Coos County Registry of Deeds, book 114, p. 151, 31 July 1903; will, Clarence W. Peabody et al. from Henry C. Peabody (Portland, Maine), Coos County Registry of Deeds, book 158, p. 100, 18 April 1911.

3. *Portland (Maine) Board of Trade Journal* 13, no. 9 (January 1901): 267, and vol. 16, no. 11 (March 1904): 432; *WWA*, 1906–7, p. 1377.

4. Obituaries, Clarence W. Peabody, *Portland (Maine) Press Herald*, 18 December 1940, and *Portland Evening Express*, 17 December 1940.

5. The author conducted research on William K. Aston at New Hampshire libraries, the New England Historic and Genealogical Society in Boston, and the New York Genealogical and Biographical Society in New York City. These efforts proved fruitless.

6. *WME* 39, no. 3 (29 July 1916): 1.

7. *WME* 28, no. 7 (19 August 1905): 8; [Merrell], *Shelburne, New Hampshire*, pp. 39–40; deeds, William K. Aston from various sellers, Coos County Registry of Deeds, grantee index volumes, 4 July 1883 to 25 August 1900. The first recorded land transfer was from William Kronberg to William K. Aston, book 31, p. 2. Apparently Kronberg acquired his first land parcel before the official name change, and deeded the property to himself under his new legal name. The Kissam and Vanderbilt families intermarried, explaining Aston's presumed connection with the Vanderbilts.

8. *NHFSH*, 1st ed. (1902), p. 31.

9. *GRM*, 17 October 1884, p. 3, 12 December 1884, p. 3, 19 June 1885, p. 3; Somers, *History of Lancaster, New Hampshire*, pp. 337, 340; *GRM*, 7 August 1885, p. 3, 25 September 1885, p. 3. John H. Smith is listed as "carpenter" in the 1875 statistics of Lancaster, but as "contractor and builder" in the 1895 directory, both contained in the Somers history.

10. Charles A. J. Farrar, *Through the Wilds* (Boston: Estes and Lauriat, Publishers, 1892), pp. 62–63.

11. Postcard photographs (c. 1930), author's collection; illustration, *WME* 28, no. 7 (19 August 1905): 1.

12. [Merrell], *Shelburne, New Hampshire*, p. 40; telephone interview with Connie Ledger, Shelburne, N.H., 4 August 1993.

13. [Merrell], *Shelburne, New Hampshire*, pp. 40, 51; *The Boston Globe*, 11 May 1960, p. 1; illustrated pamphlet, *Gordon Silver Black Fox Ranches* (Bangor, Maine), Dr. F. H. Gordon, n.d., Shelburne, N.H., author's collection.

14. Farrar, *Through the Wilds*, p. 63.

15. *Compendium of History and Biography of the City of Detroit and Wayne County, Michigan* (Chicago: Henry Taylor and Co., 1909), pp. 340–42; Silas Farmer, *The History of Detroit and Michigan . . .* (Detroit: Silas Farmer & Co.; 1884), pp. 362, 778 and 940; Robert B. Ross and George B. Catlin, *Landmarks of Wayne County and Detroit* (Detroit: The Evening News Association, 1898), p. 481. In Detroit, "Endicott Avenue" was named after Charles Endicott in 1874. The Endicotts had five children—Alice and Charles, who died in youth; Caroline, who married Charles W. Rantoul, Jr., of New York City; Grace, who became the wife of William B. Kendall of New York City; and Edith, the spouse of Gilbert M. McMillan of Gorham, N.H. The McMillans succeeded the Endicotts as owners of the property.

16. [Merrell], *Shelburne, New Hampshire*, p. 40; *GRM*, 2 November 1893, p. 3; *GRM*, 18 April 1894, p. 3; deed, Charles Endicott from Joseph Rowe, Coos County Registry of Deeds, book 28, p. 268, 4 October 1883; Charles Endicott from Otis Evans, book 28, p. 270, 15 October 1883; Charles Endicott from Susannah, Charles E., Augustus E., and Fanny Philbrook, et al., book 31, p. 312, 26 October 1883. The tracts totaled over fifteen acres and cost $1,300. Endicott negotiated additional land purchases in Shelburne in 1885 from Alfred E. Evans (book 41, p. 147, 21 February), Moses Wilson (book 53, p. 213, 20 September; book 28, p. 271, 1 December), and Charles E. Philbrook (book 28, p. 269, 1 December; book 33, p. 246, 1 December). Whereas the 1883 purchases were north of the main Gorham-Bethel highway (today U.S. Route 2), the 1885 acreage was situated on the south side.

17. *GRM*, 25 April 1884, p. 3; *GRM*, 27 June 1884, p. 3; *GRM*, 19 June 1885, p. 3; Frank W. Foss (Portland Pipe Line Co., Maine), "History of the Stone House and Barn," typescript, 1985, in possession of current owner Scott Wilfong, Shelburne, N.H. While "The Stone House" may have originally been intended as an all-male bastion, it was also used extensively by Mrs. Endicott, who came east each summer with her children, and continued to occupy the house with her family on a regular basis after her husband's death. The cost of the house was estimated at $30,000.

18. Foss, "History of the Stone House and Barn"; interviews with Scott Wilfong, Shelburne, N.H., 3 March and 10 May 1994; [Merrell] *Shelburne, New Hampshire*, p. 31; current floor plan sketches owned by Scott Wilfong. The kitchen is believed to have been located in the cellar when the main residence was originally built. In summer 1986, the current owners added a one-story kitchen/dining ell to the rear that blends nicely with the older part of the building.

19. Interview with Connie Leger, Philbrook Farm Inn, Shelburne, 4 August 1993. After the McMillan period of ownership, the property passed to Endicott Rantoul, the grandson of Charles and Caroline Endicott. He in turn sold the buildings and forty acres to the Portland Pipe Line Company for $10,000 in 1941 for a storage depot and pumping station (see deed, Coos County Registry of Deeds, 9 July). Mr. and Mrs. Scott Wilfong acquired the property from the company in 1986.

4. RANDOLPH/JEFFERSON

1. *ATC* 28, no. 6 (14 July 1904): 1.

2. Ibid.; *WME* 28, no. 7 (15 August 1905): 2. Of this group, "Bashaba," "Onaway," "The Wayonda," "Wyndebrae," "The Maples" (later renamed "Wil-

lows"), and "The Bungalow" survive today, all in generally good condition, but with twentieth-century additions and/or modifications.

3. Evans, *History of the Town of Jefferson, New Hampshire*, pp. 222–26; *WME* 21, no. 6 (6 August 1898): 7; *ATC* 14, no. 18 (31 July 1890): 5, and vol. 20, no. 5 (15 July 1896): 1; *WML* 1, no. 2 (2 September 1897).

4. *WML* 1, no. 2 (2 September 1897).

5. *ATC* 20, no. 5 (15 July 1896): 1; *WME* 19, no. 1 (4 July 1896): 7; Evans, *History of the Town of Jefferson*, p. 224; Tolles, *GRHWM*, pp. 97–98.

6. Tolles, *GRHWM*, pp. 95–100. Gale assisted with the 1889 addition to the hotel, while Manasah Perkins acted as superintending contractor, and Moses McDonald as head carpenter.

7. H. Adams Carter, "Notes on the Carters in Jefferson," unpublished typed manuscript, c. 1992; *WML* 1, no. 2 (8 July 1897), and no. 5 (29 July 1897); *WML* 1, no. 3 (15 July 1897); Grover, "Summer Homes in Jefferson Highlands," p. 49; Evans, *History of the Town of Jefferson*, p. 212.

8. *NHFSH*, 1st ed. (1902), p. 23.

9. Deed, Carrie G. Carter from Sophia K. P. Clapp, Coos County Registry of Deeds, book 90, p. 373, 20 September 1897. Situated on both sides of the Gorham-Lancaster road, the parcel was bounded by lands owned by the Crawford family and by Sylvester P. Martin. The view from the property encompasses Cherry Mountain, and the Dartmouth and Presidential ranges.

10. Withey, *BDAA(D)*, pp. 182, 268, and 510–11; Marquis, *WWA*, vol. 10 (1918–19), p. 1212; *WWWA*, vol. 1 (1897–1942), p. 1031; Marquis, *WWA*, Vol. 12 (1922–23), p. 967.

11. *WME* 21, no. 1 (2 July 1898): 9; *ATC* 22, no. 1 (18 July 1898): 4; Grover, "Summer Houses in Jefferson Highlands," pp. 49–51.

12. Grover, "Summer Homes in Jefferson Highlands," pp. 50–51; Carter, "Notes on the Carters in Jefferson"; Rupert Corrigain, "Tower Inn," unpublished typed manuscript, 1993; Evans, *History of the Town of Jefferson*, p. 213; *ATC* 24, no. 17 (1 August 1900): 4; *WME* 28, no. 7 (19 August 1907): 8; *Historical Memories of the Town of Jefferson, New Hampshire*, p. 26. An astounding total of three hundred barrels of Portland cement is said to have been used to construct the tower. Called "Carter's Folly" by Mrs. Carter, the tower closely resembled one built about the same time on the Mount Prospect estate of John Wingate Weeks in Lancaster (see "Mount Prospect Lodge," Lancaster). Carter and Weeks were good friends, and apparently conceived the idea of constructing the two matching towers. Observation towers were very popular before World War I in the White Mountains, and numerous ones were associated with both the private cottages and the hotels.

13. *LC*, 17 May 1907, p. 1; see also *ATC* 31, no. 39 (27 August 1907): 5.

14. Grover, "Summer Homes in Jefferson Highlands," p. 51; deed, James R. Carter from Frederick P. Cabot, Coos County Registry of Deeds, book 180, p. 269, 9 October 1916; Evans, *History of the Town of Jefferson*, p. 199; *WME* 17, no. 3 (21 July 1894): 14;

WML 1, no. 2 (8 July 1897), photo of "Siwooganock Cottage"; *WML* 1, no. 5 (29 July 1897) photo of "Dartmouth Cottage"; Carter, "Notes on the Carters in Jefferson"; plans for renovations to Boismont Cottage by Hartwell, Richardson and Driver (Boston), Mrs. H. Adams Carter, Milton, Mass. All the Carter family buildings today, including two modern garages, are painted gray with maroon shutters.

The purchase from Frederick Cabot in 1916 was the same tract (with buildings) that Cabot acquired from George H. Hallowell in 1912, and that Hallowell bought from Ethan Allen and Fred P. Crawford in separate transactions in 1905 and 1906 (see deeds listed under grantees, Coos County of Registry of Deeds).

15. *NCAB* 33, pp. 197–98; *WWNE*, 1909 ed., p. 192; Grover, "Summer Homes in Jefferson Highlands," pp. 48–49; Carter, "Notes on the Carters in Jefferson"; *ATC* 22, no. 20 (9 August 1898): 5, no. 33 (24 August 1898): 4, no. 39 (30 August 1898): 4; *ATC* 24, no. 5 (18 July 1900): 1; *ATC* 25, no. 23 (7 August 1901): 4; *ATC* 36, no. 8 (17 July 1914): 1.

16. Grover, "Summer Homes in Jefferson Highlands," pp. 33–34.

17. Evans, *History of the Town of Jefferson*, p. 210.

18. Deed, Mary A. Wright from Ethan A. Crawford and wife, Coos County Registry of Deeds, book 29, p. 333, 19 October 1881; deed, Mary Wright from the Savings Bank of the County of Coos, book 33, p. 337, 8 November 1881. The tract was bounded by the highway, Crawford family lands, and land owned by Sophia K. Perkins. The deeds placed a restriction on E. A. Crawford not to erect structures on the contiguous lands that would obstruct the view (Mary Wright lifted this restriction in 1909).

19. Deed, Mary A. Wright from A. L. Martin, Coos County Registry of Deeds, book 85, p. 329, 11 December 1897; deed, Mary A. Wright from Ebenezer L. Carlton, book 98, p. 239, 9 October 1901; Mary A. Wright from Ethan A. Crawford, book 138, p. 348, 4 June 1908; Mary A. Wright from Carrie G. Carter, book 143, p. 269, 13 August 1909; Mary A. Wright from A. L. Martin, book 149, p. 260, 29 August 1910.

20. Grover, "Summer Homes in Jefferson Highlands," p. 34; *Historical Memories of the Town of Jefferson*, p. 26. A sampling of Wright's publications: "The Birds of the Jefferson Region of the White Mountains," *Proceedings of the Manchester* (N.H.) *Institute of Arts and Sciences* 5, Part 1, 1911; "Morning Awareness and Even-Song," *The Auk* 29 (July 1912): 307–27; "Birds of Jefferson Highlands," *The Auk* 30 (March 1913): 512–37.

21. Grover, "Summer Homes in Jefferson Highlands," p. 34.

22. Evans, *History of the Town of Jefferson*, p. 210. Only a remnant of the shield of trees remains today.

23. Interview with Rupert Corrigan, Jefferson, N.H., 4 August 1994. "Nollis Cottage" is painted the same grey with maroon trim as the Carter/Bridgman family buildings on the opposite side of the road (today Route 2).

24. Horace and Mary Wright had two brothers, Edmund Wentworth and Augustus Hunt Wright, both of whom predeceased her. Augustus' son,

Edmund Wright of Abington, Massachusetts, was named executor of Mary Wright's will in 1928, and was bequeathed the Jefferson property. Edmund sold the cottage plot, as well as the other five parcels of land in 1936 to Snell and Anna M. Smith of Washington, D.C. There have been at least three other owners of the house since. The identities of the architect (if there was one) as well as the builder are unknown.

25. Grover, "Summer Homes in Jefferson Highlands," pp. 36–37; Evans, *History of the Town of Jefferson*, pp. 210–11.

26. Deed, Coos County Registry of Deeds, William G. Hopple from John W. and Charlotte Crenshaw, book 58, p. 238, 28 September 1891. Hopple augmented this first parcel with an additional purchase in 1893 from the Crenshaw family (book 67, p. 172, 30 September 1893). Today Route 2 runs through the community of Jefferson Highlands.

27. Gale, "Memoirs of a Master Builder," *NHP* 2, no. 4 (April 1953): 46, and no. 5 (May 1953): 62. Gale also built or remodeled numerous warehouses, barns, garages, schools, tenement houses, churches, and libraries in the White Mountain area.

28. Evans, *History of the Town of Jefferson*, p. 211; Grover, "Summer Homes in Jefferson Highlands," pp. 38–46.

29. Evans, *History of the Town of Jefferson*, pp. 213–14.

30. Deed, Gertrude B. McCabe from John W. and Lizzie M. Crenshaw, Coos County Registry of Deeds, book 62, p. 200, 18 October 1892. Gertrude McCabe acquired spring rights from the Crenshaw family two years later (book 74, p. 65, 24 November 1894). In 1901 and 1908, she augmented this real estate by purchasing two more tracts totaling about twenty acres from the Crenshaws on the north side of the road, and twelve acres from Ethan Allen Crawford at a location further removed. These land holdings totaled forty-six acres.

31. Evans, *History of the Town of Jefferson*, p. 214.

32. Grover, "Summer Homes in Jefferson Highlands," p. 47. According to the Nichols family (see "Buena Vista," Jefferson), the fire occurred the evening before McCabe was to arrive in Jefferson by train for the summer. The cause is believed to have been faulty electrical wiring. McCabe promptly replaced the house on the same site with a prefabricated dwelling, which still stands.

33. Grover, "Summer Homes in Jefferson," pp. 46–47.

34. Evans, *History of the Town of Jefferson*, p. 214. In 1897, the McCabes laid out a miniature golf course adjacent to the house for practice games (*WML*, no. 5 [29 July 1897]).

35. Gale, "Memories of a Master Builder," *NHP* 2, no. 4 (April 1953): 46.

36. Deed, William E. Bird, Jr., from Charles Ingerson, Coos County Registry of Deeds, book 180, pp. 196–97, September 1916. The sale price was $2,500. Evans, *History of the Town of Jefferson*, pp. 215–16; former date marker on granite gate posts for "Reve-Fonyah," Jefferson, N.H.; telephone interview with Evelyn Foss, Lancaster, N.H., 15 August 1994; *Directory of the Oranges, Irvington, Livingston and Millburn, 1910* (Newark, N.J.: Price & Lee, Company, 1910); *The*

Oranges (Orange, East Orange, South Orange, West Orange), *Maplewood Directory* (Newark, N.J.: Price & Lee Company, 1938); obituary, *NYT*, 1 September 1936, p. 21.

37. Telephone interview with Deborah Ives, New Boston, N.H., 9 August 1994.

38. Evans, *History of the Town of Jefferson,* pp. 219–20; "Stockin Cottage," typed manuscript, Rupert Corrigain, Jefferson, N.H.; telephone interview with Benjamin J. Sears, Jefferson, N.H., 19 August 1994; deed, Edwin Stockin from Ida M. G. Fitzgerald (Stoneham, Mass.), Coos County Registry of Deeds, book 223, pp. 231–32, 28 April 1924. The parcel was south of the Jefferson-Gorham highway, and bounded by lands owned by Charles W. Davidson, Fred Ingerson, and Ida M. G. Fitzgerald.

39. Evans, *History of the Town of Jefferson,* p. 217.

40. Evans, *History of the Town of Jefferson,* p. 217; obituary, *NYT*, 19 March 1957, p. 37.

41. Deeds, Coos County Registry of Deeds. Florence W. Fulton from Ralph E. and Effie G. Hunt, book 221, p. 259, 10 September 1923 (water rights); Florence W. Fulton from Ella S. Evans, book 224, p. 24, 10 September 1923; Florence W. Fulton from Anna Price Alburger, book 227, p. 41, 18 August 1924; and Florence W. Fulton from Anna Price Alburger, book 227, p. 141, 14 July 1926. The Evans purchase was for $1,000, and consisted of a nine-acre parcel (formerly the Gray farm) upon which the house was built (see Evans, *History of the Town of Jefferson,* p. 217).

5. BETHLEHEM/LITTLETON

1. *NCAB* 9, p. 404; Robert Sobel and John Raimo, eds., *Biographical Dictionary of the Governors of the United States, 1789–1978*, vol. 4 (Westport, Conn.: Mecker Books, 1978), p. 1353.

2. Tolles, *GRHWM*, pp. 124–25; Wilson, *Bethlehem* p. 30. Deeds, Grafton County Registry of Deeds. Henry Howard from Ezra Brooks, book 334, p. 348, 3 October 1863; Henry Howard from William O. Carleton, book 334, p. 346, 5 September 1863; Henry Howard from Joseph K. Barrett, book 334, p. 153, 8 August 1874; Henry Howard from Jonas P. Wallace, book 335, p. 374, 15 July 1875, and book 339, p. 174, 11 September 1875; and Henry Howard from Cyrus E. Bunker, book 39, p. 173, 13 September 1875.

3. Wilson, *Bethlehem* p. 62; Sims and Stevenson, *An Illustrated Tour of Bethlehem,* p. 17.

4. See McAlester, *A Field Guide to American Houses,* pp. 196–207, 254–61. "Buckeye Cottage" was sold out of the Howard family in 1881, and has changed ownership several times since (*WME* 4, no. 2 [3 September 1881]): 12; *WME* 6, no. 9 [25 August 1883]): 16; *ATC* 13, no. 8 [20 July 1898]): 1).

5. Tolles, *GRHWM*, pp. 124–28. The maximum capacity of the Maplewood during its existence was over five hundred guests.

6. Promotional leaflets, "Maplewood Hotel . . . Bethlehem, New Hampshire," 1876 and 1877; *WME* 1, no. 8 (31 August 1878): 1; advertisement, *Chisholm's White Mountain Guide Book* (Portland, Maine: Chisholm Brothers, 1883), op. p. 140; *WME* 10, no. 3

(16 July 1887): 8; advertisement, *Hand-Book of the Portland & Ogdensburg Railroad* (Portland, Maine: G. W. Morris for the P. & O. Railroad, [1888]), p. 72; *ATC* 19, no. 2 (5 July 1895): 8.

7. The cottages that survive are numbers 11, 12, and 14 (see illustrations). Number 12 is the only one of all the cottages with an off-center square tower.

8. Henry Russell-Hitchcock, *The Architecture of H. H. Richardson and His Times,* rev. ed. (Hamden, Conn.: Archon Books, 1961), pp. 277–78.

9. James L. Garvin, "The Rocks Estate," National Register of Historic Places Inventory-Nomination Form, United States Department of the Interior, National Park Service, Washington, D.C., 1984.

10. Garvin, "The Rocks Estate"; *The Book of Chicagoans* (Chicago: A. N. Marquis & Co., 1917), p. 267; *WWWA*, vol. 1 (1897–1942), p. 462.

11. Garvin, "The Rocks Estate"; *NHFSH*, 6th ed. (1908), pp. 20–23; deed, Frances H. Glessner (wife of John Jacob Glessner) from Oren H. and Urina D. Streeter, Grafton County Registry of Deeds, book 370, p. 215, 19 September 1882. The grantee books list several other land and water rights acquisitions between 1882 and 1897, all in the name of Frances Glessner. Fully developed, "The Rocks" was approximately one quarter the size of the original Webster estate in Holderness.

12. Garvin, "The Rocks Estate"; David A. Hawks, "Isaac E. Scott, craftsman and designer," *The Magazine Antiques* 105, no. 6 (June 1974): 1307–13.

13. Telephone conversation with Mrs. Charles F. Batchelder (J. J. Glessner's granddaughter, Milton, Mass.), 17 March 1994; Garvin, "The Rocks Estate."

14. *WME* 49, no. 10 (11 September 1926): 7; Garvin, "The Rocks Estate"; "Cow-Barn on Estate of J. J. Glessner . . . ," *Cyclopedia of Architecture, Carpentry and Building* 6, op. p. 39.

15. Garvin, "The Rocks Estate." Frederick Law Olmstead, Jr., was a friend and student colleague of the Glessner's son, George. See Tishler, *American Landscape Architecture,* pp. 60–65.

16. Theodore M. Banta, *Sayre Family: Lineage of Thomas Sayre, A Founder of Southampton* (New York: The De Vinne Press, 1901), p. 630; *WME* 29, no. 2 (14 July 1906): 12, and vol. 30, no. 7 (24 August 1907): 2; *NYT*, 18 July 1917, p. 9.

17. Deed, William M. Sayer, Jr., from Horace D. Wilder, Grafton County Registry of Deeds, book 402, p. 224, and book 402, p. 226, 30 August 1890. The purchase price was $800. The land abutted property owned by Mrs. Sarah P. Cleveland ("Nutwood," Jamaica Plain, Massachusetts) and Mr. Wilder, and the Franconia-Bethlehem road. *WME*, 13, no. 10 (6 September 1890): 52; *LC*, 17 September 1890, p. 1.

18. *WME* 30, no. 7 (24 August 1907): 2. *LC*, 17 September 1890, p. 1, and 8 July 1891, p. 1.

19. Deed, William Murray Sayer, Jr., from William A. French (trustee for Harriet O. Cruft), George T. Cruft, and Harriet O. Cruft, Grafton County Registry of Deeds, book 432, p. 142, 27 February 1897. The sale, for "$1.00 and other valuable considerations," stipulated that only dwelling houses and a private stable could be constructed on the land.

20. *ATC* 21, no. 7 (26 July 1897): 1; *WME* 20, no. 1

(3 July 1897): 10, *WML* 1, no. 1 (1 July 1897); *WME* 21, no. 1 (2 July 1899): 9; *LC*, 27 September 1899, p. 1; Tolles, *GRHWM*, pp. 127–28. During the first season, the cottages were let to the families of H. H. Hunnewell of Wellesley, Massachusetts, and ex-congressman Moses T. Stevens of North Andover, Massachusetts.

Edward Thornton Sanderson was born in Templeton, Massachusetts, and was trained as an architect at Rindge Technical School in Cambridge, Massachusetts. He practiced his profession in Fitchburg, Danvers, and Wellesley, Massachusetts; Parkersburg, West Virginia; Pittsburgh, Pennsylvania; Westmount, Quebec, Canada; and in Littleton. He retired to Coral Gables, Florida, where he died. See Lynn M. Case and Page Sanderson, *The Family of John Page of Haverhill, Massachusetts: A Comprehensive Genealogy from 1614 to 1977* (Baltimore, Md.: Gateway Press, 1978), p. 182.

21. Deed, William Murray Sayer, Jr., from George T. Cruft, William A. French and Harriet O. Cruft, Grafton County Registry of Deeds, book 442, p. 124, 5 August 1898. The terms of the sale were almost identical to those of the 1897 transaction.

22. *WME* 20, no. 9 (28 August 1897): 6; *ATC* 22, no. 1 (18 July 1898): 4.

23. It is conceivable that Edward T. Sanderson may also have designed "The Outlook," but this is mere speculation, lacking any documentation to date.

24. Child, *Business Directory of Grafton County, N.H., 1885-'86,* p. 34.

25. Wilson, *Bethlehem, New Hampshire,* p. 62. Sayer did not build his first rental properties until 1897.

26. *1914–1916 Resident and Business Directory of the West Side of the White Mountains of New Hampshire* (1914), p. 214; *WMD*, vol. 2 (1917–19), p. 341; *WMD*, vol. 3 (1920–22), p. 364; *WMD*, vol. 4 (1923–25), p. 418; *WMD*, vol. 6 (1929–31), p. 104.

27. Deeds, Grafton County Registry of Deeds. Leonard M. Knight from Louisa J. and Thomas W. Bean (Quebec, Canada), book 391, p. 146, 12 September 1887; Leonard M. Knight from Edgar Kethum (New York City), book 398, p. 479, 1 October 1889; Leonard M. Knight from Isaac S. Cruft (Boston), book 393, p. 538, 8 October 1889; Leonard M. Knight from Thomas W. Bean, book 400, p. 325, 11 September 1889; Leonard M. Knight from Carrie T. Wilder (Bethlehem), book 410, p. 16, 19 March 1892; Leonard M. Knight from Myron Bailey (Littleton), book 426, p. 125, 30 October 1895. The 19 March 1892 purchase was that upon which the cottages were built (bounded by South Road, plots owned by the Centennial House, Carrie T. Wilder, and George T. Cruft).

28. *WME* 13, no. 1 (5 July 1890): 7; *WME* 16, no. 12 (16 September 1893): 6; *WME* 18, no. 1 (6 July 1895): 5; *WME* 19, no. 1 (3 July 1897): 10; *WME* 20, no. 1 (2 July 1898): 9; *WME* 24, no. 2 (13 July 1901): 12; "Handsome Homes in Bethlehem of the Hills," *WME* 28, no. 7 (19 August 1905): 3; "Bethlehem Cottage Colony," *WME* 30, no. 7 (24 August 1907): 2. *LC*, 26 March 1890, p. 1; *LC*, 2 April 1890, p. 1; *LC*, 21 May 1890, p. 1; *LC*, 13 September 1893, p. 1. In 1906, Mr. and Mrs. H. Jessup Stevenson of New York City rented Knight's 1901 South Road cottage for their first year.

29. *WME* 28, no. 7 (19 August 1905): 3; telephone

interviews with Rodney Haywood and Frances Marszalkowski, Bethlehem, N.H., 19 August 1994.

30. *WME* 18, no. 8 (24 August 1895): 2.

31. The house was built on a ninety-by-one-hundred-foot parcel of land acquired from Frank H. and Emma A. Abbott for $300 (see deed, Grafton County Registry of Deeds, book 426, p. 550, 7 November 1892).

32. *ATC* 16, no. 13 (25 July 1892): 4.

33. *WME* 15, no. 1 (2 July 1892): 8.

34. Ibid.; Sims and Stevenson, *An Illustrated Tour of Bethlehem*, p. 19; *LC*, 4 May 1892, p. 1.

35. C. Bancroft Gillespie, *A Century of Meriden* (Meriden, Conn.: Journal Publishing Co., 1906), p. 173; obituary, *NYT*, 23 July 1904, p. 3; obituary, *WME* 27, no. 4 (30 July 1904): 18; *WME* 17, no. 8 (25 August 1894): 19.

36. *WME* 29, no. 6 (11 August 1906): 2.

37. *WME* 30, no. 7 (24 August 1907): 2.

38. *WME* 15, no. 5 (30 July 1892): 6.

39. *ATC* 16, no. 3 (13 July 1892): 4.

40. *WME* 15, no. 5 (30 July 1892): 6.

41. *ATC* 16, no. 3 (13 July 1892): 4.

42. *A Record of the Harris Family Descended from John Harris, Born in 1680 in Wiltshire, England* (Philadelphia: Press of George F. Lasher, 1903), pp. 57, 74–75.

43. Deeds, Grafton County Registry of Deeds. J. Campbell Harris from John M. and Catherine E. Rowe (Bethlehem), book 376, p. 148, 5 November 1883; J. Campbell Harris from John J. Blandin (Bethlehem), book 376, p. 146, 5 November 1883; J. Campbell Harris from Allen and Melvina Peabody (Bethlehem), book 376, p. 144, 5 November 1883; J. Campbell Harris from Moses C. and Julia C. Noyes (Bethlehem), book 376, p. 136, 6 November 1883; J. Campbell Harris from Charles and Mary E. Herbert (Bethlehem), book 376, p 572, 8 January 1884; J. Campbell Harris from Moses C. and Julia C. Noyes (Bethlehem), book 391, p. 342, 24 October 1887. Harris also acquired rights to a spring near "The Lodge" from the West Providence Land Company on 24 March 1897 (book 429, p. 169).

44. *WME Tourists' Registers*, 1883–92. Published during July, August, and September in weekly issues of the newspaper, these listings document the quite consistent presence of the Harris family at the Maplewood Hotel, with gaps when they apparently remained in Philadelphia or were traveling.

45. *ATC* 18, no. 2 (16 July 1894): 4; *LC*, 18 October 1893, p. 1; *Holbrook's Newark City and Business Directory* . . . (Newark, N.J.: The Holbrook Printing Co., 1891), p. 655; obituary for Mrs. William H. Kellner, *NYT*, 30 March 1932, p. 17; *Newark* (N.J.) *Sunday News*, 7 September 1958; deed, Clara Kellner from Frank E. Derbyshire (Lowell, Mass.), Grafton County Registry of Deeds, book 418, p. 50, 13 July 1893. Derbyshire had bought the land from Sarah D. Wilder, et al., on 30 September 1889 (book 398, p. 478).

46. *LC*, 18 October 1893, p. 13, 8 November 1893, p. 1, 15 November 1893, p. 1, 11 April 1894, p. 1, and 24 October 1894, p. 1; *WME* 16, no. 12 (16 September 1893): 6, and vol. 17, no. 3 (21 July 1894): 5, and vol. 27, no. 3 (16 July 1904): 12; *ATC* 18, no. 2 (16 July 1894): 4; Sims and Stevenson, *An Illustrated Tour of Bethlehem*,

p. 17. The Kellners used the house sporadically during the summers until 1906, when advertisements first appeared offering the property for sale (*WME* 29, no. 10 [8 September 1906]: 8). Apparently, no sale was consummated at this time, however, as local newspapers continued to associate the house with the Kellners until about 1910, after which it was closed for several years. In 1912, it was sold to Mr. and Mrs. John A. Secor of Laporte, Indiana (deed, Grafton County Registry of Deeds, book 514, p. 500, 18 September 1912). Later it was used by the owners of The Howard hotel as a guest annex. Today, the building accommodates a bed-and-breakfast business.

47. "Felsengarten," National Register of Historic Places Inventory-Nomination Form, United States Department of the Interior, National Park Service, Washington, D.C., 1973.

48. *WME* 17, no. 11 (15 September 1894): 6; Taylor, *Early History of Bethlehem*, p. 32; deed, Rose Fay Thomas from Charles L. Whitcomb, Grafton County Registry of Deeds, book 420, p. 472, 8 September 1894. The purchase was for $800. This first tract was expanded to about twenty-five acres by later acquisitions—see deed, Rose Fay Thomas from Charles L. Whitcomb, book 428, p. 503, 9 September 1896 (water privileges); deed, Rose Fay Thomas from Charles L. Whitcomb, book 435, p. 357, 24 August 1897; deed, Rose Fay Thomas from Mercy A. Oakes, Laurentius F. Swett, and Simeon A. Gould, book 441, p. 179, 3 September 1898.

49. *WME* 19, no. 6 (8 August 1896): 4.

50. Thomas, *Our Mountain Garden*, pp. 18–23. The house and gardens fell into a state of total neglect during the 1970s and 1980s but are being meticulously restored under new ownership. While only Mrs. Thomas' rough floor plans (see illustration) remain for the house, a sketch plan of the gardens (with plant species placed and identified) fortunately has survived.

51. *DAB* 9, pp. 424–26; *NCAB* 2, p. 139; "Felsengarten," National Register of Historic Places Inventory-Nomination Form; "Hidden Away from the World," *Yankee* 53, no. 3 (March 1989): 116–17; obituary, *Chicago Daily Tribune*, 5 January 1905. See also George P. Upton, *Theodore Thomas: A Musical Autobiography*, 2 vols. (Chicago: A. C. McClurg & Co., 1905).

52. "Felsengarten," National Register of Historic Places Inventory-Nomination Form; Wilson, *Bethlehem*, p. 62; *Woman's Who's Who in America*, p. 812; *WME* 27, no. 4 (9 July 1904): 7, and vol. 28, no. 7 (19 August 1905): 3; obituary, Bethlehem scrapbooks, White Mountain Collection, Dartmouth College Library, Hanover, N.H.

53. Cleveland Abbe and Josephine G. Nichols, *Abbe-Abbey Genealogy* (New Haven, Conn.: The Tuttle, Morehouse & Taylor, Co., 1916), p. 386; *ATC* 28, no. 15 (9 August 1904): 4; *WME* 27, no. 6 (6 August 1904): 16; *ATC* 19, no. 1 (15 July 1895): 4; deed, George E. Abbe from George T. and Harriet O. Cruft (sister of George), Grafton County Registry of Deeds, book 461, p. 595, 19 March 1903. The rectangular lot formed part of the former Bailey farm, and measures 100 by 250 feet. The Cruft family was associated with the origins and early history of the Maplewood Hotel in

Bethlehem. The deed restricted the use of the land for a "private dwelling house, outbuildings and stable" (same terms as the Poor purchase, see "Edgemont").

54. Obituary, Sylvanus D. Morgan, *Lisbon Courier*, 7 November 1940, p. 1; *WME* 26, no. 1 (4 July 1903): 3; Sims and Stevenson, *An Illustrated Tour of Bethlehem*, p. 21.

55. Obituary, Sylvanus P. Morgan, *Lisbon Courier*, 7 November 1940, pp. 1, 12; Paul A. Williams, "The Saga of 'S. D.' Morgan," *New Hampshire Echoes* 1, no. 4 (Winter 1970): 10–13. See Tolles, *GRHWM*, for more detailed information about Morgan's hotel projects. "S. D.," as he was commonly known, was a protégé of Frank H. Abbott, the builder of "The Bells," and subsequently owner/manager of The Uplands hotel in Bethlehem.

56. *WWWA*, vol. 1 (1897–1942), p. 981; *ATC* 31, no. 15 (30 July 1915): 1.

57. *WME* 30, no. 7 (24 August 1907): 3, and no. 11 (21 September 1907): 7; *NYT*, 28 June 1941, p. 15; deed, Ida M. Poor (wife of Ruel W. Poor) from Emily S. Perkins, Grafton County Registry of Deeds, book 484, p. 350, 25 September 1907. The lot, slightly less than one acre, is situated on the gentle slope of Strawberry Hill facing north across Main Street. The deed contained a restriction specifying that the lot could be used only for a private dwelling, with a stable and outbuildings.

58. Deed, Emily S. Perkins from William A. French, trustee, book 453, p. 454, 1 October 1902; *WME* 27, no. 5 (6 August 1904): 16.

59. Sims and Stevenson, *An Illustrated Tour of Bethlehem*, p. 22. In 1903, Morgan built the Abbe house, across the street from "Edgemont," and in that general period was responsible for the construction of a number of other houses on Strawberry Hill. An article published in the 4 July 1903 issue of the *WME* refers to the houses recently built on Strawberry Hill above The Uplands hotel. One is documented as being the Abbe house; the other was more than likely "Edgemont" for Perkins.

60. *NCAB* 13, p. 505.

61. "John Jacob Glessner," *The Book of Chicagoans* (Chicago: A. M. Marquis & Company, 1917), p. 267; deed, Kate V. Macbeth (wife of George A.) from G. Allen and Louise M. Noyes, Grafton County Registry of Deeds, book 467, p. 437, 12 August 1904. The purchase price was $2,500.

62. *WME* 27, no. 12 (6 August 1904): 4; National Register of Historic Places Inventory—Nomination Form for "The Rocks" Estate, National Park Service, Washington, D.C., 16 May 1984; obituary, "Sylvanus D. Morgan," *Lisbon Courier*, 7 November 1940.

63. *WME* 27, no. 1 (9 July 1904): 7. While waiting for the completion of "The Glamis," the Macbeth family rented one of Leonard M. Knight's cottages on Main Street, Bethlehem.

64. David Van Zanter, "The Early Work of Marion Mahoney Griffin," *The Prairie School Review* 3, no. 2 (Second Quarter 1966): 11–12; H. Allen Brooks, *The Prairie School: Frank Lloyd Wright and his Midwest Contemporaries* (Toronto and Buffalo: University of Toronto Press, 1972), p. 86; sketch of H. V. Von Holst, Architecture Department, Burnham Library, The Art

Institute of Chicago. See Hermann V. von Holst, *Country and Suburban Homes of the Prairie School Period* (New York: Dover Publications, 1982).

65. The Art Institute of Chicago purchased the pencil-and-water-color rendering on auction in 1987. The *Cyclopedia of Architecture . . .* was published in ten volumes, the photo and plans appearing in volume 2, p. 288, and between pp. 297 and 301. The fact that von Holst was on the editorial board for this reference work virtually assured that his designs would be represented somewhere in the volumes! The Macbeth house was also called "Stonecrest" by later owners.

66. *WME* 31, no. 2 (18 July 1908): 13.

67. Interview with Tim McKeever, owner of the Sylvanus Morgan house, Lisbon, N.H., 29 December 1993.

68. *WMD*, vol. 5 (1926–28), p. 100.

69. *WME* 31, no. 11 (19 September 1908): 1. The land upon which the house stands was purchased in the name of Annie T. Kenney (wife of John W.) from Clara L. and Henry P. Smith, Grafton County Registry of Deeds, book 484, p. 316, 13 September 1907. The deed stipulated that the "house or cottage" be built on the "described premises" within two years of the date of the transaction. The price was $500.

70. *WME* 31, no. 2 (18 July 1908): 13.

71. Obituary, Alvin W. Ivie, *NYT*, 2 June 1954, p. 31. Upon the premature death in 1924 of their daughter, Florence, who had just married hotel impresario Karl P. Abbott (see "Upland Cottage," Bethlehem), Alvin and Henrietta Ivie donated funds toward the building of the Ivie Memorial Church (1930) in Bethlehem (see Tolles, *New Hampshire Architecture*, pp. 315–16).

72. *ATC* 35, no. 8 (19 July 1913): 1; Sims and Stevenson, *An Illustrated Tour of Bethlehem*, p. 7.

73. *WME* 31, no. 11 (19 September 1908): 1.

74. Photographs of the house document the approximate date of its enlargement. The house lot was purchased for $1,150 by Alvin E. Ivie from James M. Turner (Bethlehem), Grafton County Registry of Deeds, book 487, p. 504, 8 January 1908. The deed set the restriction that buildings erected must be "family dwelling houses, private stables and garage."

75. *WME* 31, no. 11 (19 September 1908): 1. The Beaumont cottage plot (200 by 135 feet) was purchased from Rufus N. and Effie B. Gordon (Bethlehem). See deed, Grafton County Registry of Deeds, book 479, p. 276, 16 October 1906.

76. Probate notice, *NYT*, 9 April 1918, p. 23; *LC*, 14 October 1909, p. 1; *WMD (1920–1922)*, vol. 3, (1920), p. 370; deed, Julia Shaw from Marie H., Clarence C., Minnie B., and James E. Viall, Grafton County Registry of Deeds, book 492, p. 586, 25 June 1909; deed, Julia Shaw from William M. and Elsie M. Phillips, book 496, p. 8, 1 July 1909. The land was located on both sides of the Bethlehem-Franconia highway (Mount Agassiz Road). The price for the June 25 purchase was $2,000. Both tracts contained older farm buildings. The Shaw land abutted the Frank McCullock and Ellsworth Wright farms (see Wilson, *Bethlehem*, p. 63).

77. Taylor, *Early History of Bethlehem*, p. 32; *1914–16 Resident and Business Directory of the West Side of the White Mountains*, vol. 1 (1914), pp. 15, 16, 97, 116, and 226; *LC*, 14 October 1909, p. 1. The house is believed to have cost over $20,000 to build.

78. Telephone interview with Roland Shick, Bethlehem, N.H., 7 September 1994.

79. Sims and Stevenson, *An Illustrated Town of Bethlehem*, p. 29.

80. *LC*, 16 August 1917, p. 7, and 6 September 1917, p. 3; *WME* 40, no. 8 (8 September 1917): 4; telephone interview with Curt Gowdy, Bethlehem, 9 September 1994; *WMD*, vol. 3 (1920–22), p. 365; deed, "The Five Associates" (A. D. Locke, Minnie Idelle Locke, Ellesbree D. Locke, Lucy E. Locke, Dr. Francis M. Morris) from Fred D. and Alice M. Lewis of Bethlehem, Grafton County Registry of Deeds, book 515, p. 368, 23 July 1912. The purchase price was $1,500. The sale included a right-of-way to Lewis Hill Road (the Bethlehem-Franconia highway). The tract was bounded by lands owned by H. E. Whitcomb, Peter McPherson, and F. D. Lewis & Company, and was located one-fifth of a mile from the highway.

A consortium consisting of Albert D. Locke, Fred D. Lewis, Francis M. Morris, and Frank J. Hale (Newton Highlands, Mass.) made two additional land purchases (former farms with buildings) east of this highway on 31 March 1914 (book 528, p. 112), and 14 October 1914 (book 531, p. 308).

81. Hattie Whitcomb Taylor scrapbooks, White Mountain Collection, Dartmouth College Library, Hanover, N.H.; Jane Bacon MacIntire, ed. *Waban: Early Days, 1681–1913* (Waban, Mass.: n.p., 1944), pp. 103–5.

82. Interview with Mrs. Victor R. (Ruth) Whitcomb, Bethlehem, 21 June 1994; telephone interview with Michael ("Mickey") Whitcomb, Bethlehem, 20 October 1994; Wilson, *Bethlehem*, p. 63; Taylor scrapbooks, Dartmouth College Library; Taylor, *Early History of Bethlehem*, p. 32; *LC*, 16 August 1917, p. 7.

83. *LC*, 17 June 1917, p. 3.

84. *LC*, 16 August 1917, p. 7; *1914–1916 Resident and Business Directory of the West Side of the White Mountains*, pp. 21 and 119. Prior to the completion of the main house, "The Five Associates" stayed at a temporary "camp" on the property (*LC*, 28 June 1917, p. 3).

85. The house was sold to Norman H. Read of Amarillo, Texas, and New York City for $30,000 in 1949, before being acquired by Mr. and Mrs. Curt Gowdy of Boston in 1972.

86. Deed, Elizabeth B. Lemen (wife of William S.) from Leonard M. and Helen W. Knight, Grafton County Registry of Deeds, book 537, p. 181, 11 May 1916; deed, Elizabeth B. Lemen from Helen W. and Leonard M. Knight, book 538, p. 301, 19 August 1916. The first lot sold for $1,100, and measured approximately 150 by 420 feet. The second was acquired for the same price, and had rough dimensions of 150 by 350 feet.

87. Frank B. Lemen, *History of the Lemen Family, of Illinois, Virginia and Elsewhere* (Collinsville, Ill: By the Author, [1899]), p. 297; *WMD*, vol. 6 (1929–31), p. 105; telephone interview with Mrs. Mark Salton, Hartsdale, N.Y., 23 August 1994.

88. William B. Lemen is listed in *WMD*, vol. 2 (1917–19) as residing on South Road.

89. *WMD*, vol. 3 (1920–22), p. 365. The house is listed by name for the first time in this edition.

90. *WMD*, vol. 4 (1923–25), p. 430; Hattie Whitcomb Taylor scrapbooks, White Mountain Collection, Dartmouth College Library, Hanover, N.H.,; Taylor, *Early History of Bethlehem*, p. 32.

91. Telephone interview, Mrs. Mark Salton, 23 August 1994.

92. A second Lemen cottage stands on the lot to the south of "Dawn Cottage." Displaying a similar form, color scheme and features, it was erected around 1940 by contractor B. L. Harvey from plans by architect H. K. Wheeler of Newton Center, Massachusetts. A complete set of plan sheets and specifications dated 1939 are in the possession of the current owners.

93. Sims and Stevenson, *An Illustrated Tour of Bethlehem*, p. 20; *LC*, 26 October 1916, p. 6, and 19 July 1917, p. 3; date on corner stone, "Upland Cottage," Bethlehem, N.H.; Tolles, *GRHWM*, p. 128–29; Tolles, *New Hampshire Architecture*, pp. 315–16; deed, Florence Ivie Abbott (wife of Karl P. Abbott) from Frank H. Abbott, Grafton County Registry of Deeds, book 547, p. 473, 22 October 1918. The house is located on the corner of Main and Strawberry Hill streets. The site of the former "Upland Terrace," which burned in 1990, is next door, just to the west. After the purchase was made, and before "Upland Cottage" was built, a small Victorian dwelling on the parcel was moved across Strawberry Hill Street onto new foundations, where it still stands today. Soon after his first wife's death, Karl Abbott sold the house to J. Elmer Harrington of Bethlehem (Grafton County Registry of Deeds, book 594, pp. 10, 261, 278, 26 June 1926).

94. Karl P. Abbott, *Open for the Season* (Garden City, New York: Doubleday & Company, Inc., 1950), dust jacket essay; George H. Clark, "Karl P. Abbott," *GM* 58, no. 6 (June 1926): 175–76.

95. Telephone interview, Professor Richard Guy Wilson, School of Architecture, University of Virginia, Charlottesville, 17 March 1994; letter, Richard Guy Wilson to Leonard Reed, Bethlehem, N.H., 24 February 1983; interview, Leonard Reed, Bethlehem, 29 August 1993; letter, Leonard Reed to author, 16 January 1981; Pamela F. Mannix, "Abbott House, Bethlehem, New Hampshire," student course paper, School of Architecture, University of Virginia, c. 1980. For a full biographical monograph on Gustav Stickley, see Mary Anne Smith, *Gustav Stickley: The Craftsman* (Syracuse, N.Y.: Syracuse University Press, 1983).

The 19 July 1917 edition of the *LC* (p. 3) observed that the structure was "modeled after a house the Abbotts saw while motoring through California." This house may well have been a Greene and Greene design.

96. Mannix, "Abbott House."

97. *WME* 47, no. 1 (12 July 1924): 7.

98. Deed, Edgar E. Frank from James V. and Mary W. Wilson, Grafton County Registry of Deeds, book 555, p. 593. The purchase was for $8,000, and included unidentified buildings on the parcel. The land was bounded by Main Street on the north, and tracts owned by George H. Tusser on the west, the Smith family on the south, and Hattie M. Cilley and Dr. and Mrs. John W. Kenney on the east.

99. *WME* 47, no. 1 (12 July 1924): 7.

100. Hattie Whitcomb Taylor scrapbooks, White Mountain Collection, Dartmouth College Library, Hanover, N.H.; *WMD*, vol. 5 (1926–28), p. 95.

101. *Lisbon Courier*, 7 November 1940, p. 12.

102. Taylor scrapbooks; first floor plan, Frank House, Timothy McKeever, Lisbon, N.H. Morgan's own Lisbon house, which he designed and built in 1891, is located at 31 Highland Avenue.

103. For documentation of the land purchase, see deed, Frank J. Hogan from Elmer E. and Blanche M. Crane, Grafton County Registry of Deeds, book 599, p. 138, 11 March 1927, and book 599, p. 139, 11 March 1927. Secured in two separate real estate transactions, the tract was located on the north side of Bethlehem-Littleton highway, opposite and slightly northwest of "The Rocks," the Glessner estate. When the property left Guider family ownership in 1992, it comprised approximately 160 acres.

For comprehensive biographical information on Frank J. Hogan, see *Frank Hogan Remembered: Reminiscences by Lester Cohen* (Washington, D.C.: Hogan and Hartson, 1985); *WWWA*, vol. 2 (1950); *NCAB* 33, pp. 132–33; Donald C. Dickinson, *Dictionary of American Book Collectors* (New York, London and Westport, Conn.: Greenwood Press, 1986), pp. 163–64.

104. Architectural drawings for "Adair" (April 1927), Hardy Banfield, Bethlehem, N.H. These include cellar, first floor, second floor, and third floor diagrams; front, rear, east end and west end elevations; a site plan; and detail schematics (molding cross-sections; doorways; stairway balusters; fireplace surrounds and panels).

Clifford Peck was born in Lyme, Connecticut, and married Lydia Boardman of East Haddam in 1919. Peck was a jack-of-all-trades, after apparently mixed success as an architect. In 1934 he and several others founded the company, C. A. Peck, Inc., in East Haddam, to lease, own, rent, acquire, and possess real estate, conduct a jobbing machine shop, manufacture and sell wood products, and carry on a general contracting and building business. At the same time, the Pecks erected a small factory for the manufacture of clothes pins and operated it until around 1939, when they moved to Cummington, Massachusetts. See Karl P. Stofko, "Peck Family," unpublished essay, Municipal Historian, East Haddam, Connecticut, September 1894.

105. Floor plan for addition to "Adair" by Stanley Orcutt (1 November 1963), Hardy Banfield, Bethlehem, N.H. A new east wing, to create eight additional bedrooms, was designed in 1994 by Benjamin Nutter Associates, Architects of Topsfield, Mass., was planned for construction in 1997 or 1998, and has not yet been built. Stylistically compatible with the main house, the new wing was to be two stories in height, and set at an angle with the longitudinal axis.

106. Illustrated marketing prospectus for "Adair," Sotheby's International Realty, Boston, Mass., 1991; interview and house inspection with Hardy Banfield, Bethlehem, N.H., 19 March 1994.

107. "Adair," Olmstead Brothers Collection, Job 7843 (Guider, Bethlehem, N.H.), Microfilm 404, Library of Congress, Washington, D.C.; general planting plan for "Adair," Olmstead Brothers, Landscape Architects (Brookline, Mass.), 17 April 1928, Hardy Banfield, Bethlehem, N.H.

108. *NCAB* 57, pp. 98–99; obituary, John W. Guider, *NYT*, 20 January 1968, p. 29; "The History of Adair," promotional packet, Hardy Banfield, Bethlehem, N.H., 1994.

109. *LC*, 5 April 1907, p. 1; *WME* 30, no. 1 (13 July 1907): 4; deed, William B. Dickson from George G. and Addie J. Corey, Grafton County Registry of Deeds, book 483, p. 350, 6 April 1907. The purchase price was $4,500. Over the next two years, Dickson added to his farm holdings in Littleton by acquisitions from Frank and Julia B. Fitch (book 484, p. 308, 10 September 1907, water rights); James Brown, Mary Brown, and William J. Brown (book 429, p. 425, 29 September 1909); and James Brown, guardian, and William J. Brown (book 498, p. 209, 29 December 1909). His real estate holdings comprised over 250 acres at the end of 1909.

110. *NHFSH*, 10th ed. (1912), p. 11; Colby, *Littleton*, p. 35; *LC*, 11 November 1909, p. 1. The Dicksons were initially attracted to Littleton as a result of their friendship with Mr. and Mrs. W. I. Lincoln Adams, residents of Montclair as well as Littleton. Construction of the house was not completed until November 1910 as the Dicksons delayed decisions about interior finishing.

111. *NCAB* 31, p. 159; obituary, William B. Dickson, *NYT*, 28 January 1942, p. 19; Colby, *Littleton*, pp. 35–36.

112. *LC*, 11 November 1909, p. 1, and 20 October 1910, p. 1. The house measures eighty-five by approximately fifty feet, and cost nearly $60,000 to build. The construction job was undertaken by the Littleton firm of (Lewis J.) Myott and (L. Joseph) Crane, contractors, carpenters, and builders. See *1914–1916 Resident and Business Directory of the West Side of the White Mountains*, pp. 16, 86, and 115.

113. Set of nine blueprint drawings, n.d., "Bungalow for Wm. B. Dickson, Esq., Littleton, N.H." (front elevation; east elevation; west elevation; rear elevation; longitudinal section; cellar plan; first floor plan; roof framing plan; second floor framing plan), Walker and Chichester, New York City, Neil and Joan Winton, Littleton, N.H.

114. *WWWA*, vol. 3, p. 884; *NCAB* 42, p. 352; obituary, *NYT*, 7 January 1954, p. 31.

115. Obituary, *NYT*, 28 August 1916, p. 9. Chichester was born in Brooklyn, New York, and graduated from Columbia University. He lived on the upper west side of Manhattan, and was a member of the West Side and New York Golf clubs. He died of dysentery while on New York National Guard assignment in Texas.

6. FRANCONIA/SUGAR HILL

1. Tolles, *GRHWM*, pp. 196–98.

2. Ibid.; *WME* 44, no. 3 (23 July 1921).

3. *WME* 5, no. 6 (5 August 1882): 14, and vol. 18, no. 1 (6 July 1895): 5; *ATC* 22, no. 6 (23 July 1898): 4, and vol. 25, no. 3 (15 July 1901): 4; Moses F. Sweetser,

Chisholm's White Mountain Guide Book (Portland, Maine: Chisholm Brothers, 1902), p. 79; *WME* 26, no. 1 (4 July 1903): 1, and vol. 28, no. 7 (19 August 1905): 3.

4. *ATC* 27, no. 7 (20 July 1903): 1.

5. *NHFSH*, 6th ed. (1908), p. 40.

6. Karl P. Abbott, *Open for the Season*, (New York: Doubleday & Company, Inc., 1950), pp. 162–63; Tolles, *GRHWM*, pp. 200–201; *LC*, 9 August 1923, pp. 1, 12. The cottages were large, containing over twenty rooms in some cases.

7. *The White Mountain Clarion*, vol. 1, 5 August 1896.

8. Tolles, *GRHWM*, pp. 160–64; Pearson, "A Sketch of Franconia," p. 156; Welch, *A History of Franconia*, p. 83; *ATC* 26, no. 10 (23 July 1902): 4; *WME* 28, no. 7 (19 August 1905): 8; *LC*, 10 June 1891, p. 1.

9. *The Great Resorts of America (Illustrated) Together with Places of Interest in Colorado, New York, Maine, New Hampshire and Canada* (Portland, Maine: Wilbur Hayes, 1894), advertisement.

10. Photographs of "The Lodge," *WML* 1, no. 10 (2 September 1897); and, *WME* 24, no. 2 (13 July 1926): 1, and vol. 29, no. 7 (18 August 1906): 3.

11. Abbott, *Open for the Season*, p. 158; *WME* 48, no. 3 (30 August 1925): 5, and vol. 49, 8 (28 August 1926): 16.

12. *WME* 49, no. 6 (14 August 1926): 9. An examination of the house suggests that old framing timbers from "The Lodge" were employed for the construction of its successor. The original brick chimneys apparently also were rebuilt and reused.

13. *WME* 13, no. 2 (12 July 1890): 9. Independent of plumbing, the cost of the building was estimated at $7,000.

14. Telephone interview with Mrs. Virginia Sohn, Beverly Farms, Mass., 30 March 1994. "Gale Cottage" has unusual spatial arrangements on its interior, with the major rooms on the first and second floors extending the width of the building. On the first floor is a large east end room (the "Great Room") with wide stairway to the floors above, and a west end parlor. Initially, there was no kitchen, as Prime and his guests took their meals next door at the Mount Lafayette House (a separate kitchen building was later added to the west end off the porch). The second floor contains a large east bedroom, a hallway, and two other bedrooms and two bathrooms. Under steep-pitched, gabled roofs in the attic story are two smaller bedrooms. Much of the original furniture remains. It is unlikely that a professional architect designed the house. Prime probably undertook this task in collaboration with local builders.

15. *DAB* 8, pp. 228–29; *NCAB* 13, p. 254; Obituary, *ATC* 29, no. 44 (1 September 1905): 4. One of Prime's older brothers was Samuel Irenaeus Prime (1812–85), a Presbyterian minister, editor, and author.

16. Jeffrey S. Wallner, "Butterflies and Trout: Annie Trumbull Slossen and W. C. Prime in Franconia," *Historical New Hampshire* 32, no. 3 (Fall 1977), pp. 129–39. Slossen was the author of several popular White Mountain books, including *Fishin' Jimmy* (1888), *The Heresy of Mehetabel Clark* (1892), and *White Christopher* (1901).

17. Deeds, Grafton County Registry of Deeds,

William C. Prime from: Marshall A. Bowles (book 342, p. 447, 22 August 1876); Maria Richardson (book 379, p. 395, 18 July 1884); Osmon Parker, Wilbur F. Parker, and E. B. Parker's estate (book 381, p. 594, 5 January 1885); Osmon and Wilbur F. Parker (book 386, p.17, 4 December 1885); Veranus Clark (book 388, p. 263, 17 August 1886); Ebenezer, Josiah B., and Albert Richardson (book 398, p. 499, 3 October 1889—the house lot); Seth R. and Josiah R. Elliott, and Josephine C. Herrick (book 400, p. 442, 3 October 1889); and Albert and Josiah B. Richardson (book 424, p. 323, 6 September 1895). The house lot is situated on the southwest side of the road from the village of Franconia to Franconia Notch, near the bridge over the Gale River and the site of the Mount Lafayette House.

18. Wallner, "Butterflies and Trout," p. 139; Welch, *A History of Franconia*, pp. 84, 87–88. The Lafayette House was built about 1882, and burned in 1911. Despite the physical tie with the hotel, "Gale Cottage" survived the fire. See also *LC*, 1 June 1911, p. 1, and *WME* 18, no. 3 (20 July 1895): 5. Bradford Torrey authored a number books with White Mountain references, including *Birds in the Bush* (1885), *A Rambler's Lease* (1889), *The Foot-Path Way* (1892), and *Nature's Invitation* (1904).

19. Wallner, "Butterflies and Trout," pp. 142–43; "Mountain Home of the Late Dr. Prime," *Boston Herald*, 12 March 1905. Slossen sold the Lafayette House in 1908 to James Smith of Franconia, the former caretaker of "Gale Cottage" for Prime (*WME* 31, no. 3 [25 July 1908]: 4).

20. Tolles, *GRHWM*, pp. 132.

21. Ibid., pp. 131–34.

22. *WME* 20, no. 1 (3 July 1897): 9, and vol. 29, no. 7 (18 August 1906): 2; *WML* 1, no. 1 (1 July 1897).

23. *WME* 12, no. 2 (13 July 1889): 14. For the documentation of the acquisition of the house lot, see deed, Joseph B. Harden from Leonard and Simon Bowles, Grafton County Registry of Deeds, book 392, p. 552, 8 October 1888. The purchase was for $1,000, and amounted to four acres, with the right to access water on the sellers' adjacent land. On 17 April 1906, Joseph Harden's widow, Alison Cleveland Harden, transferred title of the property to Frances Harden (her daughter) but continued to use the cottage until the 1940s.

24. *WME* 13, no. 2 (12 July 1890): 5, and vol. 20, no. 5 (31 July 1897): 7.

25. *ATC* 20, no. 7 (17 July 1896): 4.

26. *WME* 14, no. 4 (11 July 1891): 11; deed, Caroline B. Adams (wife of Hugh White Adams) from Henry H. Bowles and Seth B. Hoskins, book 399, p. 232, 23 November 1889. Bowles and Hoskins granted the Adams the right to use water from the Sunset Hill House tank (behind "Lindhurst"), agreed not to erect any buildings to obstruct the view in front, and guaranteed a road right-of-way. The purchase price was $600.

27. *WME* 14, no. 4 (11 July 1891): 11.

28. *LC*, 4 February 1891, p. 1.

29. *WME* 18, no. 2 (13 July 1895): 14, vol. 22, no. 2 (15 July 1899): 16, and vol. 28, no. 4 (29 July 1905): 6.

30. *WME* 29, no. 7 (18 August 1906): 2.

31. *WME* 26, no. 3 (15 July 1903): 15, and no. 6 (8 August 1903): 14; *WME* 28, no. 7 (19 August 1905): 24.

The land on which "Allbreeze" was constructed was purchased on 15 September 1902, Albert H. Wheeler from Henry H. Bowles, and Seth F. and Martha E. Hoskins, Grafton County Registry of Deeds, book 458, p. 294. The sale price was $1,200. The lot was between "The Pavilion" and "Lindhurst" behind a plank walk running to the Sunset Hill House. The Wheelers also acquired the right to use water from the hotel supply, and to use the hotel road for access. The view east and north was protected by the deed terms.

32. *WME* 26, no. 1 (4 July 1903): 7, and vol. 29, no. 7 (18 August 1906): 2.

33. *WME* 29, no. 7 (18 August 1906): 2. It is possible that Sylvanus D. Morgan had some connection with the construction and design of the other Sunset Hill House cottages. In 1886–87, he built and may have designed the nearby Hotel Lookoff in Sugar Hill for the firm of Hiram Noyes and Sons. He was known also to have done other work in Sugar Hill, but these commissions have not yet been documented.

34. *WME* 13, no. 2 (12 July 1890): 5 and 8. The architect and builder of "The Bungalow" have not yet been identified. The land for the house was acquired in 1889 in the name of Harriet N. Andrews, wife of James F., for $800 from Leonard and Simon Bowles, the latter the co-owner of the Sunset Hill House. See deed, Harriet N. Andrews from Leonard and Simon Bowles, Grafton County Registry of Deeds, book 398, p. 332, 24 August 1889.

35. Obituary for James F. Andrews, *NYT*, 12 February 1915, p. 11; *WME* 20, no. 1 (3 July 1897): 9; *WME* 24, no. 1 (6 July 1901): 4; *Club Men of New York, 1901–02* (New York: W. S. Rossiter, 1901), p. 65.

36. *Tercentenary History of Maryland* (Chicago and Baltimore: The S. J. Clarke Publishing Co., 1925), vol. 2, pp. 269–70; *White Mountain Outlook* 12, no. 1 (17 July 1941): 20.

37. *WME* 28, no. 7 (19 August 1905): 24; deed, Rufus M. Gibbs from James F. Andrews, Grafton County Registry of Deeds, book 483, pp. 261 and 266, 13 March 1907. The property (a little more than one acre) was sold "for $10 and other valuable considerations."

38. Deeds, Isaac H. Davis from Anson A. Whipple, Grafton County Registry of Deeds, book 399, p. 546, 11 February 1890; Isaac H. Davis from David B. Hildreth, book 399, p. 548, 11 February 1890 (water rights); Isaac H. Davis from Osro E. Streeter, book 414, p. 31, 8 November 1892; Isaac H. Davis from Silas D. Spooner, book 413, p. 97, and book 414, p. 537, 26 December 1892; Isaac H. Davis from James W. Aldrich, book 413, p. 91, 19 January 1893; Isaac H. Davis from George C. Bowles II, book 413, p. 99, 1 February 1893; Isaac H. Davis from George G., Kate M., and L. D. Quimby, book 414, p. 502, 13 February 1893; Isaac H. Davis from Hiram and William H. Noyes and Charles H. Jepperson, book 413, p. 371, 4 August 1893. It is clear from the deed that there was a farmhouse, and perhaps other farm buildings on the roughly eight-acre Whipple tract when Davis purchased it. Prior to the construction of "Wayside Lodge," Davis apparently had these structures removed.

39. *WME* 22, no. 8 (22 August 1899): 20, and vol.

29, no. 2 (14 July 1906): 4; *Ladies Home Journal*, May 1899, p. 24; *Cyclopedia of Architecture, Carpentry and Building* 2, op. p. 228.

40. Interview with Robert Whitney, Sugar Hill, 18 March 1994; telephone conversation with Mrs. Roger (Nancy) Aldrich, 23 March 1994; *WME* 22, no. 8 (26 August 1899): 20. The Taylors were from Melrose, Massachusetts. Eben Taylor worked as an accountant in Boston.

41. *WWWA*, vol. 1 (1897–1942), p. 1324; *WWA*, vol. 17 (1932–33), p. 2418; Wheeler Preston, *American Biographies* (New York and London: Harper & Brothers, Publishers, 1974); *WME* 28, no. 7 (19 August 1905): 24.

42. Deeds, Henry H. Westinghouse from Isaac H. Davis, Grafton County Registry of Deeds: book 416, p. 198, 1 April 1897; book 413, p. 369, 1 April 1893; book 416, p. 200, 1 April 1893; book 413, p. 367, 11 November 1893; book 413, p. 387, 11 November 1893; and, book 419, p. 378, 23 April 1894. Many of the tracts were the same ones acquired by Isaac Davis from various landowners between November 1892 and March 1893. The fact that Davis sold these tracts so quickly after the purchases suggests that he was engaging in real estate speculation, or that he had suffered a financial reversal of some kind.

43. *WME* 28, no. 7 (19 August 1905): 24; deed, Henry H. and Clara L. Westinghouse to Amelia E. Winterbotham (Chicago), Grafton County Registry of Deeds, book 485, p. 379, 28 April 1908. The purchase price of land and buildings was $6,000.

44. Interview with David Mallery and Rosemary Mallery Gregg, Sugar Hill, N.H., 4 August 1994.

45. Plan of the Quimby Place, Sugar Hill, N.H., Ray T. Gile, Grafton County Registry of Deeds, book 530, p. 27, 1908; deed, Otto T. Mallery from Bowles and Hoskins Company, Herbert C. Merrill, Fred G. and Hattie E. Sanborn, and the Lisbon Savings Bank and Trust Company, Grafton County Registry of Deeds, book 535, p. 393, 15 December 1915; deed, Otto T. Mallery from Henry H. and Clara Westinghouse, book 535, pp. 396 and 397, 20 December 1915 (land, including water privileges); deed, Otto T. Mallery from Simon Bowles, and Daniel M. and Alice B. Tefft, book 536, p. 12, 7 January 1916 (water privileges); *WME* 40, no. 6 (25 August 1917): 1.

46. Tatham and Moss, *Biographical Dictionary of Philadelphia Architects*, pp. 312–13; interview with David Mallery and Rosemary Mallery Gregg, 4 August 1994. Graham's papers and drawings are housed at the University of Pennsylvania Archives.

47. Interview with David Mallery and Rosemary Mallery Gregg, 4 August 1994. George H. Handy of Sugar Hill was the stonemason for the main house, and may also have been the chief contractor for the entire building project.

48. Interview with David Mallery and Rosemary Mallery Gregg, 4 August 1994; blueprint plan for the "Music Room" for Otto Mallery, Esq., Paul P. Cret, Architect, Philadelphia, Penn., May 29, 1919; Tatham and Moss, *Biographical Dictionary of Philadelphia Architects*, pp. 172–75; Withey, *BDAA(D)*, pp. 149 and 506; blueprint plan for the "Log Cabin" by Rich and Mathesius, 320 Fifth Avenue, New York, N.Y., 7 June

1926; letter, Otto T. Mallery to Paul P. Cret, 8 November 1919, in which George Chamberlain is identified as the supplier of materials and builder of the "Music Box"; blueprint plan for the "Flower Pot," E. F. Hodgson Co., Boston and New York, 17 June 1930.

49. Interview with David Mallery and Rosemary Mallery Gregg, 4 August 1994; *NCAB* 44, pp. 90–91.

7. CAMPTON/WATERVILLE

1. Interview with Carol H. Newcomb, Campton, N.H., 6 November 1994. The name(s) of the contractor(s) of the cottages remains a mystery.

2. *WWNE*, 1909 ed., p. 637; *WWWA*, vol. 1 (1897–1942), p. 788; obituary, *NYT*, 21 August 1932; *WML* 1, no. 1 (1 July 1897).

3. Deed, F. Schuyler Mathews from Joseph C., Jennie S. (his wife), and Henry W. Blair, Grafton County Registry of Deeds, book 377, p. 210, 8 November 1883. The tract was three-eighths of an acre in size and sold for $37.50. Mathews added to this initial purchase on 30 May 1885 when he acquired a larger piece of land for $535.00 from Thomas S. Pulsifer of Campton. Like the first plot, it was located on the west side of the Plymouth-Franconia main road.

Mathews was introduced to Campton by virtue of many summer vacation stays at Blair's Hotel with his parents, starting in 1868 when he was fourteen years old. He quickly became interested in birds and hiking, and was an early member of the Appalachian Mountain Club.

4. Interview with Carol H. Newcomb, 6 November 1994; letter, Carol H. Newcomb to the author, 28 January 1995; *WME* 22, no. 5 (5 August 1899): 8. Prior to the front bedroom enlargement, there was no window on the second-floor front of the cottage. Had the new bedroom not been added on, the Mathews family might not have survived the fire of around 1892. According to family sources, Mathews, while in the bedroom, saw the reflection of the fire in the window glass of the house close by next door. At first he thought the other house was burning, but quickly realized that it was his house that was ablaze, and led his family to safety.

5. Deed, Mary F. Reuter from F. Schuyler Mathews, Grafton County Registry of Deeds, book 459, p. 551, 6 October 1902. Reuter acquired the land for $3,400, assuming a $1,400 mortgage from the Laconia Savings Bank as part of the purchase price. The size of the parcel is not specified in the deed.

Between 1905 and 1910, Reuter sold off sections of this tract to several parties. In 1922, she sold the remaining land and cottage to Emily S. Scott of Westchester, New York (book 568, p. 466, 3 May 1922). At the time Reuter's address was listed as Edgartown, Martha's Vineyard, Massachusetts, suggesting that her preference for vacation environment may have shifted from the mountains to the seashore. Margaret K. Campbell assumed title to the property about 1960.

6. Letter, Margaret K. Campbell to the author, 17 September 1994; interview with Margaret K. Campbell, Campton, N.H., 6 November 1994; interview with Carol H. Newcomb, Campton, 6 November

1994. The present name of the house is "Blair Cottage." It is not known if the house had a formal name during the Reuter or Scott periods of ownership.

7. Reginald H. Elphinstone from Lovain A. and Maud F. Werden (Henniker, N.H.), Grafton County Registry of Deeds, book 495, p. 334, 11 September 1909. The house and land were sold by Edith Elphinstone to the Breitenberger family in 1936 (book 660, p. 402, 15 July 1936) after her husband's death. Reginald Elphinstone was a vice president of the Prudential Insurance Company.

8. Interview with Carol H. Newcomb, Campton, N.H., 6 November 1994.

9. Tolles, *GRHWM*, p. 170–71. This was the second hotel in Waterville Valley. The Greeleys built the first in 1860 and it was destroyed by fire a year later.

10. Bean, *The Town at the End of the Road*, p. 21.

11. Goodrich, *The Waterville Valley*, p. 65; Bean, *The Town at the End of the Road*, p. 220 n. 10, and p. 221 n. 14. The Peloubet property was acquired in the name of Mary Peloubet from Merrill Greeley. An ardent golfer, Rev. Peloubet was instrumental in the creation of the Waterville golf course. He was widely recognized as the author of *Selected Notes on the International Lessons* used in Congregational and Presbyterian church Sunday schools, and wrote a Bible dictionary. The Peloubets called their new house "Glen Eyrie."

The Briggs family was associated with the administration of the Hampton Institute in Virginia (see Bean, *The Town at the End of the Road*, p. 152).

For background on Carrie Elliott's real estate in Waterville Valley, see Bean, pp. 25, 43, and 51, and Goodrich, *The Waterville Valley*, pp. 12–13.

8. HOLDERNESS/SANDWICH/ MOULTONBOROUGH

1. Alice Carey, "The Webster Estate," National Register of Historic Places Registration Form, United States Department of the Interior, National Park Service, Washington, D.C., 1989; *NHFSH*, 11th ed. (1913), pp. 24–25. In addition to serving as the Webster family summer vacation retreat, the Holderness estate has also been a working farm and timber tract.

2. Carey, "The Webster Estate"; *WWNE*, 1909 ed., p. 982; *WWWA*, vol. 1 (1897–1942), p. 1314.

3. Carey, "The Webster Estate"; obituary of George Canning Wales, *New York Herald Tribune*, 22 March 1940, p. 18. The Frank G. and Laurence J. Webster houses are two of only a few documented commissions of the firm of Wales and Holt, although Wales' obituary states that "he designed many homes." See *Boston Architectural Center Yearbooks*, 1890 and after.

4. Carey, "The Webster Estate"; plans, Frank G. Webster cottage, Peter and Mary W. Kampf, Holderness, N.H.; plans, Laurence J. Webster cottage, Laurence J. Webster III, Holderness, N.H. "The Homestead" measures 124 by 32 feet, and the Laurence Webster cottage is of comparable dimensions.

5. Carey, "The Webster Estate." "The Homestead" was provided with a north wing and ice house around

1912. In about 1917, portions of the verandas were enclosed, and a sleeping porch added above the veranda on the south end. Starting in 1987, the current owners completed a major exterior restoration of the house, replacing roof and wall shingles, decking, and architectural elements.

The Laurence Webster house retains its original floor plan, except for 1916–18 changes, which enlarged the living room, added sleeping porches and a bath to the bedroom above, enclosed a covered veranda, and removed a north elevation porch. The exterior was reshingled in 1950 and 1987. The Websters completed a major extension, restoration, and some interior remodeling in 1987, about the same time that "The Homestead" underwent the same process.

6. Carey, "The Webster Estate"; *NCAB* 38, pp. 582–83; Stone, *History of Massachusetts Industries*, vol. 2, pp. 1479–81.

7. Carey, "The Webster Estate"; telephone conversation with Jack and Betty Valentine (Carlisle, Mass.), 15 March 1994.

8. Withey, *BDAA(D)*, pp. 119 and 220; obituary, "Horace S. Frazer," *NYT*, 9 June 1931, p. 27; *NCAB* 27, p. 345; *AABN* 50, no. 1036 (2 November 1895): 49; Kevin D. Murphy, "Chapman and Frazer," *A Biographical Dictionary of Architects in Maine*, vol. 6 (Portland, Maine: Maine Citizens for Historic Preservation, 1991). J. H. Chapman was born in New York City, graduated from Yale College, and received his architectural training at the Sheffield Scientific School (Yale) and the Royal Academy of Stuttgart, Germany. Before joining Frazer in partnership, he worked in the offices of Ware and Van Brunt in Boston.

9. *Twentieth Annual Excursion of the Sandwich Historical Society* (Sandwich, N.H.: Sandwich Historical Society, 1931), p. 22.

10. Ibid.; interview with Judy Coolidge (daughter of Joseph R. Coolidge), Sandwich, N.H., 1 April 1993.

11. *Twentieth Annual Excursion*, pp. 22–23; 34–35. Joseph R. Coolidge made the house suitable for winter use by excavating a cellar and installing an oil heating system.

12. *Twentieth Annual Excursion*, p. 33; *American Art Annual* 25 (1928): 36. *NCAB* 26, p. 213; Withey, *BDAA(D)*, p. 38.

13. *Sketches of Sandwich, New Hampshire* (Center Sandwich, N.H.: Quimby School, 1928), p. 11; *Twentieth Annual Excursion*, p. 22.

14. Deeds, Carroll County Registry. Benjamin F. Shaw from William H. Orne, book 73, p. 409, 3 September 1879; Benjamin F. Shaw from Eleazar and Eliza Davis, book 73, p. 425, 10 September 1879; Benjamin F. Shaw from Albert H. Horne, book 73, p. 588, 11 October 1879; Benjamin F. Shaw from Moses and Betsey Witham, book 75, p. 95, 7 July 1880; Benjamin F. Shaw from Samuel L. Whitton, book 77, p. 91, 11 October 1881 (water rights); Benjamin F. Shaw from Jacob Manson, book 87, p. 165, 16 March 1886. The purchases were all from local residents and consisted largely of farm and forest lands, some containing older buildings. Originally, this large tract was referred to as the Lee settlement.

15. *Summer Saunterings by the B. & L.*, 1st ed. (Boston: Passenger Department of the Boston & Low-

ell Railroad, 1885), pp. 68–69; W. S. Hawkes, ed., *Win-nipesaukee and About There . . .* (Boston: Passenger Department, Boston & Lowell Railroad, 1882), p. 52; Merrill, *History of Carroll County*, p. 398; Matthews, *Moultonborough to the 20th Century*, pp. 7–10.

16. Hawkes, *Winnipesaukee and About There*, electroplate engraving, op. p. 52; cabinet view, "The Hall and the Lodge," in series, "Views in Ossipee Park, Mt. Shaw, Moultonborough, N.H." (c. 1885), photographed by L. O. Churchill, Lowell, Mass.; plate, *Lake Winnipesaukee* viewbook (Boston: G. W. Armstrong Dining Room and News Co., 1909).

17. Matthews, *Moultonborough to the 20th Century*, p. 10; Wilken, *The Castle and the Club*, pp. 2–5; Paul E. Estaver, "King of the Castle," *NHP* 7, no. 5 (May 1958): 13.

18. Harriete F. Farwell, *Shaw Records: A Memorial of Roger Shaw, 1594–1661* (Bethel, Maine: E. C. Bowler, 1904), pp. 226–30; [William F. Moore, comp.], *Representative Men of Massachusetts, 1890–1900* (Everett, Mass.: Massachusetts Publishing Co., 1898), pp. 370–72. The Shaws had six children, three boys and three girls, born between 1853 and 1867. By the mid-1880s, the Shaw Stocking Company achieved worldwide prominence in textile manufacturing, with a capital of $360,000, 275 operating looms, and nearly 500 employees. Shaw's loom and its products were exhibited in England to manufacturers from all over Europe.

19. "Castle in the Clouds, Moultonborough, New Hampshire," real estate sale prospectus, Sotheby's International Realty, New York City, c. 1990; Stan and Maryjane Bean, "Lucknow: Castle in the Clouds," *Appalachia* 40, no. 8 (15 June 1974): 151–55. The mansion is located at an elevation of 1,300 feet above sea level.

20. Telephone interview with Mrs. John Scott, Moultonborough, N.H., 20 September 1994; *NCAB* 40, p. 571; Stone, *History of Massachusetts Industries*, vol. 2, pp. 1485–86; Wilken, *The Castle and the Club*, pp. 1–2; Ann Malaspina, "A Dream with a View," *NHP* 35, no. 6 (June 1986): 36–38. Olive Plant moved to her home state, Illinois, after her husband's death, and died in California in 1976.

"Lucknow" was sold to Fred C. Tobey, of the New Hampshire family, in the early 1940s who used it as a summer residence and timber farm. In 1956, the property passed to Richard S. Robie, a car rental company executive and real estate investor from Massachusetts, and his brother, Donald, who undertook major restoration projects, and opened the main house and grounds to the public. The current owner, Albert W. Hopeman Corporation (owner of Purity Springs, L.P., the spring water bottling business) of North Carolina, bought the estate in 1991 and continues to operate it as a tourist attraction (see *Manchester Union Leader*, 7 June 1991, p. 1).

21. Wilken, *The Castle and the Club*, pp. 5–6; Topolian, *People, Places and Moultonborough*, p. 138; Jim Cunningham, "Castle in the Clouds," *NHP* 22, No. 7 (July 1973): 78–80.

22. "Castle in the Clouds" real estate prospectus; Wilken, *The Castle and the Club*, pp. 6–7; Paul E. Estaver, "King of the Castle," *NHP* 7, no. 5 (May 1985): 12–14; "Castle in the Clouds," *New Hampshire*

Premier 4, no. 40 (September 1993): 32–33; "Lucknow—A Mountain and Lake Estate," *Country Life* 46, no. 6 (October 1924): 7–14; Rodrique, *Tom Plant*, pp. 168–73.

23. "Castle in the Clouds" real estate prospectus; Wilken, *The Castle and the Club*, p. 7; Topolian, *People, Places and Moultonborough*, pp. 138; *Lucknow . . .* (n.p: n. pub., [c. 1925]), sale prospectus, Dartmouth College Library; telephone interview, Barry Rodrique, Quebec City, Quebec, Canada, 26 September 1994. One of Plant's most illustrious guests was former President Theodore Roosevelt, with whom he shared an interest in hunting and fishing.

Interior woodwork and decoration were by Irving and Casson, A. H. Davenport Co. of Boston; bronze and tile work by William Jackson & Co.; electric fixtures by Edward F. Caldwell; and glass decoration by Tiffany Studios (see "Lucknow," *Country Life* 46, no. 6 [October 1924: 14).

24. Cunningham, "Castle in the Clouds," p. 79; Rodrique, *Tom Plant*, pp. 167 and 182.

9. TAMWORTH/CHOCORUA

1. Deeds to Elliott C. Clark, Carroll County Registry of Deeds. From Abbie F. Cooley, book 97, p. 489, 14 June 1892; from Silas R. Thornton, book 97, p. 490, 14 June 1892; from Elmira, M. E., and J. F. Marston, book 97, p. 463, 20 June 1893; from Mary F. Edgell, book 99, p. 533, 4 May 1893; from Elmira, M. E., and J. F. Marston, book 99, p. 206, 2 February 1893; from Nancy S. and F. A. Huckins, book 103, p. 85, 16 October 1894; from Ernest Storer, book 103, p. 108, 16 October 1894; from Nathaniel Dillaway, book 104, p. 581, 6 November 1895; from James Henry Wallace, book 104, p. 594, 12 November 1895; from Mary F. and C. H. Edgell, book 104, p. 595, 18 November 1895; from Levi E. Remick, book 106, p. 83, 20 May 1896; from William Herbert Rollins, book 107, p. 13, 7 November 1896; from John F. Sanborn, book 109, p. 203, 21 December 1898. For a plan of Great Hill, see book 99, p. 533, 4 May 1893.

2. *WWWA*, vol. 1 (1897–1942), p. 226; W. T. Davis, *Professional and Industrial History of Suffolk County, Massachusetts* (Boston: The Boston History Company, 1894), p. 441.

3. McGrew, *If Walls Could Speak*, pp. 26–27. A driveway with a small family cemetery to the east runs along a stone wall to the house and outbuildings. This was originally the main road, formerly passing directly in front of the house. During the early years of Clark family ownership, this road became a private lane, and a bypass road was laid out to the southeast. The route is known as "Great Hill Road."

4. Interview with Wayne Mock, Tamworth, N.H., 22 June 1994; undated plans for "Addition to House for E. C. Clarke, Esq., Tamworth, N.H., Peabody & Stearns, Architects," Wayne and Anne Mock (sketches and selected originals in the Peabody and Stearns Collection, Boston Public Library, eight drawings). The northeast service wing was likely altered and expanded at this time, but it is unlikely that Peabody and Stearns were involved with this project.

5. Set of plan sheets (four drawings), "Proposed Addition for Mrs. E. C. Clark, Tamworth, N.H.," Albert C. Fernald, Architect, Devonshire Street, Boston, 12 March 1901, Wayne and Anne Mock. At the time, Albert Fernald's offices were at 186 Devonshire Street in Boston.

6. Set of plan sheets (four drawings) for "Amusement Hall and House, for Mrs. E. C. Clarke, Tamworth, N.H.," Albert C. Fernald, Architect, n.d., Wayne and Anne Mock.

7. *NHFSH*, 4th ed. (1906), p. 10.

8. *NHFSH*, 8th ed. (1910), p. 11.

9. *NHFSH*, 4th ed. (1906), p. 10; deed, John H. and Martha Boyden Finley from Grover and Frances T. Cleveland, Carroll County Registry of Deeds, book 126, p. 571, 26 October 1905. The tract of land, of unspecified acreage, was bounded on the north by land formerly owned by Sylvester K. Jackson, on the east by the Cleveland farm, on the west by additional Cleveland land (formerly the Ladd place), and on the south by Stevenson (subsequently Cleveland) Hill Road.

10. *NHFSH*, 4th ed. (1906), pp. 10, 12.

11. Withey, *BDAA(D)*, pp. 300–301 and 342–43; Herbert Croly, "The Work of Kilham & Hopkins"; obituary, Walter H. Kilham, *Architectural Record* 104, no. 5 (November 1948): 170; Candee, "Kilham, Hopkins & Greeley."

12. A photograph of "Kilmarnock" accompanied the Croly article (see note 11) on Kilham & Hopkins in the 1912 *Architectural Record*. The house is owned today by descendants of the President Finley and his wife.

13. *DAB*, vol. 11 (suppl. 2), pp. 185–86, *NCAB* 30, pp. 89–91.

14. Telephone interview with Margaret Johnson, Wonalancet, N.H., 27 June 1995; deed, Gertrude and Marjory Gane from Ira B. and Alice L. Tilton (St. Cloud, Fla.), Carroll County Registry of Deeds, book 141, p. 17, 12 January 1912; deed, Gertrude and Marjory Gane from Julia P. Lombard (New York City) and Katherine S. Walden (Tamworth), book 141, p. 285, 30 March 1912; deed, Gertrude and Marjory Gane from Arthur T. and Katherine S. Walden, book, 141, p. 285, 30 March 1912; and deed, Gertrude and Marjory Gane from Ira S. and Alice L. Tilton, book 141, p. 286, 30 March 1912. The lands purchased were situated in the towns of Tamworth as well as Albany.

15. Deed, Marjory G. Harkness to Seward B. Collins, Carroll County Registry of Deeds, book 226, p. 312, 12 March 1942; deed, Marjory G. Harkness to Seward B. Collins, book 226, p. 521, 23 March 1942.

16. Telephone interviews with Margaret Johnson, 27 June 1995, and George Zink, Wonalancet, N.H., 26 July 1995. The house is constructed largely of local materials. The two end chimneys possess an interesting and unusual feature—penetrating the flues on the second floor are small windows, in each case necessitating the splitting of the flues, which, above the window frames, become single flues once more.

17. Interview with George Zink, 26 July 1995; Christine Nasso, ed., *Contemporary Authors: Permanent Series* (Detroit: Gale Research Co., 1978), vol. 2, p. 241; dust jacket, Marjorie G. Harkness, "*A Brook of*

Our Own" (New York: Alfred A. Knopf, 1945); obituary, *Carroll County (N.H.) Independent,* 27 June 1974; *Smith Alumnae Quarterly* class notes, 1912–1974, Smith College Archives, Northampton, Mass.

18. Harkness, *"A Brook of Our Own,"* p. 12.

19. Harkness, *The Tamworth Narrative,* pp. 222–23; interviews, Samuel I. Bowditch, Chocorua, N.H., 22 June 1993 and 5 March 1994; deeds, Carroll County Registry of Deeds, Marshall S. Scudder from John H. and Clarinda Nickerson, book 64, p. 89, 9 September 1874, and Marshall S. Scudder from Stephen H. and Annie M. Allen (Boston), book 64, p. 91, 9 September 1874. The acquisition from the Nickersons was for the purchase price of $357.50, and comprised a little over four acres on the west side of the Chocorua Village–Conway road, bordering Chocorua Lake. The purchase from the Allens (brokered by John H. Nickerson) was for $1,540.62, and included slightly more than twenty acres, "part of Emery farm, so-called," on the east side of the road. This second parcel contained the Emery farmhouse, and the future site of "Birchentower." On 4 February 1875, the Scudders purchased an additional piece of land (less than two acres) from the Nickersons on the east side of the road to supplement their property holdings.

20. Harkness, *The Tamworth Narrative,* p. 223; interviews with Samuel I. Bowditch, 22 June and 7 July 1993.

21. Franklin Ware Davis, "In Chocorua County," pp. 179–80.

22. Harkness, *The Tamworth Narrative,* p. 223; interview, Samuel I. Bowditch, 22 June 1993; *ATC* 16, no. 18 (30 July 1893): 41; *DAB* 8, pp. 522–23; *NCAB* 1, p. 283; Wilson and Fisks, *ACAB* 5, pp. 443–44. Horace Scudder's brother, Samuel Hubbard (b. 1837), was a renowned entomologist. Although he occupied "Birchentower" after around 1880, Horace Scudder did not actually secure title to the property until about 1897.

23. Interviews with Samuel I. Bowditch, 22 June and 7 July 1993; obituary, "Lois Lilley Howe," *Progressive Architecture* 45, no. 10 (October 1964): 118; Schrock, *Architectural Records in Boston,* p. 150. Miss Howe designed the new wing when she was a partner in the firm of Lois Lilley Howe and Eleanor Manning, which existed from 1913 to 1926. For a comprehensive treatment of Howe's career as an architect, see Elizabeth W. Reinhardt, "Lois Lilley Howe, F.A.I.A., 1864–1964," *Proceedings of the Cambridge* (Mass.) *Historical Society* 43 (1980): 153–72.

24. Interviews with Samuel I. Bowditch, 22 June and 7 July 1993, and Alan Smith, 21 June 1993 and 4 July 1994, Chocorua, N.H.

25. Merrill, *History of Carroll County,* p. 738. Deeds to Isabel F. Sherwin, Carroll County Registry of Deeds (Ossipee): from Charles E. Beck and Moses C. Varney, Est., book 84, p. 115, 16 May 1885; from Loretta S. Varney, book 84, p. 119, 16 May 1885; from Bowditch and Walley, book 84, p. 504, 13 October 1885. Additional land purchases in Chocorua made by Isabel F. Sherwin, presumably after the house was constructed: from Edwin Sherwin, book 96, p. 122, 19 September 1891; from Annie E. Allen, book 26, p. 128, 19 September 1891; from Stephen M. and Annie E. Allen, book 96,

pp. 503 and 517, 19 December 1891; from Loretta Varney, book 97, p. 277, 19 April 1892. Also, Thomas Sherwin from Susan S. Wainwright, book 118, pp. 55 and 56 (mortgage deed), n.d.; Thomas Sherwin from Susan S. Wainwright, book 110, p. 311, 27 August 1898 (mortgage deed); Thomas Sherwin from Mark E. Robinson, book 117, p. 113, 4 November 1901. The 16 May 1885 purchase was made for $1,400, and comprised one hundred acres of land, with shoreline on Chocorua Lake.

26. *NCAB* 17, pp. 12–13; *WWNE,* 1909 ed., p. 846. After General Sherwin's death, Mrs. Sherwin sold the house to Frederick S. Bigelow, editor of the *Saturday Evening Post* (Harkness, *The Tamworth Narrative,* p. 227).

27. Deed, Mary H. Loring (wife of Charles G.) from Henshaw B. Walley and Charles P. Bowditch, Carroll County Registry of Deeds, book 105, p. 239, 17 January 1896. This tract is bordered on the west by Philbrick Hill Road. Subsequent Loring purchases in Chocorua included Charles G. Loring and Charles P. Bowditch from John G. Nickerson, book 112, p. 413, 10 October 1899; Mary H. Loring from Joseph Noble, Jr., book 120, p. 327, 13 April 1903; Mary H. Loring from Charles P. Bowditch, book 120, p. 387, 6 May 1903. These lands all abutted each other to form the current Loring holdings.

28. *NCAB* 25, pp. 301–2. The Lorings' year-round residence in Beverly Farms, Mass., was erected in 1881 from plans by William Ralph Emerson (1833–1917), the talented and increasingly recognized architect of houses in eastern Massachusetts, along the Maine coast and other locations in New England, including Jackson, N.H. (see "Maple Knoll" and the Fitz cottage). See Zaitzevsky and Miller, *The Architecture of William Ralph Emerson,* pp. 12–14, and plates 13–15. The scale, proportions, and detailing of "Greycroft" do not convey the consistently creative nature and picturesque quality of Emerson's work; hence, an attribution to Emerson is inappropriate in this instance.

29. Deed, Susan S. Wainwright (wife of Wilton P. Wainwright), Carroll County Registry of Deeds, book 105, p. 168, 28 December 1895. The land was on the south side of Philbrick Road, bordering the properties of Henshaw B. Walley and Hattie Davis. The mortgage (dated 4 March 1902) was satisfied, the estate of Susan S. Wainwright to Thomas Sherwin, Carroll County Registry of Deeds, book 133, p. 306, 5 September 1908. When the property was acquired in 1965 by its current owners, it was expanded by two acres at the rear of the house (interview with Alan Smith, Chocorua, N.H., 21 June 1993).

30. *WME* 22, no. 3 (22 July 1899): 2; *WML* 1, no. 2 (1 July 1897); interviews with Alan Smith, 21 June 1993 and 4 July 1994.

31. Telephone interview with Scott Paul, Chocorua, N.H., 4 June 1994; interview with Samuel I. Bowditch, Chocorua, 22 June 1993. The Weed work crew consisted of him, his sons, and other local artisans. The original Walker plans and related documents for the house are believed no longer to exist. To the north of the house is a large wood-framed and shingled carriage and horse barn. To the rear is an ice house/storage building, attached to the house by means of a

narrow pitched-roof walkway cover extending across a driveway between the two buildings.

32. *NCAB* 12, p. 368; *DAB* 2, p. 588.

33. *WML* 1, no. 2 (1 July 1897); *WME* 15, no. 5 (30 July 1892): 7; deeds, Carroll County Registry of Deeds, James R. Chadwick from John H. and Clarinda Nickerson, book 93, p. 512, 16 August 1890, and James R. Chadwick from Lowell Ham, book 94, p. 338, 11 November 1890. Chadwick secured lake access through additional land purchases in 1895 and 1896 (book 104, p. 206, 29 July 1895; book 104, p. 236, 15 August 1895; book 107, p. 47, 16 November 1896). The house has had three owning families: the Chadwicks; the Farlows of Boston (Professor William G. Farlow taught cryptogamic biology at Harvard); and the Macgregors. Tamworth historian Marjorie G. Harkness (*The Tamworth Narrative,* pp. 227–28) relates that sculptor Truman H. Bartlett built "a rough cottage studio" on the Chadwick property which was a gathering place for a talented circle of writers and artists, including the poet Edwin Arlington Robinson.

34. *NCAB* 14, p. 285; Withey, *BDAA(D),* pp. 623–24; Placzek, *MEA,* vol. 4, p. 362.

35. Ibid. The firm was known as Walker, Walker and Kingsbury from 1925 to 1930, and as Walker and Walker from 1930 to 1936.

36. *NCAB* 14, p. 285; Withey, *BDAA(D),* p. 624; Placzek, *MEA,* vol. 4, p. 362; "C. Howard Walker: A Memoir by Dr. Thomas Adams," *Journal of the Royal Institute of British Architects,* 3rd series, 23 May 1936, pp. 768–69; *American Architect* 148 (May 1936): 109; obituary, *NYT,* 13 April 1936, p. 17.

37. Microfilm of sketchbooks (1870–1924) of C. Howard Walker from family originals, roll no. 1049, Archives of American Art, Smithsonian Institution, Detroit, Mich., repository.

38. Deeds, C. Howard Walker from John N. and Mehitable A. Perkins, Carroll County Registry of Deeds, book 96, p. 107, 15 September 1891, and book 96, p. 107, 22 May 1893. The right-of-way was granted in 1891, and rights to it surrendered outright to Walker around 1893. He acquired additional land from his neighbor Charlotte P. Bowditch in 1906; see deed, Carroll County Registry of Deeds, book 127, p. 419, 27 January 1906.

39. Visit to "Pine Cone" and conversation with current owner, Mrs. Richard T. Gill, 21 June 1993.

40. [Eleanor G. W. Matthews], "Some Facts about the Chocorua House" (1983), pp. 1–2, photocopied typescript, Alan Smith, Concord, Mass.; deed, Gustavus Howard Maynadier from David H. and Mary J. Gilman, Carroll County Registry of Deeds, book 596, p. 328, 29 October 1891. This parcel of land was bounded by the Henshaw B. Walley farm and other tracts. The right-of-way access appears to have been acquired outright by Gustavus H. Maynadier from Walley on 29 September 1901 (Carroll County Registry of Deeds, book 114, p. 474). Gustavus H. added to his land holdings in Chocorua in 1903 when he purchased the nearby Ross farm for $1,000 (Carroll County Registry of Deeds, book 126, p. 36). See also, Plan of the Maynadier Estate, Carroll County Registry of Deeds, plan book 15, p. 63.

41. [Matthews], "Some Facts," pp. 2–3; *Thirty-*

Sixth Annual Excursion of the Sandwich Historical Society (Sandwich, N.H.: Sandwich Historical Society, 1955), p. 38; *Thirteenth Annual Excursion of the Sandwich Historical Society* (Sandwich, N.H.: Sandwich Historical Society, 1932), pp. 6–7, 18–19.

42. [Matthews], "Some Facts," pp. 3–4; *WWNE*, 1909 ed., p. 641.

43. *ATC* 16, no. 18 (30 July 1892): 4.

44. *WME* 15, no. 2 (9 July 1892): 6. Hammer was reported to have spent $20,000 on the construction of the house and outbuildings. The outbuildings were completed before the house was erected, and were presumably used for the storage of building materials, equipment, and tools.

For a record of the Hammer's real estate transactions, see deed, Martha P. Hammer (wife of Emil) from John H. Nickerson, Carroll County Registry of Deeds, book 93, p. 539, 22 August 1890, and deed, Martha P. Hammer from John H. and Clarinda Nickerson, book 99, p. 217, 15 February 1893. The first purchase of nine and one half acres of land on the east side of the Chocorua Village–Conway highway (south of the Scudder property) was for the house site, and also included a right-of-way to Chocorua Lake, and water rights on the Nickerson's Chocorua House tract to the south. The second purchase was a small, square parcel on the lakeshore, with strip access from the highway.

45. Photo collection for "Cairncroft" (c. 1890–1920), Mr. and Mrs. Jack M. Wellinghurst, Chocorua, N.H.

46. *The Jeweler's Weekly* (New York and Chicago), 18, no. 4 (18 April 1894); *WME* 16, no. 12 (16 September 1893): 6.

47. Withey, *BDAA(D)*, pp. 370–71; *WWWA*, vol. I (1897–1942), p. 726; plans for "Cairncroft," Chocorua, N.H., Mr. and Mrs. Jack M. Wellinghurst. Inscribed with Lewis' name and office address (but undated), the plans consist of west, south, east, and north elevation drawings; floor diagrams; and framing schematics. With the south wing angled from the principal axis to take best advantage of the mountain panorama, the first floor included a front porch, large parlor, study, entrance and stair hall, dining room, kitchen, pantry, and screen porch (termed "The Lookout"). The second floor accommodated a large master bedroom, three smaller bedrooms, sewing room, upper hallway, servant's room, and studio. The attic above is completely open and used exclusively for storage today, though with angled ceilings beautifully finished in soft wood. Over the years, owners have made some alterations in interior spatial arrangements.

48. McGrew, *If Walls Could Speak*, p. 52; Harkness, *The Tamworth Narrative*, pp. 222–23.

49. Harkness, *The Tamworth Narrative*, p. 223; interview with Alan Smith, Chocorua, N.H., 21 June 1993; Merrill, *History of Carroll County*, p. 738.

50. *WME* 16, no. 12 (16 September 1893): 66; interview with Mrs. Leonard (Cornelia B.) Wheeler, Chocorua, N.H., 9 October 1994. In recent years, the house has been called "Toad Hall." The original Walker plans consist of eleven drawings (cellar, first, second, and attic floor plans; front, rear, and end elevations; floor and elevation framing diagrams), and are being preserved by the current owning consortium of Charles P. Bowditch descendants.

51. *WME* 15, no. 5 (30 July 1892): 7; *ATC* 16, no. 18 (30 July 1892): 4. The house is reputed to have cost $25,000 to build.

52. Designs for an addition to the Charles P. Bowditch House, n.d., Chocorua, N.H., by Peabody and Stearns (Boston), Boston Public Library. The plans consist of ten drawings (two floor plans, and side and rear elevations). For information on the firm of Peabody and Stearns, see notes accompanying "Willowgate," Chocorua.

53. *WME* 22, no. 3 (22 July 1899): 2; *DAB*, vol. 1, p. 492; *NCAB* 1, pp. 290–91. To the north of the main house is the small "Brown Study" guest house, which was originally next to the Cone farmhouse on the main road. It was moved up the hill after "Conni Sauti" was built.

54. Harkness, *The Tamworth Narrative*, p. 227; Placzek, *MEA*, vol. 3, pp. 438–39; deed, Joseph Hutchinson, Percy S. Grant, Lilias Page, and George H. and Mary H. Page from Robert T. Hay (Boston), Carroll County Registry of Deeds, book 113, p. 7, 2 November 1899. Additional deeds registered the same date (book 113, pp. 1–6), and conveyed rights for a well and the privilege to lay aqueduct or waterpipe across neighbors' land.

55. Placzek, *MEA*, vol. 3, pp. 438–39; Withey, *BDAA(D)*, pp. 475–76; Croly, "The Work of Charles A. Platt"; Morgan, "Charles A. Platt, 1861–1933"; Van Vynckt, *International Dictionary of Architects and Architecture*, vol. 1, pp. 674–76. For an up-to-date book treatment, see Keith N. Morgan's *Charles A. Platt: The Artist as Architect*.

56. Placzek, *MEA*, vol. 3, p. 439.

57. Morgan, *Charles A. Platt*, p. 242; *WME* 22, no. 5 (5 August 1899): 5; plan sheets for the Mr. and Mrs. George H. Page house, Charles A. Platt Collection, Avery Library, Columbia University, New York City.

58. Morgan, "Charles A. Platt, 1861–1933," p. 3.

59. Interviews with Samuel I. Bowditch, 22 June 1993, and Bernice M. Burke, 15 October 1993, Chocorua, N.H.; Grant sketch, *DAB* 4, pp. 490–91; "Rev. Percy Stickney Grant," *Men of Affairs in New York* (New York: L. R. Hamersley & Co., 1906), pp. 283–84; Arthur W. Hafner, *Directory of Deceased American Physicians, 1804–1929* (Chicago: American Medical Association, 1993), vol. 2, p. 1495.

60. Harkness, *The Tamworth Narrative*, p. 221–22.

61. *Commemorative Booklet: Bicentennial of Tamworth, New Hampshire, 1766–1966* (Tamworth, N.H.: Bicentennial Commission, 1966), p. 76; *WWWA*, vol. 1 (1897–1942), p. 1066; Albert N. Marquis, ed., *The Book of Chicagoans* (Chicago: A. N. Marquis & Co., 1917), p. 589; *NCAB*, current volume B, pp. 109–10; George W. Smith, *History of Illinois and Her People* (Chicago and New York: The American Historical Publishing Co., 1927), vol. 5, pp. 105–6. The Runnellses had four children; two of them married Chocorua summer neighbors—Mabel (Mrs. Robert I. Jenks), and Alice (Mrs. William James, Jr.). While in Iowa, John Runnells specialized in railroad and telegraph law.

62. *WML* 1, no. 2 (1 July 1897); *WME* 22, no. 3 (22 July 1899): 2; deed, Helen R. Runnells (wife of John S.) from Mary J. Gilman, Carroll County Registry of Deeds, book 98, p. 447, 13 October 1892. This initial purchase was supplemented by the acquisition of additional abutting land from Charles P. Bowditch on 9 August 1899 (book 112, p. 197). Both parcels were originally part of the Gilman family farm.

63. *WME* 22, no. 6 (12 August 1899): 20. The first Runnells cottage was said to have cost $50,000, with an additional $15,000 spent on beautifying the grounds.

64. Van Vynckt, *International Dictionary of Architects and Architecture*, p. 648; designs for the J. S. Runnells House, Chocorua, N.H. (136 drawings, 5 rolls), by Peabody and Stearns (Boston), 1899, Boston Public Library.

65. Van Vynckt, *International Dictionary of Architects and Architecture*, pp. 648–50; Weston F. Milliken, "Peabody and Stearns," *A Biographical Dictionary of Architects in Maine*, vol. 6, no. 2 (Augusta, Maine: Maine Historic Preservation Commission, 1987); Placzek, *MEA*, vol. 3, pp. 380–82; Withey, *BDAA(D)*, pp. 462–63, and 568.

66. Milliken, "Peabody and Stearns," p. 3.

67. In 1916–17, unused spaces in the attic story were finished off, and a small service wing was added to the rear. Again, Peabody and Stearns did the design work. The house was demolished by its then owners to save on taxes.

68. Interview, Samuel I. Bowditch, 22 June 1993, Chocorua, N.H.; Morgan, *Charles Platt*, p. 242; deed, Lilias Page from Robert T. Hay (Boston), Carroll County Registry of Deeds, book 113, pp. 14–17, 2 November 1899.

69. Morgan, *Charles Platt*, p. 242; Morgan, "Charles A. Platt, 1861–1933," pp. 1, 3.

70. Plan sheets for the Miss Lilias Page house, Charles A. Platt Collection, Avery Library, Columbia University, New York City.

71. The name "Avoca," bestowed on the house by the Scudder family, is believed to have been inspired by its use as a town name in the United States.

72. Deed, Margaret J. Thayer from Henshaw B. Walley (Newton, Mass.), Carroll County Registry of Deeds, book 161, p. 257, 5 July 1905. This piece of land was bordered by Fowler's Mill Road, and parcels owned by Walley, and the estates of Thomas Sherwin and Helen B. Runnells. Before Bowditch acquired the land it was owned by the Nickerson family.

73. The agreement was originally made 16 October 1905, and corresponds to the date of the house (interview with Stephen Weld, Chocorua, 9 October 1994). The deed reference cites Margaret J. Thayer from Henshaw B. Walley, book 131, p. 480, 22 November 1907.

74. Deed, Margaret J. Thayer from Henshaw B. Walley, 5 July 1905, above. Scudder ultimately transferred the legal ownership of the property to his second wife, Alice McCutcheon Scudder (d. 1960), who in turn sold it to Steven M. Weld of Milton, Mass., in 1948 (Steven M. Weld from Alice M. Scudder, book 257, p. 420, 30 December 1948). "Avoca" is still owned and occupied during the summers by the Weld family.

75. *NCAB* 44, p. 58.

76. Interview with Stephen Weld and visit to "Avoca," 9 October 1994. On the interior, on the underside of a living room settee, the inscription "Fred R. Eastman, North Conway, N.H." appears. It is clear that Eastman was responsible for at least this piece of furniture, and possibly other interior finishing work.

77. James Bronson Reynolds, Mary Berenson, and Salome Machado Warren, *In Memoriam: Florence Dike Reynolds, September 29, 1919* (n.p., 1919), p. 7.

78. *NHFSH*, 1913 ed., p. 30.

79. Deed, James B. Reynolds from Frederick LeRoy Sargent (Cambridge, Mass.), Carroll County Registry of Deeds, book 129, p. 154, 3 October 1906. This parcel abutted land owned by John Albee and Charles P. Bowditch. Reynolds also made a special agreement with Bowditch for a right-of-way from the house to the main Chocorua-Albany road, so that the Reynolds could put in a driveway (see George P. Hyde [Controller, Smith College] to C. E. Gilman [Surveyor, Silver Lake, N.H.], typed letter, Northampton, Mass., 8 May 1925, Smith College Archives). This first purchase was later added to, so that the total parcel reached nearly forty acres.

80. Letter and enclosure, Mrs. Thomas (Donna T.) Rourke, Venice, Fla., to the author, 19 July 1994.

81. *Salem* (Mass.) *Evening News*, 23 September 1907, p.1.

82. Bryant F. Tolles, Jr., *Architecture in Salem: An Illustrated Guide* (Salem, Mass.: Essex Institute, 1982), pp. 83, 128, 171, 223, 258. The Blake Memorial Chapel is a Gothic Revival building, while his other work in Salem is in the Colonial Revival style.

83. *Salem* (Mass.) *Evening News*, 23 September 1907, p. 1.

84. Reynolds, et al., *In Memoriam*, p. 6; letter and enclosures, Mrs. Thomas Rourke to the author, 19 July 1994.

85. Harriet Atwood, "Chocorua," *Carroll County* (N.H.) *Independent*, October 1980, p. 7; interview with Mrs. John (Susan) Peter, Chocorua, N.H., 22 June 1994.

86. Reynolds, et al., *In Memoriam*, pp. 19–20. From Montclair, New Jersey, Florence Dike Reynolds was a special student at Smith College in 1883 and 1884. For much of her life she suffered from poor health and died at a relatively young age. Like her husband, she was interested in social and municipal problems, and literary matters. While residing in New York City, she was a member of the St. Ursula, Cosmopolitan, and Wednesday Afternoon clubs, and was president of the Inwood House. She was interested in music and art of all forms, and once took up painting as hobby.

87. The house also features four fireplaces and five bedrooms, and is supplemented by a small guest house ("Hermitage"), garage, ice house, wood house, and spring house on the property.

88. *NCAB* 10, pp. 235–36; *WWWA*, vol. 1 (1897–1942), p. 1024.

89. Harkness, *The Tamworth Narrative*, pp. 275–76; interview with Samuel I. Bowditch, Chocorua, N.H., 22 June 1993; Annual Reports for Juniper Lodge, 1967, 1975, 1980, Smith College Archives, Northampton, Mass.; telephone interview, Mrs.

Thomas Rourke, Portland, Maine, 12 July 1994; typed letter, James Bronson Reynolds to President William Allen Neilson, Smith College, 16 October 1923, Smith College Archives; codicil to the will of James Bronson Reynolds, North Haven, Conn., 31 December 1923, Smith College Archives; "Juniper Lodge," *Christian Science Monitor*, 24 July 1948; Anna A. Cutler, "The Summer of 1925 at Juniper Lodge," *Smith Alumnae Quarterly*, November 1925, pp. 29–30. In 1975, the use of "Juniper Lodge" was extended to include male members of the faculty and administrative staff.

90. Harkness, *Tamworth Narratives*, p. 228; Galusha B. Balch, *Genealogy of the Balch Family in America* (Salem, Mass.: Eben Putnam, 1897), p. 414; *WWWA*, vol. 3, p. 44. The Balches had six children (three boys and three girls), including twin boys born in 1896.

91. Interview with Mrs. Leonard (Cornelia B.) Wheeler, Chocorua, N.H., 9 October 1994; set of five undated blueprint plan sheets (northeasterly elevation; southwesterly elevation; southeasterly and northwesterly elevations; first floor plan; second floor plan) for a "Residence for Dr. Franklin G. Balch, 99 Commonwealth Avenue, Boston, C. Howard Walker, Architect, Devonshire Street, Boston," Mrs. Leonard (Cornelia B.) Wheeler, Chocorua, and Cambridge, Mass.

92. Interview and house tour with Virginia B. Harlan, Chocorua, N.H., 9 October 1994.

10. OUTLYING LOCATIONS

1. *WME* 33, no. 8 (3 September 1910): 20.

2. Florence Morey, "Samuel A. Bemis, Lord of the Valley," *Appalachia* 32, no. 1 (June 1958): 122; Campbell, "Dr. Samuel Bemis: Renaissance Yankee," pp. 142–45.

3. Campbell, "Dr. Samuel Bemis," p. 146; Morey, "Samuel A. Bemis," pp. 122–23. Deeds, Carroll County Registry of Deeds. Samuel A. Bemis from John C. Davis, book 22, p. 276, 1 June 1853 (assignment of mortgage); Samuel A. Bemis from Nathaniel T. P. Davis, book 26, p. 166, 5 March 1855; Samuel A. Bemis from Nathaniel T. P. Davis, book 26, p. 489, 12 March 1855; Samuel A. Bemis from Leavitt H. Eastman, book 27, p. 312, 18 September 1855; Samuel A. Bemis from John N. Glidden, book 69, p. 10, 6 April 1877; Samuel A. Bemis from Hiram Parker, book 72, p. 259, 29 November 1878.

4. Morey, "Samuel A. Bemis," p. 123; Campbell, "Dr. Samuel Bemis," p. 146. *WME* 33, no. 8 (3 September 1910): 20.

5. "The Mountain Hermit," *WME* 4, no. 1 (2 July 1881): 7; Morey, "Samuel A. Bemis," pp. 124–25; Campbell, "Dr. Samuel Bemis," pp. 146–153. Supposedly, about 1840 Bemis took the first picture of the famed "Old Man of the Mountain" in Franconia Notch. For his apple cultivation, he was awarded a silver medal by the Massachusetts Horticultural Society in 1860. Portions of the original orchard remain, and still bloom each spring. Bemis was buried near his house, and his grave is marked by a granite shaft.

6. In recent years, the Bemis house has accommo-

dated The Inn Unique, at what is now called Bemis Station on the former Mountain Division route of the Maine Central Railroad.

7. Tolles, *New Hampshire Architecture*, pp. 118–19; Cutter, *Genealogical and Personal Memoirs*, pp. 252–53; "New Hampshire Necrology," *GM* 47, no. 7 (July 1915); *Men of Massachusetts*, 279; Browne, *The History of Hillsborough, New Hampshire*, vol. 2, p. 183.

8. *NHFSH*, 5th ed. (1907), pp. 43–44; Pinette, *Northwoods Echoes*, p. 15.

9. Pinette, *Northwoods Echoes*, p. 14; *Errol on the Androscoggin*, p. 123; deed, Harry Dutton from Ralph D. Thurston, Coos County Registry of Deeds, book 85, p. 143, 20 October 1897. The sale price was $200. The land had been deeded to Thurston by the executors of Joseph Keppler's estate (31 July 1895). Dutton added to his Metallak Island purchase by the acquisition of a mainland tract in Errol where he laid out a nine-hole golf course (from Alva M. Coolidge, book 93, p. 102, 22 October 1898), and Bear Island in Umbagog Lake (from Frances W. Russell, book 108, p. 149, 24 June 1901).

10. *WME* 24, no. 2 (13 July 1901): p. 20, and vol. 25, no. 3 (18 July 1903): 3; *NHFSH*, 5th ed. (1907), p. 43; Pinette, *Northwoods Echoes*, pp. 15–16; *Errol on the Androscoggin*, p. 123.

11. Pinette, *Northwoods Echoes*, pp. 15–19.

12. Pinette, *Northwoods Echoes*, pp. 15–19; *NHFSH*, 5th ed. (1907), p. 43. The island was reached from the mainland by the Dutton family boat, "The Ojibway," a twenty-six-foot wooden craft with a polished brass cannon mounted on its deck. Water was furnished the island from a spring on the mainland by means of pipe running on the lake bottom. The island passed out of the family around 1940. The camp was demolished when its new owners, the Union Water Power Company, which controlled the lake level, started implementing plans to built a larger dam for the lake in Errol. Had the project been completed, the lake level would have risen, and the island flooded. This never occurred, however, and the island, with the stonework remains of the estate, is still visible today.

13. Tolles, *GRHWM*, pp. 213–23; Withey, *BDAA(D)*, p. 233. The hotel formally opened on 1 August 1902.

14. *The Bugle of Bretton Woods* (hotel newspaper), 1 October 1902; Tolles, *GRHWM*, p. 221; typed letters, John Anderson (proprietor of the Mount Pleasant House) to Robert I. Jenks (treasurer, Mount Pleasant Hotel Company), Ormond, Fla., 23 April 1903; Edward Betts (superintendent for Charles A. Gifford) to Robert I. Jenks, New York City, 26 June 1903; Charles A. Gifford to Robert I. Jenks, New York City, 7 August 1903; Charles A. Gifford to Robert I. Jenks, New York City, 9 October 1903; Edward Betts to Robert I. Jenks, New York City, 11 February 1904. All letters are in the archives of the New Hampshire Historical Society, Concord.

15. Tolles, *GRHWM*, pp. 223–34.

16. *WME* 29, no. 3 (21 July 1903): p. 14.

17. Interview with Stephen P. Barba, The Balsams Grand Resort Hotel, Dixville Notch, N.H., 7 July 1994. "The Wind Whistle" received a small, two-story extension to its west end in 1980, eliminating a one-

story connected sun porch and open veranda. In recent years, the interior has been altered to provide housing for members of the hotel staff.

18. Interview with Stephen P. Barba, 7 July 1994; Tolles, *GRHWM*, p. 231. "Beaver Lodge" is easily reached from the hotel complex by means of a graded path through the woods along the lakeshore. To the south of the house is a one-room cabin with porch, used by the Hales for entertainment and recreation. Formerly attached to the rear of the cottage was a substantial porte cochere, removed some years ago.

19. Interview with Stephen P. Barba, 7 July 1994. From 1907 to at least 1911, there are references in the annual promotional/informational booklets for The Balsams to plans for cottages, to be built "on some of the many fine sites near the hotel." No further specifics, however, are provided in these publications. The Tillotsons lived in "The Stone Cottage" from 1954 to 1960.

20. James L. Garvin, "The Weeks Estate," National Register of Historic Places Inventory-Nomination Form, United States Department of the Interior, National Park Service, 1984; brochure, "John Wingate Weeks State Historic Site," New Hampshire Division of Parks and Recreation, 1993.

21. Ibid.; *Two Hundred Years . . . Lancaster, New Hampshire, 1764–1964*, pp. 52–54; "Summer White House," *NHP* 2, no. 2 (February 1953).

22. Garvin, "The Weeks Estate." The hall features massive fieldstone fireplaces at either end, and a dark oak floor, trim, and pieces of original furniture. The complete building measures approximately forty-four by eighty-eight feet. The names of the architect and builder of "The Lodge" are unknown despite a thorough search of the Weeks family papers at the time of the National Register nomination.

23. Garvin, "The Weeks Estate"; Robert I. Sobel, ed., *Biographical Dictionary of the United States Executive Branch 1774–1977* (Westport, Conn.: Greenwood Press, 1977), pp. 350–51; *Biographical Dictionary of the United States Congress, 1774–1989* (Washington, D.C.: U.S. Government Printing Office, 1989), p. 2022; Don and Inez Morris, *Who Was Who in American Politics* (New York: Hawthorne Books, Inc., 1974), p. 601; *WWWA*, vol. 1 (1897–1942), p. 1316; *DAB* 10, pp. 601–2; *NCAB* 20, pp. 4–5; *Beautiful Newton: The Garden City of Massachusetts* (Newton: Newton Graphic Publishing Co., [c. 1920]), p. 141; *GM* 46, nos. 9–10 (September/October 1914), pp. 295–96; obituary, *WME* 49, no. 2 (17 July 1926): 8. For a full biography, see Washburn, *The Life of John Wingate Weeks*. John Weeks' son, Sinclair (1893–1972), followed in his father's footsteps, as alderman of Newton (1923–30), mayor of Newton (1930–35), Republican National Committee member (1941–53), United States senator from Massachusetts (1944), and secretary of commerce (1953–58) in the administration of Dwight D. Eisenhower. He also passed away in Lancaster. See *NCAB*, current volume 1 (1953–59), pp. 366–68; Morris, *Who Was Who in American Politics*, p. 601; Sobel, *Biographical Dictionary of the United States Executive Branch*, p. 351; *Biographical Dictionary of the United States Congress*, pp. 2022–23.

Bibliography

This bibliography lists, by general categories, the most significant and substantive printed materials employed as sources in the compilation of this book. Included are selected book, pamphlet, newspaper, magazine, and journal titles. Citations for marginally important printed materials (used for only one or two references), as well as all manuscripts and visual materials, are contained in essay notes elsewhere in the volume.

I. REFERENCE WORKS

Avery Index to Architectural Periodicals (Columbia University). 2nd ed., enl. and rev., 15 vols. Boston: G. K. Hall & Co., 1973.

First Supplement, 2nd ed., enl. and rev., 1975. Second Supplement, 2nd ed., enl. and rev., 1977.

Third Supplement, 2nd ed., enl. and rev., 1979. Fourth Supplement, 1979–82. 4 vols., 1985.

Avery Obituary Index of Architects (Columbia University). 2nd ed. Boston: G. K. Hall & Co., 1970.

Blumenson, John J.-G. *Identifying American Architecture: Pictorial Guide to Styles and Terms, 1600–1945.* Nashville, Tenn.: American Association for State and Local History, 1977.

Cyclopedia of Architecture, Carpentry and Building: A General Reference Work. 10 vols. Chicago: American Technical Society, 1909.

Hanrahan, E. J., ed. *Bent's Bibliography of the White Mountains.* Somersworth, N.H.: New Hampshire Publishing Co., 1971. (A new edition of Allen Bent's *Bibliography of the White Mountains*, first published by the Appalachian Mountain Club, Boston, 1911. Supplements by Bent, 1918, and Walter W. Wright, 1947, Appalachian Mountain Club.)

———, ed. *Hammond's Check List of New Hampshire History.* Concord: New Hampshire Historical Society, 1925; Somersworth, N.H.: New Hampshire Publishing Co., 1971.

Haskell, John D., and T. D. Seymour Bassett. *New Hampshire: A Bibliography of Its History.* Boston: G. K. Hall & Co., 1979.

Hitchcock, Henry-Russell. *American Architectural Books: A List of Books, Portfolios, and Pamphlets on Architecture and Related Subjects Published in American Before 1895.* Enl. ed. New York: Da Capo Press, 1976.

Johnson, Allen, et al. *Dictionary of American Biography.* 20 vols. New York: Charles Scribner's Sons, 1928–36.

Supplementary volumes, 1–8, 1944–88. *Index* volume, 1990.

Leonard, John W., et al. *Who's Who in America.* Vols. 1–20. Chicago: A. N. Marquis & Co., 1899–1938.

———, ed. *Woman's Who's Who of America, 1914–15.* New York: The American Commonwealth Co., 1914.

Marquis, Alfred N. *Who's Who in New England.* Chicago: A. N. Marquis & Co., 1909.

Men of Massachusetts. Boston: The Boston Press Club, 1919.

The National Cyclopaedia of American Biography. 62 vols. New York and Clifton, N.J.: James T. White & Co., 1898–1984.

Current volumes, A–N, 1930–63. *Index* volume, 1984.

Placzek, Adolf K., ed. *Macmillan Encyclopedia of Architects.* 4 vols. New York: The Free Press, Macmillan Publishing Co., 1982.

Schrock, Nancy C., ed. *Architectural Records in Boston: A Guide to Architectural Research in Boston, Cambridge and Vicinity.* New York and London: Garland Publishing Co. for the Massachusetts Committee for the Presentation of Architectural Records, Inc., 1983.

———, ed. *Directory of Boston Architects, 1846–1970.* Cambridge, Mass.: Massachusetts Committee for the Preservation of Architectural Records, 1984.

Sobel, Robert, and John Raimo. *Biographical Dictionary of the Governors of the United States, 1789–1978.* 4 vols. Westport, Conn.: Meckler Books, 1978.

Supplementary volume, 1978–83, 1985.

Sokol, David M. *American Art and Architecture: A Guide to Information Sources.* Detroit: Gale Research Co., 1976.

[Talbot, E. H., and H. R. Hobart, eds.]. *The Biographical Dictionary of the Railway Officials of America for 1887*. Chicago: The Railway Age Publishing Co., 1887.

Tatman, Sandra L., and Roger W. Moss. *Biographical Dictionary of Philadelphia Architects: 1730–1930.* Boston: G. K. Hall & Co., 1985.

Van Vynckt, Randall J. *International Dictionary of Architects and Architecture.* Vol. 1, *Architects.* London and Washington, D.C.: St. James Press, 1993.

Whiffen, Marcus. *American Architecture since 1780: A Guide to Styles.* Cambridge, Mass.: MIT Press, 1969.

Who Was Who in America, Historical Volume, 1607–1896. Chicago: The A. N. Marquis Co., 1963.

Who Was Who in America, Vols. 1–3. Chicago: The A. N. Marquis Company, 1943–60.

Index volume. Chicago: Marquis Who's Who, 1993.

Wilson, James G. and John Fiske, eds. *Appleton's Cyclopaedia of American Biography.* 6 vols. New York: D. Appleton and Co., 1888–89.

Withey, Henry F. and Elsie R. *Biographical Dictionary of American Architects (Deceased).* Los Angeles: Hennessey & Ingalls, Inc., 1970.

Wodehouse, Lawrence. *American Architects from the Civil War to the First World War: A Guide to Information Sources.* Detroit, Mich.: Gale Research Company, 1976.

II. GENERAL WORKS

Anderson, Dorothy M. *The Era of the Summer Estates: Swampscott, Massachusetts, 1870–1940.* Canaan, N.H.: Phoenix Publishing, 1985.

Aslet, Clive. *The American Country House.* New Haven and London: Yale University Press, 1990.

Candee, Richard M. "Kilham, Hopkins & Greeley." *A Biographical Dictionary of Architects in Maine.* Vol. 4, no. 8. Augusta: Maine Historical Preservation Commission, 1987.

Comstock, William T. *Country Houses and Seaside Cottages of the Victorian Era.* New York: Dover Publications, Inc., 1989. Originally published as *American Cottages* (New York: W. T. Comstock, 1883).

[Croly, Herbert]. "The Work of Messrs. Carriere and Hastings." *Architectural Record* 27, no. 1 (January 1910): 4–120.

Croly, Herbert. "The Work of Charles A. Platt." *Architectural Record* 15, no. 3 (March 1904): 181–244.

———. "The Work of Kilham and Hopkins." *Architectural Record* 31, no. 2 (February 1912): 97–128.

Cutter, William R. *Genealogical and Personal Memoirs Relating to Boston and Eastern Massachusetts.* New York: Lewis Historical Publishing Co., 1908.

Downing, Antoinette F., and Vincent J. Scully, Jr. *The Architectural Heritage of Newport, Rhode Island, 1640–1915.* 2nd ed., rev. New York: Clarkson N. Potter, Inc., Publisher, 1967.

Foley, Mary Mix. *The American House.* New York: Harper & Row, Publishers, 1980.

Gill, Brenden, and Dudley Witney. *Summer Places.* New York: Methuen, 1978.

Gillon, Edmund V., Jr., and Clay Lancaster. *Victorian Houses: A Treasury of Lesser-Known Examples.* New York: Dover Publications, Inc., 1973.

Gowans, Alan. *The Comfortable House: North American Suburban Architecture, 1890–1930.* Cambridge and London: The MIT Press, 1986.

Gregory, Jane. "The Shingle Style." *Down East* 32, no. 7 (February 1986): 49–51, 69, 71, 110. (Cottage architecture of John Calvin Stevens.)

Hamlin, Talbot F. *Greek Revival Architecture in America: Being an Account of Important Trends in American Architecture and American Life prior to the War between the States.* New York: Oxford University Press, 1944; reprinted, New York, Dover Publications, Inc., 1964.

Handlin, David P. *American Architecture.* New York: Thomas and Hudson, Inc., 1985.

———. *The American Home: Architecture and Society, 1815–1915.* Boston: Little, Brown and Co., 1979.

Haynes, George H. *Souvenir of New England's Great Resorts.* New York: Moss Engraving Co., 1891.

Helfrich, G. W., and Gladys O'Neil. *Lost Bar Harbor.* Camden, Maine: Down East Books, 1982.

Hepburn, Andrew. *The Grand Resorts of North America.* New York: Doubleday & Co., Inc., 1965.

Hewitt, Mark Adam. *The Architect & the American Country House, 1890–1940.* New Haven and London: Yale University Press, 1990.

Hitchcock, Harry-Russell. *Architecture: Nineteenth and Twentieth Centuries.* 3rd ed. Baltimore: Penguin Books, 1968.

Kaiser, Harvey H. *Great Camps of the Adirondacks.* Boston: David R. Godine, Publisher, Inc., 1982.

Lancaster, Clay. *The American Bungalow, 1880–1930.* New York: Abbeville Press, Publishers, 1985.

Lewis, Arnold. *American Country Houses of the Gilded Age (Sheldon's "Artistic Country-Seats").* New York: Dover Publications, Inc., 1982. (Republication of George William Sheldon's *Artistic Country-Seats: Types of Recent American Villa and Cottage Architecture with Instances of Country Club–Houses* [New York: D. Appleton and Co., 1886–87].)

Lewis, Arnold, and Keith Morgan. *American Victorian Architecture: A Survey of the 70s and 80s in Contemporary Photographs.* New York: Dover Publications, Inc., 1975. Originally published as *L'Architecture Americaine* (Paris: André, Daly fils Cie, 1886).

Limerick, Jeffrey, Nancy Ferguson, and Richard Oliver. *America's Grand Resort Hotels.* New York: Pantheon Books, 1979.

Loth, Calder, and Julius Trousdale Sadler, Jr. *The Only Proper Style: Gothic Architecture in America.* Boston: New York Graphic Society, 1975.

Maddox, Diane, ed. *Built in U.S.A.: American Buildings from Airports to Zoos.* Washington, D.C.: The Preservation Press of the National Trust for Historic Preservation, 1985.

———. *Master Builders: A Guide to Famous American Architects.* Washington, D.C.: The Preservation Press of the National Trust for Historic Preservation, 1985.

McAlester, Virginia and Lee. *A Field Guide to American Houses.* New York: Alfred A. Knopf, 1984.

Morgan, Keith N. *Charles A. Platt: The Artist as Architect.* New York: The Architectural History Foundation, and Cambridge and London: The MIT Press, 1985.

———. "Charles A. Platt, 1861–1933." *A Biographical Dictionary of Architects in Maine.* Vol. 5, no. 17. Augusta: Maine Historic Preservation Commission, 1988.

Murphy, Kevin D. "Chapman and Frazer." *Biographical Dictionary of Architects in Maine.* Vol. 6. Augusta: Maine Historic Preservation Commission, 1991.

Newton, Page Hale. "Our Summer Resort Architecture: An American Phenomenon and Social Document." *Art Quarterly* 4: 297–321.

Oakes, Donald T., ed. *A Pride of Palaces: Lenox Summer Cottages, 1883–1933.* Lenox, Mass.: Lenox Library Association, 1981.

Owens, Carole. *The Berkshire Cottages: A Vanishing Era.* Englewood Cliffs, N.J.: Cottage Press, 1984.

Platt, Frederick. *America's Gilded Age: Its Architecture and Decoration.* South Brunswick, N.J., and New York: A. S. Barnes and Company, 1976.

Poppeliers, John C., S. Allan Chambers, Jr., and Nancy B. Schwartz. *What Style is It?: A Guide to American Architecture.* Washington D.C.: The Preservation Press for the Historic American Buildings Survey and the National Trust for Historic Preservation, 1983.

Porter, Phil. *View from the Veranda: The History and Architecture of the Summer Cottages on Mackinac Island.* Mackinac Island, Mich.: Mackinac State Historic Parks, 1981.

Reed, Roger G. *A Delight to All Who Know It: The Maine Summer Architecture of William R. Emerson.* Augusta, Maine: Maine Historic Preservation Commission, 1990.

———. *Summering on the Thoroughfare: The Architecture of North Haven, 1885–1945.* Portland, Maine: Maine Citizens for Historic Preservation, 1993.

Roth, Leland M. *The Architecture of McKim, Mead & White.* New York and London: Garland Publishing Co., 1978.

———. *A Concise History of American Architecture.* New York: Harper & Row, Publishers, 1979.

Roth, Leland M. "McKim, Mead & White." *A Biographical Dictionary of Architects in Maine.* Vol. 2, no. 5. Augusta: Maine Historic Preservation Commission, 1985.

Scully, Vincent J., Jr. *The Architecture of American Summer: The Flowering of the Shingle Style.* New York: Rizzoli International Publications, Inc., 1989.

———. *The Shingle Style and the Stick Style: Architectural Theory and Design from Downing to the Origins of Wright.* Rev. ed. New Haven and London: Yale University Press, 1971.

Shettleworth, Earle G., Jr. *The Summer Cottages of Islesboro, 1890–1930.* Islesboro, Maine: Islesboro Historical Society, 1989.

Stevens, John Calvin, and Albert Winslow Cobb. *American Domestic Architecture: A Late Victorian Stylebook.* New York: Comstock, 1889; reprint, Watkins Glen, N.Y.: The American Life Foundation & Study Institute, 1978.

Stevens, John Calvin, II, and Earle G. Shettleworth, Jr. *John Calvin Stevens: Domestic Architecture, 1890–1930*. Scarborough, Maine: Harp Publications, 1990.

Stickley, Gustav, ed. *Craftsman Bungalows: 59 Homes from* The Craftsman. New York: Dover Publications, Inc., 1988. (Articles from *The Craftsman*, 1901–16.)

———, ed. *Craftsman Houses: Architecture and Furnishings of the American Arts and Crafts Movement*. New York: The Craftsman Publishing Co., 1909 (as *Craftsman Homes*, 2nd ed.); New York: Dover Publications, Inc., 1979.

———, ed. *More Craftsman Homes*. New York: The Craftsman Publishing Co., 1912; New York: Dover Publications, Inc., 1982.

Stone, Orra L. *History of Massachusetts Industries*. 4 vols. Boston and Chicago: The S. J. Clarke Publishing Co., 1990.

Tishler, William H. *American Landscape Architecture: Designers and Places*. Washington, D.C.: The Preservation Press of the National Trust for Historic Preservation, and the American Society of Landscape Architects, 1988.

Youngman, Elise P. *Summer Echoes from the 19th Century: Manchester By-the-Sea*. Rockport, Mass.: Don Russell for the Manchester Historical Society, 1981.

Whiffen, Marcus, and Frederick Koeper. *American Architecture, 1607–1976*. Cambridge, Mass.: MIT Press, 1981.

Zaitsevsky, Cynthia, and Myron Miller. *The Architecture of William Ralph Emerson, 1833–1917*. Cambridge, Mass.: Fogg Art Museum, 1969.

III. NEW HAMPSHIRE HISTORY

Anderson, John, and Stearns Morse. *The Book of the White Mountains*. New York: Minton, Balch & Co., 1930.

Bulkley, Peter B. "A History of the White Mountains Tourist Industry, 1818–1899." Master's thesis, University of New Hampshire, 1958.

Catalogue of New Hampshire Farms for Summer Homes. Concord, N.H.: Edward N. Pearson for the Agricultural Department, State of New Hampshire, 1894 and 1895 eds.

Catalogue of New Hampshire Farms for Summer Homes. Manchester, N.H.: John B. Clarke for the State Board of Agriculture, 1902.

Catalogue of New Hampshire Farms for Summer Homes. Concord, N.H.: J. Phoneuf & Son for the State Board of Agriculture, 1903 and 1904 eds.

Campbell, Catherine H., and Donald D. Keyes, et al. *The White Mountains: Place and Perceptions*. Hanover, N.H.: Published for the University Art Galleries, University of New Hampshire, by the University Press of New England, 1980.

The Enterprise of the North Country of New Hampshire. Lancaster, N.H.: White Mountains Region Association, 1982.

Gale, Eugene. "Memoirs of a Master Builder." *New Hampshire Profiles* 2, no. 3 (March 1953): 64–66; no. 4 (April 1953): 45–46; no. 5 (May 1953): 62.

Kilbourne, Frederick W. *Chronicles of the White Mountains*. Boston and New York: Houghton, Mifflin, Co., 1916.

New Hampshire Farms Available for Farming or Summer Homes. Concord: Rumford Press for the State Department of Agriculture, 1915.

New Hampshire Farms Available for Farming or Summer Homes. Concord: Evans Printing Company for the State Department of Agriculture, 1916, 1919, 1921 eds.

New Hampshire Farms Available for Summer Homes. Manchester, N.H.: John B. Clarke Co. for the State Board of Agriculture, 1905.

New Hampshire Farms Available for Summer Homes. Nashua, N.H.: Telegraph Printing Co. for the State Board of Agriculture, 1906.

New Hampshire Farms Available for Summer Homes. Concord, N.H.: n.p., 1908.

New Hampshire Farms for Sale. Manchester: Granite State Press for the State Department of Agriculture, c. 1922.

New Hampshire Farms for Summer Homes. 1st–13th eds. Concord: Rumford Press for State Board of Agriculture, 1902–1916.

New Hampshire Farms for Summer Homes or Agriculture. Manchester, N.H.: Arthur E. Clark for the State of New Hampshire, Board of Agriculture, 1899.

North Country Directory (Including Nine Towns). Vols. 1 and 2. Beverly, Mass., and Portland, Maine: Crowley and Lunt, 1928 and 1931.

Pillsbury, Herbert. *New Hampshire: Resources, Attractions and Its People*. 5 vols. New York: Lewis Historical Publishing Company, 1927.

Poole, Ernest. *The Great White Hills of New Hampshire*. Garden City, N.Y.: Doubleday & Co., 1946.

Tolles, Bryant F., Jr. *The Grand Hotels of the White Mountains: A Vanishing Architectural Legacy*. Boston: David R. Godine, Publishers, Inc., 1998.

———. *New Hampshire Architecture: An Illustrated Guide*. Hanover, N.H.: University Press of New England for the New Hampshire Historical Society, 1979.

Town and City Atlas of the State of New Hampshire. Boston: D. H. Hurd & Co., 1892.

Williams, Paul A. "The Saga of 'S. D.' Morgan, Master Hotel Builder of the North Country." *New Hampshire Echoes* 1, no. 4 (Winter 1970): 10–13.

The White Mountain Directory. Vols. 1–6. Beverly, Mass., and Portland, Maine: Crowley & Lunt, 1914–29.

Wood, James A. *New Hampshire Homes*. Concord, N.H.: James A. Wood, 1895. 2 vols.

IV. LOCAL HISTORY

Bean, Grace H. *The Town at the End of the Road: A History of Waterville Valley*. Canaan, N.H.: Phoenix Publishing, 1983.

Bennett, Ann. "A Revitalized Tradition: Wentworth Hall's Restoration Project." *Mountain Ear*, June 1983.

Bethlehem, New Hampshire, In the Heart of the White Mountains. Bethlehem, N.H.: Board of Trade, [c. 1921, c. 1922, and c. 1925 eds.].

Bolles, Rev. Simeon. *The Early History of the Town of Bethlehem, New Hampshire*. Woodsville, N.H.: Enterprise Printing House, 1883.

Browne, George Waldo. *The History of Hillsborough, New Hampshire, 1735–1921*. 2 vols. Manchester, N.H.: For the Town by John B. Clarke, Printers, 1922.

Campbell, Catherine H. "Dr. Samuel Bemis: Renaissance Yankee." *Historical New Hampshire* 41, nos. 3 and 4 (Fall/Winter 1986): 142–53.

Casanave, Suki. "Romance in the White Mountains." *New Hampshire Profiles* 40, no. 3 (May/June 1991): 13, 18.

Child, Hamilton, comp. *Gazetteer of Grafton County, N.H., 1709–1886*. Syracuse, N.Y.: Syracuse Journal Co., 1886. (Contains *Business Directory of Grafton County, N.H., 1885–86*.)

Clay, Paul R. *Picturesque Littleton and the White Mountains*. St. Johnsbury, Vt.: C. T. Ranlet, 1898; reprinted, with additions, Littleton, N.H.: Littleton Area Historical Society, 1968.

Colby, John H., ed. *Littleton: Crossroads of Northern New Hampshire*. Canaan, N.H.: Phoenix Publishing, 1984.

Cooper, J. M. "Jefferson." *Granite Monthly* 25, no. 2 (August 1898): 64–78.

Corrigain, Rupert, ed. *Jefferson, New Hampshire Before 1996*. Jefferson, N.H.: By the Town, 1995.

"Cottage for M. C. Wentworth, Esq., Thorn Mt. House, Jackson, N.H., Wm. A. Bates, Arch't." *American Architect and Building News* 9 (no. 262) (1 January 1881): op. p. 7. Plate.

Cross, George N. *Randolph, Old and New: Its Ways and By-ways*. Randolph, N.H.: By the Town, 1924.

Davis, Franklin Ware. "In Chocorua County." *Granite Monthly* 19, no. 3 (September 1895): 176–86.

Dethier, Mary Nichols Hardenbergh. *A Chronicle of Concordia by the Decade, 1888–1988*. North Conway, N.H.: n.p., 1988.

Errol on the Androscoggin. Errol, N.H.: By the Town, 1974.

Evans, George C. *History of the Town of Jefferson, New Hampshire, 1772–1927*. Manchester: Granite State Press, 1927.

Garland, Margaret B. *Yesterdays: Lodging Places of Jackson and Their Recipes*. Jackson, N.H.: Jackson Historical Society, 1978.

Garvin, James L. "A Significant Place in New Hampshire's Past." *Forest Notes* (Society for the Protection of New Hampshire Forests) 156 (Spring 1954): 2–4. (On "The Rocks" estate, Bethlehem.)

Gifford, William H. *Colebrook: "A Place Up Back of New Hampshire."* Colebrook, N.H.: The News and Sentinel, Inc., 1970.

Goodrich, Nathaniel L. *The Waterville Valley: A Story of a Resort in the New Hampshire Mountains*. Lunenberg, Vt.: The North Country Press, 1952.

Grover, Kathryn. "Summer Homes in Jefferson Highlands." Undergraduate winter study paper, Kirkland College, Clinton, N.Y., 1973.

Hardon, Charles. "Lancaster: One Hundred and Fiftieth Anniversary, Celebrated August 12 and 13,

1914." *Granite Monthly* 46, nos. 9–10 (September–October, 1914): 269–336.

Harkness, Marjory G. *The Tamworth Narrative (New Hampshire)*. Freeport, Maine: Bond Wheelwright Co. for the Tamworth Foundation and the Tamworth Historical Society, 1958.

Haynes, George H. *East Side of the White Mountains*. North Conway, N.H.: Board of Trade, 1892.

Historical Memories of the Town of Jefferson, New Hampshire, 1796–1971. Jefferson, N.H.: Anniversary Committee, 1971.

Hoyt, Joseph Bixby. *The Baker River Towns*. New York and Los Angeles: The Vantage Press, 1990.

Jackson, James R. *History of Littleton, New Hampshire*. 3 vols. Cambridge, Mass.: Published for the Town by the University Press, 1905.

Kilbourne, Frederick. "A Closed Chapter of White Mountain History: The Franconia Notch as Summer Resort." *Appalachia* 16, no. 2 (February 1926): 298–313.

Kingsbury, Mabel Hope. "Wonalancet: One of Fair Nature's New Hampshire Recreation Grounds." *Granite Monthly* 46, no. 7 (July 1914): 197–206.

Koop, Jennifer. "Randolph, New Hampshire, A Special Community: Founded by Farmers, Transformed by Trailmakers." *Historical New Hampshire* 49, no. 3 (Fall 1994): 133–56.

Lehr, Frederic B. *Carroll, New Hampshire: The First Two Hundred Years*. Carroll, N.H.: Carroll Bicentennial Committee, 1972.

Lewis, Bea. "Jackson's Wentworth Hotel Recalls Another Era." *The Valley Visitor*, 23 June 1988, p. 3.

Lucknow. N.p.: n.p., [c. 1925]. Printed by the Barta Press, Cambridge, Mass.

Maplewood Hotel and Cottages at Maplewood, New Hampshire. Bethlehem, N.H.: Maplewood Hotel, 1910.

Matthews, Helen S. *Moultonborough to the 20th Century*. Moultonborough, N.H.: Moultonborough Bicentennial Commission, 1963.

McGrew, Lilian C., ed. *If Walls Could Speak*. Tamworth, N.H.: Tamworth Bicentennial Commission, 1976.

[Merrell, Margaret]. *Shelburne, New Hampshire, Its First Two Hundred Years*. Shelburne, N.H.: Bicentennial Committee, 1969.

Merrill, Georgia Drew, ed. *History of Carroll County, New Hampshire*. Boston, Mass.: W. A. Fergusson & Co., 1889.

[Merrill, Georgia Drew.] *History of Coos County, New Hampshire*. Syracuse, N.Y.: W. A. Fergusson & Co., 1888.

Moses, George H. "A Lost Town: A Sketch of Bethlehem." *Granite Monthly* 17, no. 1 (July 1894): 16–33.

———. "Lisbon." *Granite Monthly* 20, no. 5 (May 1896): 311–24.

———. "On the Ammonoosuc: A Sketch of Littleton." *Granite Monthly* 17, no. 3 (September 1894): 165–94.

Nevins, Winfield S. *The Intervale, New Hampshire*. Salem, Mass.: Salem Press, 1887.

Peabody, Mrs. R. P. *History of Shelburne, New Hampshire*. Shelburne, N.H.: Mountaineer Print, 1882.

Pearson, H. C. "The Warder of the Pass: A Sketch of Franconia." *Granite Monthly* 21, no. 2 (September 1896): 148–62.

Pinette, Richard E. *Northwoods Echos: A Collection of True Short Stories and Accounts of the North Country*. Colebrook, N.H.: By the Author, 1986.

Randolph, N.H., 150 Years. Randolph, N.H.: Sesquicentennial Committee, 1974.

Reminiscences of Jackson, 1900–1950. Jackson, N.H.: Jackson Conservation Commission, [1950].

Rodrique, Barry H. *Tom Plant: The Making of a Franco-American Entrepreneur, 1859–1941*. New York and London: Garland Publishing, Inc., 1994.

Sims, Louise, and Nancy Stevenson. *An Illustrated Tour of Bethlehem, Past & Present*. Bethlehem, N.H.: The Board of Selectmen, 1992.

Somers, Rev. A. N. *History of Lancaster, New Hampshire*. Concord, N.H.: The Rumford Press, 1899.

Taylor, Hattie Whitcomb. *Early History of Bethlehem, N.H.* Bethlehem, N.H.: n.p., 1960; reprinted, n.p., 1988.

Thomas, Mrs. Theodore [Rose Fay]. *Our Mountain Garden*. 2nd ed. New York: E. P. Dutton & Co., 1915.

"Thorn Mountain House and Cottages, Jackson, N.H. for Gen. M. C. Wentworth, William A. Bates, Architect." *American Architect and Building News* 18, no. 520 (12 December 1885): 282; supplement, op. p. 3. Plate and identification notice.

Topalian, Naomi G. *People, Places and Moultonborough*. Watertown, Mass.: Baiker Publications, 1989.

Two Hundred Years: A Bicentennial Sketchbook—Lancaster, New Hampshire, 1764–1964. Lancaster, N.H.: Bicentennial Executive Committee, 1964.

Vincent, Jane, et. al. *Sugar Hill, New Hampshire—A Glimpse into the Past (1780–1986)*. Sugar Hill, N.H.: Harrison Publishing House, 1986.

Washburn, Charles G. *The Life of John W. Weeks*. Boston and New York: Houghton Mifflin, Co., 1928.

Welch, Sarah N. [Brooks]. *A History of Franconia, New Hampshire, 1772–1972*. Littleton, N.H.: Courier Printing Co., 1972.

Wilken, Elizabeth Crawford. *The Castle and the Club*. Melvin Village, N.H.: By the Author, 1964. (On Bald Peak Colony Club, Moultonboro/Tuftonboro.)

Wilson, Gregory C. *Bethlehem, New Hampshire: A Bicentennial History*. Bethlehem, N.H.: By the Town, 1974. Rev. edition, Littleton, N.H.: Bondcliff Books for the Town, 1999.

V. NEWSPAPERS

Among the Clouds (Mount Washington, N.H.), Vols. 1–39 (1877–1917).

Gorham (N.H.) Mountaineer. Vols. 1–40 (1877–1916).

The Idler (North Conway, N.H.). Vol. 1 (1888).

Littleton (N.H.) Courier. Vols. 1–42 (1889–1930).

New York Times. Obituary index references, 1880 +.

The White Mountain Clarion (Sugar Hill and Franconia, N.H.). Vols. 1–2 (1896–97).

The White Mountain Echo and Tourists' Register (Bethlehem, N.H.). Vols. 1–50 (1878–1927).

White Mountain Life (North Conway, N.H.). Vols. 1–3 (1897–99).

VI. OTHER PERIODICALS

American Architect and Building News. Vols. 1–138 (1876–1930).

Appalachia (Appalachia Mountain Club, Boston). Vol. 1 (1876–).

Architectural Forum. Vol. 1 + (1917 +).

Architectural Record. Vols. 1–68 (1891–1930).

Architectural Review (Boston). Vols. 1–30 (1891–1921).

Architecture. Vols. 1–62 (1900–1930).

Boston Architectural Club Year Books. 1890–1930.

Brickbuilder. Vols. 1–11 (1906–16).

Building. Vols. 1–62 (1884–1932).

The Craftsman. Vols. 1–31 (1901–16).

Granite Monthly. Vols. 1–63 (1877–1931).

Granite State Magazine. Vols. 1–7 (1906–14).

Historical New Hampshire (New Hampshire Historical Society). Vol. 1 + (1944+).

Inland Architect (Chicago). Vols. 1–52 (1883–1908).

Magnetic North, The Magazine of the White Mountains. Vols. 1–8 (1983–90).

Mount Washington Observatory News Bulletin. Vol. 1 + (1960 +).

New Hampshire Echoes. Vols. 1–5 (1970–75).

New Hampshire Profiles. Vols. 1–40 (1952–90).

New Hampshire Troubador. Vols. 1–21 (1931–51).

Outlook: The Magazine of Northern New Hampshire. Vols. 1–11 (1975–85).

Pencil Points (Progressive Architecture). Vols. 1–11 (1920–30).

Index

Page numbers in italics indicate illustrations.

LIBRARY OF CONGRESS CATALOGING-IN-PUBLICATION DATA

Tolles, Bryant Franklin, 1939–

Summer cottages in the White Mountains : the architecture of
leisure and recreation, 1870 to 1930 / Bryant F. Tolles, Jr.

p.   cm.

Includes bibliographical references and index.

ISBN 0–87451–953–5 (cloth : alk. paper)

1. Vacation homes—White Mountains (N.H. and Me.) I. Title.

NA7575.T65   2000

728.7'2'097422–dc21   99–35371